A ROYAL SEASON

Randy Jackson

To my dream girl Tracy

Thanks for loving me and being by my side through it all.

To the Royals' players, coaches, and board members

Bitte Schön for letting me be on the team.

To Fast N' Wide Coaches

You guys know.

FAST N' WIDE

Use the same offensive system the Potsdam Royals did to dominate the GFL!

CLIENTS ALL OVER THE WORLD ARE SCORING MORE, GAINING MORE YARDS, AND WINNING MORE GAMES WITH THIS PROVEN SYSTEM. YOU'LL LEARN AND BE ABLE TO IMPLEMENT A SYSTEM SO SIMPLE AND EXPLOSIVE...IT'LL BLOW YOUR MIND.

WHAT OTHERS ARE SAYING ABOUT 'A ROYAL SEASON'

"This book is not a book about football, but a journey about a coach, and his connection with his players that will last a lifetime. Coach Jackson has been able to inspire a team of different backgrounds through building relationships with players and coaches first before ever winning games on the field. This book is inspirational in so many ways and should be read by coaches everywhere. Coach Jackson is intelligent and committed, which shows in his coaching style and philosophies. Winning a Super Bowl in the NFL is about having great communication, a tremendous work ethic, an attitude to compete, and a conviction for what you believe in. Coach Jackson exemplifies all of these qualities."

Doug Pederson
HC Jacksonville Jaguars
SB LII Champion

"This book is a phenomenal look at how Coach Jackson helped the Royals set records! It's a true must-have handbook that has provided me with valuable insights and strategies. Randy's unique approach to the game sets him apart as a coach, which is why I have always trusted his evaluations of my teams in the past. A Royal Season provides a comprehensive view of how he creates winning teams, leaving no stone unturned in his 360-degree analysis. It's a must-read for any serious football fan or coach."

Sonny Dykes
HC TCU Horned Frogs
2023 Fiesta Bowl Champions

"Randy has always been at the forefront of team-building and did it again in soccer-crazy Europe with professional players who barely knew each other. This book is a step-by-step blueprint with tons of strategies any coach can use with their team. A Royal Season takes readers through team meetings, pregame speeches, hard conversations, and the importance of accountability. Read this book to be a master team-builder and discover how the game is played in Europe. Time after time, the stories Randy shares will make you say, "Really? That just happened?"

Matt Rhule
HFC University of Nebraska

"Randy turned around programs at every stop in Texas, and now he's done it again at the highest level in Germany. This book is not only a fascinating story of how the game is played in Europe but also a manual for coaches to see how he inspires players and creates a team-first culture."

Joey McGuire
HFC Texas Tech University

"I always reference Randy's first books Culture Defeats Strategy 1 and 2. They've been a great source of knowledge and inspiration to me. Now, he's written a third book that will help the Roadrunners. There are a ton of stories Randy used with the Royals that any coach can "plug and play" with their team. A Royal Season shows how Randy turned around program and after program as a high school head coach. As a proud former Texas High School coach, I loved reading about how one of us went to Germany and brought some Texas football to Deutschland."

Jeff Traylor
HC University of Texas San Antonio
2021, 2022 Conference USA Champions

"At Starbucks, we believe "The one sweeping the floor should pick out the broom." This approach can be incredibly effective in creating a positive and productive workplace or team. This book has story after story of how Randy gave ownership to the players, and they responded with amazing results. A Royal Season is how a group of individuals becomes a team, which is what every business owner should be striving for. If you want to take your leadership skills to the next level, read this book!"

Howard Behar
President Starbucks International, retired

"This book is a Hero's Journey played out in Europe. Coach Jackson slays the dragon of fear by finding the courage to retire from a great job as a darn good head football coach at a well-known Texas high school program to test his skills on an international level. In Coach Jackson's journey, the "death" of his American high school coaching career led to a transformation with the Royals. His use of the What's App to teach and communicate with his players to build an intentional culture is a lesson anyone can use in their own personal life and business."

Newy Scruggs
10x Emmy Winning Sports Broadcaster
NBC Sports

"Whether you are looking for something specific when you begin this book, or just wanted to something to read, you will definitely be glad you did. It has processes for coaches, stories for readers, and is in itself a motivational piece that we can all draw on later. From how the story of Randy Jackson came to coach in Germany to the relationships he had to build and showed us a light into who some of these men are, all the way to the record setting performance in a country that loves the "other" sport of football, it truly is an awesome read."

"I may be biased because Randy is a coach that is always trying to learn more and get better and is not afraid to try new things in a sport where a few years ago, no one would do that. We have spent hours talking analytics, strategy, and relationships that could help our team, and our players be better on and off the field. I love that Randy embraces the analytics side of the game while it is still in its infancy stage in that area.
This is one that when you are finished, will be glad you read!"

Kevin Kelley
"The Coach Who Never Punts"
9x State Champion

"Coach Jackson's impact on European football cannot be overstated. He did what few coaches have been able to do, introduced a completely new offensive style to the GFL, and the Royals absolutely dominated. The Fast N' Wide offense that he implemented set a new standard for the entire league and kept opposing teams guessing and struggling to keep up with their high-tempo approach and explosive plays. The Royals were the class of the Northern Conference in 2022, but Coach Jackson's influence on European football will be felt for years to come. I have a great deal of respect for Randy and consider him a good friend. As an American who coached in Germany for years, I am glad he's back in the States!"

Troy Tomlin
HC New Yorker Lions
Eight-time GFL Champion and Five-time Eurobowl Champion Coach

"Randy Jackson is a coach's coach. I had a front row seat for this entire "Royal" journey. Every coach, business and community leader needs to read this fascinating book. He took a simple offensive philosophy combined with a transformative culture and revolutionized German football. Our team played for a Louisiana State championship after incorporating all of these principles."

Dennis Dunn
HC North Desoto High School, North Desoto, Louisiana
2022 Class 4A State Finalist, 9x State Champion

"I'm thrilled to say that I'm a part of the FNW team and am grateful for the community of coaches worldwide. This is our fourth season in Fast N' Wide, and I couldn't be happier we joined. Since 2020, we've averaged 52 points per game and broken every offensive record. We were state finalists in 2021 but were able to 'Ring the Bell' and bring home the big trophy in 2022. None of this would have been possible without Randy's help and Fast N' Wide!"

John Lilly
HC Independence High School, Independence, WV
13-0 State Champions
West Virginia Coach of the Year

"Randy has been a servant leader to the "Fast-N-Wide" community. Taking his leadership style and offensive philosophy to Europe was going to be an adventure! What he was able to do in Germany in the locker room and on the football field was unprecedented. His ability to pull back the curtain, so that his American colleagues could learn and grow as coaches, was life-changing and career altering for many coaches. Randy is a connector, a tireless worker, and a winner who inspires those around him. Our run to the state finals was powered by some incredible kids, dedicated coaches, and a 'Fast-N-Wide' mindset that gave our offense the edge we needed."

Neil Weiner
135-67 Career Record
President - Louisiana Football Coaches Association
3x State Coach of the Year (2013, 2019, 2022)
7x District Coach of the Year

ISBN: 9798398219579

Printed in the United States of America

"Either write something worth reading

or do something worth writing (about)."

Ben Franklin, Poor Richard's Almanac, 1738

FORWARD

As soon as I started reading Randy Jackson's incredible book, "A Royal Season," I started thinking about what it reminded me of . . .

Then, in a blinding flash of the obvious, it came to me – Ted Lasso!

Look at this . . .

- Ted and Randy are both American football coaches.
- Ted and Randy both leave the Good Ole U.S.A. to coach in Europe.
- Ted and Randy both hate hot tea.
- Ted and Randy both have great stories to tell about their adventures.

But there's one BIG difference between Ted and Randy: Ted's story is fiction while Randy's story is fact! It's all real!!!

It's been said that there are only two types of people in the world:
#1. Those who absolutely love Ted Lasso.
#2. Those who haven't watched it yet!

Here's another commonality . . .
There are only two types of people in the world:
#1. Those who absolutely love "A Royal Season."
#2. Those who haven't read it yet!

Congratulations on starting to read "A Royal Season." You're going to love it!!!

Robert Gilbert, Ph.D.
Professor of Applied Sport Psychology
Montclair State University (NJ)
Founder of The Success Hotline

ACKNOWLEDGMENTS

Thank you so much, Dr. Rob Gilbert, for all of your incredible guidance and support throughout the writing process of this book. Your expertise and insights have been invaluable, and I am endlessly grateful for the countless hours you have dedicated to helping me bring this project to fruition. Your kindness and generosity have truly made a difference, and I cannot thank you enough for all that you have done.

Thank you, Phil Blue, Drew Douglas, and Jay Zeller. My 'case study' readers who gave me corrections and ideas that truly improved the project.

THANK YOU ALL SO MUCH!

Where there is no guidance, the people fall,

But in the abundance of counselors, there is victory.

Proverbs 1

Contents

PART 3 - THE FIRST HALF OF THE REGULAR SEASON

PART 4 - THE SECOND HALF OF THE REGULAR SEASON

THE PLAYOFFS

INTRODUCTION
By Randy Jackson

"I WOULD HAVE FIRED ME ON THE SPOT."

"Field goal, field goal!" I yelled after the ball fell incomplete in the back of the end zone.

"That was fourth down, coach." Michael Vogt, the Potsdam Royals head coach, told me with a look of disgust.

WHAT?!?!? I thought that was third down. It HAS to be third down.

If I'd called a play on fourth down thinking it was third down, I should immediately walk off the sideline and head directly to the Berlin airport back to the States.

No legitimate coach is this stupid.

Although we snap the ball as fast as any team on the planet, there's no way I wouldn't know it was fourth down. I'm too smart not to understand what dang down it is. After all, I'm a veteran coach from Texas, where we get fired if we make mistakes that lose games.

The play before, the actual third down, was from the 10-yard line going in to score. We were in the red zone in the season's first game versus the defending German Football League champions, the Dresden Monarchs.

I called a pass play that fell incomplete but didn't realize it was third down, so I called a pass play on fourth down so quickly that no one on our sideline could get the field goal team out for an easy three points.

Lord, have mercy on my soul. How could I have made a blunder of this magnitude?

Embarrassed doesn't begin to describe my emotions, but I didn't have time to wallow in it; I had to p*ark the mistake* and go. "So what, next play" in my mind.

It was the first quarter of the first game in my new pro football coaching career, and I'd already made a rookie error that could cost us the win. I've been reminded several times the Royals haven't defeated the Monarchs. What if we lost to Dresden again, and my stupidity was the deciding factor?

Although I'd coached for 31 years, the last 21 as a head coach, I hadn't called plays in several seasons and let the moment get the best of me. Dresden was the defending GFL champions that the Royals had never defeated, and this was a massive game if we were going to make the playoffs. Not only was it the home opener, but I'd relentlessly reminded our team how good we'd be if they trusted me and our Fast N' Wide offense. I'd preached for months about how we'd be the most explosive unit in Europe and terrorize the GFL with the highest-tempo offense anyone had ever seen.

If I were the head coach, I would've exploded on our offensive coordinator for not paying attention to the down. There's no way a seasoned veteran could cost us a chance at an easy field goal and not feel my wrath. Although I would've felt bad later, at the moment, any attempt to keep a neutral mindset would've flown out the window.

On a bright note, I was thrilled Coach Vogt wasn't giving me the business end of a well-earned butt-chewing. He walked away and began calling a defensive play, leaving me to sort out how to pick myself up and shake it off.

I felt 3" tall at this moment, and to make things worse, I was about to have to face the offensive players who were headed over to see me for our routine sideline meeting after each offensive series.

What did I tell them?

You'll find out because you'll be on the bench with them.

I'll unpack this and much more. You'll get to sit in our Zoom meetings, attend practices, listen to our pregame speeches and be in our sideline huddle before an offensive series. You'll "take a knee" with us after practices and games. You'll feel the anguish when one of us gets injured and celebrate with us after a big win.

You'll be a member of the 2022 Potsdam Royals.

A Royal Season is a three-prong story:

- It's my journey of installing and overseeing an offensive system unlike anything ever seen in the German Football League.
- How we created a player's creed that convinced a team of men from literally all over the world who had just met each other to unite as a "band of brothers."
- Lastly, it's a story of people. Europeans somehow found the American football game, which got in their DNA. I'll introduce you to American players whose college careers were over but couldn't hang up their cleats. You'll meet coaches and volunteers who work tirelessly to make the Royals' small budget stretch far enough to produce success.

To my knowledge, *A Royal Season* is the first book written by an American coach in the German Football League. My heart for *A Royal Season* is to serve coaches and leaders. It's also my attempt to pull back the curtain for anyone who wants to know how American football operates on the highest level in Europe. I'll tell the story of my fish-out-of-water experience of navigating the culture shock of life in Potsdam, Germany.

The structure of *A Royal Season* will be from the perspective of me wearing a white coat in a laboratory. I'll describe how I transitioned from the American football hotbed of Texas to the soccer-obsessed culture of Europe, which was nothing short of eye-opening.

You'll get a front-row seat on the entire process from when I signed my contract in October until the season's final whistle. You'll be in the room when we install the offense and create our players' creed. I'll give you a *paint-by-numbers* system of how we went from not knowing each other to a tribe mentality. You'll hear the pregame pep talks and watch the movie clips we used to bring the messages home. In short, you'll be a member of the 2022 Potsdam Royals.

A Royal Season is based on a true story. There will be some fictionalization of characters and events for ease in the flow of the story, but the tactics, stats, and game results are all 100% accurate.

My time with the Royals had its highs and lows. Returning to Texas after six months in Europe, I found myself a changed person in many ways. The experiences and lessons I learned during my time abroad profoundly impacted how I view my role as a coach, husband, and father. Throughout the six-month season, our team, much like a family, went through a roller coaster of emotions and experiences. The highs and lows we faced together ultimately shaped us into a stronger, more united group.

Bitte schöen (thank you), for coming on this adventure with me. I hope you'll learn as much as I did and enjoy it almost as much as I did!

1

LOOKING FOR A NEW LABORATORY

I was walking down the hall of North Forney High School in the spring of 2021 with a college football recruiter. We were on our way to meet a rising senior athlete. As we walked past the cafeteria and the library, we turned a corner, and there it was; our newly remodeled state-of-the-art science laboratory. It had everything a student could want to analyze, test and conduct experiments on anything under the sun. Although science was never my thing, being in this classroom was inspiring. It made me want to fire up a Bunsen burner and memorize the periodic table again.

That's when it hit me. I have been in a laboratory my entire career!

Texas is a football-crazed state, an elite laboratory for all things gridiron. We not only had access to our lab during football season but for the entire school year. I've been in a state-of-art research facility for 31 years as a high school coach. Our budgets have been more than most; our number of coaches has been larger than some college staff, and all our coaches have been on campus the entire day as full-time teachers (most states do not require coaches to be full-time employees). Athletics, as the class is known state-wide, is part of the school day, just like English, history, or math. In Texas, athletes and coaches of all sports not only practice before or after school but are allowed to use it for a physical education credit. In the offseason, programs are permitted 60 minutes a day to increase strength, conditioning, and athletic development.

Would the same laws of football, team building, and leadership work in a place where football doesn't have near-religious status? Could I go to a laboratory without all the advantages and have the same success my teams have had in Texas?

I've always been a builder. I rarely stayed in a program for more than four years because the train was on the tracks by year four, so to speak, and I began to get bored.

It was year four for me at North Forney.

Being a head coach is similar to being a company CEO with over 200 employees. Both roles require strong leadership, effective communication, and the ability to make tough decisions in high-pressure situations. As a result, I was focused on maintaining the status quo and resolving routine challenges. Much of my time was spent addressing the day-to-day issues instead of having a sense of mission and creating something new.

The past season was fun, but not as much as it should've been. We'd just completed a

10-2 season in ever-present Covid restrictions. I was eligible for retirement and started asking my financial advisor about crunching the numbers to see how it would affect my pension if I got out or stayed another year.

I decided to retire from coaching. I pulled the trigger and didn't look back.

Walking away from being the head coach at North Forney High School was the most significant professional decision I've ever made. I had a great job in a tremendous school district, Forney I.S.D. The administration supported and treated me well. I loved our coaching staff and parents. Unlike some coaches in Texas, I was not on a hot seat coaching to keep my job every year.

I could make over six-figures and win enough games to keep my job for as long as I wanted to stay.

Some athletes and even coaches go past their prime because they can't walk away from the sport that has been in their blood for decades. Nothing in the world comes close to being in the locker room before a game or celebrating with a team after a big win. But I wouldn't be the guy who burned out and didn't give it my all.

Although I had security and contentment, it wasn't fueling my fire. I wasn't going to allow my love for the crowd's roar to keep me from chasing a new dream.

Now what? I wanted to write more, but could full-time writing satisfy my need to serve others? I have been coaching coaches with my Fast N' Wide offensive system, but it's not like being on the sideline with a team. Could I live with being home during the day and not in a huddle?

Within a couple of months, I had my answer.

Nope.

I wanted to lock arm-in-arm again with a group of players and coaches.

I began researching where I could go for a season and test my laws of football. Where could I find a laboratory with only a fraction of the things that make up how we do football in Texas?

There were several possibilities for me to consider; my first thought was researching how it would be to coach in a state where football isn't king. In almost every area of the country, the structure of high school football isn't Texas-like. Coaches are not full-time employees of the schools, and sports are not allowed a class period during the school day.

What about the college level? How would coaching college-age athletes be? I contemplated what my laboratory would look like if I were an offensive coordinator at a junior college, NAIA, or Division III program. I didn't doubt the Fast N' Wide offense at the next level, but would the leadership principles I believe in work?

Would my tactics work with 18-22-year-old men? Would college-age athletes buy into my ultra-simple offensive system? Could I get them to believe in an authentic team culture and lay in traffic for each other?

I know football and how to transform teams, so my fear and anxiety were not bigger than my dream. The more I thought about it, the more I wanted to go somewhere that would absolutely prove my theories. I wanted to find a place where dad and grandpa didn't play, so the game was not spoken of at the dinner table. An area where they have been getting their butt kicked for years or where football isn't a big deal. Maybe even somewhere that they barely know what football is.

I needed to find my laboratory because, after all my years of coaching, I was ready to conduct the greatest experiment of my life. This next chapter would be an incredible experience to teach my consulting clients and make a terrific third book!

Three days after my epiphany, this comment came across the Fast N' Wide group chat:

"I know this is a long shot, but is anyone here interested in coaching in Germany?"

2

ANYONE WANT TO COACH IN GERMANY?

October 2021

"I have a buddy who is a general manager of a professional team in Lübeck, Germany. They're looking for a head coach. I know the chances are slim that anyone in our group wants to move to Northern Europe, but I thought I'd post it anyway."

Pro football in Germany? I've always loved to travel but haven't ever been to Europe. Soccer-crazy Germany could be just the lab I needed to prove my laws of football and team building.

I texted Seth and asked him more about the situation.

"I've got a buddy who runs the Lübeck Cougars in northern Germany. It's a GFL 2 franchise, so it's not the highest level of ball over there, but you'd have guys who love the game and are good athletes."

Seth helped me set up a Zoom meeting with Mark Holte, his buddy and general manager of the Cougars.

I was still deciding if I wanted the responsibility of being a head coach again, but it was worth a call to find out more. Within a few days, I had an informal interview with Mr. Holtze. He'd grown up in the U.S., so speaking with him was easy. He understood my questions from an American football perspective. I'd soon realize this would not always be the case.

"We're looking for someone to come and live in Lübeck full-time. The head coach isn't only for our GFL 2 team but also the man in charge of our youth teams."

Wait a minute; the Cougars have several teams? I was about to get an education on how team sports are played in Europe.

"How many teams does your organization have?" I asked.

"We have six teams total in Lübeck and cheerleading programs for kids to participate in. We offer a co-ed flag team for all ages. We have groups for ages 13 and under, 16 and under, 19 and under, Prospects, the equivalent of an American junior varsity squad, and our main GFL 2 team. Our teams regularly compete against others from around the region and beyond. Basically, all team sports in Europe are structured in the club model. We have to grow our top team from the ground up. We need this position to oversee the development of our farm system as much as winning games with our GFL 2 team."

I knew a little about the European culture of sports, but this was enlightening and fascinating to me. I didn't realize local clubs were the primary method for organizing and participating. Instead of playing for their school team, a German teenager joins a local club and practices at night. It sounded like the organization of a professional team in Germany was a combination of a youth league, middle school, high school, and small college football in the States.

Oh my, this situation sounded like a lot of work and stress. This was way more than I wanted to do a few months after retirement. I wished Mr. Holtze the best, but the Cougars needed someone wanting to build several teams, recruit players and coaches, and be the face of the organization. I was hoping this would be something I could do for four or five months, then come back home. Now what? What are the odds of someone else I knew having a connection like this? I needed a laboratory but didn't want to run the whole science department.

I told Seth I wasn't the correct fit for his friend in Lübeck.

"They need someone who will be all in like I have been the last twenty-one years. Mark seems like a great guy, but I'm looking to help an organization at this point in my life, not run one."

Seth had another idea.

"You need to post your resume online. Go to the website Europlayers and upload it. A few teams are most likely looking for an offensive coordinator for next season. All European clubs use Europlayers to help them find players and coaches."

A few days ago, my conversation showed me that I didn't know squat about football in Europe. The odds of finding the right laboratory were slim, but if you don't ask, the answer is always no, so I hit send and crossed my fingers.

3

COACHING FOR SCHNITZEL

October 2021

In the meantime, I decided to Google American football in Europe and do a little research.

I needed help gathering information about how the average club plays and organizes our brand of football. I found lots of social media posts from teams in virtually every European country, but finding something of substance was more challenging than I thought it would be.

I understood the laboratories wouldn't be similar, but would they resemble in the least bit what I was used to in Texas?

I did find an actual book on American football in Europe written by John Grisham titled, *Playing for Pizza.* Grisham, the famous author with nearly 50 straight #1 best-sellers, departed from his typical courtroom dramas to write a book on American football in Italy. The story is based on a real-life American football team. When researching the book, Grisham even went to Parma, watched a game, and met with Head Coach Andrew Papoccia, a graduate of Illinois State University.

It's the story of Rick Dockery, a 28-year-old, 3rd-string quarterback who the Cleveland Browns cut after he blew a 17-point lead in the AFC championship game. He asks his agent to find a team that needs him anywhere in the world. The team his agent found was the Parma Panthers. The Panthers play in a mid-level Italian football league. Rick soon learns that Parma loves fine wines, tiny cars, and good pasta. While his teammates love football, the city or country doesn't.

By the novel's end, Rick learns to love the Italian lifestyle. He and his teammates enjoy 4-hour dinners with several courses and create a bond that doesn't exist in the NFL. Parma wins the league championship, Rick meets a love interest and stays in Italy for another season.

Playing for Pizza does not paint a pretty picture for a guy spoiled to a laboratory with everything a coach could need in a state that loves football as much as BBQ and guns. It was crystal clear from chapter one that small-town Italian football would be a hobby as much as a team. My goal wasn't to become the next Rick Dockery. I was excited about a challenge to test my coaching and leadership skills, but be careful what you wish for ran through my mind as I turned each page.

The Lubeck Cougars' GFL 2 team only practiced two days a week, and they sounded more professional than Grisham's Parma Panthers. As much as I wanted to see Europe for the first time, I needed to find a situation where football wasn't a hobby.

Sometimes God takes care of a fool. This time it was my turn for His favor because I received a message from the Potsdam Royals a few days later.

The Royals are a GFL 1 team that had been to the semi-finals in 2021 and were hungry to take the next step.

Saul Goodman, the general manager and assistant head coach, reached out through the Europlayers website to ask if I'd be interested in a Zoom interview.

"We're looking for an offensive coordinator. The coach we hire will have carte blanche to run his system. Let me know if you're interested in speaking with me. We'll move quickly."

A couple of days later, I was face to face in a Zoom interview with Saul, originally from London, so he had a thick British accent. For a Texan, speaking with him was different, but English is his first language, so the conversation was easy.

"What do you know about football across the pond?" Coach Goodman asked me.

"Not much other than it's always something I've wanted to do. I haven't traveled much and felt like this would be my "semester abroad-backpack through Europe" experience."

I also mentioned reading *Playing for Pizza* as part of my research.

"I've read the book, and we're nothing like Grisham's story. We're a legit organization that'll spend the money to win. Some teams operate on a shoestring budget, especially in the GFL 2 and leagues in other countries. With us, you'll get a plane ticket to come here and one to return home. We'll pay your apartment rent, electricity, cell phone, and medical. All you have to do is get to DFW airport, and we'll pay for everything for you for the next six months, other than your meals. Not only will we do this for you, but for around 25 of our players. We take care of our team. Our roster will have guys from at least 15 different countries. The Royals spend a lot to get them here and back."

"Overall, the quality of football here compares roughly to Division 2 or 3 NCAA ball. We'll have a few ex-Division 1 players, some of the best native Germans, and other outstanding players from all over Europe."

We discussed many subjects; the Royals' organizational structure, how GFL teams recruit players, what he felt they needed to take the next step, and much more. I was getting a crash course on how different the game is outside of the U.S., which was fascinating.

Although I am always reluctant to bring up money in an interview, after several minutes, I asked, "What does this pay?"

David Saul

"Well…our OC last year was an ex-NFL guy who didn't need the money, so he wasn't paid anything."

After a few seconds of silence, I determined we had started negotiations. I'm historically terrible at asking for money, but I countered with, "I'm a retired high school coach, so I'll need to earn a salary if I'm going to eat.

“What did y'all pay the guy before the last one?"

"He made 1,000 euros a month, which is way more than enough to pay for food. Potsdam was behind the wall, which was part of East Germany. Expenses here are less than what they are in former West Germany. You can get a good meal at a restaurant for around $12. In Cologne or Munich, the cost of living is probably 25% higher."

Within a few days, I was in another Zoom with Saul and the Royals' head coach, Michael Vogt, who goes by “Berti." To say Berti loves the Royals would be an understatement. He not only played for the team for several years but founded the Royals from scratch in 2005.

Coach Vogt was quiet and reserved. He didn't speak much in the interview, and this concerned me.

Why? Because head coaches are usually alphas. To describe a head coach as quiet and reserved is an oxymoron. The outstanding ones I knew or witnessed coaching on T.V. were type-A personalities with a big presence. The leader must command the situation throughout a season or even a single practice. I could sense I'd like Berti and enjoy getting to know him, but I wondered if he would bring the juice or drop the hammer when necessary.

Coach Vogt didn't quiz me about the details of the offense or what plays I'd call in certain situations. He listened, nodded, and was very polite. He then explained his role within the organization. "My #1 job is logistics. Saul finds the players, and I figure out how to get our board to approve the money to pay them. After they sign a contract, I secure their flights and flats."

Michael 'Berti' Vogt

It was time for me to ask a few questions so I would clearly understand what to expect when we started training camp in April.

"What is the #1 thing you both feel has to happen for the Royals to take the next step and win a championship?"

Coach Saul answered first, "The professional answer is we need help scoring more points, team culture, and practice efficiency. The answer from the heart is we need someone to help us beat Dresden for the first time, create energy in Potsdam and put more butts in the seats. We want to take the next step and hope you're the right guy to take us there."

That statement fired me up immensely. I knew I'd be an assistant for the first time in over twenty years, but I'd hoped to have some input in the day-to-day operations.

"Coach Saul and I know what our strengths are. We understand the GFL, how to maximize our budget, and the administration's need for a worldwide roster. We also know we don't see the game like a coach with your experience does in some areas. We're very interested in you teaching us more than offense," Coach Vogt added.

The Royal laboratory was sounding better and better.

"How many coaches did you guys have on staff last year?"

"We were short last season at some spots. We had three on offense and two on defense."

"What days did you practice?"

Again, Saul answered quickly, "We will train on Mondays and Wednesdays and have a 60-minute 'get ready' type session the day before the games. The schedule has yet to be publicized by the league, but we'll play most games on Saturdays."

Potsdam sounded like real football. It seemed like this situation would allow me to investigate and analyze in a place where very few American coaches have ever studied. The Royal lab would allow me to test the Fast N' Wide offense and an even more challenging experiment, a True North team culture.

Our conversation didn't last more than 45 minutes. A contract was emailed to me that day; I printed it, signed it, and sent it back. I was now officially a Potsdam Royal for the 2022 season.

I felt like I'd just put on my white lab coat for the very first time, and right above the pocket, it said, "Coach Jackson, Offensive Coordinator - Potsdam Royals."

Looking back, the initial zoom with Saul a few days earlier was when I had landed the job. The second interview with Berti was so he could get to know me and make everything official to tell the Royals' board.

My heart was racing as I stepped out of my comfort zone. I'd left the security of being a head coach in Texas to the great unknown. While I've heard of many major German cities like Berlin or Munich, I couldn't point them out on a map for a million Euros. I thought I'd heard of Potsdam from the movie *Bridge of Spies*, but I'd have to google to make sure.

"We'll have a press release in a few days. After that, you'll be free to share it on social media and announce it to your family and friends."

I was grateful for the opportunity Coach Vogt and Saul gave me, but one thing bothered me as I did a post-event debrief of the entire interview process…

GFL
Kiel Baltic Hurricanes
Berlin Rebels
Braunschweig NY Lions
LIONS
Potsdam Royals
Dresden Monarchs
Cologne Crocodiles
Marburg Mercenaries
Frankfurt Universe
UNIVERSE
Saarland Hurricanes
Schwäbisch Hall Unicorns
Stuttgart Scorpions
Munich Cowboys
Ravensburg Razorbacks
RAZORBACKS
Allgäu Comets

4

INSTRUMENTS FOR THE ROYAL LABORATORY

November 2021

As I prepared to immerse myself in this Royal experience, I couldn't help but wonder if it would live up to the high standards set by Texas football. Would this new environment capture the essence of big-time football, or would I find myself longing for the familiar standard of the Texas gridiron?

I wasn't sure what was next, but finding out didn't take long. Within a week or so, I received a voice text from Saul, "We need to sign a tight end. If you have the time, I'd like to send you highlight videos of a few of the guys we're considering, and you tell us which one will fit best in your offense."

I not only had the time, but was grateful to be a part of the recruitment process. Saul was wise to allow me to have some say in the personnel for our offense because to say it's non-traditional is an understatement. We have a tight end, but it's not the NFL-type most offenses employ.

I'd explained the basics of how we'd attack and score to Coach Vogt and Goodman, but getting the right pieces was vital.

"Sounds terrific," I responded. "I'll watch all three of them today and let you know."

The first tight end was from a Scandinavian league team. He'd definitely make us better in the passing game and be a threat near the goal line. He was tall and seemed reasonably athletic. When the ball was snapped, he had a good burst, was an excellent route runner, and his hands impressed me.

All of this meant one thing; he was totally the wrong fit for what we needed for this position.

Our tight end is a glorified offensive lineman who gets to wear a receiver number and catch passes in warm-ups. This guy looked like he dreamt about touchdowns. We needed someone who was a big body and loved to move people. We'd throw him the ball some, but not much.

On to the next candidate with my fingers crossed.

It was more of the same. This player was shorter than the first one but slightly faster. He was from the Italian league, which is not as strong as the GFL, so he was making plays against inferior defensive backs and linebackers. Again, he had excellent hands and played hard.

If we were to employ a traditional NFL-style offense, both candidates might have been good enough, but we'd be far different than either of these offenses. Neither of these players would have enjoyed playing tight end for us.

We needed something else. We needed a bruiser who fantasized about knocking people down.

At this point, Saul didn't know what I wanted at tight end, so he wasn't casting his net in the right place yet. I had one more player to watch, and if he didn't fit the bill, I'd have to tell Goodman we needed to keep looking.

Saul could begin looking for a quarterback or running back because it was love at first sight when I watched this bruiser on tape.

We didn't have to look any further. In about three plays, I knew this guy was what we needed. He wasn't only a big man, 6'2", 280 pounds, but was a violent run blocker who mauled defenders. He'd played for a GFL 2 team in northern Germany, so his competition wasn't exactly what he'd face in our league, but it was easy to see he was the right fit.

Jerome Valbon was 30 years old and had several seasons under his belt.

"Email him a contract today, please. Valbon's a rare breed that's becoming extinct. He's perfect for us."

"Are you sure? He's not much of a pass catcher."

"Exactly, he'll be a sixth offensive lineman who will block 95% of the time but who can still make a catch on a bootleg or down in the red zone."

"I guess I don't understand. The guy from Sweden is a stud. I thought he'd be a legitimate dual-threat tight end, which is rare in Europe."

"This offense doesn't need a dual threat type of guy. If we sign someone who thinks he is coming here to catch four passes a game, he'll be upset before training camp starts. We must be very clear we're not looking for a traditional tight end. In fact, I call this position a *pipe wrench* because he'll be a blue-collar blocker most of the time. Trust me on this one, Jerome is a pipe wrench, and we need him."

To his credit, Goodman agreed and didn't hesitate. He pulled the trigger and offered Valbon a contract the next day.

I started watching player highlights almost daily in November. The Royals were doing what they said they'd do; sign imports and improve our roster. Not only did I evaluate a lot of highlights, but I also started being included in the Zoom calls so I could explain our up-tempo offense to potential players. They allowed me to bring the juice about how simple and fun the offense would be. It was easy for me to be enthusiastic because I believed every word I was telling them.

"The Royals will be the most up-tempo team in the history of Europe! We'll score 50+ points a game and terrorize the GFL. People will talk about this offense and team for years to come. If you join us, you'll be asked one day, "So, you played in that offense?"

While Berti and Saul knew much more about the league, the logistics, and everything a new player would want to know, they didn't have high-energy personalities when speaking to potential players. When I spoke to a recruit, my goal was to transfer passion from me to them. I didn't sugar-coat or stretch the truth. I made it clear to them that this offense would be unlike any they had ever played on, or any that GFL defenses had ever witnessed.

In the next few weeks, we continued to meet with and sign players from all over Europe. We added Stefan Stefansson, a lineman from Iceland. Next, we signed a running back from Finland, Karri Pajarinen, and another offensive lineman from Australia, Brenden Oswin. We were thrilled when we added veteran center Bobby Sövegjarto from one of our rivals, the New Yorker Lions.

This was becoming a much bigger laboratory than I ever imagined.

But the biggest selling job I had to do was in mid-November when Saul texted me, *'I think I have found a quarterback; his name is Chris Helbig. I am emailing you his film. Let me know what you think.'*

I curtailed my expectations, knowing how hard the position of quarterback is to play. It's a good thing I did because watching the film made the surprise that much sweeter.

Helbig could play.

Quarterback is not a one size fits all position by any means. I've had small, fast guys, big guys who were slow and medium-sized players who all got the job done. When your team has a "dude" at quarterback, you have a chance to be very good.

Chris' size was excellent, 6'4" and 220 pounds, and his game tape showed he could make all the throws. He also extended plays with his running ability when his pass protection broke down.

Chris started at Southern Utah University in 2018 and was very productive. The Covid shutdown in 2020 derailed his career there, so he transferred to Eastern Michigan but didn't get on the field. At 25, he was looking for a chance to show he still had some tread left on the tire and wanted to play.

At first glance, he was a no-brainer, but the game film only tells part of the story.

It's not the measurables, size, arm strength, and speed that make or break a quarterback. Intangibles determine if teammates will follow him or if he has the grit to shake off a mistake in crunch time. If I were a college recruiter deciding to sign a quarterback, my career and my family's welfare would depend on offering the right player. I'd ask everyone and anyone I could about his character, work ethic, and mental toughness. It'd be my job to determine if he had the skill set, but there would be a lot more research before we'd spend a scholarship on a quarterback.

I didn't have that luxury in this situation. I can't overstate this; finding the right [1]QB1 was everything for us. We had to sign a difference-maker. I couldn't miss on my evaluation, and the Royals had to do what it took to sign whomever we determined was our guy.

I didn't have any connections with a coach at Southern Utah or Eastern Michigan, so our Zoom with Helbig would be my only shot to see if I could get a feel for what type of person he was.

Although he passed the 'yes, he can play' test, I didn't plan on spending the next six months in Germany with a quarterback who wasn't a team-first guy. We had to ask the right questions, and one of the first questions I'd ask Helbig was, "What do you want me to call on…"

---

[1] QB1 - starting quarterback.

5

WHAT'S THE CALL ON...?

November 2021

...4th and two?

Helbig was in Colorado working part-time and training to play the upcoming season. Saul told me he had other teams interested, so we needed to decide quickly if we wanted to offer him.

We started the Zoom with the routine we had established. Saul thanked him for joining us and then introduced me as the offensive coordinator for 2022. He then asked me to explain how we'd operate with our tempo and explosive play. As usual, I brought high energy and enthusiasm to the conversation. After giving Chris the basic foundations of Fast N' Wide, I gauged his interest in us.

"We'll terrorize the GFL with an offense that hasn't ever been defended on European soil. We'll play faster, hit more big plays, and score more points than anyone in the history of ever IF we find an elite quarterback."

"Are you the guy we need?"

"Yes, sir. I believe I am."

I followed with, "If this works out, you'll have won the lottery getting to direct this offense. This season you'll have the most fun you've ever had playing football. Our scheme is amazingly simple, but we'll score a ton of points, and you'll get to throw the ball deep. On 90% of our pass plays, you'll have seven teammates protecting you and only one receiver to read. You'll literally be able to stand back and play catch with our receivers. I founded a consulting group a few years ago where I teach the offense to coaches all over the U.S. It's called Fast N' Wide and will be the closest thing to playing the game as you did in the backyard as a kid. You'll have a total blast destroying defenses this season. The GFL hasn't seen anything like what the '22 Royals offense will be. I guarantee it."

After giving Chris the sales pitch, I asked him where his head and heart were after sitting out a couple of years.

"You've had some time off since Southern Utah and Eastern Michigan. Are you sure you still want to play?"

"Absolutely, coach. I love football. I always have and always will. I'm 25, so I have a few good years left. I've decided to go to Europe and get on the field again. I'm training as hard as I ever have in my life. Whoever I sign with will get a guy with something to prove."

Chris was confident but not arrogant. I liked him, so I kept firing questions at him.

"We're looking for a quarterback with the *'it'* factor. I assume you've heard this term before and know what I'm referring to?"

"Yes, sir. I 100% believe I have the *'it'* factor. As soon as I find a team, I'll reach out to every member on the roster, introduce myself and start growing relationships. I was a team captain at Southern Utah and will be one for the Royals."

"If you become our starting quarterback, what will you do between now and training camp to make us a better team?" I asked.

"I'll study our playbook, meet with you every day if you want, continue to train my tail off, and, as I said earlier, begin the bonding process with my new teammates."

"Let me give you a scenario. We are on the two-yard line, and it's 4th and goal. What do you want me to call?"

"I want the ball in my hands. I want you to put the game on my shoulders. I won't be stopped from getting the ball in the endzone."

"Bingo! That's what I was hoping you'd say. We won't run our quarterback much in our regular offense, but on 4th and short, be ready to run quarterback power."

I was sold. Not only did Helbig give exactly the right answers, but I believed every word he said. I'd buy a used car from that guy. We talked a little more, but I was ready to pull the trigger. I was hoping Saul felt the same way.

We ended the Zoom with Saul saying, "Thanks again for meeting with us today. I'll speak with Coach Jackson immediately, so expect an answer soon."

"What do you think?" Saul asked me.

"This is the first time I've recruited a quarterback, but Chris convinced me. Not only did I love what he said, but he also said it with 100% conviction, and that's what sold me. I want to coach that guy."

Saul wisely cautioned me, "We haven't talked about money with him yet or his demands, but if you like him, I'm good to start serious negotiations. I'll contact him tomorrow and see if we can strike a deal. Don't get your hopes up, though. He has other offers on the table."

The next day, I received a WhatsApp message from Saul that read...

"Chris Helbig's a Royal! We got our QB1!"

Yes sir. What a relief to get a guy who appears to be a solid piece of our puzzle. We have a chance to be good if Chris is everything he appears to be, but time will tell. I've gotten my hopes up before and been disappointed.

Over the next few weeks, Saul and I continued adding to the roster. After snagging Helbig, he told me he was looking for our other American starter. The GFL only allows two American players on the field at once, so most teams use their allotment with guys who touch the ball, like QB, running back, or wide receiver.

"Last year, we had an absolute beast of a running back who played division II college ball in Florida. His name is Jake Johnson, and we'd love to have him back. We're still waiting to see if he can find a way to join us this season, but he has major issues at home. His current girlfriend is pregnant, and he already has a child with an ex."

Oh my. Just another reminder that I'm entering a world I haven't lived in before.

"As much as I'd love to have a top-three running back in the league, our offense can get by with a 'company guy' who will get 5 yards and block for Chris. What will make us go is a wide receiver who can go deep versus the better cornerbacks we'll face."

"Are you sure?" Saul responded. "Johnson is the best we've had here. I was going to push hard to get him back."

"Our offense is based on what the defense gives us. If the defense puts more defenders [2]in the box to stop the run, we'll have one-on-one coverage outside. If we get Helbig an elite receiver, he'll lead the GFL in passing this season. We can win the German Bowl with an average running back who is coachable and disciplined, but we can't win it with average receivers."

Again, to Saul's credit, he listened and trusted me. He not only found us a speed-burner, Brandon Polk, who played a few years back at Penn State but also a holy grail dual-passport receiver from Long Island, NY, Jared Wolfe, who played at Villanova. A dual passport means Jared wouldn't count as one of our [3]A's because his grandparents had German passports.

---

[2] The 'Box' is the area between the left offensive tackle and the right offensive tackle.

[3] A' - American

Acquiring talent was job #1, and we're crushing it so far.

My dad, himself a coach for 41 years, used to say, "You can't make chicken salad with chicken manure" (edited version). Although I knew very little about the GFL, I could evaluate skill and effort. Our three American players would be significant upgrades over the same positions the Royals had in 2021.

It was still early December, but Christmas was coming early. I was feeling better and better about our American players.

A ROCKET AND A UNICORN

December 2021

I asked Saul and Berti about starting an offensive chat so we could begin getting to know each other better. Saul responded, "We have a Google Classroom where we communicate with everyone. I'll get the 2022 one up and going."

Google Classroom is a tool for uploading information. Teachers use it to post communication and assignments, but there are better places to foster back-and-forth dialogue.

"I haven't used Google Classroom, and I'm sure there's a place for it, but I want something where we can text each other daily. No one wants another email notification, but texting is different. Every one of these guys texts at least 100 times a day, so this will be right up their alley."

I didn't get the feeling that either of them was a believer, but neither objected, so I proceeded. I created a WhatsApp offensive chat group that day. WhatsApp is a global texting type platform that's very popular worldwide. I've used it for the last several years with my teams, coaches, parents, booster club, etc. It was a perfect fit to use with the Royals since it is internet based. Every player could access our group, no matter if they were in Australia or Finland.

When creating a brand for your team, you must be intentional with the words you choose. Words have energy; they can help, harm or hinder. Words matter. At North Forney, we branded our weight room the 'Collision Enhancement Center.' Why? Because it not only sounds better than the weight room, it puts into our athletes' minds why we're lifting. The title I chose for our group was *Autobahn 80*. Lots of teams in the GFL are no-huddle, but they don't snap the ball all that fast or run a high number of plays during a game. Our Fast N' Wide offense relies on us to play with a ludicrous tempo. Our goal is to run 80 plays per game.

"If we get to 80, we will score 50", is what they were going to hear me say from now till the end of the season.

I started with posting messages about coaching points of NCAA and NFL games (all the European players keep up with both). I would post a picture of a player holding the ball loosely and ask, "What's wrong with this picture?" or a quote about tempo or a clip of a play we would run from a past game I'd coached.

All of this generated lots of terrific dialogue. Just as has been the case with my other teams, they loved texting back and forth. Chris, Brandon, and Jared led from the front by commenting on posts and generating their own topics for discussion.

Chris and I had Zoomed a few times, but I was eager to get to know some other Royals, so I put a message on WhatsApp that I'd love to visit one-on-one with anyone who had the time.

ROCKET MAN

My first Zoom was with 25-year-old Brandon Polk, our 4.3 receiver from Penn State. Brandon grew up in Virginia, which is where he was living then. He was invited to training camp with the Los Angeles Rams, but after getting cut was no longer in football.

"Brandon, I am thrilled you are a Royal. Your speed jumps off the screen, even versus Ohio State and Michigan."

"Thank you, coach. You can just call me Polk; that's what everyone's called me since I can remember. I was always the smallest guy in the receiver meeting room but usually the fastest."

Polk was humble and very likable. He had two computer monitors running on both sides of him, so I asked about them. I'd intentionally discuss more than football in these 1-1 meetings. I also needed to know about their personal life to have a more than surface-level relationship.

"I'm a day trader. I use algorithms and a system to trade stocks. It's been a good living for me."

"Wow, that's awesome. I've always been in mutual funds and periodically an individual stock or two, but I don't know anyone who makes their living by day trading. That's fascinating."

"Yes, sir, I can show you sometime how I do it for sure."

"Very cool. I assume you'll continue to do this while we're in Germany?"

"Yes, sir, the 7-hour time difference will be somewhat of an issue, but I'll work around it."

Polk and I visited for about an hour. I asked him about his mom and dad, siblings, and a little about his upbringing.

"I'm lucky, my dad is an attorney, and my mom could stay home and care for my brother and me. We played everything growing up."

"I assume you ran track in high school?" I asked.

"Yes, sir. In my junior and senior years, I won the Virginia state championship in the 100 meters."

Oh, heck, yes. I knew Polk was fast, but I loved hearing he was "state champ fast" in high school. I now asked for his help in my mission of creating a team. "One thing I'll help bring to the Royals is an intentional culture. Tell me about the brand or culture at Penn State."

"It was phenomenal. In every daily meeting, we heard what it's like to be a Nittany Lion. Our head coach, James Franklin, constantly preached his message."

"Tell me about how it was playing for Coach Franklin."

"Coach Franklin's the real deal. He's a leader in every aspect and has his finger on the pulse of the team at all times. Sometimes, you might not like what he told you, but you respect the source. We were held accountable, but we all knew it was to get us to a place we wanted to go."

I expected Polk to say something like this about his experience at Penn State. He would be someone I leaned on to help us establish our culture or "The Royal Way" this season.

"That's awesome. Coach Saul and Coach Vogt say the Royals haven't ever had a set of core values or a players' creed. The edge most teams don't utilize or understand is mental performance and team connection. I'll ask guys like you, Helbig, and Wolfe to help me sell the importance of all of this. It'll be a work in progress, so I'm not sure how it will all unfold but be ready to be an assistant coach when we begin creating the Royals culture for 2022."

"I've noticed you're putting things in our WhatsApp to get the culture started. I'll make sure and chime in more often."

I liked Polk a lot. He was bright and seemed well-grounded. I texted Saul and Berti my thoughts and congratulated them again for finding and signing him.

SIX POINTS > SIX FIGURES

My next Zoom was with our other American receiver, Jared Wolfe. Jared was a finance major from Long Island who'd turned down a six-figure job on Wall Street to play one more season.

"Jared, it took me twenty-five years to make over 100k. You're coming to Potsdam to catch passes instead of starting your career and building your 401k?"

"I am, indeed, coach, and fired up about it. There'll be a time when I will ride the train to Wall Street every day, but I have a bigger dream I am chasing now. With the XFL and USFL starting back, I want a shot to play again, but I need to get on the field and put up some numbers to get a tryout."

"Saul explained that you're what they call a [4]unicorn because you have a dual passport and won't count as one of our A's. How do you have one?"

"My grandparents on my father's side immigrated here from Germany after the war.

Because of this, I qualify for a German passport, making me very marketable in the GFL. I had a few offers, but after hearing you speak about Fast N' Wide, my decision was easy."

"Tell me about your playing career from Peewee through college," I asked him.

"My dad started taking me to play at six years old, and I loved it from day one. I played other sports, baseball and basketball, but when I got to high school, I began to focus on football. I was a three-year varsity starter on a decent team but had few offers. From there, I played at Division 3, Western New England, in Springfield, Massachusetts. After two seasons at WNE, I transferred to Villanova. I earned a scholarship after the first year but never cracked the starting lineup as a receiver. I returned punts and kickoffs but only caught a few passes. I'm ready to make my mark at receiver."

"How did you connect with the Royals?"

"I've been working with the Long Island Receiver Academy for a few years, and the owner, Mike Vanucci, is friends with Coach Goodman.

"I've heard of Vanucci. He has a reputation for developing elite receivers. Lucky for us, they're buddies. I'm beginning to realize Coach Goodman has connections all over the world."

"Are you a Jets or Giants guy?"

---

[4] *Unicorn is a dual-passport player who grew up in the States but doesn't count as an American on the field where there is a limit of two.

"Giants all the way! I'll be at the Super Bowl rooting us to victory in a few years."

I was a little nervous about his ability, especially after hearing he didn't play much at a lower-level, Division 1 school. What I could sense, though, was his drive and ambition, which I loved. Jared was a hungry player running down big dreams, and I was ready to help him.

Just like Polk, Jared was more intelligent than most of my former players and myself, for that matter. At 24 years old, he was mature and would be a player-coach for me in Germany. When I signed my contract, I knew coaching professionals in a laboratory 5,500 miles from Texas would be drastically different.

But, the more I learned about our A's, the more I believed all three had some Texas football in them.

7

OUR FIRST OFFENSIVE MEETING

January 5, 2022

It was January, and although the season didn't kick off until May 20, it was time to get to work. One thing I never brought up to the recruits on our Zoom calls was my lack of pedigree compared to the Royals' offensive coordinator in 2021. Coach Brian Moon had worked with the Tampa Bay Buccaneers the year before coming to Potsdam. He helped lead the Royals to the GFL semi-finals for the first time, and the offense averaged a healthy 30 points per game.

In 2022, the play-caller would be a retired high school football coach.

On paper, no one would say we upgraded. Coach Moon had been with millionaires studying a game plan to win *Monday Night Football.* I'd been on the same practice field with high school kids barely shaving and studying to get their driver's licenses. No matter how closely they read it, a high school coach's resume wouldn't impress anyone. Our A's all played major college ball. The returning Royals from last year, had an ex-NFL assistant coaching them.

I've never lacked self-confidence and wasn't going to start doubting myself now.

OUR SECRET AK-47

I knew we'd take the league by storm, and our players would eventually believe in me 100%. But I had a secret weapon that would blow everyone's mind. Have you ever heard of the phrase, "Always bring a gun to a knife fight?" We wouldn't bring a pistol to the fight but an AK-47 machine gun. Our ultra-simple offense was something no defense had ever faced in Germany. Defensive coordinators were going to hate defending us. They'd never had to stop our #1 pass play, the choice route, but they'd also absolutely despise our tempo. We'd snap the ball faster than anyone in the history of Europe.

Why did I believe the Fast N' Wide offense would be so effective? FNW has been a near-secret offense developed and run at a Division 1, Big 12 program from 2010 - 2016. They led the NCAA's largest division in scoring and yards gained almost every year during this span. They also did a fantastic job of not telling anyone about it. I learned it in 2017 at North Forney High School when we hired a former assistant with the program. The offense changed my career ever since. In the first year, we scored 53 points and an equally insane 547 yards per game. In 2020, I took it a step further and started a consulting business called Fast N' Wide, where I teach it to coaches all over the United States. It was the perfect system for a German football laboratory.

But at this moment, today, the 2022 Royals didn't know any of this. Today, I'm just a retired high school coach with a Texas accent they haven't ever heard before. All of us are in sales whether we sell a literal product or not. As a seasoned coach, I always stress to my clients the importance of making a powerful first impression during their initial team meeting. Sales are about relationships, and my #1 job at this meeting was to sell myself and the offense. I needed the players to 'buy into me' and the system of play I was teaching. I advise client coaches they have one goal with their initial team meeting: to have the players go home and tell their parents, "We hired the right guy. I can't wait to play for Coach Smith." My mindset at this meeting was the same. I'd be the head coach of the offense, and I needed to build excitement. I wanted these guys to be fired up to get on the field in April and go Fast N' Wide. I also wanted to share a little about my personal life with them because connection creates bonding.

In this first group session, I would also use who would become a vital assistant in Potsdam, Chris Helbig. He'd been true to his word. We'd Zoomed a few times in December, and he was very sharp and conscientious. Chris always took notes and asked excellent questions. He might not have been invited to an NFL training camp but he had an NFL attitude and mentality. I'd hoped he could help with game-planning when we signed him, but now I had no doubt.

On January 5, we had our first offensive team meeting. The lab was opening for business, and it was time for me to deliver.

In 2021, Coach Moon's scheme was similar to a typical NFL offense. They didn't play fast. In fact, they huddled up between each play. We were going to be the exact opposite. We were going to terrorize the GFL with our lightning attack.

We had 21 players and two coaches, Vogt and Goodman. This session, and all others, would be recorded, so it wasn't critical, but I was hoping for a larger turnout. I knew we had a few guys, like Brenden Oswin, who couldn't join us. Brenden, one of our import offensive linemen, was in Australia and fourteen hours ahead of us, so it was the middle of the night for him.

THE FIRST MOVIE CLIP

I started the meeting with a clip from the movie Talladega Nights. When the team lost their driver during a race, the pit boss asked the crew…

"Who here wants to GO FAST?"

Will Farrell's character, Ricky Bobby, raised his hand and responded, "I do, sir. I want to go fast."

I then asked the team, "Who here wants to go faster than any team in the history of Europe?"

Movie clips stick in people's minds. Anytime I'm hired to be a keynote speaker at a conference or speak to a team, I will always use the power of visual storytelling. "Facts tell, stories sell," and nothing does a better job than a short video. Kids today don't even speak to their friends! They text each other with emojis when they sit beside each other at lunch. One of my favorite philosophies is Pete Carroll's "You must fascinate your players every day". Jesus, the greatest teacher ever, used parables [stories] because they stick in our brains. P.J. Fleck, head football coach at the University of Minnesota, spoke at a clinic I attended in Minneapolis on the impact of movie clips in team meetings. He convinced me they are the modern-day parable.

Next, I told them a little about my history, professionally and personally. I told them I'd been a head coach in Texas for the last 21 years and had written two books on creating a team culture, Culture Defeats Strategy and Culture Defeats Strategy 2. But most importantly, I shared my heart that my goal is to serve each of them.

I firmly believe that vulnerability wins when leaders interact with followers, so I went there early in the meeting.

The next slide was a picture of my fiancé', Tracy, our daughter, Coco, and myself.

"I'm engaged to the most beautiful woman on the planet, Tracy, and we have a five-year-old daughter, Coco. Back in the fall, Tracy and I were split up. I accepted this position, and then we got back together. To say Tracy's being amazing by allowing me to keep my commitment is the understatement of the century. They'll be coming over to watch a game or two this season. I can't wait for you guys to meet them both."

"Last year, I quit football out of the blue. I've worked over 100 hours a week to win games since I can remember. My teams weren't average because our staff wouldn't let them be. I'm not doing all of this to be average. I'm not coming here to experience Europe or see German landmarks for the first time. I'm coming to Potsdam to serve and win. My mission will be to help the Royals break barriers and set new records. I'll work my butt off to help us win the German Bowl for the first time, for Coach Vogt to be the coach of the year, and for Coach Saul to be the general manager of the year."

“Once we meet individually and I understand your personal goals, I will also work tirelessly to help you achieve them. The tattoo on my right forearm reads, *Anteambulo*. It’s a Latin word that means “clear the path for others.”

"Not only am I a football guy, but I’m also a certified mental performance coach. You’ll benefit from some mental training if you’re unfamiliar with how vital positive self-talk, mistake releases, and “so what next play” mindsets are. We’ll work on mental performance as an offense, but I’d also be honored to help any of you with one-on-one training."

"Let's get to the offense now."

As I clicked on the next slide with a picture of several cars driving very fast, I told them, "There’s only one way we can play as fast as some of you drive on the Autobahn: to be uber simple."

The following slide was a quote by German Albert Einstein, "Genius is making complex ideas simple, not making simple ideas complex.”

"Guys, you’ll hear me say this regularly, "Football isn't hard, don't make it hard.”

“We’re going to be simple. Some football coaches want to make others think they’re smart by having a complex-sounding offense."

BACKYARD BALL

As I said this statement, I advanced to the next slide. It was an example of an actual play from an NFL offense: “Green right x shift to viper right 382 x stick lookie.”

I was careful not to have them think I was being disrespectful to Coach Moon, the previous offensive coordinator, but I wanted them to know our offense wouldn’t be wordy in verbiage or complex in the scheme.

"No joke, fellas; football doesn't have to be this difficult. I’m not too proud to say I’d struggle to articulate a play this long without stuttering or forgetting half of it. We're not going to try to outsmart our opponents but bludgeon them with relentless execution."

The next slide showed families playing in a traditional Thanksgiving Turkey Bowl in their backyard. At the bottom was a Leonardo DaVinci quote, "Simplicity is the ultimate sophistication."

"You'll be in absolutely the most fun offense you've ever been a part of or ever will. Remember when you played in the backyard and how much fun you had just playing?"

"Wait a minute, did you guys in Europe ever play football in your backyard growing up?"

German running back Von Heiko Bals, one of the few who spoke up in this first meeting, said, "Thanksgiving or turkeys are not common things here. When we played outside, it was football, but not American football, coach. You'd call it soccer."

"Thanks, Von Heiko. I knew as soon as it came out of my mouth that I might be missing the mark on that analogy. So, let's all pretend you played American football at recess with your buddies when you grew up. How deep would you run when you didn't have a coach to tell you where to go on your route?"

Silence for a few seconds, then New York receiver Jared Wolfe spoke up, "Deep, coach. Anybody in P.E. or at the park in a pickup game that ran a short pass pattern wasn't any good, and they weren't getting the ball thrown to them."

Boom! We were getting things done.

I then explained more about the offense: when a receiver was single-covered, we would refer to him as being *Michael Irvin*. I'd heard Troy Aikman say in an interview that when they were teammates and Irvin had single coverage, he was throwing him the ball no matter the situation.

"Everyone in the stadium knew I was throwing the ball to Michael. The defensive coordinator and the cornerback certainly knew it, but they couldn't stop it because Irvin would win one-on-one matchups. NFL offensive coordinators today, in my opinion, don't allow the game this simple. Get your best receiver in a one-on-one situation and throw him the ball," said Aikman.

"Just like Troy said with Irvin, when one of you is single covered, with no possibility of the corner getting help from a safety, we'll call your number."

Next, I had still shots of the '21 Royals offense in a pre-snap alignment vs. different teams and began asking for more participation using the chat feature on Zoom.

"Here are the Royals versus Dresden from last season. Can you spot the player who is the *'Michael Irvin'* of this team? Please put the jersey number of the receiver you believe I'm referring to in the chat."

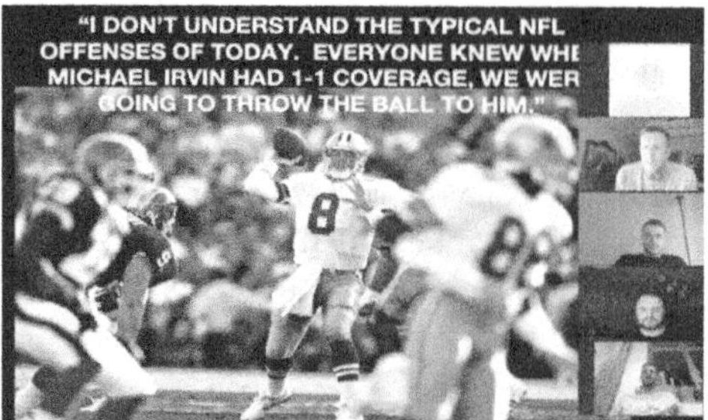

The chat started rolling with responses, and most were correct.

"Put in the chat how many of the defenders you believe they've committed to playing the run."

Again, most were correct. I wanted them to understand exactly how we would decide whether to call a run or pass. We'd take advantage of how the defense aligned and attack them there.

"Von Heiko, I know Christmas is a thing here. Did Santa think you were good enough last month to leave you some presents?"

"Ha, he left me a few. Probably more than I deserved."

"This offense will be like we all have a lot of presents with different wrapping paper, but the actual gift inside will be the same. The wrapping paper is how we change formations and the different ways of using each of you, but the gift, which is our basic plays, remains the same.

"One more thing I would like to see in the chat, please put your #1 individual goal for 2022. I don't want to see German Bowl Champions, but what you'll strain to achieve individually."

As the meeting started to wind down, I felt like I'd accomplished all three goals: they could feel my passion for the offense and my heart for coaching. They also understood how we'd play with warp speed because of our simplicity. Finally, they all had a firm grasp of our *Michael Irvin* philosophy and how I'd determine if I should call run or pass.

I wanted more confirmation, so I asked Chris, "You and I have met a couple of times, Chris. Have you ever run an offense this simple?"

"No, sir. I can't wait to unleash this. Dresden and NY'er won't know what hit them in a few months."

"Polk, was playing receiver this simple at Penn State?"

"Not at all. Nothing was simple there. This is going to be a blast. The defensive backs in Germany better start working yesterday on speed development."

One more movie clip to end the session; another *Talladega Nights* clip, but this time Ricky Bobby is in his Nascar uniform and behind the wheel. The pit boss tells him, "You're new to this, so take it easy."

Ricky punches the accelerator and goes full speed immediately. He goes for it and has a look of excitement and determination on his face.

"If you want to take it easy and gradually get up to speed as the pit boss suggested, please resign now. No hard feelings, I'll still love you and say "hi" to you on Facebook, but you aren't the right fit for us. If you're an *all-gas, no-brakes* type of player and ready to push the accelerator to the floor, let's go!" I said jokingly.

"Thanks, guys, for taking the time to be on this Zoom. Our goal will be to get 1% better each day. Today we got 1% and then some. Next week, we'll continue unpacking everything."

After the players exited our Zoom call, Saul, Berti, and I remained to debrief a little.

"Whew," I said. "I threw a lot at them, but we made some headway."

Saul, who had a sly, sheepish look on his face, said, "Coach, not sure if you noticed some of us giggling a little during the meeting, but in Germany, sometimes "Von" is put in front of a name, sort of like "sir" would be in English. You kept saying "Von Heiko" because that's what his Zoom name is, but his actual name is just Heiko."

LET'S BLITZKRIEG SOME GERMANS

February 2022

We'd met several times as an offense and in position groups. These meetings were to lay the foundation of Fast N' Wide. It was paramount that all of them understood what the "studs of our house" would be before training camp began. FNW differs significantly from the standard European scheme, which is no huddle but not a fast tempo, four wide receivers, and a non-physical style. We were going to snap the ball faster, be more 'blue collar,' and throw the ball downfield farther than anyone on our team had before.

On one Zoom, we were watching the 2021 Royals versus the Cologne Crocodiles. As always, I was very respectful of their style of play the year before, but I pulled up a clip of the Royals huddling, breaking out and getting to the line of scrimmage very slowly, then running a play. It was precisely like NFL teams do it, so there was no arrogance in my voice when I pointed at the fattest, most out-of-shape-looking player on the Crocodile defense and asked, "Do you guys think he wants us to huddle again this year or go lightning fast?"

After a few seconds of silence, Heiko responded, "I don't think he'll enjoy how fast we'll play, coach. Last year after the game, I saw him smoking in the parking lot."

"Heck, yea, Heiko! That's what I'm talking about! He'll hate playing against us! But…wait a second, I have to ask, did you actually see him smoking after the game?"

"I did. That's not all that uncommon. Smoking is customary in Germany, and some older players occasionally light up."

Not only did Heiko's statement shock me that players smoked after games and make me laugh out loud, but his comment reinforced the Royals were buying into their new laboratory of fast football.

All teachers know this: keeping students engaged and interested is more challenging now than ever. Competing with YouTube, TikTok, Instagram, and everything else they watch on a screen makes it more demanding than ever to fascinate them. One tactic I used with the Royals was to do weekly quizzes.

"I don't care if you play receiver, running back, or offensive line; you should know how we teach our choice route. I will pause the film when the receiver gets to his depth.

Write in the chat what route you think he runs."

"This one is for our offensive line. As you know, our first step is determined by how the defender aligns over us. I have numbered each OL 1-5. Write in the chat what step each lineman should take."

"Here's a still shot of the Berlin Adler defense aligned to a 2x2 offense last season. Write which receiver to which we would consider throwing the choice route in the chat box because he is "Michael Irvin (man-to-man coverage)."

I also intentionally used humor, jokes, and phrases they hadn't heard before. When asked a question that had an obvious answer, I'd respond with, "Do 100 kilos of flour make a big biscuit?" When someone would answer incorrectly, I would say, "Don't feel bad, like my momma always said, "You're not worthless. Even body parts sell for a lot on the black market." When I wanted to ensure they were following along with my point, I'd ask, "Are you picking up what I'm throwing down?" or "Do you smell what I'm stepping in?"

THEY WOULD RATHER STAY STUPID

Even after a few weeks of me bringing high energy to meetings, using our *Autobahn 80* chat for daily interaction, and my attempt at witty sayings, I still wasn't getting a lot of back and forth with most of our German players. I not only used quizzes with written answers, but I also asked open-ended questions to generate engagement. When I called on a player specifically, he'd have the correct answer, so I knew it wasn't fear of not knowing or the language barrier.

"Coach Vogt, how can I get our German players to ask more questions? I'm working hard to engage them, but I'm not used to so much silence during meetings."

"Getting Germans to communicate with you openly won't happen overnight. Germans would rather stay stupid than ask questions. It's maddening at times as a coach. I don't understand it, but we're too prideful and worry too much about looking foolish from not knowing the answer."

At the time, I didn't realize how meaningful this statement by Berti was. I should've written this on every practice schedule to remind me that I'd have to coach differently than I ever have.

I'd begun getting to know Bobby Sövegjarto, a GFL veteran of ten seasons, all with the New Yorker Lions, where he'd won five German Bowls and other European championships. NY'er released Bobby this winter, so we grabbed him to give us a veteran who'd seen it all and been through the wars of the trenches.

I messaged Bobby privately on WhatsApp and asked, *Am I going to have to force you guys to talk to me? I don't want to be the annoying American, but the more trust we have, the more we'll fight during a game not to let each other down.*

(Bobby) Be patient with us. As I said in our one-on-one Zoom call, most Germans are quiet and speak only if spoken to first. We give our opinion if asked, but we'd never tell someone what we think if not asked. I know you're asking, but your style differs from the coaches here.

(me) How is my style different?

(Bobby) You're trying to do more than teach the plan. You want us to understand why the offense will work and get us to believe in it. A couple of years ago, we had an ex-NFL coach in New Yorker who sent us teaching modules on recordings in the winter, but we never spoke to him until we met in person. Most coaches don't care if we know each other or not as long as we execute the plays and work together in unison.

A short time later, in another Zoom, I told the guys my plan to write a book about the season.

"Most Americans are just like I was a couple of months ago; they have no idea how American football operates in Europe. Taking them on this journey with me will be a fascinating read. I'm still searching for a title that represents football in Europe, Germany, and how the GFL works. Fast N' Wide and our tempo will be a central focus, so I'm considering the title *Blitzkrieg Football.*

"Blitzkrieg literally means *lightning war*. I looked it up, and it's defined as "a surprise attack using a rapid, overwhelming force." Germany captured so much territory at the beginning of WW2 with this shock and awe tactic. The more I read about it, the more I fell in love with the term. It's the perfect German word for FNW. What do you guys think?"

Patrick Jones, a quarterback on the prospects team, instinctively yelled out, "No, coach, no! Blitzkrieg is very offensive here! If you use any term from our Hitler era, it won't be popular with Germans."

"Really? It's that bad?" I responded, shocked.

"100% that bad, coach. Most Germans today view World War 2 as a liberation from Nazism. We're all still embarrassed and ashamed about that time in our history. Some of us have ancestors who were active Nazis, so we don't talk about it. When you get here, you'll notice there aren't a lot of German flags displayed. We joke about how patriotic Americans are and how you'll fly a flag for almost anything."

"Wow, ok, thank you very much for the heads up. Blitzkrieg's out. I hope I didn't offend anyone with that suggestion. I'll apologize in advance for not understanding the culture. I want y'all to know my heart will always be in the right place, but I'm the typical American who doesn't think about WW2 or the tough past of Germany."

"I did have another idea about a celebration prop to use for pics after a touchdown, like the 'turnover chain' used by many teams. Since our mascot is the Royals because [5]Potsdam was the capital of Prussia and many kings lived here, could we use an old helmet with the [6]Prussian spike" for players to wear on the sideline after a TD?"

"NOOOOOOOO!!!!!"

[5] Potsdam is the home to 17 palaces spread across three parks and its city center. The conglomeration is one of the largest UNESCO World Heritage Sites in Germany. Every Prussian ruler has left his own legacy to the city with his buildings.

[6] The German *pickelhaube, or* spiked helmet, is one of the most enduring symbols of WW1. To Germany's enemies, the helmet quickly became associated with "Hun barbarity" as propaganda artists filled British, French, and American newspapers with illustrations of *pickelhaube*-wearing Germans committing all manner of atrocities upon French and Belgian civilians.

FOLLOW US

February 2022

Max Evenhuis, a returning center, and guard from The Netherlands, sent me a text message that read…

Coach Jackson, I have something I'd like to run by you if you don't mind.

(me) Sure. What's up?

(Max) It's too detailed to explain in a text. Can we do a Zoom together soon?

We set up a one-on-one Zoom meeting for the next day.

"I have an idea for the offensive line I'd like to ask you about. When the Allies landed on Normandy in WW2, the officers had a white stripe on the back of their helmets. The enlisted men were told there'd be so much smoke and chaos when they hit the beach the odds were high that they'd need help finding their commanding officer. If or when they get lost, follow a white stripe. They would take them where they needed to go."

"This visual seems perfect for the OL to have a white stripe on the back of our helmet to tell the running back to follow us, and we'll take him where he needs to go," Max said.

"Max, I absolutely love this. Do you think the Germans and other non-Americans will be ok with something like this? After all, the white stripe at Normandy was a tool to defeat Germany. I was slightly embarrassed after last week's blitzkrieg and Prussian helmet ideas."

"The U.S. and Germany are great friends now, so I don't see a problem. If there was a radical, neo-Nazi type on the team, we might have some resistance, but there won't be. Last year's group, I know, would've had no problem with the white stripe meaning."

"This is one of the best unit bonding ideas I've ever heard. Getting a stripe for our helmets shouldn't be a problem. My mind is racing now, but we'll figure out a way for each lineman to earn their stripe."

I had a scheduled meeting with the offensive line in a few days, but before, I asked our most seasoned lineman, Bobby, to get his thoughts about the idea. I wanted his opinion, but I also wanted to establish a relationship where I could go to find advice on things. I was learning quickly, but I knew there were lots of things where "I didn't know I didn't know"...yet.

Bobby had no issue with it being something from the U.S. military. "I don't think anyone will have a problem with it. It'll be well received and something we can use as a mantra. When I was in New Yorker, they used to tell us not to hang our heads. The coaches said, "When animals hang their heads in a fight, they're ready to die." This white stripe will be another reason to keep our heads up. It'll be a reminder we're leading the way."

"Is earning the stripes too 'high schoolish'? Do you think it's corny?"

"I like the idea of having to earn the stripe. This is something none of us has experienced before, our offensive line having something just for us. It's good."

ALL HELL BREAKS LOOSE

A few days later, I started our position meeting with a movie clip, which they were now expecting. Finding the right video is sometimes tricky, but this one was a no-brainer. At the beginning of the meeting, I didn't say a word. I just hit play, and we watched five minutes of the most incredible battle scene ever: the opening scene of *Saving Private Ryan.*

Hall-of-Famer Steven Speilberg directed the film, and most experts consider the first 20 minutes the best of his career. Speilberg didn't storyboard the scene to ensure the beach landing on Normandy would be unrelenting and intense, with images and sounds to put the viewer on the beach and on the edge of their seat. He allowed improvisation from the 1,000 actors to help show the brutality of war. Imagine how chaotic it would have been on June 6, 1944, if the great Speilberg allowed actors to 'free-lance' the landing scene to give it the most realism possible.

Saving Private Ryan begins with the troops on the landing ship. Tom Hanks' character's hands are shaking as he takes a drink, two soldiers vomit, and they start taking fire before they ever disembark from the craft. Once they exit, several soldiers are shot within seconds, and all hell breaks loose.

We watched a few more minutes so they could get the exact emotion I was looking for when I hit pause and said, "Max had an excellent idea the other day. He taught me something about the D-Day landing I didn't know. The American officers had a white stripe on the back of their helmet so their company could find them and proceed correctly during the beach landing from hell."

The guys were now looking at the next slide of the PowerPoint, a picture of an officer on a landing craft with a white stripe on the back of his helmet.

"This system wasn't something for "just in case." It was necessary. We all know there'll be games this season where 'the crap hits the fan', and I want our skill position players to know they can count on us up front. What do you guys think about our offensive linemen and tight ends having a white stripe on the back of their helmets like this?"

"I like it. The stripe is a very good way to convince our running backs we'll take care of them," said Stefan Stefansson, a tackle from Iceland.

"Are we going to call this white stripe system anything?" Yasir asked.

"Follow Us if you guys are good with it," I replied.

Max and Bobby were correct. Our German and other European offensive linemen loved the idea as much as they did. I changed the name of our OL WhatsApp group to "Follow Us" and, with Saul's help, began making a graphic on the back of a Royals helmet for the group icon photo.

Our offensive line having its own brand would help bring us closer together. It creates a mini-fox hole, in essence. It's even better when it's organic and a player helps create it. I couldn't be more excited about how we were bonding.

Within a week, in a meeting with our skill players, Polk, maybe our smallest player, asked, "How do I get in the white stripe club?"

Polk asking this was music to my ears. Guys who score touchdowns don't ever envy the "grunts in the trenches." This was a very good idea. Max's white stripe was already having an impact...

10

NECESSARY EVILS

March 2022

I don't know if I should call this chapter "Arrogant Americans" or "Necessary Evils."

In less than a month, I'd be in Potsdam, and one thing that hadn't happened yet that was borderline shocking; there hadn't been one meeting for the coaching staff.

Saul and I continued our consistent communication. Coach Vogt and Saul even asked me how my teams had practiced fast for the past several years. They admitted that in prior seasons, the Royals only got around 30 minutes of good work in a two-hour practice. They asked for my help with a more efficient plan.

While I was thrilled to have the input on practice, I was becoming concerned about staff organization, so I asked Saul about it.

"Will we ever have a full coaching staff meeting before training camp?"

"Probably not. Our coaches have full-time jobs, so getting them together would be difficult."

"It would be difficult to Zoom with them all at once?"

"I can ask Berti (Coach Vogt's nickname), but normally we don't meet much. He's a head coach that hires you for the job and doesn't look over your shoulder."

Ok. This was one way the Royal laboratory was different than I expected. Most football staff in Texas, or anywhere I'd ever heard of, meet for several days before training camp begins. There are a million, and I'm not exaggerating much, things to discuss and be on the same page with before any coach puts a whistle around their neck.

"I know we have a couple of guys hired to help with the offense. When can have our first offensive meeting to discuss Fast N' Wide?"

"Whenever you want to. You're the boss on that side of the ball like I'm with special teams. Berti won't ever tell me to have a special teams meeting or tell me I can't have one. Anything that happens with the offensive staff is up to you."

OUR FIRST COACHES' MEETING

Message received. I'd done way more than most getting our players ready for the start of the season but hadn't forced the issue with our wide receiver coach, Chris Genau, or our running back and tight end coach, Jonas Heck. Time wasn't on our side. It was a miscalculation I'd made waiting on Berti or Saul to organize a meeting. This took my mind back to Bobby's comments about Germans waiting until they are asked. I still hadn't realized how different the typical German personality was from mine. It wasn't that either Chris or Jonas was being insubordinate. Both were waiting for me to invite them in. This wouldn't be the last time I made the mistake of not realizing my "the answer is always no if you don't ask" mindset was uncommon in my new lab.

Luckily our offense was straightforward because it would be challenging to coordinate a meeting with our newly hired offensive coaches, who were working in a seven-hour time zone ahead of me.

Chris and Jonas were easy to work with, and we had our first offensive staff meeting within a day or two. David, who'd be coaching the running backs, was also present, but Michael was not. It was becoming more evident that he'd be the most hands-off boss I'd ever had.

I started the meeting by having us get to know each other. We're about to spend the next several months together and need to have a bond every bit as much as we have with our players.

"Let's start by introducing ourselves and saying something interesting or unusual about ourselves. I'll go first to break the ice. I'm a native Texan who hasn't ever been to Europe. Both of you guys will need to be ready to hold my hand and help me navigate daily life and how to coach Europeans. I'm excited about this next chapter but humble enough to know I'll need help from both of you and David. My goal is to create a relationship where any three of you can tell me during the fourth quarter of a tight game, "Hey, idiot, what are you doing? We discussed this last series, and you aren't doing it!"

I could sense both Chris and Jonas, and even Saul, being surprised by this statement, but it was vital for me to establish this would be a team effort, not a dictatorship.

"I'm Chris Genau. I recently moved to Berlin to continue my path toward becoming a doctor. I'll be doing my residency, but I can adjust my schedule to coach our receivers. I've been on one of the offensive meetings and am excited to see us go fast."

"Coach Saul told me you played for the Dresden Monarchs?" I asked.

"I did. I was a wide receiver there until Covid shut the season down in 2020. My football career began at age 19 when I injured myself playing handball. During rehab, one of my friends who had just joined an American football team kept asking me to come to a practice. I finally did and joined the team the next week."

Next, I asked Jonas to introduce himself and tell us how he came to coach with us this season.

"My name's Jonas, an ex-player who still loves the game. I live in Fulda and am the head coach of our local team, the Fulda Saints. I've been an assistant coach for the New Yorker Lions for the past three seasons. I stay under the radar, but I've been in several offensive meetings and am excited to see what we do this season."

Jonas Heck

"Jonas, Saul tells me you'll be full-time with us. I'm excited that we'll get to watch a film and meet during the day. What other duties will you have with the Royals?"

"I'll also coordinate our injuries with the doctors and physios. When a player gets injured, I'll see that he has an appointment and his prescriptions if needed."

"If this isn't putting either of you guys on the spot, tell me something about the GFL I don't know. Imagine if you were coming to coach in the States, and someone gave you a nugget early that kept you from making a big mistake. I need this from you before we start discussing our favorite plays and how to teach them."

Jonas jumped in, "Instead of practicing five times every week and having off-season workouts as a team, we'll have two, maybe three practices a week. There's no off-season program; our players lift weights on their own if they are motivated. Lastly, we mainly coach adults who play football in their spare time as a hobby. They either attend the university or work full-time jobs. Like all GFL 1 teams, we'll have 12-15 actual professional players."

"Thanks, Jonas. Yes, that's helpful. I'm learning how different this is going to be. I wouldn't have realized we have an edge with most of our offensive guys being imports."

Next, Chris said, "This is a big deal, Coach Jackson. On every team I have been on that had American players, they were arrogant, which hurt our team chemistry."

"Really? Every American?"

"Well, maybe not every American, but most of them are spoiled and cocky. Americans learn the game early and don't have patience for Germans who've played for just a few years. They make more money, score more touchdowns, and get more attention from fans. If somehow we can get our American players to be team-first guys, it would help us tremendously."

Oh my, this was precisely the type of information I needed to know. I've always believed if 'your best players are your best leaders,' the team has a chance for greatness. It hadn't crossed my mind that the typical American receiver or quarterback was the most disliked player on the team. I was even more grateful now that Helbig, Polk, and Wolfe appeared to be team leaders.

"So, you're telling me on the teams you've played for that if the players elected captains, none of the American players would've been chosen a captain?"

"That's what I'm saying. Most Americans have been "necessary evils," if it's not too harsh. We all cheered when they scored a touchdown, but we also didn't miss them after the season ended."

I contacted Chris, Jared, and Polk almost immediately after this meeting to discuss the 'Arrogant American' epiphany.

"First, I want to thank you even more for who you are. Chris, you've done something I've never seen before and reached out to every Royal, regardless of whether he's on offense, a starter, or whatever. That's leadership at its finest. Before these guys shake your hand for the first time, they're already ready to fight alongside you.

Polk, you've even been in some of our *Follow Us* meetings, and I know you're coordinating online *Call of Duty* games with some German players and making connections. Jared, you're leading by example big time. I love how you were the first to video yourself running the 10-yard track meet drill and running choice routes versus a cornerback. You're a former Division 1 player and asking for coaching. All three of you are leading from the front. Thank you."

Chris replied, "Coach, if you don't mind me asking, you've known about us doing all of this for a couple of months now and have praised us. What inspired you to get us together today?"

"I was just about to get to that. Yesterday, I met with our two new offensive assistants for the first time. Our receiver coach, Chris Ganeu, is a former GFL receiver and told me the typical American in the GFL is an arrogant jerk. From the bottom of my heart, I appreciate all three of you for being leaders and not entitled team cancers. Y'all have already convinced the team you're not the Americans they've played with before, but I want you to keep Coach Ganeu's comments in your head. We'll win the German Bowl because we'll be a true team that cares about each other. You guys are creating that, and I'm grateful."

"We got your back, coach. I've heard things like this from some of our teammates already. At Penn State, we got rid of the jerks, but I guess teams over there have to put up with them," Polk said.

Jared followed up, "The guys I'm getting to know are amazing. They're asking questions and want to be good. This is going to be fun."

"The more I get to know each of you, the more I know I will lean on you as assistant coaches. We're creating something special here, and I want to thank each of you in advance for everything you'll do to help. I think we should meet with the entire team about…

11

NEIGHBORHOOD OR BROTHERHOOD?

March 25, 2022

“Establishing a culture and not just having a few slogans.”

I was learning that if it were going to happen, I’d have to initiate, so I asked Coach Vogt if we could meet as an entire team. It was time to discuss an intentional *True North* team culture. This was too important and foreign to 95% of our roster to wait until training camp for them to hear about it for the first time.

Sixty Royal players and coaches were present when we met in late March. I began the meeting by thanking all of them for attending, introducing myself briefly, and reiterating how excited I was to be a Royal for 2022.

"Thanks for being here tonight. It’s difficult for 60 guys worldwide, in different time zones, to be in one place, even virtually. What we’ll discuss this evening has nothing to do with scoring touchdowns, intercepting passes, or kicking field goals, but it has everything to do with us winning the German Bowl. If you’ve ever played on a team that was not close-knit or had bad chemistry, then you know it not only sucks to some degree but affects the team's win/loss record. Tonight, we’ll break down some tactics we’ll use this season to have a “band of brothers” mentality."

They were now looking at a slide that said, “Why do you still play American football? Why are you a Royal?”

I knew it was essential to get them involved, and I also knew most of them didn't want to talk, so I had them all answer questions in the Zoom chat.

"We must all answer these two questions in our hearts and minds. Some of you have full-time jobs, some will commute over an hour to practice, and some will travel 1/2 way around the world to get to Potsdam to be a Royal. Please explain in the chat why you still play football and why you’re choosing to be a Royal."

The chat started filling up with responses.

- *I play to stay a kid as long as I can.*

- *I play to be on a team and win games alongside friends.*
- *I still play to help feed my family.*
- *American football is the game for me. I like hitting other people and making them hurt.*
- *I'm still playing to enjoy the game as long as possible.*
- *I know I have a few good years left and will not look back wishing I would have played while I could.*
- *The Royals and Coach Vogt have been good to me. I enjoy being a Royal.*
- *I began playing for the Royals when I was 16. I will be a Royal for life.*

DAS WORT

I used German on the next slide; "What is *Das Wort* (one word) you want the Royals to be known for?" Again, players responded quickly in the chat.

- *Tough* *Speed* *Physical*
- *Family* *Fast* *Champions*
- *Legendary* *Resilient* *German Bowl Winners!*

"In one month, we'll all converge on Potsdam. We'll be coming from an amazing 18 different countries! Coach Vogt's allowing me to implement the systems I've used in the past with my teams to create a bond and a brotherhood. Here's the bottom line, if we "hope for the best" to have team chemistry, we won't. Our team is as varied an assortment as any in the history of the world. We'll have guys who have played for this team for several years and have grown up a Royal, guys who played Division 1 collegiate ball in the States, guys who have two kids, and teenagers who literally are still kids. If we're going to get in the foxhole together, we must know why we're fighting together. Today's meeting is going to start that process."

Ruben De Ruyter Heiko Bals

Next slide. It was an old black-and-white photo of two soldiers in a foxhole. I copied and pasted two players' faces on the soldiers. It was symbolic for sure, but because I couldn't help myself, humorous as well. There were several giggles from the guys. For around half of them, it was their first introduction to me. I wanted to be fun-loving and let them know I'd be approachable.

"Coach Saul, I know the guy on the left is Ruben, but I need to find out who the guy on the right is. I just grabbed a face from the internet that worked well with this photo."

"It couldn't be more spot-on, coach. The guy on the right is who you refer to as Von Heiko."

That was perfect. I had gotten to know Heiko and knew he was a loyal team member.

The following slide was a three-minute video of the University of Alabama football team walking through a tunnel onto the field for the national championship. There was no commentary, just sights and sounds. It was a powerful few minutes.

"You can feel the bond this team has with each other. All are giving positive affirmations to teammates. We'll walk through a tunnel similar to this in October as we head to the field for the German Bowl. Are we going to be this united?"

Next slide. Separate pictures of Aaron Rodgers and Antonio Brown [wearing an over-the-top mink coat]. Also in the frame is a quote of Aaron Rodgers saying, "Green Bay isn't a huge destination. Players are coming here to play with me."

"Coach Ganeu dropped a bombshell on me the other day. He says 95% of all American players he has played with are conceited and overbearing, especially toward their European teammates. I don't personally know Aaron Rodgers or Antonio Brown, but I wouldn't enjoy coaching the attitudes they show on camera or the quotes I read that come out of their mouths. I'm adding this to the presentation today because the American players on offense that I've come to know are polar opposites of what Coach Ganeu has experienced. This is another reason we're going to shock the world."

NEIGHBORHOOD OR BROTHERHOOD?

Next slide. A picture of then-Atlanta Falcon head coach Dan Quinn and some of his players. The words "Neighborhood or Brotherhood?" are at the bottom.

"I'm sure all of you remember when the Atlanta Falcons were up 28-3 and lost the Super Bowl a few years ago. Their head coach then was Dan Quinn, now the Dallas Cowboys defensive coordinator."

I read aloud an article from Bleacher Report on Coach Quinn's epiphany.

"As the Falcons cleaned up the slop from a disappointing season last January, Quinn watched players say farewells. He was taken aback when he noticed many of them exchanging phone numbers. How could they have been teammates all season long and not have each other's numbers?"

"At this moment, he completely understood his team wasn't close to each other. The Falcons, he realized, were a group of individuals who shared space with one another but didn't share themselves."

"When we started the offseason, we were like a neighborhood," Quinn says. "Hey, man, good to see you" is not a brotherhood. We weren't tight. So, the challenge was getting from a neighborhood to a brotherhood."

"Are we going to be a neighborhood or brotherhood? The Falcons had hats printed that said *The Hood* on them. If we wear GFL championship rings a year from now, it'll be because we established a brotherhood. Please list a teammate who has worked already to create our brotherhood in the chat and how he has done it."

Again, the chat had many examples of our American players and others. It was affirmation overload and was fantastic.

The meeting continued with our daily practice core values we would use:

- Tell the Truth Monday - The film doesn't lie. We see the "whole truth on film and nothing but the truth." We'll review performance grades from the previous game each Monday.

- Juice Tuesday - Juice is a powerful, modern word for energy. Our emphasis for each week's first practice is "Bring the Juice!"

"How important is it to be juiceful? A long-time friend, Jeff Traylor, takes being juiceful so seriously that he has one camera devoted solely to filming their sideline during games. Jeff is a legendary name in Texas football circles. His teams won multiple state championships when he was a high school coach in East Texas, but he's now the head coach at the University of Texas San Antonio. He enthusiastically told me that when I interviewed him for my coaches' mastermind, UTSA brings the most juice at every game. He told me, "When they score a touchdown or create a turnover, everyone on the sideline better be cheering and celebrating."

The Roadrunners are 30-10 since he took over in 2020. They've won Conference USA titles and gone to bowl games all three years. Everything important to winning must be coached and celebrated. That's why he coaches being juiceful more than anyone I know. When you create energy and enthusiasm around making plays, you can positively impact the game. Every Sunday, when the team reviews game film, Coach Traylor shows clips of guys who are celebrating the most on the sideline before they split up into position meetings. If there are any instances of players not bringing the juice when they should, they get called out in front of the team as well. That's how important it is to be juiceful."

"While we may not have the resources to film our sideline as Coach Traylor does, we can still emphasize maniacal energy in every practice and game. As they say, 'champs are useful because they're juiceful!' Let's bring that same energy to everything we do and see where it takes us."

- Competition Wednesday - "Always Compete," as Coach Pete Carroll says. The offensive staff will wear yellow coaching shirts, and the defensive ones will wear red.

- Fast Friday - On Friday, it's time to get our central nervous system firing again so we don't feel sluggish on game day. Our Friday training session will be a mock game emphasizing perfect reps and laser-like focus.

When you think of our team in twenty years, I hope brotherhood or family comes to mind. But when you think of our offense, it better be schnell or fast!!

The following slide was a picture of Usain Bolt, considered the fastest man in history who's won several Olympic and World championship gold medals. On the bottom, it read, *Are there any gold records for being slow*?

"We're going to play fast, fellas! I don't know which GFL team has played the slowest in league history because no one cares! We'll be the fastest and be remembered years from now."

REMEMBER THE NAME

I closed the meeting with the new *Follow*

Us identity for our offensive line, changes to how we'll practice, and a video clip from the movie *Troy*.

Brad Pitt's character, Achilles, asleep in his tent with two female companions, was awakened by a young boy. The king was summoning him to fight the giant, Brogrius. Achilles was irritated by having to leave his tent when the boy asked, "Are the stories about you true? They say your mother is an immortal goddess. They say you can't be killed," as he handed Achilles his shield.

Achilles answers, "I wouldn't be bothering with the shield then, would I?"

The boy continues, "The Thessilonian you're fighting; he's the biggest man I've ever seen. I wouldn't want to fight him."

Achilles ends the conversation with, "That's why no one will remember your name," and rides off to battle.

The next slide is a video of Achilles defeating the giant, then taunting the Thessalonian army by shouting, "Is there no one else?... Is there no one else?"

The enemy king asks, "Who are you, soldier?"

"Achilles, son of Peleus."

"Achilles? I'll remember the name," the king says.

I have used this clip for a few years, and it never disappoints. We all want to be remembered, especially alpha male athletes, so I knew this scene would resonate with the team.

"Achilles is known as the greatest of the Greek warriors. Two thousand five hundred years later, we're still talking about him and making movies about him. Who's known as the second or third greatest Greek warrior? I don't know him either, and neither does anyone else. No one still talks about the 2019 Royals. In-fighting, lousy leadership, arrogant Americans, and selfishness are forgotten as quickly as possible. We have the players, the coaches, and the scheme to win the German Bowl for the first time in the Royals' history. It'll be up to this team if it happens. It'll only happen if we all point to True North. It'll only happen if we want to be remembered."

Within a few minutes of signing off the Zoom, Tracy, my fiancé, asked, "How was your meeting, babe?"

"It was good, thanks for asking. I think we're gaining ground for sure. Today some of these guys were introduced to team culture for the first time."

"Your flight is in two weeks. Do you have everything you need as far as COVID-19 requirements?"

12

SORRY, BUT YOU CAN NOT GET ON THE FLIGHT

April 10, 2022

"Oh yea. I've got proof of vaccination, so I'm all good to go."

"Are you sure that's all you need? You might also have to show proof of a negative result?" Tracy asked.

"I've looked at the websites. I think I'm fine."

I was single when I uploaded my resume on Europlayers.com in October 2021. Two months later, Tracy, my fiancé, and I got back together and soon became engaged again. As the days on the calendar continued to count down to April 10th, I dealt with the emotional struggle of "Do I go" or "Do I stay?" Coaching football overseas is a great adventure, but it isn't for a man who will leave a family behind. After getting back together with Tracy, I should have backed out of my commitment, but I selfishly continued on my path to Europe. The lure of coaching again, especially in the German Football League, drew me in like a bug to a purple light. Bonds were forming between myself and Royals from our Zoom sessions and WhatsApp.

The problem was I also had a team at home. I convinced myself our separation would pass by quickly. After we got through the first two months, we'd see each other on a semi-regular basis. Tracy could come to Germany twice, and I'd go home in July for two weeks. Not only did Tracy not guilt-trip me or give me an ultimatum to stay, but she was a huge help in my preflight prep.

"Things are not easy in Europe like they are here. You don't know how much more difficult things will be over there until you experience it. We're spoiled here, trust me," Tracy warned me.

Finally, the morning of April 10th arrived, and it was time for me to head to the airport.

"Your order will be right out, sir," said the cashier at Whataburger near the airport. Tracy, Coco, and Tracy's mom, Gaye, were on our way to the DFW airport when we stopped for my last U.S.

meal for a few months.

On the way to the airport, Tracy reminded me, "Things are going to be more challenging in Germany. Be ready to figure things out and jump through hoops for things we take for granted here."

Within 30 minutes, Tracy's words were already ringing true, and I was still on American soil.

"Sir, your last COVID test was more than nine months ago. You'll not be able to board until you get a negative test result," said the American Airlines attendant.

My heart sank. I thought I had everything in order. I missed the part where a vaccine or negative test must be within nine months of departure. Masks were still required on flights, but the vaccination standards were all over the map when entering each country. Regardless, I wasn't going to get on my flight to Paris and then to Berlin.

"There is a testing center in the airport. You can make an appointment and get tested. I can help you get on another flight."

It took me an hour to get a negative result. Then I headed back to the attendant.

She said, "Let me see... I can get you on a flight to London, but it doesn't take off for six hours. Your itinerary is now a nine-hour flight, a nine-hour layover, then a three-hour flight to Berlin. You'll arrive at 10:20 P.M. local time in Germany."

I started adding up the hours it would take to get to Berlin...27 hours from now, I'd be landing, then the 40-minute drive to Potsdam. Luckily, I don't believe in omens because I hadn't left the airport yet, and things weren't going my way. I called Tracy and said, "If y'all aren't already headed back home, do you think you could come pick me up and spend a few more hours together?"

Luckily for me, they returned, and we spent a few more hours together. Eventually, I had to say goodbye to Tracy and Coco and finally took off for London.

When I arrived at Heathrow Airport at 10:00 a.m. local time, I'd been up for 17 hours and was ready for a shower and a place to lay down. The ticket the Royals provided me was a window seat, but I was too cheap to upgrade to an exit row for more legroom. Nine hours later, I was rethinking the cost-to-value equation of this decision.

"Ma'am, can you help me find a lounge where I can shower and rest?"

"Yes, sir. It's in terminal two. You will need to take a shuttle to get there."

I made my way to the Heathrow VIP lounge. The attendant informed me that the showers were out of order, so I decided to pass on spending the 40 Euro admission. After walking around the terminal and looking for a place to lie down, I realized there was absolutely no carpet anywhere in the airport. An hour later, Tracy's warning of "It's harder in Europe" was on replay in my ears. I made the best of the situation and bought wet wipes to feel as clean as possible. I returned to the "not so VIP" lounge and somehow slept in two chairs I carefully positioned just so. Finally, at 7:00 p.m. local time, I drug myself onto the plane bound for Berlin. After a three-hour flight, we touched down at 2200 (10:00 p.m.).

I was confident as I approached IMMIGRATION CONTROL or the customs area. All U.S. visitors staying in Germany longer than 90 days must secure a visa. The Royals had provided me with a letter explaining I'd be working in Potsdam for up to six months, so I'd be getting a work visa. I placed it on the counter with the satisfaction of knowing, finally, something would be easy on this trip.

"What is your business in Germany, sir?" asked a uniformed customs agent.

"I've been hired to coach for the Potsdam Royals," I replied, knowing it would impress him.

"Who are the Potsdam Royals?" the agent asked.

Well, so much for that. "They're a professional American football team who brought me to coach this season."

"Is this your first time in Germany?" he asked me.

"Yes, sir. It's my first trip to Europe."

"You are from Texas?"

"Yes, sir. Near Dallas."

"I see. Do you have any Euros, sir?"

"Euros? No, sir. I haven't been anywhere to need them."

"I shouldn't let you in without Euros. Didn't they tell you to have some Euros on your person?"

"No, sir. They didn't. I can get some, though. I have some dollars on me that I can exchange."

"That won't be necessary. I'm stamping your passport, but I will not allow you in next time without Euros."

I thanked the customs agent with a grateful heart for access to Germany; then, I made my way over to baggage claim.

"Wann kommen unsere Taschen an?" I heard someone ask. It didn't take me long to realize the translation of this is "When will our bags arrive?"

I'd been texting Tracy during my trip, so she knew the trip was kicking my butt. *(me) Hey, honey. I'm on German soil, finally. Things seem to be very difficult in Europe. Who knew?*

(Tracy) It's impossible getting things through your head sometimes. You realize this, right?

(me)I know I'm about to lovingly hear, "I told you so", but my bags aren't here. Can you send me some underwear and get it here in a few hours?

I filled out a form to be contacted when my luggage arrived, then made my way to find Saul, who was picking me up. Not only was Saul waiting to greet me, but Ruben as well! We shook hands, hugged, and Saul gave me a Royals Fast N' Wide t-shirt he had printed as a welcome to the Royals present.

"Welcome, coach! We're glad you finally made it!" Saul said.

When I told Saul and Ruben about my customs agent experience, Ruben said, "So, he said you must have Euros to enter?"

"The letter we gave you works every time for players and coaches. I'm not sure what he was doing, but I think he might've been having some fun at your expense," Saul said.

Thirty-two hours after I left my home, I'd finally arrived in Berlin. I'm not sure if the customs agent was messing with me, but there wasn't anything funny about how tired I was and not having a change of clothes or a toothbrush.

"My girlfriend, Anna, made this for you. We're vegan, but it is very tasty," Saul said, handing me a Tupperware-type container with beans, rice, and peppers.

"Oh, wow. Please tell Anna thank you for me. In Texas, you get extra credit for owning longhorn cattle, but I'm sure this will taste amazing," I said, smiling.

13

I'M NOT IN TEXAS ANYMORE

April 12, 2022

Day one in Potsdam started with me waking up around 9:00 a.m. as my body tried to recover from the 30-something-hour journey from Dallas. I met Saul for coffee, and then he took me to the Royals' office. In exchange for marketing, the Royals use two rooms in a shared workspace [Simplioffice] building built less than a year ago.

"Here's some start-up money to help you with groceries until the 15th." Saul slid me an envelope with 200 Euros in it. I'd be paid 500 Euros in cash twice a month.

After about 30 minutes, a man with a black Royals polo came in and introduced himself.

"Welcome to Potsdam, coach! My name is Jens Müller. I'm the president of the Royals, and we're glad you're here!" Jens greeted me with a hearty handshake. Jens is my age, so he's not as comfortable with English as the younger generation who learned it in school after the Berlin Wall fell in 1989. What he lacked in English skills, he more than made up for with enthusiasm.

"Please let me know if I can do anything to help you with your transition. Forgive me for my broken English. I'm not as good as I should be when speaking with our American coaches and players."

I responded, "No problem, sir. I'm honored to be a Royal and grateful you brought me over. This is going to be a fun season."

"We plan on it! I've been told this is your first time in Europe. I'd love to show you around when you have the time. Please allow me to take you around Potsdam and buy you a good meal soon."

As Jens left, Saul said, "Jens is a good guy, but like the rest of the board, Berti and I struggle to get them to understand what it takes to win a GFL championship."

"How does the board work? Are they paid or volunteers?" I asked.

"Our board is made up of several volunteers. They do things such as organize uniforms for game day, pre-game and post-game meals, print and social media, our youth teams, and many other things. As president, Jens' main job is finding sponsors to pay our players."

"This reminds me of a booster club board back home. They're all volunteers that help make the program go. I've always said elite teams have elite parents. GFL boards, I'm sure, are vital."

"Well...they have their place. I appreciate our board, but they need to trust more, raise more money, and ask fewer questions."

"Is there a separate board for the GFL 1 team?"

"No, but that might help. They're all good people, don't get me wrong, but GFL championships aren't won by grooming the 13U team into 20-year-olds. The elite teams here have four stud Americans, one or two American coaches, European imports, and the best Germans from all over the country."

"That makes sense. Even in Texas, most 13-year-olds don't continue playing all the way until they graduate high school. The best booster clubs I've had were the ones who said, "You tell us how much you need, and we'll raise the money. We're here to serve."

"Berti and I know we need to spend money on the youth programs, but for some board members, it's their priority."

"I get it. I would think the GFL is the ultimate transfer portal when it comes to 50 or so elite players in the country."

"That's not a bad analogy. We have a few players who've come up through the system, but not many."

"Will I be able to meet Coach Vogt in person today?" I asked.

"No, he's at his day job. He's a director in the German social welfare system. He helps take care of Ukrainian refugees with housing and jobs. He can work from home most days and be up here when we need him."

"Really? Wow, I assumed he was full-time since he is the head coach. Do most GFL head coaches have other full-time jobs?"

"It varies. I think it is probably around 50%," Saul responded.

Berti was not only the head coach, but he founded the Royals in 2005. He helped take them from the 5th league, a level where players barely know anything about football, to the GFL first league. He wasn't the head coach because of his love of football. The club was his baby. The fact there was not enough money generated for him to work at his passion 80 hours a week was stunning. Berti loved the Royals with all his heart and soul.

"I know you said Jonas and I are full-time, but what about the rest of the coaching staff? Will we have enough here to meet about practice and game plans?"

"Probably not. Everyone works during the day, and most don't live in Potsdam. Our linebacker coach, Paul Kruger, will take a train three hours to practice...one-way."

As I prepared to leave and get to my flat alone for the first time, I asked Saul how to ride the train home.

"It is only a 15-minute walk, but there is a stop within a few hundred meters from here. Get on the 96 and get off at the first stop. It'll be at the Aldi grocery store. Your flat is across the street."

"That's it? Is it that simple? You know, we don't have trains in Texas for the most part. The German public transportation system is all new to me."

Saul assured me I wouldn't have a problem, so I headed out to learn how to get around Potsdam and, more importantly, get home.

I walked up to the stop and saw a train with *96* on it sitting there. I attempted to board, and the driver said something in German that I didn't understand but was not inviting me to get on the train. This would be my first encounter, but not my last, with frustrating "Texan to older German communication." The driver was around 60-65 years old and spoke no English. He gave me a look of confusion and said something else in German.

I did what any good American would do. I pointed at the *96* and repeated it louder and slower. Finally, he gave me a walking motion with his index and middle finger. He was trying to get me to go to the pickup area less than 100 yards away. Exasperated, I finally understood what he meant and walked over and waited. Within a minute or two, he pulled the train forward, stopped, and motioned for me to get on (the train system has exact times for departure). The doors opened, and I entered and sat down. I was relieved to be figuring out how to get around Potsdam on the train. We made it to the Aldi; I stood at the door to get off, but it didn't open. I wondered if I would still get home when someone finally came up and pushed a green button that spread the doors open.

Although I'd spent the night at my flat, I wondered which building was mine in the large complex across the street when I got off. After a little searching, I found my building and made it to my third-floor apartment. I was exhausted when I sat on the couch. Tracy, Coco, and Texas seemed a long way away and a long time ago. (all within 24 hours)

Before long, I had a knock on the door. Our other full-time coach and offensive assistant, Jonas, agreed to help me navigate the grocery store.

"This flat is nice. Most in Germany have the living room, bed, and kitchen all in one room. You're lucky you have a separate kitchen. You're also lucky to have a lift (elevator). Most buildings with five floors or less only have stairs. The communists saved money when they built anything. I've been told this is a complex for retired people, so I'm sure that's why they added the lift."

"This place looks like it was used by the military at one time," I replied.

"It was originally built to house troops. It is called the *Red Barracks* because of all the red brick exterior. It was built in the 1890s for Prussian troops. Later, German soldiers used it, then after WW2, the Soviet military lived here. It was vacant for several years when the wall fell until a developer bought it and made flats."

I love military history, so living in the same complex as soldiers from three countries was fascinating. Like a curse, my mind instantly shifted to the task at hand...the Royals.

"When the guys start arriving in the next few days, I want to be at the airport to greet them. Saul has agreed to make t-shirts for everyone when they land, but I plan to be at the terminal if it's feasible. It looks like our stadium is amazing, so we could stop by and let them get on the grass on the way into Potsdam. They can see where we'll unleash hell on the GFL, and I'd also like to see it. Saul isn't saying much when I mention the idea to him. What do you think?"

"You haven't heard, have you? We'll not be allowed to play at Karl-Liebknecht Stadium this season. I don't know all the details, but the soccer club has denied us access. I think it's something to do with us getting more subsidization from the city. I'm hearing we'll be playing at Sportpark Luftschiffhafen. It's not nearly as nice as Liebknecht, so I'm sure that's why they haven't told you."

"Well, crap. I hate hearing that, but we'll make do as long as the field is 100 yards long and 53 yards wide."

"I'm about to go meet Ruben for lunch. Do you want to join us?"

"No, thanks. I've got to get some things in order at my flat. I'm picking up my air conditioner and installing it along with some other things."

"Wait a minute; you have an air conditioner?"

14

I MAY EITHER GET PUNCHED IN THE FACE OR KICKED OFF

April 14, 2022

Our first team meeting wasn't until the next day, so I messaged the offense and asked anyone in town if they'd like to meet for coffee in the main shopping area of Potsdam, Brandenburger Strasse (street). Eight guys, including Coach Jonas, showed up, and the mood was light. After seeing each other only on a screen for months, we were all glad to be sitting together face to face in Potsdam.

Like yesterday, I was about to learn a ton. I'd leave our meeting with more questions than answers.

"Thanks for taking the time to show up this morning, fellas. Some of us are still getting over the long flight, but getting together for coffee and hanging out is more important than tomorrow when we're in an official meeting."

"If you guys don't mind, I'll ask some GFL and Royals vets questions to get us going. I'm on information overload and want to continue discovering everything I can before training camp begins in a couple of days."

"Bobby, how did you learn about American football and decide it was for you?"

Bobby Sövegjarto, our 35-year-old center, was present. "When I was 19, I read a Sports Illustrated article on football. It seemed like a sport I'd enjoy, so I began looking for a team. The closest club was 50 kilometers away, but I didn't have transportation, so I saved money for about a year. I bought a car and started playing. As I improved, I played for teams in higher divisions until I joined the New Yorker Lions when I was 24. I've been there until now but am excited about helping the Royals win a championship for the first time."

"What's your #1 individual goal for this season?"

"That's easy, coach. Kick the Lions' ass at their stadium."

Our best player, at least on paper, Yasir [an Islamic name that means wealthy] Raji, was present [another good sign for our chemistry]. Yasir was an all-Europe offensive lineman in 2021 in his first season with the Royals. I directed my attention to him next.

"Coach Saul told me you are a native of Nigeria. How did you come to live in

Germany?"

"Both of my parents are teachers and decided to move our family to Dresden when I was three. When I was 16, they returned to Nigeria, but I liked it here, so I stayed and kept the flat."

"I grew up loving soccer, but although my coach said, "If you come to practice, you'll get to play," I wasn't playing much. To be fair, I was a fat kid and not built for the game."

"You were fat?" I asked incredulously.

Yasir is no longer fat. He's 280 pounds of chiseled steel and looks like an Under Armour mannequin.

"Yes, my nutrition was horrible, especially living on my own. The Dresden Monarchs, who I know you've heard all about, liked me being large, so I began to play American football. I was with them for several years before enrolling at Potsdam University last year and joining the Royals."

“Let’s get back to your parents allowing you to live on your own. You’ve lived by yourself since you were 16?” I asked.

“Sure, it was no big deal. It made me grow up a little faster.”

"Yasir, tell coach about what we did with the OL coach last year in training camp," Max Evenhuis said.

Yasir got a sly smile and responded, "Well, the coach we had last season was so bad, we kicked him out of practice early in training camp. He was terrible. We knew more than he did, so we didn't need him."

I'm sure I didn't hide my shock as I said, "Y’all did what? Y’all fired your OL coach after a few days? Did you guys meet with the offense and decide to do this or ask Coach Vogt first?”

"We didn’t ask anyone. The offensive line just kicked him out. None of the other players really knew about it or cared. He sucked. I knew I could coach us better, so I did."

Before I could respond, Chris asked, "YOU were the offensive line coach last season?"

"I was. It was no big deal. I knew the drills and took us through them. I’ve also worked with some of our youth teams and trained local guys this winter. Eventually, I’d like to become a coach when I graduate."

“Let me get this straight. At the end of practice, you approached him and told him not to come back? What did Coach Vogt say about it?" I asked again with still a little shock in my voice.

"We didn't wait until the end of practice. There were three or four of us who told him during our individual drill time that his drills were shit and we had better ones. I probably said it first, but Max and others stood with me. The OL coach left before the practice was over. I'm not sure if Coach Vogt tried to convince him to come back, but he trusted us to get it done, and we did," Yasir said.

Saul had told me that Yasir was one of our alpha males, and it didn't take long to see it. He was very polite and respectful, but there was little doubt in my mind that he wouldn't be asking me for tips or advice on improving his game.

I'm a [7]confront and demand type of coach and always have been. Confront and demand means I had no problems giving my players high expectations and demanding the expectations be met. Human nature means all players will not meet expectations. When this happens, a coach or leader must be willing to have hard conversations. They must be willing to confront the player and hold him accountable. How would this work if Yasir had been the OL coach last year? Will he be ok with being held accountable and a challenging style of coaching? Getting Yasir on board with the new offense and our players' creed would be vital for our success this season.

"Max, what brought you to Potsdam?" I asked.

"I played for one of our rivals, the Cologne Crocodiles, in 2018 and '19. When the league started back up in 2021, the Royals offered me more money, so I moved to Potsdam. I have my own business that I operate online, which allows me to play anywhere."

"What position do you prefer on the offensive line?"

"I'm happy to play center if the team needs me there, but guard is my best spot. Identifying the defensive front and snapping the ball removes some of my aggressiveness. With Bobby here, I'm sure I won't have to worry about it."

"Max, this could be very helpful for all of us. I like to get players to rank themselves and aspects of the program on a scale of 1-10. Ten being the highest and one being the lowest."

"Rank yourself as a player from 1-10."

"8, but I plan on improving. Yasir is a 9.9, so I'm working to catch him," Max said.

---

[7] Confront and demand - "People don't like to be held accountable. You must confront bad behavior, but that's only half the battle. You must also demand the behavior changes."

“Rank the Royals last season.” I said.

“7.5…maybe an 8.”

“What is one thing we can do to take it to a 10?” I asked.

“Do you mean offensively or as an entire team?” Max asked.

“Whatever you want to answer.”

"Let me think about that for a second, coach. For me, offensively, the continual moving around the offensive line last season hurt us. We could have gelled quicker if we had stayed with the same five. Regarding the entire team, I hope Coach Vogt changes a few things, but not his style.”

“What's his style?” I asked.

"Coach is very laid back, and we appreciate it. He’s a player's coach. I once was on a team where a coach constantly yelled. Once, he got in a player's face screaming and got punched in the mouth."

Max and I had developed a reasonably strong bond in the months before I arrived, but his comments sounded off some alarms for me. We’ll earn our right to play each week and laid back is not a way I’ve ever been described. After a couple of days of living in Potsdam, I was learning on the run about the Royals' operation and culture. The comments by Max and Yasir were as shocking as Berti having a day job.

As impossible as it seemed, was Max warning me not to raise my voice too loud when coaching him, or would he punch me in the face? Who allows a player revolt where they kick a coach off the team?

One thing I know for sure is that I don’t think I will have any problem getting them emotionally ready for a game. If they had enough energy to kick a coach off the team, then I know they have enough energy to kick our opponents’ butts.

15

SHUT THE 'F___ UP'

April 15, 2022

I sat with the other coaches, waiting for Berti to begin our first team meeting at Simplioffice. He stood before our 60+ players for a few seconds and waited for the guys to notice him and get quiet. Most didn't see Berti standing there or didn't bother to end their conversation.

After waiting a few moments for the room to quiet down, Berti gave a thundering command of...

"SHUT THE F____UP!"

The room fell silent. This was different from the guy I had gotten to know in the few interactions with him over Zoom calls. Yet another "I'm not at a-high-school-in-Texas" moment for me.

After a few comments about our training camp schedule and expectations, Berti introduced the coaching staff, the board members who were present, and our head physio [athletic trainer], Taka. He allowed Saul and me to say a few words, along with the team president, Jens. We then split into offensive and defensive team rooms.

The team meeting was informational but not motivational. There wasn't an emphasis on energizing the room to begin the season. Day one with the team is a special time to create a "moment of wow," something they'll remember after the season ends. I was learning inspiration, team culture, or branding wasn't the "norm" for Berti or the Royals.

It was my turn with the offense to show them my heart and how fired up I was to be the offensive coordinator this season. I felt good about the hours and hours of Zoom meetings we'd done together to learn the offense, but it was now time for them to feel my passion for football in the flesh. They must leave the room knowing I was the guy they could trust and count on to get it done.

When everyone was settled in our reserved room, which needed to be much larger for the 30 of us, I hit play on slide #1 of my presentation.

An old, grainy, black-and-white video with only ominous music for audio appeared on the screen. A wooden ship was being crushed on all sides by ice. Both of the masts were also breaking under intense pressure. Slowly, the old wooden vessel was sinking into the ice. A few sailors were visible, attempting to salvage what they could before it was too late.

“The ship you see here is the British *Endurance*. It was on an expedition in 1914 to explore the South Pole. One of the men you see in the film was Captain Ernest Shackleton, the expedition's leader.”

I advanced to the next slide. It read *Men wanted for hazardous journey, small wages, bitter cold, long months of complete darkness, constant danger, safe return doubtful. Honor and recognition in case of success.*

"Return was doubtful. You guys saw in the video that the want-ad was correct. With a promotion like this, how many do you think he had that responded and applied?"

"I doubt many blokes stood in line for this job," said Australian lineman Brenden Oswin.

"Actually, over 5,000 men wanted to be on the ship *Endurance*, and if reports are correct, “three sporty females” also applied. Twenty-seven men won the right to be on the ship we saw being crushed and were probably facing certain death."

I then talked about the type of person the ad targeted. "All of the 27 on board were alpha males. All were precisely the type we must have in this room to shock the GFL this season. Now, let's talk about how we’ll make it happen."

"This meeting will be less about our scheme and more about what you can expect this season from me and how we’ll do things. We'll start with how I want it to look on the practice field Monday. This next video is about a team that's the fastest tempo in Division 1 college football. We will play with this pace and be the most feared offensive machine in Europe."

The next slide was the University of Tennessee football team’s spring game. The offense was playing extremely fast. We watched three plays in about 40 seconds when I hit pause and asked...

"How will we play this fast?"

Stefan answered, "We'll be simple."

"We'll have two base running plays and one base pass play," Chris responded.

Jared chimed in, "We'll have three-play series memorized that we run in order."

"All of you are correct. We'll have a walk-through practice tomorrow to show everyone the logistics of our new training system, but on Monday, our two running plays will be inside zone and zone lead. Our one-pass play will be choice. We've met for hours and hours over all three, and we're ready."

The following slide had four words on it in large print - MY FOUR PROMISES.

"Promise #1 is I will be EXTREME."

"All of you are on this team for two reasons. The order may be different for some, but all of you are here to 1. win the GFL championship and 2. improve as a player. I promise to be an extreme coach for each of you. We will not leave a stone unturned. Whatever it takes, I'll do, and whatever you need from me, you'll get."

"Promise #2 is I will ATTACK THE PROBLEM, NOT THE PERSON

"I promise to coach and correct, not criticize and attack. I'll also not ask "why" in our conversations. Coaches who say, "Louis, why did you do that?" aren't coaching. They're blaming you for the mistake. An elite coach should look internally to see where he let Louis down. Together, we'll fix the issue. When something is good, I'll say, "Great job, Karri."

When something needs correcting, it'll be..."Ludi, your right foot isn't flat enough here, and it's my fault I didn't coach you properly. We're going to get that right foot fixed tonight at practice. You have my word."

I'll coach you this season. Intensity is a part of my personality, but I'll yell positive more than negative."

"Promise #3 is I WILL COACH EACH OF YOU DIFFERENTLY-THE WAY THAT WORKS BEST FOR YOU."

"Elite coaching is custom-tailored for each individual. It's not one size fits all. The only way I can do this is to get to know you. Some of you've told me you want to be coached hard. A few of you'll need to be trained with precise instructions, "Step here," or "Place your hand here," while others will have a more natural feeling for the game and be told, "Get it done." And others, if you're like me, will crave encouragement."

"Promise #4 is I WILL BRING THE JUICE."

"I'll always be fired up to coach you in a meeting or on the field… every single time. I retired because I thought I could live without coaching, but I was wrong. Being in front of you right now is my second chance, and I'm grateful. I promise to be the most juiceful person in the group. Be ready for me to coach fast, be intense and excited."

PERFORMANCE VS. TRUST

"Once upon a time, Fire, Water, and Trust were walking in the woods. They started talking about what they'd do if they got separated.

Fire said, "If we get lost, look for smoke because where there is smoke, there is fire."

Water said, "If we get separated, look for green grass because where there's green grass, there must be water."

Trust said, "Don't lose me because if Trust becomes lost, you'll never find it again."

"Have any of you ever been let down by someone you trusted? Have you been on a team and a teammate or coach said or did something they promised they wouldn't?

An aspect of coaching in high school that I don't miss at all is some 16 and 17-year-olds are still very immature. Sometimes a very good player would be hard to trust when he wasn't with us. He'd be fine around the coaching staff at practice, but it'd be a different story when he walked through the double doors to leave the athletic wing and head into the school building. Teachers and principals would see a totally different kid. They'd see one that constantly caused disruptions in class or skipped class altogether. They'd have to deal with a spoiled, undisciplined teenager who lacked the maturity to make the correct choices or care about others.

I'd tell the player, "I don't want to trust you on the field if I can't trust you away from the field. The guy you can't trust when you're not around is the same guy who will jump offsides on 4th and one or get an unsportsmanlike penalty when the game is on the line. If your wife or girlfriend is 99% faithful, is that good enough? Of course not! True trust is *24/7-365*."

Next, I brought up a video of author Simon Sinek. He's at a whiteboard and says, "I've worked with the Navy Seals. I asked them once, 'how do you pick members of 'Seal Team 6?' We all know they're the best of the best of the best of the best!"

Sinek continues, "They drew a graph for me. On one side, they wrote the word *Performance*. On the other side, they wrote the word *Trust*. They defined performance as skills *on* the battlefield. They defined trust as skills *off* the battlefield. In other words, what kind of person are you? How good are you at your job? The way they put it is, "I may trust you with my life, but would I trust you with my money and wife?"

"No one wants the *low performer, low trust* guy in the group, and of course, everyone wants the *high performer, high trust* teammate. But they've learned it is much better to have a *medium performer, high trust* teammate than a *high performer, low trust* one."

"This is a question for the group. What is your take home from this?" I asked.

Polk was first, "The arrogant American isn't what's best for the team."

"Agreed," I responded. "The most elite unit in America is looking for trust over performance. What are some ways we show trust to each other?"

"When someone tells you it's okay after you make a mistake. I will likely throw an interception at a bad time this season, and the teammate who pats me on the back is someone I will trust," said Chris.

"Trust is gained in drops and lost in buckets. As the season plays out, we will learn who the high-trust guys are. I'm still determining when, but you will elect our 2022 offensive captains in the second half of the season. The high-trust guys will get the most votes."

MERITOCRACY

The next slide was a video of Tony Romo addressing the media after being benched for rookie Dak Prescott. Romo says, "You see, football's a meritocracy. You aren't handed anything. You earn everything every single day, over and over again. You have to prove it. That's the way the NFL and football work. A great example of this is Dak Prescott and what he's done. He's earned the right to be our quarterback. As hard as that is for me to say, he's earned that right."

"Let's unpack this. Why is Romo talking about meritocracy?"

Jared responds, "He realizes Dak has performed so well that he should be the starter. Even if Dak got the job because Tony was injured, he's playing too well for Tony to get his job back."

"Yes, sir. I agree. This offense is going to be a meritocracy. It isn't going to matter if you're a returning starter, an American, or have been with the club the longest or the highest-paid. How you perform during training camp will be what determines if you're on the field for play one or one play vs. Dresden."

The meeting concluded with slides with a typical weekly schedule of our Zoom meetings in the mornings, practice days at 7:00 p.m., and their off day [Thursday].

"Let's go back to Earnest Shackleton's expedition. By the way, all 27 on board survived the trip. The man who stood in line for a chance to endure hardship, low pay, and little recognition is the same man I'm hoping is in this room. We're going to take an adventure together. Sometimes, we'll have to change plans and figure it out as Shackleton's team did, but we'll do it together."

16

THE MIDDLE FINGER

April 16, 2022

It was a beautiful Saturday morning, and we were finally on the field. Berti, Saul, Jonas, and I had met a few days earlier and agreed to make today a practice logistics day. The schedule we installed for this season was much faster, with a lot more moving parts than they'd used before. We sensibly used today as a walk-through for all 70+ players and coaches to be on the same page.

There was *day one* excitement in the air. We were doing a dry run of the same 41-segment practice we'd done on Monday when we went live and in color for the first time.

I can't emphasize enough how different this structure is from how the typical team trains. Most coaches use five or ten-minute blocks for individual position technique, small groups, and full 11 on 11 team sessions. Our practice periods were short, with lots of moving parts. We have two, three, and four-minute periods with tons of transitions.

There are several offenses vs. defense or good-on-good competition segments. An elite practice is like a boxing match; offense and defense meet in the middle of the ring. They "go at each other" and then return to their respective corner for correction.

After a while, we meet back in the middle of the ring and get each other better. Then we return to our corner for specialized teaching and correction.

Games aren't played in five or ten-minute blocks, so I've always wondered why coaches train their teams that way.

I always want to begin each practice by speaking to the team first. They need to hear reminders, encouragement, and our specific daily goals. Our routine would be to have an offensive meeting on the field a few minutes before we officially started.

"Don't worry about where to go or if you're in the right spot. We'll have two walk-through practices today. The first session will have one-minute periods to get everyone acclimated. The second will be two-minute periods where we have time to get a few things done. Our only goal today is for Monday to be a great practice because we all know where to be and what to do. Most of you haven't experienced practice with this tempo before, but we'll figure it out. When in doubt, move fast!"

"One last thing, we'll have four agility-type stations after our first walk-through today. They'll be five minutes each. I lobbied for these to give us some extra conditioning but mostly to see who is ready to go physically. Not to start with a negative tone, but we should all be in the best shape of our careers today. You'll give us a virtual middle finger if you struggle to make it through these stations. We're all grown men, and all have responsibilities to the team. I made sure I was ready for today. I hope you did as well. Most of you have worked your butts off and will destroy the stations. The offense must lead the way. Remember, we're about to embark on a hazardous journey, but it'll be the adventure of a lifetime! Before they all dispersed, I looked at them and screamed, "ENDURANCE!"

A whistle blew, and Berti called all of us up to speak about the day and explain to the team what I had just said to the offense.

Berti is a man of few words. His message today was short and sweet, like usual. "There's no pressure today to be perfect. Just pay attention and listen to instructions."

We coached fast, and the players moved quickly. Our head physio, Taka, blew a whistle every 60 seconds, so everyone was in perpetual motion. After 41 minutes, the walk-through ended, and Berti called the team to the middle of the field.

"Excellent job. I know there was some confusion, but we'll be ready for Monday after we repeat this in our second practice today. Coach Jackson will now explain what we'll do next before we take a short break."

I organized the team into four groups based on their speed and ability. Each group needed to have a mix of offensive and defensive players so that everyone could see the level of effort put in by each other. The coaches managed the drills while I timed everything and signaled the athletes to rotate between stations.

I was pleased to see Helbig, Polk, and Jared crushing the stations. They must have put in a lot of work over the winter because they were in fantastic shape and clearly leading the pack. While a few other players were also doing well, some Europeans were struggling with the new type of training, and I had to provide them with some assistance. However, my offensive linemen were having a tough time. Without a proper off-season to prepare them for the cardiovascular demands, some were sticking to what they knew best, lifting weights or doing nothing at all.

After the second station, I realized it wasn't going well. It wasn't "shared suffering as we fight through this together" but genuine agony for some. A few players were in danger of being unable to do the second walk-through in about 30 minutes. Our tight end, Jerome Valbon, was off to the side throwing up, and a few more were on a knee, totally exhausted. I only allowed the third drill to go four minutes and the final station three minutes. By now, a few more were vomiting, and it looked like a bomb had gone off with several bodies lying on the ground.

I walked up to Berti and said, “Sorry, coach, that didn't go as planned. About 20 of them gave us the middle finger by not being ready to go today.”

Berti didn't say anything, but I knew he didn’t love the stations, and I couldn’t say I blamed him. It might not have been the best idea after all. There’s a difference between *conditioning* them and *discouraging* them. We used training camp to get in shape in the 1980s when I was in high school. I just discovered many Europeans also use the first month of preseason practices to condition their bodies like we did back in the day. I wonder if the elite soccer teams have the same mindset?

The fact most of our offensive linemen weren’t cardio-ready didn't concern me from a tactical standpoint. I knew we’d have their big butts ready to play in four weeks, but it bothered me from a team culture aspect. Were my expectations too high for pro football in Europe? Texas high school players lift, run, wrestle and train physically and mentally over 1,000 hours from December to August in an organized off-season program to get ready for the season. The next few months will be a tug-of-war with me and some of the players and coaches. Will I impose my culture on them, or will their culture be imposed on me?

Let the games begin!

POTSDAM ROYALS

6:30 KICK MEETINGS
6:45 UNIT MEETINGS
7:00 TEAM MEET
7:10 WALK THRU
7:20 PRACTICE BEGIN

IF YOU'RE JUICEFUL YOU'RE USEFUL!

HELMETS

LB	DL	MIN	PD	PERIODS	OL	PIPE	RB	WR	QB
		4	1	CO. FAIR	WALK THRU - 15-12-10-8-6-4-2 / RIVERSIDE				
		3	2	WARM UP					
		1	3	Break					
		3	4	PUNT					
		1	5	Break					
		5	6	BLITZ	OL/R/Q v. DL/LB				
		1	7	Break					
		5	8	LAUNCH					
		1	9	Break					
		3	10	CIRCUIT	BIRD DOG			PERFECT	PERFECT
		3	11		OVERLAP			PAT N GO	PAT N GO
		3	12		CHAIR			SWITCH	SWITCH
		1	13	Break					
		3	14	BALLDOWN					
		3	15	2' B. DOWN					
		3	16	BALLDOWN					
		1	17	Break					
		4	18	INDY					
		4	19						
		4	20						
		4	21						
		1	22	Break					
BIG BOY HULL		6	23	2 v. 2	BIG BOY HULL				
		3	24	TURNOVERS					
BIG BOY HULL		6	25	1 v. 1	BIG BOY HULL				
		1	26	Break					
		4	27	KO					
		4	28	KOR					
		1	29	Break					
		4	30	BALLDOWN					
		6	31	1/2 TIME					
		1	32	HIGH KNEES					
		1	33	KOR					
		1	34	Break					
		5	35	B'DOWN - O					
		1	36	Break					
		3	37	TEAM APART					
		3	38						
		3	39						
		1	40	Break					
		3	41	FG					

#ROYALSFAMILY

17

NO LINES ARE NO PROBLEM

April 19, 2022

Monday morning, I woke up feeling like it was Christmas day. Our first real practice was finally going to happen that evening. We would use our drone to video the team sessions (11 vs. 11). There'll be 50 to 60 repetitions to evaluate each player. We'd built up to this moment with hours of preparation by coaches and players. Our first offensive meeting occurred over three months ago, so I was on pins and needles. I was eager to see us execute.

It was *GO TIME.*

Berti didn't give me or Jonas specific requirements for being in the office, nor did we have official staff meetings. I decided to go in when needed, which was around three times a week at this point in the season. This morning was sunny and a little cool as I made the 15-minute walk to the complex. There is a bakery on the way, so I was getting in the habit of stopping by and grabbing a swine ear pastry, a pretzel roll, and a brötchen (roll topped with cheese) to tide me over til I left, which was usually around 1:00 p.m.

Saul and Jonas arrived about the same time as me, and we began planning practice for that evening. About 15 minutes into our discussion, Berti walked into the office and said, "We have a problem. Our field is not available tonight. There's a conflict with our schedule and an adult men's football league. The city tells me we don't have the field reserved for Monday nights this spring."

Wait, what? Are we being bumped for an over-60 soccer league?

"You've got to be kidding me. I thought we had the field set for Mondays and Wednesdays from now on. What happened?" Saul asked.

Berti responded, "You know the drill. The city does what the city does. There's no telling if they made a mistake or if we didn't get the request for Monday nights as we were supposed to. Either way, we aren't going to practice tonight. We need to focus on finding a field for tomorrow night."

As Berti left, he was getting his phone out to do what he does best, correct the logistics. Within a few minutes, he returned and said, "We have a field for tomorrow night, but it's a soccer-only field with no American football markings. We must decide if we want this or wait until Wednesday to return to our normal field."

Saul, who sets the calendar and does an excellent job keeping us organized, is irritated as he says, "Crap, this is such rubbish. We're the second-highest attended pro franchise in Potsdam, and they act like we don't exist unless we bitch and complain. The next time they do something to help us will be the first time."

"I'm good with tomorrow and no lines. It's time for us to get going. We'll *monitor and adjust* what we have to do. This will be my first time without lines, but offensively we'll be fine," I said.

"We had to practice without markings from 2005 to 2017, so it's no big deal for me, but I appreciate your understanding. Let's communicate with our players now so they can make the adjustments," Berti said.

American football in Europe is about overcoming obstacles most of the time. The Royals don't own a practice facility or stadium for games, so they must rent both. Players bring their pads to and from practice and dress when they arrive. We have access to a restroom but don't have our own locker room.

The following day, we began our morning meetings with the offense. I met from 9:30 am-10:15 am with the offensive line and from 10:15 am - 11:00 am with the skill position players. Chris and Karri, our running back, were always in both meetings.

"Tonight will be an excellent opportunity to show Coach Vogt and the defense where we are. Field markings or not, we will roll! All I care about on our official day one is seeing us play fast! Don't worry about me grading you on anything tonight but how fast you move."

Around 5:30 p.m., Saul stopped by my flat to take me to the field. The practice officially began at 7:00, but traffic in Potsdam can be tricky. The ten miles take around 30 minutes on a normal day. "Do we have everything?" I asked. The head coach in me knows there is much more to having a practice than football. Saul wears a lot of hats for the Royals. He's the general manager, special teams coordinator, receiver coach, equipment manager, video coordinator, and whatever else needs to be done.

"I think we're all good for tonight. I've checked and double-checked everything. What a minute... did I tell the guys to bring water?"

I responded, "Our guys bring their water to practice? No, I don't remember ever hearing that."

"Yes, since COVID, they have brought a water bottle. It reduces our risk of spreading the virus. I'll call Jonas and ask him to pick up some water for tonight."

Our makeshift digs for the night were in a beautiful area that bordered the Havel River. The German Olympic bobsled training facility and a track were also nearby. Soon after we arrived, players began to show up. Most rode the train, but some in cars and others on bicycles.

After getting out of the Royals' van, I heard something I didn't expect to hear again for a long time, a loud Texas-sounding voice that said, "Hey, Coach Jackson!"

I stopped in my tracks and looked around. A man around my age walked up and stuck out his hand.

"Coach, my name's Buddy Carroll. I grew up in Ft. Worth but have been living here for a few years. My son, Stephen, is the quarterback for the 15U team. Welcome to the Royals!"

"Thanks, Buddy. I'm excited to be here. I think we have a chance to make some noise this season if we stay healthy," I said.

"I've followed your career and all the successes you've had. When you retired last year, I was shocked. I figured you were too young to stop coaching. I've also read your two books on culture. I still can't believe you're in Potsdam coaching the Royals. I told all the other board members about you when I found out you were hired."

"I appreciate the kind words, Buddy. You're making me feel famous for the first time since I arrived in Germany," I said, smiling.

Buddy reminded me of many guys I knew in Texas who were consumed with high school football and knew more about it than they did about the NFL

"From speaking with Berti and Saul, I think we're going to score a bunch of points! I'm excited to see how the fast pace affects the defenses in the GFL. I know you must get to the field, but I want you to know this Texas High School football junkie is glad you're a Royal!"

"Thank you, that means a lot. I hope we can visit again soon," I responded.

"Yes sir, coach! If you need anything, please let me know. I know navigating Germany for the first few weeks can be tough. Have a great practice!"

Within 15 minutes of practice beginning, we huddled on the sideline. We were about to run our season's first team session (11 v. 11). We'd have four team sessions in most practices, but I wanted to set the bar high right then.

"You guys ready to shock and awe our defense? Relax and have fun. It doesn't have to be perfect, but it can be warp speed fast."

We always huddle on the sideline before the first play of a team session or of a drive during games, but I only talk briefly. Reminders and confidence are my main objectives, and I don't want the defense waiting on us.

Helbig added, "I haven't enjoyed playing football in a long time. This is why we're all here. Move fast and have fun."

We did both.

Chris was amazing. The ball was like a laser coming out of his hand. Jared and Polk were also, as advertised, both ripping the secondary with big catch after big catch. Our defense was without an American starter for the time being, and it was a glaring mismatch when Chris targeted Jared or Polk. We literally blitzkrieg-ed our defense. We stayed simple and moved faster than even I expected. We ran 10 or 11 plays in the four-minute segment and gained nearly 150 yards. I high-fived the offense as they came off the field. I knew this was only the first of a hundred of these sessions we'd have during the season, but I was proud and let them know it.

Our offense gained at least 10 yards per play when we finished for the night. We even ran a perfectly executed trick play named *Schnitzel,* where Chris threw a backward pass to Jared, who then threw to a wide-open Karri down the middle of the field. After having a complicated, NFL-style offense the year before, the guys needed to believe Fast N' Wide would function as advertised from day one. We executed like we knew what we were doing, which is saying something considering we barely know each other or the offense.

The only issue on the night was a one-on-one drill where the offensive line pass blocked versus the defensive line rushing an imaginary quarterback. I stood in front of the offensive lineman and behind the defensive player and held up a number representing the snap count. It was a new drill for everyone, so there'd be some learning on the fly for the players. We had to vary when the ball was snapped, or the faster defender would have the advantage.

After a few reps, Max was up. I gave him the snap count of one and then started the cadence, "Go, Hit!" Max was a bit slow off the ball, and the defensive lineman got past him to Jonas, our substitute quarterback.

"Let's go again. Fast feet, Max. Stay in the middle of him; you got this," I said. This time I held up a closed fist which meant the ball would move on first sound, hoping to give Max a slight advantage.

"Go!" I yelled. Max was quicker this time, but the defender gave him a *right, left* move, and got past him again. To be fair, Max is a large interior guard who isn't built to win one-on-one battles against faster defenders. I'd be a bad coach if I had us run plays where he didn't get help in pass protection. But this was still an essential drill for him to be ready in the rare instance when he had to hold his own with no help.

"I don't know where he is coming from!" Max angrily shouted at me.

I'm sure this is how the offensive linemen spoke to the coach they booted last season, but Max's outburst was also a test to see what I'd tolerate from him and the others. He was embarrassed by his performance and wanted to blame me and the new drill. It was in front of every offensive and defensive lineman. It was a test I had to pass. I had to respond accordingly. All eyes were on me when I said...

"Let me tell you something. I didn't come 6,000 miles, or however many kilometers that is to be yelled at by a player who gets his ass kicked in a drill. I'm not sure what you don't understand, but keep your mouth shut next time or talk to me like you want me to respond. I won't be yelled at for the next six months. I promise you that."

After practice ended, I saw Polk picking up pylons and yard markers. I said to him, "Hey man, it's awesome you're being a servant leader after having such a terrific practice. Thanks for being the humble American we need."

"You got it, coach. I'll help pick up stuff after every practice. It's what I do," Polk said, smiling.

"Coach, can we talk for a second?" I turned around to see Max holding his shoulder pads and helmet.

"Of course. What's on your mind?" I responded.

"I just want to talk to you as a man and say I think you took my confusion to the drill wrong tonight," Max replied.

"Max, I'm not sure what you expected to get from me, but Yasir isn't the OL coach this year. I'll coach you and everyone else as if y'all want to improve each practice. We'll do competitive drills against the defense, where we win some and lose some. I knew this would be a different experience with coaching grown men, but I can't tolerate you shouting at me. Are you going to let me coach you hard this season without snapping back at me?"

"I will coach. I want you to coach me hard. The drill was new and confusing, and I wasn't sure how to win. My reaction was 100% wrong, and I'll fix it. I appreciate you talking to me man to man."

It was a relief Max approached me after the workout and wanted to visit about the incident. I was proud we shook hands and moved forward. Coaches in high school, 99% of the time, must go seek out a player and patch things up if need be, but Max is a mature adult and acted like it. He was also one of our five best linemen who I needed to get on board with our culture.

I graded the film in the office with Saul and Jonas the following morning. On each play, I evaluated all five of the offensive line for correct first step, face placement, did they block the proper defender and effort. After an hour, the grading was complete. We began to discuss what plays we would run and who should be in the starting lineup at our next practice, Friday, when Berti came into the room.

"We can't get either field for Thursday. I am working on finding a field for Friday now."

"Speaking of not practicing, Coach Genau won't be practicing with us if we find a field or not. Check your phone and see if he texted you," Saul said to me.

There was indeed a WhatsApp message to Saul and me that read...

I'm sorry to say this, but my intern responsibilities at the hospital are more than I anticipated. I won't have the time to coach this season after all. Undoubtedly, you guys will be an excellent team, and I'm disappointed I won't be on the staff, but I don't want to do anything I cannot give 100% effort towards. Thank you for the opportunity, but regretfully, I must focus on becoming a doctor. Good luck this season.

You've got to be kidding me. So, the coaches here throw in the towel after one practice? And they do it with a text message? I didn't need a lab experiment to know this is ridiculous. If our players have the same commitment level, this will be the most frustrating season of my life.

18

50 STRONG

April 26, 2022

We were ahead of schedule on the field but needed to get into high gear to create a player's creed. Elite behaviors don't happen by accident. In our 'Name, Image, and Likeness' society, everyone brands themselves and essentially acts as an independent contractor. Today, more than ever, we must be *on purpose* with setting a vision for all members of our organization to understand what it means to be a team. Programs without a vision or mission react poorly when the crap hits the fan.

"Coach, I'm sorry, but I forgot to mention to the defense that you have a players' creed meeting tonight. I'll post it now." Berti told me as I was leaving the office for the day.

"It's ok, coach. Tonight will be the start of something they'll enjoy. My job will be to inspire them to invite others next week."

I scheduled voluntary meetings for the next three Tuesday evenings since it was an off day. We met in the office complex with a clear goal in mind. Our mission was to create something revolutionary - something I believe had rarely, if ever, been done before in the GFL or pro sports teams in Europe. Tonight would be our first gathering to create a players' creed for the season.

We met in the common area on the ground floor, where we held our team meeting a couple of weeks prior. I was pleased with the turnout. There were 18 offensive and six defensive players in attendance. I purposely didn't hound any of my guys to attend because I wanted to see who was buying into the culture we were establishing. To be honest, I wasn't concerned with how many showed up but *which* ones did.

I opened the meeting with a story.

"Thank you very much for taking the time and effort to get here on an off day. In 1981, Lakers assistant coach, Pat Riley, was promoted to head coach. He had been the Lakers TV *color guy* just a few years prior, so he wasn't a slam-dunk choice, no pun intended, to get the job. The Lakers became a dynasty in the 80s, winning five NBA titles. According to Coach Riley, the #1 reason he was accepted as the head coach was that his two best players, Magic Johnson and Kareem Abdul-Jabbar, were on board with him. Once they bought into his shared vision, the rest of the team followed suit."

"On elite teams, the best players are the best leaders. Our best players are here tonight, and that excites me."

On the defensive side, Tibo Debaillie, a beast of a defensive lineman from Belgium, was present. We all were ecstatic when he signed with us just a few weeks ago. He played collegiately at Towson State in Maryland and had American-type talent. Tibo was already establishing himself as a team leader. His attitude was incredible. He was humble but would be a top-3 defensive lineman in the league. Any player-maker who wasn't an 'A' is a big bonus in the GFL.

Yasir, our all-Europe tackle and maybe the best player I had ever coached, was present. This was huge. I needed him to be here. He was an influencer x 100 for our returning Royals. Yasir was a certified destroyer on the offensive line. He was smart, strong, violent, and extremely quick for his size. NFL teams draft left tackles early in the first round and pay them millions to solidify their OL for a decade. Yasir was that guy for us. He would protect Helbig's blind side, and we would run behind him the majority of the time in critical situations. He was Kareem or Magic for me to get on board. The fact that he had made the effort to take a 30-minute train ride to get here spoke volumes to the rest of the team.

Jerome Valbon, our French-Canadian tight end, and Brenden Oswin, a guard from Australia, were in the room. Somehow, they'd played in the GFL 2 the year before, although their film from 2021 was very good, it a great feeling they were actual "dudes" who'd be two of our most productive guys. They were also best friends and roommates, so it was a package deal on getting them to buy into our creed.

Our three A's, of course, were leading from the front and sitting up close. I can't stress this enough, the fact Chris, Jared, and Polk were unselfish rockstars was huge in getting this going. All three of them had played on college teams with intentional cultures. They would help me sell how important it is and help us create it. Many other imports were also in the room that were current and future starters. Locals who were not working were also present. We even had a few guys make the trip from Berlin.

What was also screaming at me was who was not present. Our all-GFL dual passport defensive end from Colorado, TK Thompson, was a no-show. Max, who needed an attitude adjustment of late, was also AWOL.

If our creed was going to be more than a slogan on a t-shirt or a Twitter hashtag, I had to deliver tonight.

"I need you all to stand up and close your eyes. Turn around until I say stop."

Twenty-four players and three coaches started slowly spinning around. After a few seconds, I said, "Stop! Keep your hand over your eyes."

"Now, take your other hand and point to the direction you believe is *True North*."

They all reached out their hand, and fingers went in every direction.

“Open your eyes and see where everyone’s pointed." There was laughter because fingers were everywhere.

"Why are you laughing? Is it because most of us don't know where True North is? But that doesn't matter. What matters is that we begin to all point in the SAME DIRECTION."

“If some of us will point in the same direction, we will IMPROVE. If most of us point in the same direction, we will be MUCH BETTER. If ALL of us will buy in and point in the same direction, we will be UNSTOPPABLE.”

"Let me give you some background on why a players’ creed is so important to me. In 2014, I read the book *Always Compete* by Pete Carroll, which emphasized the significance of a player's creed. Inspired by this, I decided to implement core values for our team. I selected four values: compete, family, honor, and tough. These were printed on everyone's locker tags alongside their name and number. This might be a stupid question, but can anyone guess how effective these core values were for us?"

"I bet they weren't amazing. Just words to most of them," Chris said.

"Correct! Why do you think that, or if anyone else wants to jump in," I replied.

"Because your guys didn't spend any time on them. They were just values without meaning," Jared responded.

"Exactly! No one washes a rental car! I was curious if anyone would get where I was heading. The four words didn’t do anything for our team. We never talked about them, and 99% of them probably wouldn’t have been able to tell me what they were at the end of the season. It was a total waste of time and energy. But, in 2015, I hired a mental performance coach and learned how to create a team's core values or a set of standards. When I learned a system on how to create a culture that came from the players, it changed everything.”

"What we’ll do the next three weeks is create a compass for the Royals. Championship teams know where they're going. We will make history in Potsdam with guys from 18 countries who’ve just met each other, but all point True North. We'll create a team that's never been assembled before, and our creed will be like the Magna Carta of 1215. It’ll set the standard for how pro teams in Europe should operate. I'm excited about what we're about to undertake, and we'll use this system to make a written proclamation of what the Royals and the game of football mean to us."

"I'm looking forward to seeing what you all come up with, and I hope you can appreciate the importance of this endeavor. Together, we can create something truly special."

“Let’s begin with this. Nothing can be accomplished unless it can be defined. What do you guys think a creed is? How would you define a creed?"

Faces stared back at me, but that was all. No one said a word.

"For this to work, it has to be a discussion and dialogue. I’ll facilitate or show you the way, but this has to be your document (as I pointed at them) if our team is going to point to it when times get tough. You guys will name it, decide what pillars we agree on, and define them. I don't believe elite leadership is just showing up and performing. Real leaders bring energy, are engaged, and make teammates better. I need you guys to be vocal and make this process better."

Jared jumped in, "I'm going to say a creed is something that says what a group or team believes in, how it operates on a day-to-day basis."

"That's really good. You’re right on the mark. A creed is “a set of beliefs or aims that guide someone's actions. A few months after I retired, Sonny Dykes, now the head coach at TCU, asked me to embed with his team and give him a fresh set of eyes on everything and anyone I could observe the weekend of a game. I spent the night in the team hotel, ate meals with them, attended meetings, and stood on the sideline. I also did this for Rice University and head coach Mike Bloomgren. I told both coaches if I could speak to their team and ask them, "What is this team about? What do you guys think TCU, or Rice football is?" If I get several different answers, then there's no culture. Teams and organizations must have a few characteristics that make it go, and everyone must know what they are.”

"This next question is for a Royals vet. What were the Royals' core values last season? Every team has a set of principles that guides it, whether they're written down, specifically talked about, or not."

Ludi, one of our offensive linemen who’s been with the Royals since he was 16, said, "We didn't have a creed, of course, but we played hard and didn't blame each other when things went bad."

"Let’s start going from a *neighborhood to a brotherhood* right now. Get in a group with two people you don’t know. Guys who don’t play your position or, even better, your side of the ball. Introduce yourself and get out your phone. Google core values used by a championship team. Find the most elite team you can, regardless of sport, and see if you can determine their core values.”

The guys got up and moved around the stadium-type bleachers we were sitting in. Within a few minutes, I began asking for responses.

"The All-blacks rugby team in New Zealand. I found their core values," Stefan said.

"The Golden State Warriors' core values are *joy, mindfulness, compassion,* and *competition*," said Canadian defensive back Cody Cranston.

Polk was next, "I sort of went 'insider trading', but I can tell us the core values of Penn State football."

“Excellent. What are they?” I asked.

"Attitude, work ethic, compete, and sacrifice!" Polk said confidently. "I’ll know them until the day I die."

“Why will you know them until you die?”

“They were all over the locker room, weight room, meeting rooms, and even the stadium. We talked about them every day. I almost got a tattoo of all our core values," Polk said.

"Good stuff, guys. Although it isn't publicized much, most collegiate and professional teams in the U.S. have core values. Once, I was allowed to tour the Dallas Cowboys training facility. They had a large framed “blue star” with their team's core values for the season. Our tour guide told us the captains took six to eight weeks to create them. Around the logo were the thumbprints of every team member. We’ll do something similar when we finish.”

"Before I forget, let's start a WhatsApp group with everyone here. I’ll label it “Players Creed” until we create an awesome name for all of this. I’ll make you an admin so you can admit others, but you must be “present to win,” as they say. We should have 24 players in the group and no one else. Next week, we’ll add others."

Although I did this with them in the core values Zoom back in March, I felt we needed to discuss it again. I wanted them to see what the end could look like in their minds and then figure out how to make it happen.

"Get your phone back out. Put in our chat one word you want the 2022 Royals to be known for."

- *Brotherhood*
- *Champions*
- *Terrorize*
- *Strong*
- *Finish*
- *Legacy*
- *Ring*
- *Family*
- *Fun*
- *Trophy*
- *Record-setting*

"Let's see what we have in the chat. Are most of the words *root* or *fruit* words? What I mean by that is, are most end-result, what we want to accomplish words or adjectives that describe what we must do to achieve it?"

"Most are fruit words. But we must take care of the root first, and then the fruit will happen. We will have to take care of the roots to be a great team," said Jerome.

"Who in here has played on a team with an intentional value system or creed?" I asked.

"We had one at Southern Utah that was in place when I arrived. It helped our team chemistry quite a bit. I'm not positive, but I believe it was from the head coach and not player-created," said Chris.

"What was something in it you liked the most?"

"The mentality of a united team. The one that resonated with me the most was 'unity.' We didn't hope for togetherness, but captains and coaches made sure we did things together. We were a tight-knit group, and it helped on the field."

"Perfect example, Chris. That is a good segway into the areas we need to address. My goal isn't for us to create anything tonight, but we can start on what we know must be included for us to be special. What is a characteristic of a team that's important to you? Something you believe we must have to win the German Bowl? Let's work in our groups again. I'll give you a few minutes to collaborate on this. These are just ideas, but areas like, practice habits, attendance, weights, film study, sleep, and hydration are things we must do better than our competition. That said, I'd like each group of three to give us one suggested pillar in a few minutes."

The guys were warming up now and more talkative. After a little while, I asked, "What did you guys come up with?"

"Our group wants to make sure compete, or competition is in the creed," said Yasir. I was thrilled to see him joining the discussion.

"Shared emotions," said Jared, speaking for his group.

"Fun," said Tibo.

"High Trust," said Heiko.

Polk said, "Relationships are for the boys."

"Positivity," said Stefan.

"1/11, which means we all have our job to do. If I do my 1/11 and Ruben does his 1/11, and everyone else does, then we are good," said Dutch lineman Mads Högen, one of my big boys.

Jerome was next, "Do your job. Everyone has a job, and we must do it every day in practice or game day."

"I love it, fellas. Now we have a starting point for next Tuesday. We'll decide on the pillars and a name for our creed next week to give you an idea of where we are heading. Thanks again for being here tonight."

Just then, I noticed Jared's hand in the air, "Yes, sir, Wolfe, what's up?"

"I'm not sure if the group will like this, but at Villanova, we dressed out 88 guys, so our creed was called *88 Strong*."

It was perfect, and everyone nodded their heads in agreement. "Coach Vogt, how many can we dress on game day?" I asked.

"50."

"I have to be careful here because this is not my creed or Coach Vogt's creed or anyone else's but yours. Do we want to marinate on 50 Strong and see if anyone has something else to consider for next week?"

"50 Strong it is!" confidently declared Jerome and Leo simultaneously, indicating their decision had already been made.

19

DID HE GET TREATMENT OR NOT?

May 2, 2022

A few days later, the offense met at the office to review practice. We gathered there once a week to be face-to-face so that all meetings wouldn't be a Zoom call. Attendance was always 100%, but Max was absent that morning. He had injured his ankle a few nights before, but there should be no reason he couldn't watch the video with us.

"Does anyone know where Max is?" I asked.

"He still isn't moving well on this ankle. His flat is on the other side of Potsdam, so it takes him around 40 minutes to get here. I'm sure he didn't feel like coming over this morning. He could also be getting treatment, but I doubt it," Yasir said bluntly.

Later that evening, Max was at practice but dressed only in our team sweats. I approached him and said, "I've got a few questions. Why weren't you at our meeting this morning, and why aren't you dressed to practice tonight?"

"I haven't been cleared to practice and didn't feel well this morning, so I stayed home," Max replied.

My voice was getting louder than it should have, but I was being tested again by Max. "It's not ok to miss our meetings because you don't feel well without letting me or Coach Jonas know. What did the physio or doctor say about your timetable to return to the field?"

"I still haven't been able to see a physio. I'm waiting for the doctor's office to call me to come in." Max replied.

Now, this was maddening. A starter wasn't practicing because he couldn't get an appointment?

"Do any of the coaches know more about this than I do? This is the first I am hearing of this, and it pisses me off that you are skipping film this morning and practice tonight."

"I'm not skipping tonight. Taka won't allow me to practice until I see a doctor."

"I can't believe this," I muttered under my breath. This can't be ok in any laboratory anywhere in the world. I was beyond frustrated. I'd never dealt with a player returning to practice when he felt like it. It just didn't make any sense.

I walked over to Saul and asked him, "Max just told me he isn't practicing tonight because he hasn't seen a doctor. Were you aware he hasn't had any treatment on his ankle?"

Saul calmly replied, "I didn't know he hadn't received treatment. It’s not my job to know.”

I was getting fired up when I said, "It's been over a week since his injury. Does he just hang out until he decides to see a doctor?"

"Sometimes it's difficult for our players to get in to see a doctor. I suspect Jonas would know more about this since it's his responsibility," Saul replied.

I was still trying to hide my frustration when I said, "What is our protocol with injured athletes? Is there any accountability for ensuring they’re trying hard to return?"

Saul was now getting irritated with my questions. "Look, Berti has assigned Jonas to help us sort out injuries. Last year it wasn’t very good at times, and we struggled to keep up with it all.”

I was equally frustrated with my response, "So, let me get this straight. We’re about to start practice, and Max is not dressed out because he has been injured for over a week and hasn't been to the doctor. No one knows he hasn’t seen a doctor, and it feels like no one cares. What the hell are we doing if we don't have systems for this?"

Saul continued to remain very calm and deliberate with his answers. It was almost as if he wanted me to get the message that it wasn't his job, nor was it something he worried about when he said, "Coach, I would appreciate it if you would lower your tone with me. Jonas is responsible for knowing if Max has seen a doctor or physio, so I would appreciate it if you would stop yelling at me."

I turned towards Jonas and loudly asked, "Did you know Max hasn’t even seen a doctor yet?"

I hated putting Jonas on the spot. He was becoming a good friend and, as a native German, someone I depended on to help me understand the cultural differences among the players here. After practice, we sometimes went to a döner kebab cafe and debriefed how we thought everything went. Jonas was eager to learn everything he could about the game from me, and I was anxious to know everything about the GFL and the culture from him.

"Max has been told to keep me updated, but he hasn't done so. I wasn’t aware if he had been to his appointment yet, " Jonas said.

I snapped back, "You have to know! We have to know! We cannot allow someone to hang out because they don't want to practice!" I looked back at Saul when I said, "You're the general manager of this organization but don't give a damn if a starter is not here? We're a joke if guys come and go with no accountability."

Saul didn't look up at me. He continued to fix a facemask on a player's helmet.

After practice, I approached Jonas and said, "Döner's on me tonight. I'm sorry for going off on you before practice. "We sat down after we ordered. I wouldn't only make this right with him but wanted to mentor him on why this is such a big deal to me.

"If we allow players to get treatment when they feel like it or come to practice when they feel like it, we might as well stop trying to create a players' creed. Nothing we put on paper will have any merit if they get to skip practice. I hope you'll forgive me for my rudeness earlier."

"It's all good, coach; I understand. You weren't wrong. I should've done a better job of making sure Max got treatment."

The next day Berti entered the office, and I asked him, "I hate to start with a negative right off, but I have to ask, do we have a system for injuries? I'm sure you've heard about the situation before practice yesterday. I will only play someone on offense I'm positive is doing their best to practice."

"I agree with you, coach. I take full responsibility for not giving Jonas and Taka more direction. I've asked Taka to be here today so we can all devise a plan."

I doubled down since we were talking about players' injuries. I also hit Berti with my concerns about the "Club Med" that was forming in the treatment area in the endzone.

"We also have an issue with players "getting injured" during practice and staying with our young female physios for the rest of the workout. Can we address this as well? More guys go over for something during a workout and don't return than I've ever seen. I have to keep up with who I have and who is getting rubbed on the physio table."

"Years ago, I had a senior running back named Manuel who severely strained his ACL in the eighth game. Usually, this injury would sideline a player for six to eight weeks. His ACL! Our physio and doctor told Manuel that if he would rehab like a madman, he might play a few plays if we advanced to the second round of the playoffs, about a month away. They would then do the surgery if it was required after the season was over. Oh, and by the way, our record was 1 win and 7 losses at the time."

"He decided to rehab with an enthusiasm I'd never seen from a player before."

"We won the last two games and qualified for the playoffs with a dreadful 3-7 record. We miraculously defeated our first opponent, who had won nine games and made it to the second round. Manuel wasn't ready to play but suited up for the game anyway. The glass slipper was off our foot by this time, and we were getting our butts kicked by 30 points in the fourth quarter. Manuel came up to me and asked, 'Coach, can I run the play 24 Toss one more time?' He limped onto the field, ran 24 Toss for one yard, and limped back to the sideline. His knee just wasn't ready. After the play, he over to me with tears in his eyes and said, 'Thanks, coach, it was worth it.' I know Max is not Manuel, and I know Potsdam is not Texas, but I do know football is football, and dammit, this is why I'm so frustrated."

We did come up with a plan. It was two weeks too late, but it was better than where we were before. After the meeting, we decided that all injured players would check in with Jonas ten minutes before the start of practice. Jonas would also give all coaches in our WhatsApp group the status of injured players during the day.

"Taka, I've never tried to override a physio's decision to return to play for an athlete. I wouldn't know either if I had the authority, but it's driving me crazy seeing so many players over there. I swear there were five or six at one point the other night," I said.

"I know what you're talking about, Coach Jackson. I've noticed it as well at times when I'm able to be at practice. I'll say something to the girls about it."

"Thanks very much, Taka. When I played in high school in the dark ages, our team had 22 total players. No one would replace you when you weren't on the field, so we didn't leave the field. We played through pain and discomfort. The other day, I half-jokingly told my guys I don't believe in injuries. We all chuckled a little, but I am seriously worn out with my big guys getting tired, so they see the physio for a rub down."

A PIZZA AND A DÖNER

An hour later, I was at lunch with Heiko and Yasir. Breaking bread with players is a tactic I've long used to create a bond and increase communication. I bought pizza and or döners for a couple of guys at a cafe about once a week the first couple of months of the season.

"Guys, I have one question that I haven't asked anyone else. Since you were both with the Royals last year, you'll be able to answer this. You knew from my comments at practice last night and with some of the things I've posted in our WhatsApp that I'm frustrated with guys missing practice or missing the last hour with an "injury" (I made the air quotes sign with my fingers)."

"We can tell for sure. We have some guys who need to step up. Some of them are used to getting away with more than you'll let them," Heiko said.

"The starters will be at practice 99% of the time. Especially since we have so many imports," Yasir said.

"It's killing me. I knew coaching guys with full-time jobs and families would be different, but it feels like it's not a big deal. It's ridiculous that "Player A" from Berlin can't come to practice because he has an unexpected job requirement or that "Player B" can't get cleared for practice because he doesn't feel like it. I know football in Europe is different from what I'm used to, so I wondered how Coach Moon handled it last year. Was he aggravated with this type of stuff like I am?

Yasir smiled and chuckled, "Oh yea. Coach Moon was always pissed off. He'd been with the Buccaneers, so not only did he think we didn't have enough commitment, but he also didn't think we were any good. At least you think we can play."

I believe some of these guys are talented, but I'm not sure if they dream about football or just think about it when they're with the team.

My fingers are crossed.

20

KNOCK ON THE DOOR

May 3, 2022

Jonas picked me up for our second players' creed meeting. I was excited to see what was in store for us this week. As we headed to our destination, I couldn't resist asking, "So, how many players do you think we'll have this week? We had 24 last time."

"Well...in my brief experience, anytime something is voluntary, the number decreases each week. I hate to say it, but I don't think we'll have as many people show up tonight. I'm curious, why haven't you said more about it in our meetings? They respect you; if you pressured them, we'd have a lot more of the team show up."

"That's the point. I want guys here who care enough to give up a couple of hours on an off night because they believe in this. The fact Max and TK weren't here last week speaks volumes."

"Did you know they're roommates?" Jonas asked me.

"I didn't. That seems strange to me, considering they don't play on the same side of the ball or are not from the same area of the world."

"Both stayed in Potsdam in the offseason, so the Royals put them in the same flat," Jonas replied.

"TK is extremely talented but is maybe the worst practice player I've ever seen. It's hard to watch how lazy he is sometimes. After a few plays of our fast tempo, he shuts it down and says, "Forget about it." When we do any of our one-on-one drills, he never goes against Yasir. If he doesn't change his attitude, he'll be a problem when guys begin to sign the creed. Why do you think the Royals put up with his attitude?"

"He is one of the best pass rushers in the GFL and is a unicorn like Wolfe. He's an American but somehow has a British passport, so he doesn't count as an 'A.' The Royals tolerate him because they feel they can't live without him."

"I've always believed that with cancer, you either have to treat it or cut it out. I hope that TK and Max can be treated. The question is whether Berti and Saul want to create a 50-strong team or if they'll turn a blind eye. I can assure you that I won't ignore Max. I'll keep working with him to get him on board, but it won't bode well for us if he doesn't show up tonight. We can't make exceptions for anyone, or the creed will be worthless."

The guys started coming in, and it looked like we had at least the same number as last time, but after I counted, we had 28, four more than last week! I gave Jonas a look of satisfaction, and he shot me back a thumbs-up.

"Thanks again for being here, men. We have a few new guys. I appreciate y'all joining us tonight. All of you already in our WhatsApp are admins, so please add anyone new to our group."

"We know we'll be a top-5 talented team in the GFL. 50 Strong will be an edge for us that no other team has. Last week, we created a foundation for our core values. It's crucial for us to have a shared creed that we can all unite behind. Tonight, we have more important work to do as we lay the foundation of 50 Strong. Let's get to it!"

YOU MUST COME IN PERSON

"I sent this to you guys earlier today so we could start immediately tonight. Unless you are Jerome, raise your hand if you can tell us anything about the French Foreign Legion."

"The Legion takes soldiers from all over the world," said Brenden.

"If you're wounded in battle, you're granted French citizenship," said linebacker Leo Bosch.

"It's considered the most elite mercenary unit on the planet," said Tibo.

"All excellent answers. Thank you for those. Jerome, now it's your turn. What's something about the Legion that resembles the group here tonight?"

"They're from all over the world but wear the same uniform."

"I agree with you, but more specifically, how does one get into the Legion?"

"I believe you have to go in person. You can't apply online, send a letter, or call. You must physically go to the building to apply."

"That's exactly right. To be a Legionnaire, you must get off your butt and go in person to France and knock on the door. This is precisely what each of you who are in this room did. Texas is 8,500 kilometers from Germany. Chris came even farther. Most of you who are imports got on a plane and left your family behind. Seventy-five percent of our Germans are from somewhere other than Potsdam. We all came here and knocked on the door."

"Think back to our True North exercise last week, where we had fingers going in all directions. How do you think the French Foreign Legion takes guys from every country and gets them to point in the same direction?"

Jerome responded, "One thing they do is make them all speak French. The only language used is French."

"Exactly! If I had to speak German to come coach here, I couldn't have come. We all use English, but that isn't enough for us to want to have each other's backs when the *crap hits the fan.* Every team in the GFL speaks English. We're going to speak 50 Strong."

"In the book of Genesis, there's a tale about the Babylonians who aimed to construct the most magnificent city on the planet. They worked on building a tower that would reach God, but God didn't approve of their plans to build a massive city. Instead, he wanted them to spread out and inhabit various parts of the world. Thus, He confused their language so they couldn't understand each other."

The Lord said, "*They are one people and have one language. This is only the beginning of what they will do. Nothing will be impossible for them.*"

"It's a fascinating example of the power of a common language. Does anyone know how the story of God confusing languages and the origin of the word 'babel' relate to 50 Strong?"

Jared responded, "Unless we speak 50 Strong, we might as well be scattered. We won't be able to accomplish much, but if we do, nothing is impossible,"

"That's right. God knew they would succeed if He allowed them to speak to each other! If we make this meaningful, 50 Strong will be our "Royal language." The French Foreign Legion and the tower of Babel are perfect examples of the power of teams speaking a common language."

"Once someone is accepted into the Legion, they're forbidden to speak their native language...*ever*. How do you understand a command in French? You figure it out. For instance, a sergeant might ask me to get him a wrench, but he'll say "clé" instead. I'd have no idea what he wants because he is pointing at an entire toolbox. I might try bringing him a screwdriver, but he'll be livid and make me run a kilometer with the entire toolbox held over my head. It's not an easy way to learn, but it's effective. After that experience, I'd never forget what "clé" means."

"Let's get into our pillars. This question is for guys like me who are new to the GFL this season. What are some things you're experiencing that have surprised you?"

"All the free time we have," said Chris.

"No team meeting facility or locker rooms has been an adjustment for me, to be perfectly honest," Polk said.

"The quality of play is better than we had in the Austrian league," said Stefan.

"Our camaraderie is higher than on teams I've played on. Maybe it's because most of us carry our pads on the train to get to practice, but we are a close-knit group," said Jared.

"I appreciate all the answers. The most significant adjustment for me has been the lack of attendance at practice. It's been borderline maddening with our backup players. I know the phrase "When in Rome, do as the Romans," but second-team JV players in Texas will walk two miles to get to practice if their truck won't start."

We had a whiteboard at the front of the room. I drew a roof with five columns.

"This is a visual for us. Get in groups of three again tonight, make sure you're with someone you don't know well, and discuss what areas we want to proclaim as those we'll stand and fight for."

We had another fantastic meeting. There was lots of discussion on several areas, but we settled on these five pillars:

1. BROTHER'S KEEPER
2. COMPETE
3. PREPARATION
4. PLAY HARD, PLAY SMART
5. HUMILITY

"To show you guys how we'll do this, let's define one of our pillars before we go. Everyone put one word that you think of for Brother's Keeper."

I knew it would be tough to define all five pillars next week. Taking one and showing the guys our system would speed up the process. This was an off night for them, so I would respect their time. Ninety minutes was the maximum length we would spend, or our attendance would suffer next week.

"Chris, will you write for me this time on the board? We're looking for one or two short sentences for a definition that we can recite to the team. Start throwing out words or phrases to help us define Brother's Keeper, and Chris will make a list."

"Love"

"Have each other's back."

Jared, the most vocal participant again this week, said, "If I'm genuinely a brother to someone, then I love him enough to tell him when he is screwing up. We need something about helping hold my brother accountable."

"I like it. Accountability," I said.

"Trust"

"Lock arms"

"Keep watch"

"Foxhole, brother"

"Family"

"I am my brother's keeper, whom I love. I will have his back and lock arms with him when he is right and wrong," Jerome said.

Jared continued, "What do you guys think of something like this? “I'm my brother's keeper. I will hold him accountable with love and trust."

"We're getting close! I like where we are headed for sure. Remember, you guys will need to memorize the creed for it to come to your mind when things get difficult," I said.

Jared continued, "I'm my brother's keeper whom I love, trust and hold accountable."

"That's good stuff, bro! Check out my fellow receiver killing the creed!" Polk said.

"I like it as well. It's short enough to memorize easily but states everything we need. Good job, Jared," Stefan said.

Of the month I've spent in Germany, and all the hours I've spent with the team, this is the first time I've felt goosebumps.

"The 50 Strong Culture built the strongest team bond I have ever experienced. It enabled us to find our True North, the shared direction we could all work and live towards."

Leo Bosch
#52 Linebacker
Potsdam, Germany
2023 Team
Potsdam Royals

21

MIDTERM EXAM

May 7, 2022

We were at the midpoint of our month-long training camp. Our practice schedule had settled into Tuesdays, Wednesdays, and Fridays. Game one versus the defending champs, Dresden, was only two weeks away, and our offense has been unstoppable up to this point, which also means our defense needs to improve. We have been in desperate need of help from American defensive backs. To their credit, Berti and Saul found two, and they'd just arrived. We all had our fingers crossed they had enough time to learn our schemes. Like most GFL offenses, Dresden is a 'spread you out and throw the ball' team.

After our Tuesday practice, Berti, Saul, Jonas, and I went to the preferred pizza place in Potsdam, PiPaSa. (pizza, pasta, salad) We ordered our favorite pizzas, pepperoni for Berti and Jonas, Margherita for Saul, and chicken and mushroom (huhn and pilze) for me.

“Can one of you update me on Max? At least he's coming to practice and watching, but he should be dressed and practicing again. I know he wasn't in great shape at the start of training camp, and that's contributing to his slow return, but Lord have mercy."

"I'll speak to him tomorrow and see how close he is to returning to play," Berti responded.

"Thank you. It's one thing to be injured and working hard to return, and maybe he is, but I don't have a clue when Max will be back."

Berti added, "He's too heavy, but he gets away with it with his ability. Max didn't prepare for the season last year either, but he slowly got in playing shape and played well, eventually."

I said, "He's a natural offensive lineman. If he trained his body like Yasir, he'd be all-Europe like Yasir. Changing the subject, I have something I'd like to suggest to everyone. I've always had a midterm exam during training camp."

They looked at me, confused.

“I mean a formal type of scrimmage. This Friday would be the perfect time to do it if you're not opposed. We could call it a red/white game, the Royal Bowl, or however Saul wants to market it. It'd be good to have one dress rehearsal before game day."

Saul liked the idea, "This could be good. We could post it on social media and have an autograph session afterward."

Berti asked, "How did you normally organize the scrimmage?"

"We make it as game-like as possible. I always tell my players that the *first time should never be the first time.* Which means everything must be rehearsed mentally and physically. We take our guys through the pregame meetings, stretching, warmups, and the whole nine yards. The mid-term would be good for Taka, the physios, and anyone like me who is new. Most importantly, we'll give it a game feel—one repetition of kick-off, then our starting offense on the field for a drive. If we score, we kick the extra point. If the defense stops us, we punt. When the night is over, we'll also have high-speed reps of each phase of our kicking game."

"Hmmm, I can see where this could be a good thing. We don't have Divine or Time (our new American defensive backs) up to speed in the secondary yet, but they'll still be better than who we have tried to play against you guys, so I feel a little better about how we'll perform."

I added, "If we have last year's jerseys, we could put them in those to dress it up some. Maybe even get the board to provide food and beer and make it a good time."

"Let's do it," Berti said.

Chris, Jared, Polk, Jonas, and I all gathered at the office on Thursday to discuss and plan for the upcoming scrimmage.

"Ok, guys, let's make sure we are on the same page for tomorrow. You know we'll throw our choice route at least 20 times, but I want to see how each of you likes it the most. Chris, what formation do you want to make sure we run it out of?"

"I like it stacked to the boundary (short side of the field). They aren't rolling the backside safety wide enough to the sideline, so I think that'll hurt them."

"We've been burning them up with Dealer's Choice out of our five-wide, empty set," Polk added.

"I vote we only get in empty after Tibo and TK are tired. I know they can't hit me, but I want to score on every possession," Chris said.

"I agree wholeheartedly. Tibo and TK are an issue during the first couple of drives each practice. We'll double-team Tibo on the inside and use Karri to help with TK on the edge," I said.

"It might be different with Divine playing safety, but he's my new roommate, so I would love a couple of choice routes from the slot so I can go one-on-one with him,"

Jared said.

We made a 10-play script of plays together to open up the scrimmage. I was going to enjoy using these guys to help formulate the weekly game plan. They were all intelligent and dedicated to film study. I might not have but a fraction of the coaching staff as I am used to, but our three A's were player-coaches in my eyes.

THE MID-TERM

Our offense jogged onto the field, looking even sharper than normal in last year's game uniforms, for the first play of the scrimmage. In our regular practices, I didn't concern myself with beating the defense, but tonight was different. This would be a game-like session, so we'd be more intentional about attacking certain players.

"Go! Hit!" Bobby, our center, yelled out the cadence and snapped the ball back to Chris. Sidenote: My center has vocalized the snap count, not the QB, for my teams for the last 15 years or more. It gives him a significant advantage to be the first to move in the line of scrimmage.

Polk, the fastest player on our team, was on the outside and running right at the defensive back, responsible for covering him. Polk stopped suddenly after ten yards, and Chris delivered a strike. The corner missed the tackle, and now Polk was in the open field. If not for Manase Time, our new safety from California, diving and clipping Polk's foot, he would've scored.

We were moving fast on offense, snapping the ball as quickly as possible. We were rotating and throwing the ball to different receivers with lightning speed. During the second play, the corner played Jared aggressively, so he ran by him and went deep. TK, the fastest defensive end in the GFL, almost stopped us in our tracks when he split our double team and nearly grabbed Chris. Chris spun to the outside and got away, hitting Jared in stride with a beautiful pass. Manase again made the tackle, pushing him out of bounds after a 42-yard gain.

"Snap it! Snap it!" I yelled as we were hurrying to the ball. Some teams claim to play fast, but we would be a nightmare for defenses with our relentless tempo.

Next, it was Heiko's turn at outside receiver. He was now facing a defensive back who was winded and frustrated after covering Polk and Jared. Heiko got inside him and went deep as well. Tibo was the problem up front this time, pushing the pocket back into Chris. Max was still not cleared to practice, so Ludi, our 5'10" guard who plays with excellent leverage and technique, was working hard, but Tibo was too powerful. We still didn't have a backup quarterback, so I was even more cautious with Chris' health. I blew the whistle right before Tibo made any type of contact. "Sack!" I yelled, and now it was 2nd and 18 from the 31-yard-line.

Next, we ran the ball with Karri right behind Yasir for a six-yard gain. Karri was showing us every day that he would be fine as our starting running back.

"Go! Go!" I yelled as I was signaling the next play, a screen pass to Polk.

Early in the scrimmage, with TK and Tibo still fresh, I knew we would need to utilize screen passes. Screen plays are passes behind the line of scrimmage where the offensive line entices the defensive linemen to rush hard, then release up-field to block linebackers and defensive backs. Screens are good play calls when the pass rush begins getting to the quarterback. Polk caught the *jail screen*, our term for a screen where our slot receiver takes three steps toward the sideline, then comes back to the quarterback in stride. Our offensive linemen did a great job of getting in front of Polk, creating a wall. No one got close to tackling him as he high-stepped into the endzone. It was a “follow us” play, if there ever was one.

"Great job! Great job, big boys!" I yelled as I high-fived the offensive line after we kicked the extra point.

The rest of the night was almost as good as the opening drive. Chris was proving each time out we hit the jackpot by signing him.

The offensive line was still a work in progress. With Max out, I was shuffling six guys for five spots. One of the trickiest parts of preseason is finding the right combination for the offensive line. Like most teams I’ve coached, we had seven guys ready to play on Saturdays. Bobby was not in midseason form yet, and I was honestly worried about him. He was making too many mental mistakes, and I wasn't convinced he was buying into my coaching techniques. Because of this, Ludi was swinging from center to guard. This was good for depth, but I needed him to get more reps at guard.

TK and Tibo continuously caused problems for us early, but our pace wore them down, and they became less of an issue. TK got "injured" late and didn't return. None of us, including Taka, believed it was severe and probably just a way for him to rest. I was grateful Tibo would be a high-trust guy, but TK was showing us quite the opposite.

Speaking of high trust, Polk was picking up field equipment like always after practice.

“Polk, I’m going to pick more yard markers than you will tonight. I’m feeling pretty fast for an old guy," I said as I grabbed a pylon.

As I was leaving, I saw Bobby walking across the field.

"Hey, Bobby! Wait up!" I yelled as I jogged over to him.

This was going to be a conversation that either brought Bobby and me closer together or farther apart…

22

WHO'S GOING TO THE CFL?

May 9, 2022

"You don't have to say it, coach. I know I sucked tonight," Bobby said as I approached him.

"Well…I wasn't going to say it quite that way, but yes. You did suck at times, and I was hoping you realized it. Tonight's game seemed to echo some of the issues you've had during training camp. We signed you because you have won five GFL championships and would be a veteran presence. Please know that I'm not upset or angry, but I want to understand what might be causing this so we can work together to address it. Either something's happening in your personal life, or you don't believe in what I'm teaching."

"I'm sorry, coach. I don't like playing this way. Finals are coming up, and I'm studying a lot to prepare for them. I'm still looking at our film and trying to be focused during practice, but honestly, any other time, I'm preparing for my exams."

"That's all I needed to know. Use the time with us as a break from worrying about your diploma. I trust you. I believe you'll be ready for Dresden in two weeks." I said.

"No worries, coach. I'll play better," Bobby replied.

The next morning, I was grading the scrimmage in my flat when I received a text from Saul. "Big trouble in the defensive line. The damn BC Lions have signed Tibo!"

"Oh, crap! How did they find out about him now?" I responded immediately.

"Tibo was selected last year in the CFL global draft but was cut by the Edmonton Eskimos. We were hoping we could hide him for a season, but we couldn't. Damn, this is not good for us! I guess someone told BC he's worth signing and bringing back over. He won't make NFL money, but he'll make a hell of a lot more than we can pay him!"

Losing Tibo for us would be devastating. It's the equivalent of how the Rams would feel if Aaron Donald wasn't around anymore. He was an incredibly talented and powerful player, and it's hard to imagine finding someone else who could match his skills. After reviewing the opponent's video from last season, it was obvious that he'd be the most dominant interior defensive lineman in the entire league. After quarterback, defensive linemen are the toughest players to find. We weren't going to be able to get on the Euro players' website and find anyone in the same galaxy.

Tibo was also a great teammate and was well-liked by everyone. He would have been one of the first players selected to sign with 50 Strong. Losing Tibo wasn't just a bad break; it was absolutely a gut-punch for our defense and our entire team.

Tibo Debaillie

I had to channel my E+R=O mindset now: Events + Response = Outcome. There wasn't anything any of us could do about losing Tibo. Every player is one play away from being done for the season with an injury. We had to focus on what we could control. I had to turn my brain into being grateful Chris was healthy, especially since we still didn't have a backup QB. At least we still had a pass-rush expert in TK. My fingers were crossed that he may become more consistent with his work ethic when the season starts.

The following Tuesday, we were back on the practice field. I noticed TK in his team sweats over by the physio table. Knowing he'd also be frustrated, I asked Saul, "Do you know why TK's not working today?" I learned from the conversation about Max being in sweats a couple of weeks ago to tread lightly.

"There's no telling. I'm sure he is saying his hamstring got tweaked in the scrimmage or something. He does this periodically when he doesn't feel like doing anything."

THAT ESCALATED QUICKLY

The next few days, it became clear TK wasn't 'feeling the Royals' anymore. He was a no-show for the following night's practice. The next morning, I texted Berti and asked if he knew what was happening.

(Berti) TK is being TK.

(me) Maybe we can get Yasir to speak to him and see what's going on.

(Berti) I'm sick and tired of dealing with him. He did this to us last season. We've bent over backward for him. He wanted to stay over the offseason, so we paid for a flat. He needed a job, so we helped him find one. He's making this not fun for me.

(me) At *the end of the day, it's all about the team. It's admirable you care about TK as*

an individual, but you're our leader. I know you didn't bring me here to preach but, leaders must make hard decisions that may hurt the individual but help the team. It's about the Royals. TK is very talented but doesn't represent any of the pillars of 50 Strong. I struggle to watch how lazy he is during practice. We're preaching brotherhood, and he's the biggest individual I've ever shared the field with. We can live without him. We will score 50+ points per game this season.

Trust me, I knew what it meant to lose a pass rusher that our opponent would have to double-team. But TK was exactly the arrogant American I've been told was prevalent in the GFL. He was the *anti-50 Strong* guy on the team. Shortly after this conversation, Berti arrived and said, "TK quit this morning. It's not official yet, but he's going to the NYer Lions."

Now, the last few days and even weeks were starting to make more sense. "We'll be fine, coach. If he hadn't left, it would have been necessary to take drastic measures in order to serve the greater mission of 50 Strong. He would've been a massive headache when we started having guys sign the creed next week. He knows he'll never become the type of guy that will be our standard and get on board with the culture we're creating. I bet the creed is one reason he's leaving."

I added, "By the way, how can he sign with the Lions? Surely, the GFL doesn't allow players to break their contract and play for another team."

"A contract is only worth the paper it's written on," Saul said with matter-of-fact emotion.

"So, you're saying a GFL contract is only binding if we sue the player in court? How in the heck does the league allow this? NFL players couldn't quit their team in training camp and join another team. I couldn't walk out on my team as a high school coach in Texas and join another one without having permission to break my contract. There's nothing we can do?"

"A contract is only worth the paper it's written on. TK owes us a lot of money for unpaid parking tickets and things like that. We won't release him until he's clear with us. We'll not make it easy for him," Saul reiterated to me.

Berti, always calm, said, "He must sit out three weeks according to league rules. It's not optimal, for sure. Right now, I'm more concerned about our defense. Losing Tibo and now TK leaves us paper thin. We've gone from having the best defensive line in the league to a bottom-tier unit."

"Isn't this some bush-league BS? If Munich or Dusseldorf calls Chris today and offers to double his salary, could he leave and sit out for three weeks?"

"I'm not sure how else to explain this; we're just going around in circles, but in theory, yes," Saul responded.

"Talk about dysfunctional. We play New Yorker in July and will face a player who walked away. Amazingly amateur-like."

Later that day, I sent a message to our three A's. *We're going to win the GFL with our AK-47 offense. We're going to rip the Dresden defense next week. But, right now, I would bet a million Euros that negative shockwaves are radiating throughout the team, worrying about our defense. We need your help to spread positive vibes. Please inject confidence more than usual every chance you get.*

Jared responded first; *We'll miss Tibo everywhere. He was in our foxhole 100%. We'll only miss TK on game days.*

(Polk) Let's remind everyone, including the defense, that we can't be stopped. They couldn't stop us in practice with Tibo and TK. We're about to roll the GFL!

(Chris) He was already spreading it around that he was signing with New Yorker. The day he sat out practice, one of our physios told Polk he was talking about how he would sack me three times when we play.

(me) Is this true, Polk?

(Polk) Oh yea, coach. He was running his mouth. We'll have something for him.

23

SEARCHING FOR THE BEST FIVE - NOT THE FIVE BEST

May 25, 2022

Other than installing the offense, figuring out our offensive line starters was #2 on my priority list. We were in the middle of training camp, and I still had a lot of work to do in the Follow Us laboratory. A good offensive line is what I refer to as *elephants on parade*. Footwork is the key to getting five guys in unison like circus elephants under the big top. When all five work like a choreographed unit, it is a thing of beauty.

The issue I was having was each of these guys had learned how to play the position from another coach. One axiom that always holds true about the offensive line is, "It's ok to be wrong if we're all wrong together." At the moment, we were all baking a cake using the ingredients from different recipe books. We had to get on the same page with our footwork and techniques. Once, Max said to me, as I was correcting his first step for what seemed like the 20th time, "Coach Alexander of the Bengals says when reaching an outside defender to get depth with your first step for leverage."

My response wasn't in a harsh tone, but it was no-nonsense, "When Coach Alexander coaches our offensive line, that's how we'll do it, but until then, we'll take a lateral step. There are always multiple ways to skin a cat, so I'm not saying he's wrong, but this is how I'm coaching it." At least Max said something to me; most of the guys just nodded along but weren't buying into my teaching techniques.

Yesterday, we had our *Tell the Truth* session, where I evaluated each offensive player's performance and graded them for every snap they took part in.

"Two more guys will get white stripes on their helmets today! Who's it going to be?" I shouted as we jogged over to our area of the field.

"We are starting with 'Athena' today, the goddess of war otherwise known as...the *CROWTHER*! "GO, HIT!" I yelled as Stefan and Ludi leaped at our two-man offensive line sled.

The Crowther sled was invented by coach Jim Crowther in 1932 and has yet to be improved, although company after company has tried. If the pad is not contacted correctly, low and in the middle, the sled, with a rounded pan-type bottom, will spin off the blocker.

"Good job! Way to get low on the pad and lift! We're getting better day by day!" I shouted.

After a few more minutes of sled work, we went to our next drill, zone boxes.

"Overlap, overlap, overlap!" I said with conviction before the drill started. "We must get our leg over his leg on the double team. A good double is a *3-legged sack race* for us with our lower body! Keep your offhand free," I said to Bobby.

"When you put it on the defender, it turns your shoulders. Never, ever, ever does a good lineman turn his shoulders."

Good offensive linemen don't grow on trees. God doesn't make many big bodies that can move. Defensive linemen are even tougher to find. We had ten *big boys* at practice most days. Some of the guys who play on our Prospects team were less consistent with their attendance. Like most all teams I have coached, we had six potential starters and one or two more who could play in a pinch.

"Play review. Give me the same five guys that started the scrimmage up first. Brenden, I know you're working right tackle and left guard, and that's not easy. I appreciate you. I still don't know who the starters versus Dresden will be. This is why I spend time grading each play of practice. We're going to figure it out. It might take till game five, but we'll figure it out. We're going to start games with the best five but the five best. This means the five who work together as a unit."

Brenden wasn't the only player working at two positions. We had to make sure if anyone was injured, we could move the puzzle pieces around and still function as a unit. If we could find a suitable right tackle where Brenden was currently starting, I could move him to left guard next to Yasir. This would be a tremendous "one-two" punch for us with them working together.

"The biggest issue I'm having at this moment is most of you show me the technique I'm looking for in drills, but in our scrimmages, you revert to something else. Either you don't understand what I'm teaching, or you don't believe in it, and it's frustrating the hell out of me."

We'd settled on adding players into *Follow Us* at our five-minute "1/2 time" portion of practice. It was the only break in our Autobahn pace schedule. It was also good to do it here to have the other offensive players be involved, but we didn't want it to interfere with 50 Strong introductions after the workout.

"Guys, I want to introduce the next two members of our *Follow Us* society! Both of these guys have worked their butts off at practice. They'll be imposing their will on defensive linemen all season. If I were a running back, I'd look for the white stripes on the helmets of these two crushers who also live together! Please put on your white stripes, Brenden and Jerome!"

Both smiled as they approached me to get their stripes.

"Please let me put them on your helmet! They must be straight and in the correct spot!" Yasir said, half-joking but also wanting them uniform, which I loved.

“Wait a second, coach! I know I’m the smallest guy here, but I’ve been asking to be let in for months now. When am I going to get into the club?” Polk asked with a big grin and a fake look of confusion.

“I’ll make a deal with you. Whenever you make a block in a game that all of the current *Follow Us* members deem has a big boy level of physicality, you’ll get your white stripe.” I said.

“I guess it’s safe to say we don’t have to worry about me having to put a stripe on his helmet then," said Yasir.

That night, after Saul uploaded the film, I edited it and separated it play-by-play so it could be graded. I hoped to see the techniques I was teaching in our individual sessions on display in the scrimmage portion of practice. I also hoped Bobby would take the starting center spot and Mads or Ludi would emerge at our other guard position. As I watched the fifth play in the video, a pain in the front of my head began to grow. My frustration was mounting, and I found myself questioning whether my guys were really listening to me. Had I been too quick to assume they were on the same page as me? Or were they just tuning me out?

24

THE ROYAL STANDARD

May 10, 2022

I texted Berti and Saul around lunchtime, "We will finish with the creed tonight. We need to start with two players being appointed by the coaching staff. The system works like this; only members of 50 Strong can invite others to join them. We need two *tried and true* Royals as our initial members. One from the offense and one from the defense. Do we have a couple of players who came up through our junior teams who would bleed Royal red if we cut them open?"

Saul responded quickly, "Ludi started playing with us at age 16. He's worked his way up. He's 100% Royal."

"For the defensive side, I like Leo Bosch. He also joined the Royals a few years back and worked very hard during the offseason. He'll be a defensive captain each week as well."

"Sounds good. I like both of those guys a lot. If either or both of you are coming to the meeting tonight, please help me announce them at the end," I said.

That evening we finished the creation of 50 Strong. We defined the remaining pillars using the same system we did for *Brother's Keeper*. Chris wrote words and phrases on the whiteboard and formed them into short definitions.

Our team leaders were all present as usual. I didn't say a word to the team about this last meeting. I didn't prefer someone to jump in the last one who hasn't been in the first two where the heaviest lifting occurred.

50 Strong was a beautiful proclamation. It evolved over three weeks, with much discussion and thought by our players who cared the most.

THE ROYAL STANDARD

Potsdam Royals 2022

- Brother's Keeper - I am my brother's keeper, whom I love, trust and hold accountable.

- Preparation - I will prepare in all aspects; eat, sleep, film, and do whatever it takes to be ready for battle.
- Play Smart, Play Hard - We will empty the tank and leave it all on the field. We will play with discipline, knowing success comes from precise execution.
- Compete - We compete as it provides an environment for growth. We either teach or learn but get 1% better each day.
- Humility - We are crumb eaters chasing perfection. We don't Blame, Complain or Defend because we are grateful to play the game we love.

"A manifesto is a public declaration. 50 Strong is the 2022 Royals declaring to the GFL what we're about. I've been honored to facilitate this process, and I couldn't be prouder of how you guys stepped up to create this. Here is what happens from here: if our creed is going to be a real, living document, we all have to live it. When you came to these meetings, you said, "I'm all in". Live 50 Strong, or they will be empty words on a piece of paper."

Jared stood up and faced the group. "Coach is 100% correct. This can be what propels us to the championship if we are 50 Strong when practice, watch film, lift, take care of each other, and play together on Saturdays."

I continued, "Thank you, Jared. We'll have to remind ourselves of the responsibility of our creed periodically."

"Here's how everyone will be admitted to 50 Strong: you must be invited to join by a member already in. I deleted everyone in our WhatsApp besides the two guys Coach Vogt and Coach Goodman said were foxhole Royals through and through. Leo and Ludi, congratulations! Y'all are the inaugural members, the first-ever members of 50 Strong! After practice tomorrow night, I'll ask you to introduce one player each to join us in 50 Strong. Once you're voted in, you'll help decide who's added to the group for the rest of the season. You'll also be admitted back into the 50 Strong WhatsApp. Coach Goodman is having a poster created with the logo and creed for you to sign."

Jerome closed the meeting with the emotion that we'd start seeing more and more in the coming weeks, "Everybody up! Get your hands in the air. I believe in this group! I'm honored to have knocked on the door with everyone in this circle! 50 Strong on three! One, two, three!"

"50 STRONG!"

Before we started our Zoom meetings the following day, I asked Leo and Ludi in our chat, "Who do you guys want to add after workout tonight? Remember, the first guys we admit will set the standard. It's not the best players *on* the team, but the players who are best *for* the team."

We talked about four or five guys who would all be excellent choices. We finally settled on three guys who were active in our meetings to create the creed and hadn't missed a single rep in training camp. All three were studs on and off the field. After each practice, admitting players into 50 Strong would be epic for us moving forward. Most of these guys haven't been on a team with an intentional culture, much less earning the right to be a member.

After our standard announcements and review of our unit's performance at the end of the workout, Berti said, "Coach Jackson will now introduce us to our new system of adding players to 50 Strong."

"Thank you, Coach Vogt. Ludi and Leo, please come up here to the front. After each practice, members of 50 Strong will introduce the new guys selected to join the group. The coaches chose our first two members, Leo and Ludi. Give them a hand! Today, Leo, Ludi, and the coaches kicked around who should be invited tonight. Several guys could've been chosen, but we finally settled on three. I'll be quiet now and turn it over to Ludi."

"I appreciate it, coach. I'm honored to be selected by the coaches. Tonight, we're adding a guy that is one of my best friends but also one of the best players on the team, on and off the field. He's always the first at practice and gives 100% every play. Yasir, welcome to 50 Strong."

Everyone clapped as Yasir came forward.

"We'd also like to ask a player who did almost as much work creating the creed as the rest of us combined it seemed...welcome to 50 Strong, Jared Wolfe."

Jared smiled, came forward and fist-bumped Leo, Ludi and Yasir.

"Congrats, Yasir and Jared," I said. "Next, we have Leo from the defense. Leo, who would you like to introduce as our newest member?"

"This person is new to our team, but it seems like he's been here for a long time. He's not only good on the field, but studies as much or more than most coaches. Welcome to 50 Strong, Ruben."

Ruben was moved by being selected. When his name was called, he dropped his head and looked down. After a few seconds, he stood up smiling, but his eyes were watery. You could hear the emotion in his voice when he said, "Thank you" and shook Leo's hand. Ruben's reaction was another sign we were becoming united. This part of the laboratory was working. Their hearts were starting to open, and my goosebumps were getting more intense.

THE ROYAL STANDARD

"The 2022 Royals season was an unforgettable experience for me. We all had such a great bond, and we were more than just colleagues; we were family. Even though we didn't reach our ultimate goal, I'm grateful for all the memories we created and having met so many
close friends for life."

Ludwig Rötzscher
#56 Guard/Center
Potsdam, Germany
2023 Team
Potsdam Royals

25

TELL US ABOUT THE GUY YOU HAVE TO DEFEAT

May 16, 2022

One innovation I came up with for the new laboratory was having each player do a scouting report on the individual defender he was most likely to face on game day. With large coaching staffs at high schools in Texas, opponent scouting reports are done by the coaches and given to the players, but this lab didn't have the same amount of manpower, so I had to improvise.

I stumbled upon the idea when I began to create our weekly game plan and needed more time to watch every player and type up a detailed dossier on them. I thought to myself, "I wonder if the players would do a good job evaluating one person they would likely face in the game?'

I quickly realized that having the guys study an opponent was an excellent way for me to see how they viewed him. Did they respect him or feel like he was *rubbish*? When teams take their opponents lightly, it can have devastating consequences on gameday.

All players had to have their opponent's evaluation posted on WhatsApp by Sunday evening. I then compiled them and made a PowerPoint for our Monday meeting.

The criteria for the scouting were as follows:

- Height / Weight
- Age
- Years of experience playing football
- Best attribute and worst attribute
- Describe his 'motor'. Does he play hard?
- What do you have to do to defeat him?
- Overall rating 1-10

Bobby, our center, reported on Dresden's middle linebacker:
#48 Ben Schmidt / 185 cm / 99 kilos / Age: 28
He had played for Dresden for three seasons, but no information was found before he joined the Monarchs.
Tall, uses strength more than agility / Shows blitz / Good vs. Run
Medium effort-much better vs. run / Lacks change of direction.

We must get on him in the run game / He is a plugger, not real fast but is physical.
Motor: 7 / Overall Rating: 6.5

One of our young receivers, Louis Christian, a 19-year-old with minimal playing experience, nailed his first report on a defensive back:
#5 Connor O'Brien / 188 cm / 84 kilos
Plays on the Irish national team / Second year with the Monarchs.
He is long but moves well / Will travel w/ Polk or Jared, most likely.
Will grab & hold, so double moves will hurt him /Emotional, we can get in his head.
Good ball skills and above average tackler
Motor: 8 / Overall Rating: 7.5

I asked Karri, a running back who must pick up pass protection blitzes, to report on the Monarch's favorite blitzes.

"I can go up to the whiteboard and draw up the blitzes I saw from the scrimmage and from a few of their games last season," Karri said.

"You were only asked to watch the scrimmage. You broke down a few games from last year as well?" I asked.

"Yes sir, they were pretty vanilla in the scrimmage. I wanted to see the blitzes they used in close games last season. I think we better work on a few of these I'm about to draw," Karri said.

I'd watched Dresden games from last season to get a feel for what we might see but didn't expect a player to be so conscientious.

After Karri reported on the blitzes, I said, "Chris, you're our opponent's secondary expert. What coverages are we going to see the Monarchs use on Saturday?

"They're a base cover-four defense. They'll show two safeties 90% of the time pre-snap but will roll one safety down for run support quite a bit. When we get in our spread formations, they'll stay two-high and keep everything in front of them. Their best corner will play man on our receiver to their sideline when we are in our three-wide set. I made a short highlight film of how they played opponents last season. If you don't mind, I can pull that up now and talk everyone through it."

"You made a cutup of their coverages? Heck, yes, I don't mind. Coach us up, brother," I said.

The reports were outstanding. The guys crushed it, and it made me wonder why I hadn't ever done this with my high school players. Then I started thinking, what other simple but powerful things have I been missing?

26

ARE YOU OK COACH?

May 17, 2022

It was finally game week, and this one had even more significance than usual. The Royals have never beaten Dresden in the program's history. Last season they lost 31-15 at home and were shellacked 63-7 in Dresden. If we lost the first one at home, we'd have to pull one out in Dresden in July to avoid being swept. This would also be a huge confidence booster for our guys with our 50 Strong culture and Fast N' Wide offense.

As always, we met for our face-to-face meetings at the office on *Tell the Truth Monday*. Since we didn't have a game to grade, we focused on the Monarchs. Unlike us, Dresden played a preseason game, so we had some game-like film to evaluate their defensive schemes and personnel. Each scouting report began with a theme of the week to set the tone for where I believed we needed to be mentally for the upcoming opponent.

This week's theme was WHO WANTS TO GO FAST?

"Fellas, this week is important. Not because we will be 1-0 or 0-1 versus a division opponent, but because we will unleash something unstoppable on the Monarchs. We've hidden this secret weapon for months, but no more. We'll improve in every aspect as the season progresses, but we can go faster than Dresden's ever seen tomorrow. I can't wait. We'll do some good things, but mistakes will also happen. The bottom line is we're going to be better afterward. We'll get your technique and effort on video and use it to improve for the future. We cannot make the playoffs with a win or be eliminated with a loss. What we will do is get better each week."

"Has anyone ever heard the story of Milo of Croton? This season, we'll be like Milo." No one responded, so I continued.

"Milo was a legendary figure in the ancient world who lived in Croton, now southern Italy. He was born around 520 BC and is known as one of the strongest men in the history of the world. Milo won six Olympic wrestling championships."

"The greatness of his story is how he became so strong. The legend is that a calf was born on Milo's farm one day. Milo lifted the small animal and carried it around their house and barn. The next day, he did the same thing. Milo continued this training program for the next four years, hoisting the calf onto his shoulders each day as it grew until he was no longer lifting a calf but a four-year-old bull. Imagine a man being strong enough to carry a full-grown bull on his shoulders!"

"How did Milo do it? He did it gradually. He did it O-D-A-T…One Day At a Time."

"We will improve each week. Our offense will get stronger and stronger. We will keep putting the offense on our back each week and become more powerful. Don't get me wrong, Dresden is undoubtedly no small calf. The schedule maker did us no favors; we have to carry a 1000-kilo bull around our stadium on Saturday."

Tuesday and Wednesday were definitely some of the best practices we've had all season. We were firing on all cylinders. We had Thursday off, and one day of prep remained. The "day before the day" where we dot all our i's and cross all our t's.

FAAAST FRIDAY

I've used a coaching phrase that my players have enjoyed for years. It's "Get your piss hot." Some might say it's a bit classless, but it's memorable. My offensive line coach at Louisiana-Monroe, JB Grimes, used to tell us, "I'm not going to pee on your leg and tell you you're sweating." Even after all these years, I still find myself quoting him.

Each day as I led warmups, I brought the juice by shouting, "Get your piss hoooooottttttttt!"

"Warm up! Get your piss hot!" I loudly roared after we completed our walk-through. Our warm-up was nothing more than a way for us to come together as a team to do a little loosening up, but more for getting some energy to prepare us for a great practice mentally.

"What do we have to do?" I shouted to the team as I walked amongst the players.

"Get our piss hot!" they screamed back.

We worked across the field during warm-up. The offense was on one sideline, and the defense was on the other. I'd give the command for what exercise we'd execute but also select a player for a word for all to clap in unison and break us out to begin the drill. I chose Jerome to give us a word to begin high knees.

"What are we going to do to Dresden tomorrow, Jerome?"

"Dominate them!"

"High knees on dominate!" I shouted back and then blew my whistle.

All the guys yelled, "Dominate!" as the first row performing the high knees clapped their hands and began the exercise.

I next chose a defensive player and asked him a question to give us some positive thoughts.

"What's the defensive line going to do tomorrow to help us get the W, Stanley?"

"Stop the run!"

"Crossover on Stop the Run!" as I blew the whistle again.

I knew we needed to lighten the mood. I sensed some anxiety and nerves as we had our last tune-up before Dresden. I decided to do something I've never done before...fake an injury.

I walked close to one of our German defensive backs, Jerry Bolten, who is also one of the best humans on the planet. I went down to one knee and became very quiet. I grabbed my chest and didn't move or say a word.

I'm the one who got practice started with energy and was the most extreme person on the field during warm-ups, so the entire team stopped and looked over at me. They had no idea if I was alright or if I was having a heart attack.

"Are you ok, coach?" Jerry asked me with a ton of concern in his voice.

I stayed in the same position and moaned a little. After a few seconds, the tension increased as Jerry got even closer and touched me on my shoulder.

"Coach?" he asked again with sincere concern in his voice.

Now, a couple of other players were also moving towards me to check on me.

"Heck, yes, I'm ok, Jerry!" I yelled as I got up fast.

Jerry smiled and now realized I'd hoodwinked him.

"My piss was just too hot, Jerry! My body could not handle it! Are you kidding me? Taka, you better get an ambulance over here! I'm so ready for tomorrow that my piss is on fire! Let's goooo!"

GAME #1
2-DEEP DEPTH CHART
LUFTSCHIFFHAFEN
MAY 21, 2022

QB	**#8 CHRIS HELBIG - U.S.-COLORADO [Southern Utah]**
RB	**#20 KARRI PAJARINEN - FINLAND** #9 HEIKO BALS - GERMANY
WR	**#3 BRANDON POLK - U.S.-VIRGINIA [Penn State]** #14 LOUIS CHRIST - GERMANY
WR	**#15 JARED WOLFE - U.S.-NEW YORK [Villanova]** #9 HEIKO BALS - GERMANY
WR	**#21 RUBEN DE RUYTER - BELGIUM** #9 HEIKO BALS - GERMANY
TE	**#89 JEROME VALBON - FRENCH CANADIAN** #81 MAT DUBICKI - POLAND
LT	**#78 YASIR RAJI - GERMANY** #53 TIM WALTNER - GERMANY
LG	**#75 BRENDEN OSWIN - AUSTRALIA** #71 MAX EVENHUIS - THE NETHERLANDS
C	**#56 LUDI RÖTZSCHER - GERMANY** #67 BOBBY SÖVEGJARTO - GERMANY
RG	**#50 MADS HØJEN - DENMARK** #71 MAX EVENHUIS - THE NETHERLANDS
RT	**#77 STEFAN STEFANNSON - ICELAND** #75 BRENDEN OSWIN - AUSTRALIA

27

"THIS END ZONE IS UNACCEPTABLE"

May 21, 2022

We were finishing up our pregame meal near the stadium. "Guys, if you have been inducted into 50 Strong, please come sign it before you leave to go to the stadium," I said to the team. Saul came up with an excellent idea for a system of having the guys sign our creed; he would bring it to each pregame meal at home. Anyone who'd been admitted into the Royal Standard between home games would sign it at the cafeteria.

Ludi Rötzscher

Finally, after 18 months, I was able to stand on the sideline again and lead a group of men. It was a great feeling to be back in action. And the weather couldn't have been any better for our game. The forecast was for a high of 66 degrees and mostly sunny.

Sportpark Luftschiffhafen, our home stadium for 2022, was constructed in 1924 as a track and soccer facility. While the home side is covered, temporary seating was brought in for our visitors. At 1,500, the crowd was typical for professional football in Germany, albeit small by Texas high school standards. What truly set this experience apart was the carnival atmosphere created by the Royals for the fans. From superheroes walking on stilts to a lively band, a bounce house in one of the endzones, and a master of ceremonies announcing all the entertainment, it was a truly unforgettable experience.

"Everything's amazing, Jens!" I shouted to our president as I positioned myself for our pregame warmups.

"I wish that were true, Coach Randy. Everything's not amazing. This end zone's very bad," Jens said, pointing and walking to the north end of the field.

Berti was also making his way towards the end zone where the head official, Mats Schweiger, and Dresden head coach Ulrich Däuber stood.

"Is there anything I can do to help?" I asked as we neared the two men who had concerned looks on their faces.

"Unfortunately, no. Damn, I have asked the city to ensure everything is suitable for today. We may have to play it tomorrow if we don't find a solution," Berti said.

It would be a public relations disaster if the opening day were canceled for field repair. Imagine the Yankees or the Rose Bowl telling their sold-out crowd to return tomorrow as they got the turf in playable condition.

"Coach Vogt, this area of the endzone looks terrible. There are lots of holes and bare spots where players could be injured," Mats said.

"I'm also uncomfortable with our team playing in this endzone," Coach Däuber said.

"I know we need to play this game today. None of us want to come back tomorrow. Jens has already called the city to help get us some sand brought in. We can fill the bad spots. It won't be perfect, but we can make it playable," Berti said to the group.

"I will give you 20 minutes to repair the turf, or we will play the game on a 90-yard field. There's no other way around it," Mats warned.

"This is unsatisfactory. The Royals had all training camp to make the field ready. Mr. Müller, as president, how did you expect this to pass inspection today? Neither the Royals nor us can afford to lose a player to stepping a hole in the endzone." Coach Däuber said, irritated.

"We're going to repair it immediately. This is a temporary field for 2022, and the city hasn't fulfilled its promises. I apologize to you and your team. We'll have it playable very soon. We'll play on a 100-yard field today," Jens said.

Within a few minutes, a utility vehicle pulled up with a pile of sand in the back. "Great! Thank you, sir! Where were you able to locate the sand?" Jens asked.

"The long jump pit at the track across the street. If you don't tell anyone, I won't either," said the stadium manager.

Royals board members began shoveling sand as quickly as they could. Coach Däuber walked away in disgust. He was very professional but understandably frustrated. After the holes were filled, Mats and Coach Daüber returned to decide if we would use the North end zone that day.

"I am reluctantly saying yes if Coach Däuber is ok with it," Mats said.

"I'm not ok with it, but it's better than playing on a 90-yard field, so we'll cross our fingers and hope we don't get a stupid injury," Coach Däuber said.

Mats looked at Jens and Berti and gave them this warning. "Tell the city to fix this field before you play here again. Next time, this field will not pass inspection."

Finally, we could focus our attention on football again. Although we would kick off 20 minutes later than we should have, we'd play on a 100-yard field.

"Everybody up!" I said to gather the offense for my final thoughts before we began our warmups.

"We're going to learn a lot about each other today. Things are tested in the fire. Iron is forged in a constant flame. I don't know how you'll react to the fire. Like a marriage, you only know about your wife once things get difficult. When this game is over today, win or lose, I'll know which of us will go through adversity together. Just like Milo carrying the calf, we'll be better after today. In week two, we'll be faster with our tempo and organization. In game three, we'll double-team a little better. Our choice routes will be more accurate by the fourth game, and when week five rolls around, we'll be a machine. But today, week one is about finding out who'll point to True North when all hell breaks loose. It's like what Mike Tyson says, "Everyone has a plan until they get punched in the face." Are we going to give the punch, or are we going to take the punch? It's our choice. This game will be the most educational game of all. We'll learn if you're ok being in the fire."

Later, on the field, Jared jogged by me and asked, "Is your piss hot today, coach?"

"You know it! Taka will have to cover me in ice to keep me from overheating, brother!"

"Who would you like to be the two offensive captains for the coin toss?" Berti asked me.

28

AN ENDZONE PROBLEM SAND COULDN'T FIX

May 21, 2022

"I'm going with Ludi and Yasir, the first two in 50 Strong. Are you still good with us taking the ball if we win the toss?" I asked.

"We've always deferred, but let's see what we do today with the ball first if we can," Berti replied.

I walked over to Chris, who was throwing with Heiko, Jared, and Polk. "Are you ready to take the first step in terrorizing the GFL today?"

"Yes, sir. I feel great. I can't wait to get going."

We won the toss and took the ball. After a good return by Polk to our 37-yard line, I said one last thing to our guys huddled on the sideline.

"This is going to be more fun than going to Disney World! You all know we're starting with three straight passes as fast as we can go, so let's do what we do," I said.

Chris had a rocky start to say the least. On first down, his pass to Polk was high and wide. He then somehow skipped the next pass to Jared on 2nd down. It was now 3rd and 10, and we were on the verge of starting the season with the dreaded "3 and out". We needed to pull through and get a first down to show that our offense could really deliver. It was crucial to set the tone for the season and boost everyone's confidence.

"Needy, not greedy," I told Heiko before the ball was snapped. This meant that his route should stop after ten yards to get the first down, unless the defender fell down.

Heiko ran full speed at the corner but throttled down after 10 yards, where Chris placed a perfectly thrown ball into the hole between the corner and outside linebacker. The corner missed the tackle, and Heiko rumbled to our 35-yard line for a confidence-boosting 27-yard gain. Now, we were rolling. Four plays later, Karri muscled his way in for a 3-yard touchdown.

After the successful point-after attempt, we were up 7-0. I high-fived the guys coming off the field. "That's what I'm talking about! Great job!" I shouted. "That was a statement drive, guys. We're going to attack just like that all season. Awesome catch, Heiko, on third down. That was big time!"

Next, I asked the offensive line, "What did they give us up front?"

Brenden responded, "They're what we expected. Both defensive tackles over our guards and both pretty strong against the run."

"It looked from the sideline like #8 was breathing hard after our big pass completion. Is he already hating our tempo?" I said as I looked at Yasir.

"Hell, yes! He's gassed already. Keep running the ball to the left, and we'll make his life miserable," Yasir said.

The next drive was the one I described in the introduction ending with me forgetting it was fourth down. Big plays win games, and I wasted a 45-yard run after the catch from Polk on the drive.

"My fault, guys. Damn, I don't have an excuse other than being stupid. I'll make it up on the next possession, I promise," I assured the group.

"You're ok, coach. We'll pick you up," Chris reassured me.

Helbig and the offense did just that. Karri scored again, this time from 2 yards out to cap a 12-play, 85-yard drive. We were now up 14-7 in the second quarter. The Monarchs added another touchdown later in the quarter, so the score was tied 14 all at halftime.

We met outside the locker room in a shaded area. "We're holding up overall, but we've shot ourselves twice in the foot in the red zone. Once was totally on me. The other was a turnover after a false start. We'll score touchdowns instead this half when we get down there. OL, what running play do y'all like the most?" I asked.

"We've got a soft edge on my side. Let's get back in our heavy formation and run it at them," Yasir said.

"I like it. Get yourself ready for a brawl in the next two quarters. They have to feel good that it's tied 14-14, considering we've probably gained twice as many yards as they have. We'll start punching the ball over the goal line and get some momentum. We'll win the game up front and bloody their noses."

"Let's break it out on finish!" Jared said to the team as we headed back into the stadium.

Our defense held them on the second half's first possession, and we went back to work offensively.

The Monarchs sent pressure on 3rd down with their best linebacker, Rashard Ashby, a GFL rookie who won all-conference honors as a three-year starter at Virginia Tech. Karri put his face between Ashby's "2" and "3" on his jersey and stopped him in his tracks. Chris let the ball fly. Jared ran a skinny post and hauled in the perfect spiral for a 34-yard touchdown that put us up 21-14.

We drove the ball once more to the red zone on the next drive, but the Monarchs' defense held to set up a critical fourth at the six-yard line. If we could convert and go up 14 points, it would be a sizable lead the way our defense was playing.

"Time out, time out!" I yelled to the side judge. Chris walked over to the sideline, and I asked, "What do you think?"

"Let's sneak it. I can get the push for a yard."

It was a good call. Chris had a look on his face that every coach dreams of seeing in their quarterback's eyes. He would find a way to get the yard. Chris started in the shotgun, then shifted under center quickly and said, "Hit!" Ludi, Max, and Brenden pushed forward, but the Monarch tackles plugged the inside. Ashby came over the top and stuffed Chris for no gain.

"Damnit!" Chris yelled as he came off the field.

The fourth quarter started, and it was like a tale of two offenses. While we hadn't punted and had moved the ball well, we only had a seven-point lead because we'd wasted several opportunities near the goal line.

It was like *Deja Vu all over again* on our next possession. We drove the ball down the field and had a 4th and goal at the six-yard line.

Again, I called for a time-out.

"Jonas, we might have them on our pop pass to Jerome. The linebackers will be playing close," I said.

"I think we have a chance with it. #23 (Ashby) is making every tackle on 4th and short. He'll be filling hard," Jonas responded.

Ashby, again was a thorn in our side. He didn't fall for our fake on 4th and 6. He leaped in the air and picked off the pass. The nightmare continued, and the score remained 21-14.

#27 Cody Cranston #19 Jonas Gacek

Dresden quickly drove to our 16-yard line, and all the juice had shifted to their sideline. But momentum is the most fickle of all mistresses. On 2nd down and seven, Cody Cranston, a safety from Canada, intercepted a pass in the endzone and began going the other way. After 75 yards and looking like he would take it all the way for a touchdown, he was tripped up at the 30-yard line by a diving Monarch receiver. The crowd and our sideline went nuts as our defense saved the day once more.

The next three plays might have been the worst drive of the season. After two unproductive run plays and a holding penalty in our only pass attempt, it was fourth and ten from Dresden's 35-yard line.

I looked at Berti and Saul to see if they wanted to go for it or try the long field goal.

"Field goal!" Saul shouted.

Oh my, I thought, can Heiko make a 51-yarder? He’s a running back, receiver, punter, and kicker. It’s not like he spends all this time working on his kicking craft.

Mads’ snap was good…Jared’s hold was good.

Heiko’s kick was…GOOD! The ball was right down the middle. Heiko passed this test of fire 100%. We had a little breathing room finally, up 24-14.

Dresden scored to close the gap to three points early in the fourth quarter. After we traded possessions, we got the ball back with six minutes left, up 24-21.

"Run the damn ball, coach. Go behind Yasir and me," Jerome said emphatically on the sideline.

"I'm listening, brother. That's exactly what we’re going to do."

Karri, Heiko, and even Chris ran the ball on critical downs and ate the clock.

But Dresden's defense bowed their neck again to force a 4th down and three with three minutes left in the game. I called our last timeout. This time, Berti and Saul joined in on my conversation with Chris and Jonas. I had no doubt Berti had his belly full of our debacles, and I didn't blame him.

"I'm tired of running into the Berlin Wall of Dresden. Let's throw choice to Polk at #20," I said to the group.

"I like it, coach. We got this," Chris said.

"If we don't connect, the Monarchs get it back with a chance to win or tie it up and send it to overtime. Do you guarantee this will work, coach?" Berti asked me.

"I can't guarantee it, but we'll throw the ball to one of our best players versus one of their worst. I like our chances." I replied. Berti walked away and allowed us to run the play. Chris threw a perfect pass to Polk on a 10-yard stop route for the first down.

"Good call, coach! We played ugly at times, but what a win!" Jonas said enthusiastically into the headset. Jonas hadn't said anything truer all day. We hadn't played well offensively, but it was a win for the first time in Royals history against a good Dresden squad, and we'd take it.

"Victory formation, victory!" I yelled, signaling to Chris to take a knee to run out the clock.

As Berti was talking to the team on the field, wet after being given a *Gatorade bath*, he said, "Coach Jackson, do you have anything to say to the team?"

I grabbed a ball and said, "Coach Vogt, if anyone deserves a game ball for today, it is you! Congratulations, sir!"

After our team meeting, I made my way over to the VIP section to enjoy the moment. "Coach, come eat and drink on the Royals!" Jens said, patting me on the back. It was a celebration that I won't ever forget. Some Royals players were drinking beer while still wearing their shoulder pads. Berti and Saul were all smiles, eating with their families. I made a plate of chicken, potatoes, brat, and a roll.

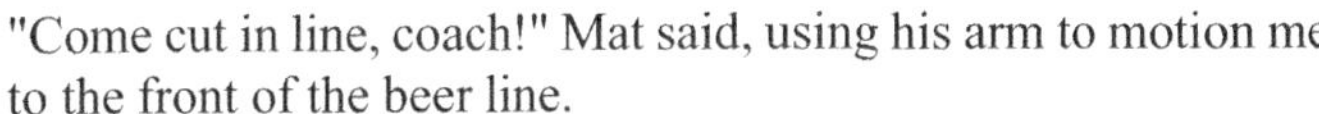

"Come cut in line, coach!" Mat said, using his arm to motion me to the front of the beer line.

"I don't drink much, especially dark beer, Mat. Is there anything light?"

"Get coach a Radler, please," he said to the Royals volunteer manning the drink station.

"What's a Radler?" I asked.

"It's half beer and half lemonade. You'll like it".

"It's what the average German calls candy in a bottle. You'll be fine, coach," said Tim, a backup tackle from Berlin I'd just cut in front of with his and Mat's permission.

I sat and ate by myself and took it all in. The euphoria I was witnessing was what makes coaching and being a part of a team so rewarding. Everyone was laughing and reliving the close victory. The faces of a small community in West Texas look just like the ones I was looking at this moment in Potsdam, faces of sheer joy. After eating and seemingly being congratulated by every Royals board member and volunteer, I began to make my way out of the stadium and head to the train station. Max, who had played about half of our offensive plays, came beside me and said, "We did it, coach. You have no idea how big this win is."

"Thank you, Max. I think you played well today. I'm glad you're back healthy."

On the way back to my flat, I called Tracy and gave her the rundown of the game that, thankfully, she could watch online back home. Eventually, the long, emotional day caught up to me, and I couldn't stay awake any longer. I said, "I love you," and went to sleep.

Around 2:00 a.m., I woke up with thoughts racing through my head. What am I doing wrong? I promised every Royal who'd listen we'd be averaging 50 points a game, and we scored 24?

How could I not have known it was fourth down? Anytime an offense doesn't punt, allow a sack, and only has one turnover, it should score at least 40 points.

Everyone was celebrating like we'd won the Super Bowl, but I knew we'd gotten lucky. There's a phrase, "Winning makes everything ok", but I wasn't ok. All I had were more questions. We had things to fix and fix in a hurry. I personally had things to improve, or the looks on everyone's faces would be much different the next time we played the Monarchs.

Was I disappointed in my players? Absolutely.

Was I disappointed in my performance? Even more.

Tomorrow would be a long day of grading the film and searching for solutions. Luckily, I fell back asleep because God didn't give me any answers.

Around 6:00 a.m., I woke up to an ambulance's siren blaring in the distance. Luckily, that ambulance wasn't for the Potsdam Royals because we dodged a bullet yesterday.

POTSDAMER TAGESSPIEGEL

(Excerpts from the Potsdam Daily Mirror)

At the start of the German Football League (GFL) season, the Potsdam Royals received the Dresden Monarchs on Saturday. It was an uprising against the crown because the royals from Brandenburg defeated the Saxon monarchs, who had arrived as reigning GFL champions, and thus also formulated ambitions for the succession to the throne. For the first time ever, last year's semi-finalist Potsdam won against Dresden.

In the end, the difference was three points. Bals made the difference with his converted field goal in the final quarter. Twice earlier in the game, the hosts missed the kick on the fourth try. Instead of bagging the supposedly easy three points, they risked a touchdown were stopped just before the endzone. "We tried to run away with the result as early as possible, we wanted to put Dresden under pressure," explained Bals. "Unfortunately, it didn't work out." But when the score was 21-14, trust was placed in his quality. He shot through the bars from a whopping 50 yards.

"The snap was good, the hold was good, and as soon as I touched the ball, I knew it was going to be good." The visitors then reduced the lead again, but Potsdam took the lead.

The defense was stable and the offense around the new quarterback Chris Helbig "marched properly across the field," said head coach Michael Vogt. "We surprised Dresden a bit with how fast we played," said Bals.

Unlike his kicker Bals, the coach did not want to rate the opening success too highly: "The first game is not yet 100 percent meaningful. But for the moment it's great for us, of course."

The rest of the season will show whether the Potsdam Royals are fit for the throne.

GFL **GAMERECAP**

vs Dresden

24 | 21

SHARKWATER GFL — SEASON OPENER

(1-0) (0-1)

EWP

	ROYALS	MONARCHS
TOTAL YARDS	484	380
YARDS RUSHING	200	209
YARDS PASSING	284	171
YARDS PER PLAY	6.6	5.6
PUNTS	0	5
PENALTIES	6-38	6-45

RUSHING	ATT.	YARDS	AVG.	TDS
PAJARINEN, K.	30	178	5.7	2
BALS, H.	5	22	4.4	

RECEIVING	RECEPTS	YARDS	TDS	LONG
WOLFE, J.	7	95	1	34
POLK, B.	6	103		45
BALS, H.	3	42		30

PASSING	COMP.	ATT.	YARDS	TDS	INT
HELBIG, C	21	33	284	1	1

#91 Stanley Aronokhale #27 Cody Cranston
#2 Divine Buckrham

#9 Heiko Bals

29

DO GERMANS NOT LIKE HAMBURGERS?

May 23, 2022

It was a relief to be back in the office Monday morning with the boys after soul-searching in my flat on Sunday. The red zone issues versus Dresden were a tough pill to swallow, but I knew we had to turn the page and focus on our next opponent, the Berlin Adler. They have a reputation for having the best coaching staff in Germany.

After the offensive line and skill position meetings, our three American players stayed behind and helped me finalize the game plan. "Guys, what am I holding up?" I asked as I held up my hand with all five fingers extended wide.

"A five?" Polk said, more of a question than a statement.

"Exactly. Do any of you know why the number five kept me awake the last two nights?"

"That is how many times we had the ball in the red zone and didn't score. We should've beat the crap out of Dresden if we'd have scored even two or three of the five," Chris said.

"Yes! Lord have mercy, fellas; let's figure this out. We had almost 500 yards and didn't punt or have a sack. But we shot ourselves in the foot time after time near the goal line. I'm lucky Coach Vogt didn't put me in a headlock or on a plane back to DFW last Saturday."

"It won't happen again. Run me more down there. I know we didn't convert on 4th and one, but it won't happen again," Chris said.

"Jared and I can win one-on-one inside the 10-yard line every time. I don't care if it is against #4 from Dresden or whoever we face," Polk said.

"I agree with both of you guys. This is why it's so important that we meet each Monday. I know we have to protect you from injury, Chris, but you'll just have to be fine and stay healthy," I said, smiling.

"I'll be fine. I promise I'm not fragile, coach," Chris replied.

"Let's watch the Adler red zone defense and come up with two plays max inside the

10," I said. We watched the film and scripted our plays for Tuesday's practice for the next half-hour.

After the guys left, I entered the office where Saul was watching Adler's special teams film. "I believe we can block a punt this week. Divine and Cody were both close against Dresden," Saul said.

"That'd be huge. The analytics of winning goes way up when you block a punt. Let me google it right now, but I believe the stat is if a team blocks a punt, they win 90% of the time. This would make it the biggest momentum shift play there is."

After a month of riding the trains, thankfully, Saul let me borrow one of his bicycles, so I began riding it to the office. After the guys left, I cycled ten minutes to Brandenburger Strasse, the main tourist area, looking for a place to eat.

"Coach Jackson!" It was weird to hear my name called in a city where I knew no one. I turned around to see Jens and Buddy Carroll, the board member from Texas, walking together.

"Hey, guys!" I said enthusiastically back. It was an unexpected treat to see familiar faces. "What are y'all up to?"

"We are about to have lunch in one of my favorite spots at a delicious German place. Please join us," Jens answered.

Here we saw old buildings made of red brick and Dutch architectural influences everywhere. Seeing how well the city blended multiple styles and cultures was interesting. "This is Zum Fliegenden Holländer. It opened in the mid-1900s, closed down in 1948 when the Soviets came, then reopened in 1996 when the wall fell," Jens explained. It was a small restaurant with outside tables (like 90% of the eateries in Potsdam).

"You may have figured this out already, coach, but most restaurants here are either Italian or Turkish kebabs. This place actually has good German cuisine," Buddy said.

"I do have a few questions about the food here. Do Germans not like hamburgers? I don't eat them all the time back at home, but I am craving a good one now," I said.

"Pork is the number one meat in Germany. Beef cows aren't plentiful. They're too expensive to feed," Jens replied.

"Good beef is almost an oxymoron here. Hamburger meat, especially, comes from old dairy cows that no longer produce much milk. Unless you go to an expensive restaurant, stay away from the burgers or steak," Buddy said.

"But you didn't come to Germany for burgers, did you coach?" Jens said, smiling. "We're going to show you what good schnitzel tastes like. There is pork and chicken. Either one will be excellent here."

"I can't wait. Thanks for allowing me to join you guys," I said.

"Let's talk about the game Saturday, coach. That was a big win for the entire Royals organization. Thank you for helping us defeat Dresden for the first time. You're making a difference in the team already. We looked much more disciplined than in the past. Everyone was talking after the game about how we, how do I say it in English? We restrained ourselves and had far fewer penalties," Jens said.

"Thanks very much. I'm honored to be here and help in any way I can," I said.

"Do you know, coach, that I played for the Royals for many years?" Jens asked.

"Berti and Saul mentioned it to me the day I met you in the office."

"Yes, I grew up snow skiing. I was actually on the East German Ski team for a while. I also, of course, played our brand of football. But in 1990, the NFL came to Berlin and played an exhibition game. The Rams defeated the Chiefs, and I knew that day I wanted to wear the armor and be an American football player. I said to myself, "This is the game for me!"

"I had no idea the NFL played in Berlin. That's amazing you fell in love with American football and began playing after seeing your first game," I replied.

"Yes! Yes! American football got in here, pointing at his heart, and never left. Now, if you can help us win the German Bowl, my heart will be full," Jens said enthusiastically.

"How about you, Buddy? How did you get here from Ft. Worth?" I asked.

"My better half is from here. We met in Texas, but she told me she wanted to come back home when we got married, so we did. I'm an electrician by day and a Royals board member for the other 16 hours."

"You told me your son plays quarterback. How does he like the brand of football here?" I asked.

"We've lived here for five years, so the only football he played in Texas was flag. I'm going to ask Chris if he will give Stephen some one-on-one coaching. After the first day of seeing Chris lead the offense, I knew he'd be able to help Stephen."

"I bet Chris can help him. He wants to be a coach when his career as a player is over. I'll say something to him about it as well," I said.

"I do have one question for you, coach," Buddy said. "About our troubles in the red zone the other day. What do you think was the issue?"

"We can't afford any more mistakes like the one I made. Despite Dresden's strong defense, we must step up our game. I've just left a meeting with our A's, and we've developed a plan to fix some things near the goal line."

"Well, I was telling Jens this morning about a few plays that worked great for us near the end zone when I played at San Angelo State that could help. Pass me that napkin, and I will draw them up for you..."

"The 2022 season was definitely the best season I have ever experienced in my football career! Working hard every day together to reach the same goal and having fun while doing it. Not only did I make brothers for life, I gained a family of 50 strong!"

Stefan Stefansson
#77 Tackle
Egilsstaðir, Iceland
2023 Team:
Potsdam Royals

30

SETTLE DOWN COACH

May 28, 2022

Our first road trip was only 30 miles to Berlin to play the Eagles. We met at the Potsdam Central train station to board our chartered bus. After I sat down, I passed around a couple of call sheets, our game plan, for guys to review one last time.

"Please make sure you're 100% on everything. Go through each play and make sure you don't have any questions. Thanks again for a great week of prep. I can't wait to see us execute today," I said.

After the short bus ride, we walked up to the historic Poststadion Berlin Stadium, built in 1929. As I would soon expect, the Royals had a spread of food for everyone to enjoy a few hours before kickoff. The Royals board member responsible for meals was Conni Wagner. Conni and other volunteers always arrived well before the team. On several long tables, they had cold cuts, buns, cheese, and scrambled eggs.

"Thank you, Conni. The food you prepare for us is delicious. Last week, during the game, we had sweets and fruit for players to eat on the sideline. I was surprised there was food in the bench area during the game. Is this something we always do?" I asked.

"Yes, last week, the boys were hungry. We went through four cakes! They ate a lot to keep up their energy in such a close game," Conni said.

After making a sandwich, I had an hour before offensive meetings, so I walked out to the game field. Something wasn't quite right about it, but it took me a second to figure it out. It was marked every 10 yards instead of five! Saul and Jonas walked up a few minutes later, so I asked, "What the hell, guys? Do most GFL teams only paint the field every 10 yards?"

"Crap, no, this is rare, thank God," Saul said.

"You see it more in the GFL 2 and lower-level teams. I'm sure the Adler coaches are also unhappy with the markings," Jonas said.

"I hope like hell this isn't going to start a trend. Not having lines every five yards would be just as likely to cause a pregame meeting as the endzone fiasco last week. There are 1,200 high schools in Texas, and if any of them only painted lines every 10 yards, it would lead off the 10:00 p.m. news," I said.

A few minutes later, Berti came out to the field, so I asked him if I could be proactive with the officials. "Do you mind if I speak to the officials during pregame? They did a good job last week, but I would like to tell them how fast we'll play if they let us," I said.

"That's fine. We'll also have the same head official, Mats, this week. He told me in an email this week they had never officiated a game with such quick tempo."

About 90 minutes before each game, the referees conduct what is referred to as a 'pass check' with both teams. Each club must have a team information card for each player that states their country of origin, birthdate, etc. Teams are allowed only ten imports who didn't play in the GFL the prior season. After our guys were all matched with their players' cards and it was determined we were compliant, I walked up to Mats and introduced myself.

"Nice to meet you, Coach Jackson," Mats said, smiling. "How are you enjoying Germany so far?"

"I love it. Everyone is very friendly unless I am walking across the street at the wrong place or forgot my mask on the train. Thanks for asking, but more importantly, thanks for allowing us to play fast last week."

"You're welcome. We met about it before the game, but it still was something we hadn't seen before. After the game, we had a long meeting to ensure our mechanics were ready for your pace. The pace of your offense still took us by surprise, despite being warned by Coach Vogt during the week. We'll be more ready this week," Mats said.

"I appreciated your demeanor during the game. As you may recall from the nail-biter last week, I struggled to control my emotions when things got sticky. Your personality helps me to be calm, and I appreciate it," I said.

"We look forward to another exciting game today. The official on your sideline is Günter Ludenbeck. If you need to speak to me, just let Günter know. By the way, I commend you on the overall play of the Royals last week. In the past, they may have found a way to lose that game. You guys were much more disciplined. I know you're not the head coach, but I'm sure you're making a difference."

"Thank you, that means a lot. Berti has allowed me to have a voice, so I'm trying my best to preach discipline."

Our offensive captains for today were Brenden and Jerome. Both of them had played against Adler in the GFL 2 (Adler moved up after winning the league championship), so this game had been circled on their schedules for months.

"They took the ball, fellas," I said on the sideline as Mats made the signal the Adler would be receiving.

"Follow Us, guys; let me speak to you for a second. We should see a four-man defensive line again this week, so we shouldn't have any issues. I expect us to improve a ton over last week. Let’s go!"

Adler received the opening kickoff and marched down the field. Our defense stiffened eventually and held them to a field goal. We were behind 3-0 when we got the ball.

It was 3rd and 7, and we were in danger of starting the game "3 and out" and having to punt for the first time this season.

We quickly aligned and snapped the ball. Jared, the outside receiver to Adler's sideline. He attacked the corner, then snapped the post. Jared was wide open, but we had an assignment bust in the offensive line. An Adler defender's hand grazed Chris' facemask as he stepped up in the pocket. Chris let the ball go and hit Jared in stride for a 67-yard score.

“Touchdown! What a way to start!” Jonas shouted into the headset.

The good guys were up 7-3, but more importantly, for the second time in as many games, we converted a long 3rd down and scored on the opening drive. This huge play was an early dagger to Adler. Teams with the most plays of plus 20 yards win games 81% of the time. We didn't have to solve any red zone issues when we scored from our 33-yard line. But, we did have problems to solve.

"They’re playing us in a three-man front. We looked confused in the middle of our pass protection. Karri tried to help, but it happened fast," Jonas said.

As the offense gathered on the bench on the sideline, the first thing I did was high-five Chris and Jared. "Great stuff, guys! Their DC is over there trying to figure out how they just gave up the big one!" I then turned my attention to the offensive line. I said, "Let's work this out, guys. Adler’s playing a different front than we expected. All we have to do is follow our blocking rules. What happened on 3rd down? Crap, Chris got hit in the face as he stepped up!"

"I made an “Ace” call. I thought I’d get help, but when I slid left, I felt the nose guard go free," Ludi said.

"Are you kidding me? What did you do, Mads?" I asked harshly.

"I had a guy on my outside shoulder, so I thought I had him," he answered.

"No! That is a four-down rule. When there's a nose over the center, you must combo and help the center, damn it! When Ludi says, "Ace," don't think, just ace!" I said in frustration.

#75 Brenden Oswin #8 Chris Helbig
#67 Bobby Sövegjarto #78 Yasir Raji

I knew I needed to end the meeting positively, so I looked at Ruben and said, "Great job capturing the safety on choice. I appreciate your unselfishness. We'll fix the issues up front, fellas. Expect them to use a nose-guard again this next drive. All we have to do is overlap him."

I liked Mads and immediately regretted going off on him. Mistakes on the field are one of two things: 1. The player doesn't understand, or 2. The player doesn't care. Mads cared, so I walked up behind him, patted him on the butt, and said, "Sorry for my rant. I believe in you."

At that moment, I heard a roar from our sideline, "We got it! We blocked the punt!"

"Fritz Cola! Fritz Cola!" I shouted. Fritz Cola is a popular brand of soft drink in Germany and the name of a gadget play we had prepared for this week. We had the ball on the Adler 32-yard line and would take a shot to the endzone.

I high-fived Saul as our players jogged onto the field and said, "Great job! You said we were going to get one!"

"Hell, yes! You can't be unsound up the middle when you punt against us!" Saul said.

"Go, hit!" Bobby, our center this offensive series, yelled as he snapped the ball back to Chris. After Karri took the handoff, he pitched the ball back to Jared on a reverse. Polk was now dragging across the field, and Jared, who we discovered had an accurate arm, hit him for a 17-yard completion.

Two plays later, Chris hit Polk on a slant route for a 3-yard touchdown and a 14-3 lead.

"That's better, big boys!" I said, high-fiving players after Heiko split the uprights on the extra point.

In the next series, Heiko, aligned as a receiver, jumped offsides, committing the biggest faux pas a wideout can make. Receivers shouldn't even know what the snap count is. They should look inside towards the center and move when the ball is snapped.

"My gosh, Heiko! Just be deaf and watch the damn ball!" I shouted.

"Louis, go get Heiko out of the game!" I said to our young German receiver.

"Come here, Heiko!" I was fired up as I continued, "What the hell? Junior high receivers don't jump offsides! If you don't have any more discipline than this, you can stay here and watch the game with me!"

Jerome approached me as I prepared to call a play, and Mats walked off the penalty.

"Coach, we know you want to win, but you can't go off like that on Heiko and Mads. We're grown men and aren't used to being coached like this. We know you're passionate, but so are we. Just talk to us like this, and we'll get the job done," Jerome said.

Wow, that hit me right between the eyes. I knew he was 100% correct. I wasn't doing well early on in this game and was grateful Jerome pointed it out. My goal in coaching the Royals was the same as dealing with the officials, to stay calm and neutral.

"Thank you, Jerome. I know you're right. I appreciate you manning up and saying something to me. It means a lot."

"Heiko, next play, go back in."

We led 24-10 at the half and pulled away for a low-stress 51-17 victory.

Chris and Jared both had monster days. Chris threw for six touchdowns and 332 yards with no interceptions. Jared would be named the GFL receiver of the week with 13 receptions, 216 yards, and a whopping four TDs.

After the game, I bought a bratwurst and a beer and celebrated with some coaches outside the stadium. I also reflected on the two outbursts I had with Mads and Heiko. I had to do better in the future. I saw Jerome out of the corner of my eye, so I approached him and said, "Thanks for speaking to me on the sideline. I love that I'm with 30-year-old grown men who'll talk to me about hard things when necessary. You were right on the money about my temper. Thanks again."

On the bus ride home, I saw Karri looking at his phone.

"What are you watching? Is there a GFL live stream on?" I asked.

"No, sir. This is Formula 1 racing in England. It's the London Grand Prix."

"I want to apologize to you about today. Some of the issues were my fault. I'll make sure it doesn't happen again," Karri said.

"What are you talking about? I'm the offensive line coach, and we're the ones who had issues today. I should apologize to you and Chris for not coaching better. I can't guarantee you much, but you have my word we'll do a better job opening holes for you next week."

GAMERECAP

vs Berlin Adler

17 (1-1) | 51 (2-0)

	ROYALS	ADLER
TOTAL YARDS	466	316
YARDS RUSHING	134	158
YARDS PASSING	332	158
YARDS PER PLAY	8.8	4.6
PUNTS	0	2
PENALTIES	8-59	8-69

RUSHING	ATT.	YARDS	AVG.	TDS
PAJARINEN, K.	17	96	5.5	

RECEIVING	RECEPTS	YARDS	TDS	LONG
WOLFE, J.	13	216	4	67
POLK, B.	7	100	2	40
BALS, H.	1	16		

PASSING	COMP.	ATT.	YARDS	TDS	INT
HELBIG, C	20	27	314	6	

"We had a great group of guys together. I loved the energy and how we got to work every week to prepare for the next opponent. We had some characters I will always remember. 2022 is a year I will always love to talk about with fond memories."

Bobby Sövegjarto
#67 Center
Germany
2023 Team
Potsdam Royals

31

REINDEER STEW

May 30, 2022

Grading the game film the next day in my flat was challenging for the second week in a row, but this time it was because of my guys, the offensive line. Follow Us performed more poorly than any unit on the offense or defense vs. Adler. My pride was hurt, and I wasn't happy. What made the situation even more difficult was I liked every one of them. They gave great effort at practice, were punctual at our meetings, and seemed to want to please me.

So, what the heck was going on? Who were these guys I was grading? We should have improved from last week but played better in week one against Dresden.

It was my fault we didn't handle an unexpected defense. I was disappointed we didn't make the corrections and adjust more quickly. We have too many smart guys for there to be confusion most of the game. Not only did we not block the correct defender several times, but when we did, our footwork and technique were incorrect.

I posted the grades in our Follow Us chat group, saying, "We're going to fix what ails us this week!"

The next morning, we met at the office, and it wasn't pretty.

"I love coaching you guys, but something has to give. Only two or three of you pop into my mind when I ask myself, "Who is trying to do it my way?". Yasir and Ludi, thank you. I see our techniques on film. Brenden, you as well. Brenden, weren't you the OL coach at Rostock (GFL 2) last season?"

"Yea, I helped out. We couldn't find an OL coach, so I took it. It was no big deal," Brenden said with his Australian accent.

"So, two of the three guys who were freakin' coaching last season aren't fighting me on 'L' steps, overlap, or if we make a "box call" versus a 3-down front. You would think they'd be the problem. I appreciate you guys for buying in," I said, looking at all three of them. "Everyone else either doesn't approve or isn't capable of doing it. Either way, it won't work. I don't give a crap about what step an NFL guru says we should take on mid-zone. I don't care if you like the Crowther or don't believe in our overlap technique. We'll find two more guys who'll do it my way, and they'll play—end of story. If you're paid the most or have the most rings doesn't matter to me. I don't give a damn if you're a good guy, like puppies, and give blood twice a week. Try me on this. Try me and see what happens."

After a few minutes of film review, I settled down. I had made my point and now had to get some good vibes going.

"Let me make one more comment about how important it is for all five to work together. Stefan, have I ever told you about when I went to Iceland and helped cook reindeer stew?"

"No, sir, I don't recall you telling me about this." Stefan said.

"Oh yea, I went on a camping trip with a few world-famous chefs."

"Did you? You once told me you haven't ever been to Iceland, but I'm sure you just forgot about this time," Stefan said, smiling.

"That's exactly right. The trip was terrible, so I blocked it out of my mind. Do you want to know why it was terrible, Stefan?"

"I do, coach. Please tell me why it was terrible."

"Because all the chefs wanted to do it their way. We planned to make the greatest gumbo-type stew in history with all these world-famous chefs. It seemed like a great idea until it became apparent they were the problem. They couldn't agree on how we should prepare the stew."

"Back to the story. I traveled to Iceland a few years ago with four legendary chefs. One was from Germany, one was from France, one was from Finland, and one was from Australia. Being from Texas, my job was shooting the reindeer and preparing the meat."

"I tracked a deer for two days in the ice and snow. I journeyed across extremely high mountains and glaciers, traversed sandy beaches, and made my way through thick forests. I even had to avoid several Viking clans along the way."

"Umm, we don't have sandy beaches or many forests in Iceland, coach," Stefan said.

"I once approached a house with Stefansson on the mailbox, but no one answered the door, so I kept trudging along in my boots with the tennis racket-looking bottoms. Let me tell you, my job was not for the faint of heart! Finally, I shot the reindeer and gutted it. As I was walking back into our campsite, victoriously dragging it behind me, I could hear them all arguing."

"We need more potatoes in the stew," said the German chef. "We need more salt and garlic," said the chef from France. "We must add more onions," said the Finn. The cook from Australia was even yelling about adding Kangaroo and a lager from Queensland!"

As I spoke, I noticed lots of eye-rolling and smiles in the room.

"Other than Brenden's crazy uncle from Melbourne, do any other chefs want to use sub-par ingredients? Of course not, but if all four cooks put whatever they want in the pot, it'll taste terrible. This is our OL, when we do it how we prefer instead of all being on the same page in the same cookbook. Furthermore, Tracy is flying in this week, and I don't want to be in a bad mood. I haven't seen her in six weeks, so for all things good in Germany, take the correct step and keep your offhand away from the defensive tackle."

Practice Tuesday and Wednesday was excellent. I started seeing improvement in our techniques upfront. Chris and our receivers were becoming more comfortable each time out.

"Good stuff today, Chris. We might've executed better tonight than we have all season," I said as we finished Wednesday's session working on our extra point and field goal unit.

"Thanks, coach. All our receivers are getting dialed in and understanding our backyard mentality."

"Everybody up!" Saul yelled for our post-practice meeting.

"I'm excited about who you guys are adding tonight. They both represent all our pillars," I said as we jogged to gather around Coach Vogt.

"No doubt, they both deserve it 100%," Chris said.

We've added guys to 50 Strong after each practice for a few weeks.

Jared had become the on-field leader of our Royal Standard. Like in our players' creed meetings, where he was the most vocal, he's taken the same role in the 50 Strong WhatsApp and on the field after practices.

"Jared, who are we inviting into the Royal Standard tonight?" I asked.

"The first guy started as a wide receiver but now plays tight end. He's bought into our standard from day one after coming to the Royals from the Berlin Rebels. But in reality, he doesn't care about where he plays. He wants to contribute in any way he can. All of you know I am describing Mat, who you also know drives over two hours from Poland to get here. Welcome to 50 Strong, Mat!"

All clapped and cheered as he came forward and Saul handed him his helmet sticker.

"Leo, who are we adding from the defense tonight?"

"Just like Mat, our defensive selection joined the Royals this season. He works extremely hard every practice. He is never late or misses with minor injuries. He always finds a way to get on the field and has improved our defense. He travels more than two hours to get here because he lives in Poland and rides with Mat. Welcome to 50 Strong, Maciek!"

"Whew! Thank God you guys chose Maciek, or the ride home might have been awkward!" I said.

Both guys were awesome teammates, and I was happy for them. Neither could be at the creed meetings with the distance they would have had to drive, but both deserved to be in.

"Just a second, Coach Vogt. Can I say something to the team?" said Hjalmar Nielsen, a defensive back we signed during training camp after Dresden cut him.

"Of course, Hjalmar. Go right ahead," Berti said.

"I first want to thank the Royals for bringing me in after the Monarchs cut me. I wasn't around during the 50 Strong meetings, so I was blown away when I saw players introduce and add other players to the group. I asked to speak tonight to say we have something special happening."

"Teams always talk about being a family, but we really are a family. They talk about it in Dresden, but they're not. Our best players are the most humble guys on the team. There are no cliques here where the studs treat the second-teamers like crap. After we beat Dresden, they are all doing BCD-ing (blame, complain, and defend). I don't hear excuses here. I just wanted to say it is incredible to be on this team. It is an honor to be a Royal."

"Thanks, Hjalmar! That was awesome, brother! You break us out tonight!" I shouted.

"50 Strong on three! One, two, three...50 Strong!"

32

SWING FIRST

June 4, 2022

Buddy drove me to Berlin Airport to pick up Tracy on Thursday morning. "How are you feeling about Kiel, coach?"

"I like our game plan. We'll get in empty (no backs in the backfield) for the first time, which will hurt them. Kiel has two good American defensive backs, but their other cover guys will need help to stop us."

"Let me know if you need help watching anything during the game. I know you have Jonas up there helping, but I don't mind if you need me also."

"I appreciate that, Buddy. We're very simple, and Jonas does a great job, but I'll keep your offer in mind."

The airport was about a 30-minute drive. "I see McDonald's and Burger King on the interstate or Autobahn but don't see them anywhere in Potsdam. Is it like this in most cities?" I asked.

"Yes, Germans have a much different relationship with food than we have in America. Bakeries and Turkish kebabs are the fast food here. You won't see people eat or drink while they are driving. Heck, cup holders in cars are optional in Germany."

BERLIN INTERNATIONAL

"Hey, honey! I yelled as Tracy appeared from baggage claim.

Tracy looked more stunning than ever after not seeing her for six weeks. We talked all the time on the phone, but the seven-hour time difference was brutal at best. I was beyond ecstatic to have the next 12 days with her.

After weeks of telling Tracy about the beauty of Potsdam, it was awesome to get to show her. We took a boat tour of the Havel River, walked through Sanssouci Palace, the famous Bridge of Spies (also an excellent movie starring Tom Hanks), and went to Cecilienhof Palace, where the Allied leaders met in 1945 to divide up post-war Germany.

We also had a great time allowing Tracy to explore the pedestrian-only Brandenburger Strasse. There are many small shops lining both sides of the brick road. We shopped, ate, and people-watched as they strolled along the street.

"Is there anywhere else you'd like to go before we hop on the train back to my flat?" I asked.

"Yes! I almost forgot. My electrical adaptor blew up trying to blow dry my hair yesterday. Let's find one that works," Tracy said. We stopped at a few stores, but we couldn't find the right adapter to be able to use it.

"Let's just buy a new dryer that we know will work. We don't need to deal with it in Paris next week either," I said.

"Do you remember me warning you Europe is hard?" Tracy said playfully.

Although Tracy wasn't going to get to see a home game, I was also excited she'd make the road trip with us to Kiel, in NW Germany. It was our only regular season away game, far enough to spend the night in a hotel. On Friday afternoon, we rode with Saul for about three hours to the outskirts of Hamburg in a Royals rental car.

"This hotel, the Van Der Valk, is pretty unusual. It has a massive indoor ski slope attached to it," Saul said as he drove us on the Autobahn.

"Wow, that's cool. How far will we travel on Saturday to get to Kiel?" I asked.

"Roughly an hour, give or take."

Tracy and I ate the buffet breakfast at the hotel restaurant around 9:00 a.m. the following day. We could see an indoor ski slope behind a massive glass wall from our booth. "Babe, we have a team meeting at 10:00, then I will speak to the offense after. We'll check out and be on the road by 11:00."

The team meeting was short and sweet. Berti and Saul explained the day's schedule, and then we split up for defense and offensive meetings.

"My guys, we'll meet right over there for about 15 minutes," I said, pointing to some chairs nearby.

After we went over the opening script and had a brief walkthrough, I closed the meeting using a movie clip.

"Get your phones out and click on the movie link I just posted in our WhatsApp," I said to conclude our meeting in the lobby between the front desk and the ski slope.

"I will wait to hit play until everyone's ready. I haven't seen this movie, but maybe one or two of you have. This clip is one a buddy told me about a few months ago."

I always give context to a movie clip before the players watch it in a meeting. I want to lead them to the point I'm trying to make.

"I have a two-minute clip for us this morning from a 1990 movie called 'Goodfellas.' Here's the deal, Henry's girlfriend, Karen, calls him crying. Her neighbor has assaulted her. He tried touching her, but she hit him and told him to stop. Henry drives Karen back home and sees the guy who got violent with her."

"Now hit play."

I let the guys watch the 20 seconds of the clip I just described. Henry gets out of the car and starts walking up the driveway, where the neighbor and two of his buddies are working on his Corvette.

"Pause it."

They all look up at me.

"Henry has to decide how he's going to handle the situation. What do you think he's going to do?"

"Henrys pissed off. He is going to beat him down for touching his girl," Brenden said.

"Hit play again and let's find out," I said.

Henry gets out of his car and puts his pistol in the front waistband. He then starts walking up to the neighbor. As Henry approaches, the neighbor says, "Hey, "f-er," you want something?" Henry doesn't say a word. He quickly removes the pistol, grabs his collar, and hits him in the head repeatedly and violently. The neighbor's two friends don't move a muscle. They just look on in shock and disbelief.

After about 10 blows to the head, Henry tells the now-bloody neighbor, "If you ever touch her again, I swear you'll be dead! He then gets up, walks back to Karen's house, and it's over.

There was silence and a good type of tension in the room. This was the first time I used a movie clip on game day. The guys were locked in and focused on the message.

"What is the take-home I want you guys to get from this?" I asked.

"Karen isn't to be messed with. Henry beat him down," Polk said.

"The neighbor won't ever touch her again," Stefan said.

"Yes, but let's break it down even more. Karen needed action, and Henry took massive action. He doesn't approach the neighbor and say, "Don't do that again." He gets out of his car, doesn't say a word, and starts beating the hell out of him. What would happen in a situation like this most of the time?"

"Henry would threaten the neighbor, and that'd be about it," Mat said.

"Exactly! Most of the time, someone would get out of the car, walk over, and verbally warn him not to do it again. Something like, "If you touch her again, I swear I will kill you. Let's discuss this angle of the scene...how did Henry approach the neighbor?" I asked.

"He didn't waste any time. He quickly got out of the car and started beating him fast," Jerome said.

"Yes! Let's be Henry today. Let's play fast, don't say a word, and just beat the hell out of them. The look on his friends' faces. Do y'all remember how astonished they looked? That's how I want Kiel's fan's faces to look. I want them to say, ""This butt-whipping is so bad I need to look away, but I can't."

"OL, we're going to follow our rules and dominate. Running backs, trust the double-team and hit it tight. Receivers attack the middle of the DB and make a decision at full speed. Chris, lead us. Put your pistol in your belt and lead us to a beating Kiel won't soon forget."

"Today we're going to SWING FIRST and KEEP SWINGING."

33

NO ONE MESSES WITH KAREN

June 4, 2022

About three hours before kickoff, Tracy and I settled into the old wooden bleachers on the visitor's side of Kilia Stadium, which, interestingly enough, was the original home side way back in 1919. We couldn't help but notice how much nicer the current home side was. With 4,000 comfortable, chair-back seats, it was clear that Kilia Stadium had come a long way since its early days.

As a Texan, I found one interesting thing about the field to be the markings. The primary white lines were for soccer, while the football lines were the less noticeable tan ones. It's funny because, in the States, it's usually the opposite.

The Kiel players and coaches were on the field having an abbreviated practice. The defense was aligning to formations, the offense was going through blocking assignments, and the special team's coordinator had a final check to ensure all units had 11 players for the day.

"Is it normal for a team to practice like this before the game?" Tracy asked.

"No, this doesn't usually happen. They're working on getting lined up quite a bit. Fine-tuning is typically done the day before. If they're still making sure of personnel packages and alignment, they're about to hate seeing us play at warp speed."

About an hour before we started warmups, I noticed Berti sitting on a bench on our sideline, so I sat beside him.

"How are you feeling?" I asked.

"I'm ok. To be honest, I'm a little nervous about this one. We haven't lost to Kiel in Kiel before, so something in my gut tells me this could be the day the streak ends."

"Berti, one day in the distant future, I'm sure Kiel will beat us on this field, but I guarantee you it won't be today." It's not that I was 100% sure we'd win, but I knew what Berti needed at that moment. He needed a confidence boost, which we all do at times.

"We'll win the toss and score in less than five plays. I'll even go one step further; I bet our streak of no sacks or punts will remain intact after this game. If they aren't, brats and Radler are on me."

"I don't drink Radler's, sir. They're like liquid candy," Berti said, smiling.

A couple of hours later, it was finally game time. I looked up in the stands and gave Tracy, who was sitting with Buddy and his wife, a wave.

After the public address announcer introduced us, it was time for the Hurricanes to take the field. "Now, let's get ready for yoooooooour Kiiiiiieeeeeelllll Ballllllltic Hurrrrrrricanes!"

The team ran out of their run-through tunnel, and the offensive starters were introduced individually. What happened next is something I've never seen before and, I dare say, won't ever see again. The Hurricanes didn't go to their bench. They went to the opposite end zone and gathered again behind a run-through sign the cheerleaders were holding up.

"What's happening here, Jonas? Why are they looking like they're going to run out again?"

"Wait a moment. It's about to be over. We never understood this when I was at NYer."

"Just like a natural hurricane blowing in, here come your Baltic Hurricanes again!" the Kiel public announcer shouted through the P.A. system (in German).

"Jonas, did we just see a team enter the stadium twice? "What is this all about?"

"A hurricane hits land, then has the eye, then hits again. It's ridiculous, but they take the field at home, and after the visitor is announced, they do it again. We Germans love the stuff before the game as much as the game itself."

We won the coin toss. I happened to see Berti and gave him a thumb's up.

Stefan had a good week of practice and got the nod at right tackle. It would be huge if he could claim this spot so Brenden could play his natural position, left guard next to Yasir.

Our game plan was to test the Kiel secondary. We were going to throw it early and often. Our first drive started at our 20-yard line. Chris completed a 26-yard strike to Polk on our sideline on our first play.

"Hurry! Snap it!" I yelled at the offense.

Jared was now the receiver on our sideline, working against the same corner who just gave up the completion to Polk. Jared planted his outside foot at 10 yards and went deep. Sitting calmly in the pocket, Chris floated the ball up, and Jared hauled it in for a 54-yard touchdown to put us up 7-0 less than a minute into the game for the second week in a row.

I jogged down the sideline to congratulate our guys when Berti, who was all smiles, said loudly, "Who's the genius here? You for installing this offense or me for hiring you?"

"You're the genius, coach! You all the way, brother, you!"

As we met on the bench, I told the offense, "We just swung first! Let's keep on swinging!"

We went 5-wide on our next series, meaning we had no backs, just five wide receivers. One of my favorite aspects of Fast N' Wide is we max protect most of the time, meaning we have our five offensive linemen pass-protecting, tight end, and running back.

Analytically, I classify a sack as a 'disaster'. In the NFL, every sack lowers a team's total scoring by 1.75 points. This is why edge rushers are the second most important position in football. Teams who give up the least amount of sacks in a game win 77% of the time. We still need a backup quarterback, so getting in empty is dicey on many fronts.

After two incompletions, it was 3rd and 10 on our 33-yard line. Chris looked to throw to Louis on his right, but almost as soon as the ball was snapped, we had pressure up the middle. Heiko adjusted his route, knowing we were in scramble mode and all the receiver's jobs were to find open grass and give Chris somewhere to go with the ball.

"Heiko! Heiko!" Jonas says in the headset excitedly as he sees him get lost by the secondary and come wide open. Chris sees him and throws another beautiful deep pass that Heiko hauls in for a 67-yard score. Heiko also nails his second PAT to put us up 14-0 after only five offensive plays.

"Chris, awesome job avoiding the pressure. Yasir, thanks for cleaning up the stunt in [8]A gap," I said to the offense on the sideline.

---

[8] A gap - the space between the center and guard.

"No one messes with Karen, coach! We're going to keep swinging!" Jerome said.

"Offense! Offense!" Jonas shouted into my headset. "They fumbled the kickoff return!"

We had the ball on Kiel's ten-yard line and had a chance to put a massive nail in their coffin in the first quarter. After a holding penalty on 2nd and a goal from the four-yard line, we were now on the 14.

"Jonas?"

"Yes, sir?"

"If I call a pass play again inside the ten-yard line. Please come down here and kick me right in my man-parts. Damn, I'm about to jump off a bridge. We need to run the ball three times in a row and get up three touchdowns."

Karri saved the drive by scoring on the next play. The score was 21-0, and there were still two minutes left in the first quarter. We were going to keep swinging.

Later in the second quarter, we started a drive on our one-yard line. "We're ok, fellas. We'll have the first 99-yard drive in Royals' history."

That's exactly what we did. Chris capped off a ten-play drive with a 19-yard scramble touchdown, further demonstrating his ability to run the ball. The score was now 29-0 after Chris threw a 2-point conversion to Jerome.

The next few minutes of the game brought me back to reality. Kiel went into desperation mode and started passing the ball on every play. It worked for them. They scored on their next two possessions to close the gap to 29-13.

"We have a ball game now! Let's get back to kicking their butts again," I said to the offense.

We worked our 2-minute offense for the first time this season. We were still up 16 points, but all the momentum had swung to Kiel. Their bleachers were full, and their fans were back in it. We quickly had 3rd and 7 with 29 seconds left from the Kiel 41-yard line. Kiel's defensive coordinator brought pressure. Chris stepped up and fired a strike to Polk, who was running a 10-yard in-cut and was wide open. Polk's speed was on full display as he outraced the secondary across the field for six points.

"Yes, sir! We needed that one! Great job stepping up in the pocket again!" I said to Chris as he came off the field.

We needed to make a statement before halftime and get the momentum back on our side. Being up 36-13 put the game back firmly in our control.

The visitor locker room could have been listed as a historical landmark. Although it had been remodeled at some point (maybe 50 years ago), we needed more room to meet, so we gathered outside.

"Everyone sit down over here," Jerome said to the offense. We had a bench that would hold about seven or eight, so the rest of the guys found a spot on the ground.

"Follow Us guys only on the bench," I said.

"I like what we've done in the first half. My fault on the 4th down call that we missed. I'm concerned that they are getting close to sacking Chris. Keep working on our technique and footwork. I want to see five guys, not just swinging, but swinging together when I grade the film."

We cruised in the second half offensively. We were up 50-19 when the fourth quarter began, but Kiel continued to attack with their passing game and hit us for two more scores.

The final score was Royals 57 and the Hurricanes 33.

Chris had another massive stat line: 31 completions for 455 yards and five touchdown passes. Heiko led us in receiving yards with 143 on six receptions. Jared hauled in ten passes for 133 yards and two scores. Polk caught eight balls for 128 yards and one touchdown. Karri was also productive on the ground. He had 79 yards and a touchdown on only 14 carries.

We gained 605 yards for the game and averaged a terrific 9.2 yards per play. We were averaging 48 points per game and 518 yards for the season. The most amazing stat of all. Though, was the fact we still had yet to punt or allow a sack. If a professional or college team achieved this feat in the States, it'd be the lead story on SportsCenter.

"Great job, babe!" Tracy said to me as she hugged me on the sideline.

"Thanks, honey. We're improving for sure. Let's go to the Kiel VIP area and see if we can get a brat and a beer."

"Berti, can I get you something to eat or drink?" I asked him as we made our way to the other side of the stadium, where other Royals' coaches were already partaking.

"Give me ten minutes, and I'll take you up on it. I have to do an interview, but I'll be over there soon. Good job today, coach!"

"Thank you! Good job to you as well!"

Tracy and I showed our VIP guest badges to the Kiel board member and entered the pavilion with covered tables and chairs. It would be an excellent vantage point to watch a game.

"What will you two do next week since we're open and don't have a game?" Buddy asked.

"We are going to the city of love, Paris," I said, grabbing Tracy's hand.

GFL **GAMERECAP**

vs Kiel-Baltic 'Canes

33 (0-2-1) | 57 (3-0)

	ROYALS	'CANES
TOTAL YARDS	605	411
YARDS RUSHING	455	120
YARDS PASSING	150	291
YARDS PER PLAY	9.2	5.6
PUNTS	0	5
PENALTIES	11-91	8-67

RUSHING	ATT.	YARDS	AVG.	TDS
PAJARINEN, K.	12	79	6.6	1

RECEIVING	RECEPTS	YARDS	TDS	LONG
WOLFE, J.	10	133	2	54
POLK, B.	8	128	1	41
BALS, H.	6	143	1	67

PASSING	COMP.	ATT.	YARDS	TDS	INT
HELBIG, C	32	41	455	5	

Kieler Nachrichten

(Excerpts from Kiel Newspaper)

The spectators saw a total of 13 touchdowns at the first home game of the Kiel Baltic Hurricanes this year in the Kilia Stadium. However, the Potsdam Royals scored eight of them. With 33:57, the Kielers had to admit defeat to the leader of the table.

"It was the expected physical game and Potsdam played incredibly fast on offense. We didn't manage to slow Them down, so we had to chase them from the start. Too often we didn't manage to make the decisive plays", summarized head coach Timo Zorn after the game.

34

PARIS TO THE NEW YORK TIMES?

June 6, 2022

We had an incredible time exploring Versailles and admiring the stunning architecture of the Eiffel Tower. The boat tour along the River Seine had breathtaking city views. However, our favorite activity on any trip is always searching for a unique antique to bring home as a forever memento. We found some beautiful pieces on this trip that we will cherish forever.

"That's a stunning piece! It looks like it was originally in a castle," Tracy commented, gesturing towards a beautiful baroque section of wood with gold leaf detailing.

Curious about its history, I asked the vendor at the flea market booth if he could tell us more about it.

The vendor smiled and began to provide a detailed history of the piece. "You're correct; it's from a castle in the 18th century," the owner explained.

"What's your best price?" Tracy, our chief negotiator, asked.

"Well, if you have cash...." the vendor replied with a smile. Tracy began negotiating, and I watched as she skillfully brought the price down to a reasonable amount. We were thrilled to take home a fascinating piece of French history.

"Where do you want to go next?" I asked.

"How about we have a quick meal before returning downtown to catch one of the Hop-On Hop-Off buses? It will be a good way to see some sights and get off our feet," Tracy suggested.

After a long day of sightseeing, we finally arrived at Avenue des Champs-Elysees, the

most famous street for shopping in Paris. The shops and cafes were packed, but we couldn't resist stopping for delicious gelato. As we sipped our drinks and enjoyed the atmosphere, we noticed a couple of street performers on the massive sidewalks. One was dancing to loud music, and the other was making incredible artwork out of sand.

After a few minutes, we continued our stroll through the city, and I said, "How about we find an Italian restaurant on our way back to the hotel? I saw one advertising truffle pasta this morning."

"That sounds great. Maybe we could stop by Zara on the way?" Tracy asked, smiling.

After leaving the store, we watched one of the many street performers and then took a picture with the beautiful Arc de Triomphe as the backdrop. It's incredible to reflect on how much my life has changed in just a few short years; I'm truly grateful for every moment.

We spotted the Italian restaurant after walking a few blocks toward our hotel. We sat down at a small table on the sidewalk and ordered drinks. Suddenly, I felt my phone vibrate in my pocket. I had a WhatsApp message from a U.S. number I didn't recognize.

Randy, this is Charlie Scudder. I'm a freelance writer from North Texas. I've had articles published in the Dallas Morning News, Texas Monthly, and others throughout the state. I've pitched your journey coaching in Germany to the New York Times, and they are interested. What do you think?

(me) Charlie, thank you for your interest! At the moment, I'm in Paris with my fiancé. Upon my return to Potsdam, I'd love to speak with you about the amazing story unfolding here. We've created a players' creed called 50 Strong, an intentional players' culture never before seen in European sports. Only members of the group can invite new players to join. It's incredible to see players from 18 countries supporting each other and forming deep connections. I'm thrilled to share more with you when I return home in a few days.

(Charlie) Excellent! I can't wait to hear more about it. Just let me know when you get back to Potsdam. I've been following your social media post about how your team is making waves in Germany, and it's such a fascinating story. I've never had an article in the New York Times, but I'm confident I could persuade them to print it.

(Me) I'm excited you like the story. Thanks for your patience. I'll get back to you very soon.

I put my phone away, turned to Tracy, and couldn't help but feel excited about the news I was about to share with her. "You won't believe it," I said, trying to sound calm but failing miserably. "A freelance reporter from Texas contacted me. He wants to write an article about me coaching with the Royals. And get this; he's pitching the story to the New York Times!"

"Wow, that's awesome! You've told me people in America would find it fascinating to hear about the differences in football in Europe. I guess this reporter agrees with you."

"Yes, he's seen some of my Twitter and Facebook posts. If this happens, it could open a lot of doors for us. More people will see this article than all my posts, blogs or books combined."

The next couple of days just flew by, and before I knew it, it was time for us to say our goodbyes at the Paris airport. Tracy had a nonstop flight home to Texas while I returned to Berlin. We only had less than a month before our two-week summer break, but the reality of being apart was tough on both of us.

WHERE AM I?

After a two-hour flight, I was back on German soil. "Just use google maps" kept going through my head as I attempted to locate a train that would take me to Potsdam. Getting on the correct train would be the simplest task ever for a European, but for me, not so much. One of the perks of coaching for the Royals was a train pass that worked in Potsdam and the surrounding areas. Berti gave me a physical ticket each month that I kept in my wallet. After getting help from a young person, who I knew would speak decent English, I made my way onto a train that would take me back to Potsdam main station.

"Can I see your ticket, ma'am?" I heard an attendant ask a lady near me. A train conductor came into our car and checked the tickets individually. I prepared for her to ask for my ticket, so I opened my wallet to get my pass. It expired two days ago! Coaches and players had warned me that being asked for a ticket on a train is unusual, but the fine is large if you don't have one. I wasn't sure how I would get out of this when the train began to slow down for a stop at a remote station. The attendant looked at me and stepped towards me when I grabbed my suitcase and backpack and exited. We were in the middle of nowhere, it seemed. There were nothing but trees, a parking lot, and a two-lane road.

The platform had a couple of covered benches, but it was an unmanned station. The only other person at the train stop was an elderly lady on a bench beside mine. I was in a rural area and had no clue what to do next. I used my Waze app to determine I was still over 20 miles from Potsdam.

"Excuse me, ma'am. Do you know how I can purchase a ticket?"

"Kein Englisch" [no English], she said with a heavy German accent.

"Danke schön." I knew it was a long shot she would speak English.

After a few minutes, I pulled my suitcase to the road and looked around. I saw a sign with a bus symbol and an arrow. I headed that way, but after half a mile of not seeing anything, I turned around and headed back to the train stop.

How do I get home? I didn't have Uber installed on my phone [German SIM card]. There was no telling when the next train was coming, but I decided to sit it out. I'd take my chances without a ticket. After around 30 minutes, another train pulled up to the platform. I got on and hoped for the best.

After almost two months in Potsdam without a car, my frustration was getting the best of me. The visit with Tracy had been amazing, but not having a vehicle limited us to where we could go and what I could show her. Getting home from Berlin was kicking my butt at the moment, so I texted Berti, hoping I wouldn't see another attendant.

(me) Remembering to have a mask and using trains to get anywhere has become exhausting. I was told using the train system is no big deal, but for this old, spoiled Texan, it's a big deal. I know y'all have been good to me, but on my way back from Berlin today, I narrowly escaped the 'ticket police' because mine was expired. Is there any way I can get a car?"

(Berti) I understand, coach. I only take a train if I absolutely have to. I will get back to you soon.

Berti sent me this message the following day: *Can you drive a stick shift?*

By lunchtime, Berti, Saul, and I were at a rental car company that was one of the team's sponsors. If I asked for something to make my life easier, the Royals would try and accommodate me. I should've asked for a car sooner.

"Do you have any questions?" the rental car worker asked me.

"No, sir, I'm good to go."

"This is the car Bobby used when driving back and forth before his university semester ended," Berti said.

I was about to be the proud recipient of a Mercedes Benz hatchback. A European model that doesn't exist in the States. I was ecstatic to be behind the wheel again. Back home, I drive a Ford F-150 truck that sits tall, but after not having the independence of a vehicle for two months, this felt like a Lamborghini. Gas is sold by the liter, but it would be roughly $8 a gallon, so there are very few gas guzzlers like full-size pickup trucks on the roads.

"Most Americans can't drive a stick. This makes it easy for us to let you use the same car Bobby had," said Saul.

"I grew up driving a stick, so this won't be a big deal at all," I said with fake confidence because I hadn't driven a manual transmission in nearly 40 years.

This model had no remote start, so I inserted and turned the key. The Benz sputtered as I put it in reverse and tried to work a clutch for the first time. After slowly turning the car around, I pulled forward to the exit, waving at Berti and Saul and putting my blinker on. I released the clutch and pushed the gas pedal. The car sputtered again, lunged forward onto the four-lane road, and died. I was blocking both lanes of incoming traffic. I glanced in my rearview mirror and saw all three guys looking worried. I wondered if they thought this car would be the death of the team's offensive coordinator.

"I'm good! I got this!" I said through the rolled-down window. Several cars were waiting for me to get out of the way. I restarted the car and slowly let go of the clutch again. The Benz jerked forward several times, but eventually, the transmission engaged.

I was on my way.

I wonder if I can turn *right on red* here...I guess we'll find out.

"Brotherhood - Brotherhood was the one thing that kept us all together through both the good times and the hard times. Made some brothers for life on this team."

Divine Buckrham
#2 Safety
Queens, New York
2023 Teams
XFL San Antonio Brahmas
ELF Tirol Raiders

35

THE TWO WORDS

June 18, 2022

The next day, I went to the Berlin Airport to welcome my longtime friend, Eric Luster. I've known Eric for over 20 years, and we had a close working relationship at North Forney. After my retirement, Eric became the head coach, previously serving as our assistant head coach. Among all the people who expressed interest in visiting me in Germany, Eric was the only one, besides Tracy, who followed through and made the trip.

“How are you liking it so far?” Eric asked.

"I'm really enjoying my time with the Royals. They treat me so well here, and it's great to be part of a team again. The best part is that I don't have to work insane hours like I did back in Texas! Plus, the weather is amazing compared to the scorching summers I'm used to."

"That's so good to hear. I was hoping you weren't homesick and wanted to come home."

"The separation has been tough on Tracy and me for sure. I wish she could quit her job and bring Coco for the summer."

“I bet y’all both wish that could happen. I guess there’s no way for her to be here for a few months?” Eric asked.

“No, not and keep her job. She can work remotely from home, but not from Germany.”

"How is the quality of football? It looks pretty good when I watch it on the live stream."

"The guys here can play. They didn't grow up with football, so the game isn't as innate for some, but the passion is there. I respect Europeans for playing American football. It isn't as easy to be on a team as for our kids in the States," I said.

"So, you're saying the game comes to you in America, but in Europe, you have to go to the game."

"That's a great way to put it. This is another reason I'm treating this experience as a laboratory of offense and culture. I've been doing experiments on both for a few months now. The early results have been fascinating."

"In what way?" Eric asked.

"It's hard to explain. You'll have to see for yourself, and then I'll ask you the same question."

Eric agreed to watch our running backs at practice that night. When we arrived, I introduced him to Karri, Heiko and Jonas. "Guys, this is my good friend, Eric Luster. He was our running back coach at North Forney but is now the head coach. He's going to watch practice tonight and give you his thoughts."

"Fist-to-chin, Karri," Eric said to him during a team session. "Tight. Stay tight on the double team. The cutback will be there if you're patient," he added.

During halftime of practice, Karri approached Eric and asked, "What do you think, coach? What can I do better?"

"Coach Jackson mentioned to me your zone path at times isn't tight enough. When you bounce, you're saying to the O-line, "I don't trust you." I saw a couple of times where you hopped outside when you needed to stay patient and have faith in the big boys up front. They might as well take off the white stripes."

"That makes sense, coach. The last team I played on had me running outside a lot, so this is a big change for me, but I'll trust the guys more."

TOUR GUIDE

"Thursday's our off day. Tell me where you want to go, and we'll do it." I said to Eric after practice.

I took Eric to some of the places Tracy and I visited the week before, but playing host with a car was much easier this week.

Wannsee Conference Villa

"If you have the time, I'd love to see the historical sites in Berlin. I taught students about WW2 and the Cold War for years, so seeing that would be great."

On the way to Berlin, at the suggestion of Jens, I took Eric to an estate where the Nazis planned to finish the mass extermination of the Jews. The villa has been converted into a museum commemorating the Wannsee Conference of 1942. High-ranking Nazi officials met here to discuss and coordinate implementing what they called the "Final

Solution of the Jewish Question." This stop was a sobering reminder of Hitler's evil deeds and what he would have done if Germany had won the war.

Our first stop in Berlin was Olympic Stadium, and it was an incredible experience. The 1936 Olympics were held during immense political tension, as Hitler's Third Reich was rising to power and using the games to showcase supposed Aryan superiority. However, the success of American athlete Jesse Owens proved to be a pivotal moment in history. Owens won four gold medals, shattered Hitler's propaganda and demonstrated that people of all races could achieve greatness.

Afterward, we visited prominent landmarks in Berlin, starting with the Brandenburger Gate and the Victory Column. Our final stop in Berlin was "Checkpoint Charlie," renowned as the most famous border crossing between West and East Berlin during the Cold War. It served as a powerful symbol of the divided city and the tensions of that era.

"Thanks for today. I know you have a game to prepare for," Eric said.

"You're welcome, brother. It was fun for me also. What was your biggest lab result from today?"

"It made me realize how big the world is. America's history started in 1776, but today we saw things that have been around for 1,000 years."

On the 30-minute drive back to Potsdam, I asked Eric, "If Berti is ok with it, what do you think about us doing a pregame speech to the team? I've talked to the offense before each game but not the entire team. I bet you and I could come up with something good. We could do half of it in the cafeteria after our pregame meal and the new 50 Strong guys sign the creed. We can finish it in the locker room right before we hit the field."

"I like it. Again, I don't want to step on anyone's toes, but if Berti is good with it, I will enjoy firing up the team."

Game day arrived, and the weather forecast was brutal. The average high temperature for Potsdam in June is 71 degrees, but today temps were expected to be near 100.

"You told me one of the things you love here is the high is usually in the 70s!" Eric said, smiling.

"The weather has been amazing. I've worn a hoodie in June for the first time! I think

you brought the heat with you."

"Didn't you tell me no one in Germany has air conditioning in their homes because they don't need it?" Eric asked as we drove to the stadium.

"That's what I've been told, but if I don't get some sort of A/C in my flat soon, I'll sleep at the office."

As the guys were finishing their lunch, Eric and I went to the front of the room.

As a humble individual, Berti wasn't someone who sought the spotlight. He didn't deliver pregame speeches to the team, but he had no issue with Eric and me bringing some energy before our home game against the Berlin Rebels.

"Gentlemen, may I have your attention," I called out. "Coach Luster, whom most of you have met, and I have the privilege of speaking today. I want to share one of my favorite stories, *The Coward and the Hero*. Former NFL head coach Bill Parcells loved this story and told it to his teams on more than one occasion. It revolves around a middleweight boxing match that took place in 1977 between Cyclone Hart and Vito Antuofermo."

To give you some history of the boxers, Ring Magazine named Cyclone Hart a Top 50 Puncher of all time. He never won a championship belt but fought guys who did. He was a "dude". Vito, on the other hand, was a middle-class boxer who had no shot of ever winning a title. He was a tough guy who loved boxing more than working a real job. According to Parcells, the only good quality of Antuofermo was that he *bled well.* But Parcells also said, "He had other attributes you couldn't see."

"Hart was the heavy favorite to defeat Antuofermo. He knocked him all over the ring early in the fight, but after a few rounds, something was happening. Antuofermo was taking punch after punch. He was absorbing the blows, and Hart was beginning to get discouraged. In the fifth round, Hart began to tire, not physically but mentally. Seizing the moment, Antuofermo attacked and delivered a series of quick blows that knocked Hart down. Although every judge's scorecard had Hart winning handily, Antuofermo won the match with a knockout."

"Now, pretend Coach Luster is Hart, and I'm Antuofermo in our locker rooms post-fight. We're actually in the same room. There's only a thin shower curtain-type material separating us, so there isn't any real privacy."

Coach Luster and I were sitting at two different tables. He had his head down in dejection. I sat down and said, "If Hart had punched me one more time, I would've quit. He was killing me with those left hooks. I don't think I've ever been hit that hard in all my life. In the third round, I thought, "I can't take much more". In the fourth round, I said to myself, "If he hits me this hard again, I'm quitting". "Then, in the fifth round, he stops hitting me."

At this point, Eric sinks his head even more. "He's hearing me say all of this to my trainer. He starts to weep quietly at first, but it becomes louder and louder," as I point at Eric.

"Why is Hart crying?" I ask but don't wait for an answer. "Because he realizes Antuofermo had felt the same way he had and worse. It sinks in that he was one punch away from victory, but he gave in to his pain, and his opponent didn't."

Now Eric stands up and begins to speak loudly, "Hart made the mistake of listening to his heart. You see, your heart has an ear in the middle of it. It doesn't have a tongue, teeth, or lips. Your heart can't speak to you."

Eric now holds up a large piece of paper with the word HEART written on it. He folds both the H and the T to the back, leaving only "EAR" to be seen. "Remember, in the middle of your heart is an ear. As long as your heart beats, it cannot speak but can listen. Your heart needs to hear two words from you when things get tough."

The entire team was locked into every word Eric was saying.

"Right before we take the field today, I will give you those two words."

"Let's go blitzkrieg some Rebels today!" I said enthusiastically dismissing the team.

"That was awesome, Coach Luster," Mat said as we exited the cafeteria.

"Great job, coach. Thanks for speaking with us today," Leo also said to Eric.

MELTING IN THE SHADE

Eric and I drove to the stadium when he asked me, "Did you guys plan anything to help deal with the heat?"

"No, we're just wearing all black today. That may intimidate the Rebels," I said, smiling. "Seriously, I think Taka and his crew will have ice towels. I will wear my Royals hoodie in warmups to show the guys I'm tougher than the heat. I hope I am." It was extra hot, even for a Texan who's coached in August for over 30 years. I don't know if the sun is more intense in Germany than in Texas, but it was a scorching 100 degrees.

I don't know if the heat played a factor, but in our first wave of warmups, tensions were escalating and getting chippy on the field.

"Hey Saul, are you ever going to play again or just run your mouth from the sideline like you normally do?" Ritchie Pollard, a Rebel receiver, asked Saul.

"Why are you worried about me, 5? Are you going to play the whole game today or fake an injury like last year?" Saul replied.

"You'll see what I'm going to do today, you little bitch."

"Oh, I'm a bitch, am I? That's what we called you in film study this week," Saul replied.

"F___ you little man. You'll see the back of my jersey as I run by your ass on the sideline today. You only think it's hot now. That scoreboard will burn up like I'm going to burn that weak-ass secondary."

"We'll see 5, we'll see."

Next, the Rebel's best defensive player, Rory Johnson, a 34-year-old American who played linebacker at Ole Miss, gets in on the craziness.

"Why you always running your skinny ass mouth, Saul? Every time we play, you start this crap. Damn, I swear you're the weakest guy out here. Just shut the f___ up and get back over to your sideline. You only talk because you don't have to see me on the field. Why don't you put on some pads so I can whip your ass and not get arrested?"

"Shut the f___ up, Rory. You're showing your intelligence now. Nobody wants to hear your crap," Saul said.

By now, the two were almost nose-to-nose. If either of them threw a punch, we'd have a 30-person brawl and a frenzy of bodies going at each other.

"I'll show you more than my intelligence. You start this s___ every time we play. If you have it in you, meet me after the game so we can settle this. I swear, I will beat your little bitch ass into the ground," Rory said.

"I'll see you after the game then, Rory. I'll be ready, trust me."

"Let's just play ball, guys," Pollard said to Rory as he pulled him back.

"C'mon, coach. This isn't worth the aggravation. We will take care of 44 after kickoff for you," Jerome said, pulling Saul away as well.

"Be thankful they saved your sorry ass, Saul! That mouth of yours is going to go get your ass kicked!" Rory said, walking away.

"What the heck just happened? Does this stuff go on before every game?" Eric asked me.

"No, this is the first time we have had any trash-talking. I'm not sure why Saul fed the fire on the stupidity of the situation."

"Me either. We wouldn't see this type of "BS" in the States. It dishonors the game and takes away from what it's supposed to be about. The word professional means something to me, but this wasn't professional at all."

"I agree. I'm learning that some things are normal, and some are a *new normal* of crazy. I have someone I want to introduce you to. You won't believe this, but so far, the officials here actually like me," I said.

"Really? Are you sure about that? This is Germany, not never-never land," Eric said jokingly.

"Mats, how are you today, sir?" I said.

"Coach Jackson! It's good to see you again. Have you gone completely mad, sir?" Mats said, pointing at my sweatshirt.

"I've been asked that on many occasions, but if you're talking about this hoodie, it's just my attempt at a mind game to convince our guys it's not too hot. Our running back from Finland told me this won't be the hottest game he's ever played in but the hottest day he has ever experienced, period."

"Mats, meet my buddy from Texas, Eric Luster. Eric and I coached together, and he took over as the head coach when I retired."

"Nice to meet you, Eric. Welcome to Germany," Mats said, shaking Eric's hand. The officials call Randy "Fast Football Randy," by the way. We haven't ever officiated the game at this speed before. Does your team play this fast in Texas?"

"We do. We believe in trying to kill the officials just like Randy does," Eric said, smiling.

"We're glad you made it to Potsdam. I hope your stay here is excellent."

"Thanks, it's been great here other than it's hotter than Texas."

"Eric and I are about to pump up the team, Mats. Good luck to y'all today," I said as we headed for our locker room.

THE LOCKER ROOM

"Quiet down, guys. Let's lock in right now," Buddy said to the team as Eric and I entered the locker room.

They quickly found a place to sit and were focused. Everyone was making eye contact when I said, "The heat today will make one team be Cyclone Hart and the other Vito Antuofermo. Keep going at them play after play today. We'll use the heat to our advantage today. When you get tired, think about the two words Coach Luster is about to share with you.

Eric stood on a box in the middle of the room and spoke with as much passion and enthusiasm as I'd ever heard from him.

"Does your heart have teeth?" Eric asked.

"No!"

"Does your heart have lips?"

"No!"

"Does your heart have a mouth at all?

"No!"

"My coach always told us we only needed two words to say to our hearts. No matter how bad things got or how tired we got. It didn't matter if we were ahead or behind. He said you don't need to tell yourself anything but these two words…

"Let's Go!!'

"Today, when you are hotter than ever on a football field, tell yourself…

"Let's Go!"

"Today, when you are on the sideline and see your brothers tired and needing some encouragement, you know what to say…"

"Let's Go!"

"Today, when you feel like you can't go hard anymore because you are so exhausted, tell yourself the same thing Antuofermo said to himself...

"Let's Go!"

"Let's leave this locker room right now screaming "Let's Go" where they can hear us!"

Eric was in full motivational mode now. He was fired up, and so were the Royals. Eric took it up another notch as the team entered the hallway leading to the field.

"Two words!" Eric yelled.

"Let's Go!" the team yelled back.

"Two words!" Eric yelled again.

"Let's Go!" even louder this time.

"Two words!"

"Let's Go!"

Eric continued to hype up the team by continuing the chant alongside them as they crossed the street and made their way to the run-through tunnel.

"Two words!"

"Let's Go!"

36

WE'RE JUST GETTING STARTED

June 18, 2022

"Thanks for allowing me to be a captain today, coach. It means a lot," Mat said.

"You're welcome, my friend. My rule is, if you played for the team last year, you get to look them in the eye at the coin toss!" I said, slapping Mat and Tim on the back; he also is a former Rebel.

"Congrats on starting today at center, Bobby. Play your butt off, and keep the spot, please. I need you to be the starter," I said as we waited on the sideline.

Mats flipped the coin, gestured it was our decision, and we took the ball. If I thought the shenanigans before the game were crazy, I hadn't seen anything yet.

After a holding call on the kickoff return, we started on our 10-yard line.

"We're fine, guys. We'll go 90 yards on this first drive. Remember, [9]flame is on “two”. Hold your water," I reminded the starters on the sideline.

The Rebel's defensive line didn't [10]hold their water and jumped into the [11]neutral zone. Bobby wisely snapped the ball, and we had a free play. When this happens, all our receivers go deep, and Chris takes a shot down the field. Since the defense is offside, there’s no risk, so offenses usually throw it deep.

"Great catch, Way to hang on the ball, Polk!" I yelled as he caught the 31-yard pass on our sideline and was immediately hit hard by a Rebels' safety.

"Let's go! Hurry, hurry!" I yelled as I signed in our inside zone play.

Bobby and Brenden, starting again at left guard, double-teamed the Rebels' defensive tackle, and Karri broke through to the secondary. The Rebels' safety, who just made the tackle on Polk, missed on Karri.

Karri cut back to his right and broke down the sideline for the 59-yard touchdown. Polk

---

[9] Flame - pass protection by the offensive line.

[10] Hold their water - this is a term used in the Southern U.S. for “not jumping offsides.”

[11] Neutral zone - the area between the ball and the offensive line.

made the key block on the corner to allow the score.

We were up 7-0 with less than a minute gone for the third game in a row.

"Polk made a big block, coach! He put the corner on skates!" Jonas shouted into the headset.

#3 Brandon Polk #20 Karri Pajarinen

"Did you see that block, coach?! Can I get that white stripe now?" Polk said with all smiles as he came off the field.

"You're dang right you can! Love it! You got hammered on the first play, then blocked your butt off the second play!"

The Rebels were very average on defense but, like us, had weapons everywhere on offense. They marched 79 yards on their first drive to tie the score at 7-7.

Two plays later, we went 4-wide, and Chris threw a perfect 60-yard touchdown to Polk to put us back in front. We faked the PAT for two points to go up 15-7.

After forcing a Rebels' punt, we were back in business on our 25-yard line.

We drove to the Rebels' 20-yard line when I yelled, "Orange Cookies! Orange Cookies! Mat had brought me some amazing orange and chocolate cookies from Poland a few times, so his gadget was aptly named. On the snap, Chris half-rolled right and threw a short pass to Mat, who aligned at left tackle in a trick formation up the seam. The safety barely clipped his ankles for a 12-yard gain. We now had first and goal at the eight-yard line.

On the next play, Karri goes untouched for the score on our inside zone to put us up 22-7. "That's trusting the double team! You look like you believe in the white stripe guys!" Eric said, high-fiving Karri as he came off the field.

"How does Karri look to you?" Jonas asked me.

"What do you mean? He looks fine."

"Before the game, the heat was kicking his butt."

"What do you guys think? Are they making any adjustments up front?" I asked the offensive line as we met on the sideline.

"Nah, coach, those blokes are just trying to get air. They are already too tired to rush hard," Brenden said.

The Rebels' offense only needed three plays; the last was a 59-yard touchdown pass to close the gap to 22-13 early in the second quarter.

#15 Jared Wolfe

On our next possession, Chris, throwing the ball better than I had seen anyone before, hit Jared in perfect stride for a 49-yard touchdown pass.

"We may get that 50 at half this week," Saul said.

"I hope so. Their QB and receivers are so good we might need 60."

I should have knocked on wood or something because Berlin's next possession lasted all of one play. A 73-yard touchdown pass to Pollard, who high-stepped into the endzone while looking at our sideline, made it 29-21.

"How you like that, Saul? How you like that, bitch?" Pollard yelled to our sideline after scoring.

Berti doesn't ask my opinion about the defense, so I don't say much, but I couldn't help myself now. I walked over and said, "We will score 75 today. Let's make them beat us by running the ball. They can't score enough on the ground."

"Yes, our safety was supposed to be over there, but he blew the coverage, dammit!" Berti responded, ultra-frustrated.

On our next drive, it finally happened. After 218 plays to open the 2022 season, we had three incomplete passes in a row and were forced to punt. Almost as miraculously as the streak, Saul seemed irritated about it. "What the hell happened there?" Saul asked me in a tone I hadn't previously heard from him.

"We dropped a screen pass on second down, and their safety made a play on third down. It's going to happen occasionally," I snapped back, irritated.

Our defense was not handling the heat any better than Berlin's was. This time, the Rebels gashed us with the run and pass and tied the score 29-29 after a 7-play 80-yard drive.

"We can only control ourselves. We knew we would eventually punt this season, so let's focus on what's in front of us, " I told the offense under a makeshift canopy to keep the sun off us. "Ludi, you're the center this next series. I was rotating guys as much as possible to keep us fresh. Max, you go back to right guard."

"Karri, are you ok? I can put Heiko at running back if you need a rest."

"I'm good, coach."

"Alright, let me know. You told me everyone in Finland has a sauna at their house. Just think, we have one here for everyone to enjoy," I said, patting him on the butt.

I had decided to keep my hoodie on for the game and felt how Karri looked, but I'd committed and couldn't take it off now. Seven minutes were left in the second quarter, and we needed to stop the bleeding on this possession. "Curse me in German if we go more than two plays in a row without handing the ball to Karri, Jonas. Scratch that, do it in English so I can understand."

Karri capped off a 75-yard drive with a 29-yard touchdown run. We went for two again on the PAT and were up 37-29.

"Yes! Great job, Karri," Eric said to him as he came off the field...limping. Once on the sideline, Karri went to the ground with severe leg cramps.

"Damn, we don't need this. We will be in trouble without Karri," I said to Eric and Jonas.

"Heiko can do it, coach. They're so gassed; his physical running style will be tough on them," Jonas said.

Our defense forced a Rebel punt, and we had the ball on our 45-yard line.

#3 Brandon Polk

On 3rd and 10, Chris hit Jared in stride with a 15-yard pass in the middle of the field. He outraced the Rebels to the endzone for a 55-yard touchdown. "Great route, Jared! You think we should call that play again?" I asked him as he came off the field after holding for the extra point, which Heiko made to give us a cushion of 44-29 with four minutes left to go in the half.

"Hell, yes, coach! They can't cover any of us."

"Four minutes gives them plenty of time to score with their passing attack," Jonas said.

"I know, we might need to start working Jared at some corner in some situations. Berti and Dave (our DB coach) are coaching their butts off, but we're leaking oil big-time."

Instead, our defense came up big and forced the Rebels to punt from their 27-yard line. The heat was even getting to their punter because the ball came off the side of his foot for a zero-yard shank. There were 90 seconds left in the half.

"We have all three timeouts left, coach," Berti said to me as our offense jogged onto the field.

"We aren't going to need them. We are going to score right here on *Pork Knuckle* to Heiko." Pork Knuckle is a flea-flicker where Heiko lines up at running back, and the ball eventually gets back to him up the sideline. Although the corner played it well, Heiko slyly 'shoved him by' to create space to make the catch.

"It wasn't pretty, but it worked!" I said to Berti as we high-fived.

"We're just getting started! We're just getting started!" I yelled at the offense on the field and the guys on the sideline.

"WE'RE JUST GETTING STARTED!"

"Good call, brother," Eric said to me as I got a drink of water at the back of our bench area.

#75 Brenden Oswin #89 Jerome Valbon
Official: Mats Schweiger

"Thanks, 50-29 feels better. Maybe they will soon get tired of the heat and say, Uncle."

They didn't say uncle or anything similar. With a minute left, the Rebels' quarterback, Darryl Isom, went back to work on our secondary. He completed a 15-yard pass on their sideline to stop the clock at their 40-yard line. On the next play, our friend Pollard flew by our secondary on a go route for a 60-yard touchdown to close the gap to 50-35 at halftime.

"Lord have mercy! You've got to be kidding me! I haven't seen so many deep passes completed in all my life," I said to Eric and Jonas as I removed my headset.

We gathered in our usual spot outside the locker room.

"Does anyone know the status of Karri?" I asked.

37

A NEW RECORD?

Second Half

"It doesn't look good for his return. He's still cramping. Heiko will get it done. " Jonas replied.

"This is a heavyweight fight, just like we said it would be. We're going to keep swinging! We have a decision to make. Do we eat up the clock and keep their offense off the field, or do you guys want to continue to attack?" I said to the offense.

"Attack always, coach!" Jerome said.

"The official told me to tell you as we were coming off the field he hopes we weren't "just getting started". They're worn out as well!" Saul told the offense, laughing.

"Ha! I love it! Let's see if we can make the big ref on our sideline cramp," I said.

"Run the ball behind me. They all suck over there. We can attack and run the ball at the same time," Yasir said and had an excellent point.

"We always talk about this. The most important part of the game is the [12]middle eight. We won the last four minutes big-time. Our defense is about to stop them. Let's go win these four minutes."

"So much for the middle eight," Brenden said, standing next to me on the sideline as #81 raced past us, heading to the endzone. The Rebels counter-punched with a haymaker on the kickoff return with an 85-yard touchdown.

"You have got to be kidding me! Dammit!" I said in frustration in the headset.

"We're good, coach. Run the ball with Heiko behind Brenden and Yasir," Jonas replied.

After Polk made a big 3rd down catch to keep the drive alive, Heiko ran over a defender at the goal line for a 17-yard touchdown run. We were back up 57-43

Our defense forced a stop on the next possession. We drove down the field again, this

---

[12] Middle Eight - the last four minutes of the first half and the first four minutes of the second half.

time a 10-play drive, but after a holding penalty, we were forced to kick a 37-yard field goal to put the score at 60-43.

"There's lots of time left. Let's score 90, coach," Chris said to me.

“How’s that hoodie feeling, coach?” Polk asked me as we gathered under the canopy on the sideline.

#81 Mat Dubicki

“Whew! I only look hot, but I’m doing great! In fact, I wish I had a Polish soccer scarf to put around my neck also!” I said, smiling at Mat. Chris just mentioned he wants to get 90 today. I won’t remove this hoodie until we score 90 or Rory (Berlin’s #44) passes out!”

We were only halfway through the third quarter when Berlin's running back broke free for a 35-yard touchdown. This brought the score to 60-49.

Our next possession ended with another score. This time it was Polk's turn to find the endzone. He set the corner up with a small fake to the inside, then faded back to the corner of the endzone. Chris laid the ball in just in time before the safety could get over to help.

"Touchdown! Good call and an even better throw!" Jonas yelled.

"Great job, fellas," I said to Chris and Polk as they came off the field. "We're just getting started, Mats!" I yelled, smiling as he drank some water from our trainers.

#8 Chris Helbig

We faked the extra point, but Heiko was stopped short. The fourth quarter began with us up 66-49. The Rebels threw another counterpunch. They went 75 yards in just four plays to keep the game in question at 66-56.

"I swear I was 54 years old when this started, but I'm 64 now. This is the craziest game I've ever seen, not just coached in," I said to Eric as I drank some water and wished I wasn't still wearing my hoodie.

"They are so freakin’ done, coach. Let's run it at them and make them like it," Bobby said on the bench.

“Rory isn’t running his mouth anymore. I predict he is about to fake an injury to get out of the game,” Yasir added.

"I agree. My heart can't take much more of this. We're going to ride your back, Heiko. Chris, be ready for me to call QB run if we need you," I said.

We finished the fourth quarter with two more scores, a 26-yard touchdown pass to Polk on third down, and an 18-yard run by Heiko to ice it finally.

The final score was 81-56.

After the game, Buddy approached me and said, "We got your 80 today, coach! It just wasn't the number of plays, but points!"

"Yes, sir! And we're just getting started!"

81 is the second-highest score in GFL history. Our stats were like *Madden's* video game numbers. We had 783 yards as a team, the most in league history. The Rebel's amassed 618, so we combined for an amazing 1,401 yards.

Chris completed 25 passes for 532 yards passing and six touchdowns. Both of our 'A' receivers had over 200 yards receiving each. Jared had 13 catches for 278 yards and two scores, and Polk hauled eight receptions for 208 yards and three touchdowns. On the ground, Karri finished with 155 yards on 15 carries and three scores in only a quarter and a half. Heiko had 90 yards and two touchdowns in the second half.

"Offense, you picked us up today," Berti said to the team in a reserved tone. He was understandably reeling from yards and points given up in the last two games as the defensive coordinator. "We're going to figure out our issues in the secondary. We must play better, and we will. We have a week off to adjust, but we tip our cap to you on offense for now. Good job."

"We owed you defense! You guys saved our butts vs Dresden in week 1. We're even now!" I said to the team.

After the game, Eric and I sat with our food and Radler at a large table in the VIP area where fans, Royals board members, and players gather post-game.

"We need Coach Luster to stay here full-time after scoring 81 today," Buddy said as he sat down.

"I agree, coach. You must have brought us some luck today," Taka added.

"Not that we want you to go, but when are you headed back home, coach?" Jens asked.

"I'm going back tomorrow afternoon. We have a clay-shooting competition I have to get home for on Tuesday," Eric said.

This comment made everyone's eyes get big at the table except for Buddy and me. Jerome, who'd just sat down, said, "You have guns, coach?"

"Oh yea. I have a few. Do any of you guys own guns?" Eric asked.

"Ha! No, sir. I've never owned a gun. In fact, I've never even held a gun before," Jerome said.

"Really? I knew guns were uncommon in Europe, but I didn't realize it was rare to see one," I said.

"They aren't just uncommon, but they barely exist. I'd be willing to bet most of the guys on the team haven't ever seen a gun before," Jerome said.

"Coach, you're in gun-free Europe! There's a little bit of hunting here, but nothing like in the States and Texas," Buddy said.

"Did you hunt in Texas before you moved here?" Eric asked Buddy.

"I did. Growing up, my family had a deer lease near Breckenridge. I had a Winchester .270 my dad gave me for Christmas. I hated to sell it when I left."

"Do you own many guns, coach???" Jens asked.

"Yes, I have 21 pistols and rifles combined," Eric said, smiling, knowing he had just astounded everyone at the table.

"What?!?! 21 guns? Why would you need 21 guns?" Jens said, astonished, almost falling from his chair.

"I almost just choked on my brat, coach. I'm the trainer, so I'm not sure anyone here could save me," Taka said.

Eric, Buddy, and I started laughing.

"Are you messing with us, coach? Do you have 21 guns at your house?" Jerome asked, looking at Eric was amazement.

"I do. I need that many because all of my kids hunt as well."

"Your children shoot guns?" Jens asked again with shock in his voice.

"My whole family loves guns. In fact, I have a picture here of my 6-year-old daughter, Nala, holding a rifle."

Eric found the pic on his phone. Sure enough, his beautiful little princess held a rifle with a scope attached.

"Oh my gosh! This is incredible! Next, you will tell me you voted for Trump!" Jens said, smiling at Eric.

"Well, I do own a MAGA hat."

Later that night, Eric and I went to an outdoor restaurant to escape the heat in my flat.

I received a text from Berti that read, *I hate to have bad news when you and Eric are probably still celebrating, but we have a problem...*

GFL **GAMERECAP**

vs Berlin Rebels

81 (4-0) | 56 (0-2-1)

	ROYALS	REBELS
TOTAL YARDS	783	618
YARDS RUSHING	251	251
YARDS PASSING	532	367
YARDS PER PLAY	10.9	10.7
PUNTS	1	3
PENALTIES	3-40	5-22

RUSHING	ATT.	YARDS	AVG.	TDS
PAJARINEN, K.	15	155	10.3	3
BALS, H.	12	90	7.5	2

RECEIVING	RECEPTS	YARDS	TDS	LONG
WOLFE, J.	13	278	2	54
POLK, B.	8	204	1	41

PASSING	COMP.	ATT.	YARDS	TDS	INT
HELBIG, C	31	42	455	5	

#56 Ludi Rötzscher #77 Stefan Stefansson #75 Brenden Oswin
#89 Jerome Valbon #8 Chris Helbig

Markish Allegmeine

(Excerpts from Brandenburger General)

Potsdam Royals and Berlin Rebels just miss a record of points

At the end of a memorable football afternoon, Michael Vogt's strength was gone. "May I sit down first?" he asked politely in view of the approaching interview. The head coach of the Potsdam Royals didn't work for hours like his players on the field in the Luftschiffhafen stadium on Saturday, but the events also affected him on the sidelines. In addition to the heat, the history of the game was to blame. "I've never experienced anything like this myself," said Vogt in disbelief.

The Potsdam Royals and the Berlin Rebels fought an absolute heat and offense battle in week 5 of the GFL season 2022. At a "cuddly" 36 degrees (98 degrees Fahrenheit) and bright sunshine, both teams competed in the Berlin Brandenburg Derby in the Luftschiffhafen stadium.

It was the second game with the most points in the history of the German Football League (GFL). The record was only missed by six points, in which the Stuttgart Scorpions and Saarland Hurricanes had even come up with a total of 143 points in their duel (83:60) in 2005. "We won today - that's the most important thing," said Ruben de Ruyter. The Belgian defender added after the fourth win in the fourth game of the season: "81 own points are crazy, but 56 for the opponent is far too many - that's crap that we have to work on."

"Our defense was nothing today"

One of the 1125 spectators on Saturday presented a suitable motto for the match day. "We not only had to deal with a physically strong opponent, but also with the weather. It was extremely hard," said de Ruyter of the ordeal in the lush football outfit under the blazing sun. Does the weather make it harder to defend than to start the offensive? "You can see it that way if you want to talk it up and make it easy," replied Vogt. "But we have to be honest: Our defense was nothing today. The excuse that some people were absent or that it was so warm doesn't count either. Sometimes the communication wasn't right – we played something different on both sides of the field. Those are stupid mistakes."

In the few moments remaining before the half-time break, the royals even got into the end zone twice, but the rebels also once. Totally wild. And because the guests managed the feat of turning the kickoff of the second half directly into a touchdown, it was tight again at 50:43 from a home perspective. "We made it unnecessarily exciting," said Vogt.

But you can rely on **the offensive around US quarterback Chris Helbig.** "We've been steadfast in that area so far this season," said the coach. Heiko Bals contributed 29 points, he scored two touchdowns per run, one after a pass, and he scored a total of eight additional points after breaking through the end zones. Karri Pajarinen had three touchdowns, Brandon Polk three and Jared Wolfe two. With successful two-point increases, Helbig and Mateusz Dubicki also joined the sprawling statistics.

With 81 points in a game, the Royals achieved the sixth-highest point total by a team in GFL history.

GFL RECORD!
Just missed the points record but broke another GFL record! The 783 yards total offense the @PotsdamRoyals are a new record (previously 2013 @unicornsfootbll 741 yards). Congratulations!

38

WHAM!

July 2, 2022

(Berti) I have repeatedly asked the board to pay for a backup quarterback. We understand your frustration about not having one. Saul and I know our offense is exceptional. Everyone is so happy today, so it'd be the perfect time to ask again. Most teams don't pay for a backup here; our board wants to wait.

After reading this, I looked at Eric and said, "I know you're tired of me saying *everything's good and bad*, but my gosh, there are some frustrating things about coaching in Germany. If Helbig gets injured, you may look up and see me at the North Forney fieldhouse."

DRESDEN 2.0

After our open date, the offense was back in the office on Monday, preparing for our huge rematch in Dresden.

"Thanks for the scouting reports, guys. I'm concerned with how we graded some of their players. Since I only implemented this in game #2, we can't cross-check how you would have evaluated them the first time. Am I wrong in thinking the Monarchs are the best defense we will see in the regular season?"

"They're good as a unit. They've used the same scheme for several years, so they don't make mistakes. I think #8 sucks, so I had to say he sucks," Yasir said.

"I think their secondary is solid. The best player might be the Irish dude, #15," Chris said.

"As long as we are respecting them. They held us to 24 points last time, and I bet that will be our season low," I warned.

"Jerome, you're the man of the hour today. I still have night sweats about our five trips to the red zone without scoring against Dresden the first time. No pressure, but please give us the best goal line scouting report ever."

Jerome stood up and came to the front of the room.

"Oookkkk...I felt good about what Mat and I came up with, but I'm a little nervous after this," Jerome said jokingly. "Seriously, you don't have to worry about Mat and me taking them lightly in the red zone."

"We all know our offense is leading the league in scoring, yards, and, most importantly, plays per game. But, in week one, we crapped our pants in the red zone against Dresden, and it almost cost us. Mat and I always thoroughly prepare our report, but we worked even harder this week."

"We appreciate you guys. Thank you! I want to stay for the entire season and not be shipped back home," I told Jerome in the room and Mat, who joined us via ZOOM.

"No problem, coach. If you could know when it's 4th down, that would help a bunch, though," Mat said, laughing.

"Jokes, the man has jokes!" Polk said.

"I own it! I agree 100%! No guarantees, but I'll do my best," I said.

"Sorry for taking the shot, coach. I couldn't resist being in Poland and all," Mat said.

Jerome was drawing on the whiteboard during the back-and-forth banter.

"Dresden is the best defense we have faced this year, including near the goal line. #99 and #95 are strong enough to clog the middle, and their 'A' inside backer, #23, hurt us, filling the gaps. Coach, if you can start the Qwikcut playlist we created, please," Jerome said.

I hit play. The video was us on the three-yard line vs the Monarchs in game one. Mat said, "They'll dare us to throw the ball inside the five-yard line like most people. They do a great job of walking their strong safety, #38, down as a fourth linebacker away from the tight end. No one they've played has accounted for him, and we didn't last time. Jerome and I charted who makes tackles for them inside the five, and #38 is their leading tackler. No one ever blocks him."

The next day, Bobby approached me before practice and said, "If you don't mind, I have a play I'd like to show you."

"Of course," I responded, thinking I would politely tell him, "Thanks but no thanks" afterward.

Bobby pulls out his phone and finds a video of the Kansas Chiefs using their tight end, Travis Kelce, "trapping" or whamming the opponents' nose guard. Kelce aligns to the right, the center avoids the nose guard, and Kelce blindside blocks him violently.

"Valbon would be perfect for this play. I know you joke with me about being 35, but I can dip my shoulder and get to the linebacker. What do you think?"

"I think it's beautiful. If I weren't engaged and afraid, Tracy would find out; I'd kiss you on the lips."

Within a few weeks, my perception of Bobby changed significantly. Initially questioning whether he truly cared, I fully embraced his enthusiasm and said, "Yes, let's run this play!"

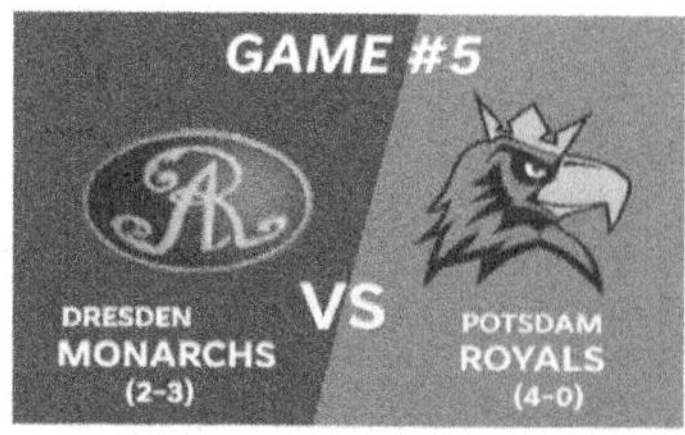

We loaded the bus early Saturday morning for the two-and-half-hour trip to Dresden. Their normal stadium was being renovated, so we'd play at their practice facility.

"Wait till you see their complex. It's very nice," Saul said to me as we arrived. "The Monarchs own this, so they are the only ones who use the locker rooms and this weight room."

We walked around, and although the locker rooms and the weight room were OK, neither compared to what a large or even medium-sized high school in Texas would have. I did have an appreciation for the hard work it took the Monarchs to raise the money for their own 'space.' Functional and not very large is what came to my mind, but I was jealous of both. The Royals don't have either, much less a practice field.

"How many of the 14 teams in the GFL own a facility like this?" I asked Saul.

"Three. New Yorker, Schwäbisch Hall, and Dresden. The only three teams that also win championships."

Before we took the field for warmups, I spoke with the offense outside our locker room.

"We know today will be a challenge. Dresden is much better than anyone we have faced on defense, and they've seen us before. The first item of business will be to see what their adjustment is to the corner away from #4. We've talked a lot about the red zone this week. I'm excited to see us score 50 today! While destroying the Rebels' defense was fun, I didn't *Knock on the Door* to pick on teams that weren't very good, and neither did you. You knocked on the door to test your mettle as a player! I'm 8,500 kilometers from home to test my mettle!"

"We're going to find out today if we're for real. We're getting a lot of publicity for averaging 48 points and having every skill player either leading the league or near the top. But today is the day the real football people will know if we're legitimate contenders."

"I showed you a clip of Achilles earlier in training camp saying to the young boy who was scared of the giant. What did Achilles say to him?"

39

"WE KNEW WHAT YOU WERE DOING"

July 2, 2022

"No one will remember your name," Jared responded.

"Exactly! No one is going to remember us beating Kiel or the Rebels. We all *Knocked On The Door* to help the Royals create a legacy! We'll be tested today!"

"Today's game, like all of them, will be determined by three or four plays. Including the kicking game, the ball will be snapped 175 times or more today. The magic of football is that only three or four will determine the winner and loser, and we don't know which three or four plays it'll be! We must play with fanatical effort on every play today! You might be the guy who makes one of the three or four critical plays work for us!"

Like we do every chance we can, we started by taking the ball.

On the drive's fourth play, it was time to see if Bobby's wham play would work.

"Benz, Wham," I told Jonas in the headset and signaled to the offense.

"Whack!" You hear the sound of the collision on the sideline as Jerome blocked the defensive tackle, who had no clue what was coming after Bobby immediately released to the linebacker. Starting at right guard, Max blocked his linebacker, and Karri burst through the big hole for a 16-yard gain.

"That was nice!" Jonas yelled into the headset.

"Dang sure was. Getting help on #23 was big there."

Four plays later, it was 2nd down and goal at the two-yard line.

Chris faked to Karri, followed Max, our pulling guard, and got into the endzone to put us up 7-0 after the successful kick.

Berti and the defensive staff made a few changes to simplify our scheme. Our defense performed better in practice this week and was ready to prove themselves today.

Our defense started well, forcing a Monarch "3 and out." We started at our 27-yard line.

Dresden blitzed off the edge, and Chris threw the check down to Polk on a quick slant. Polk, possibly the fastest player in the league, made one guy miss and then went up the Monarch sideline for a 67-yard touchdown. We faked the extra point, but Dresden held us out, so the score was 13-0 still in the first quarter.

The Monarchs put together a seven-play drive capped off by a 16-yard touchdown pass early in the second quarter. The score was now 13-7.

Bobby's 'Wham' play was still working very well. I called it three times on our next possession. We were marching down the field again and had the ball on the eight-yard with a 1st and goal. After a one-yard Karri run and two incompletions, Heiko booted the 25-yard field goal to increase our lead to 16-7.

On Dresden's next possession, their running back made an impressive 48-yard touchdown run through the middle. That brought the score to 16-14 with only a few minutes remaining in the first half. After being up early, 13-0, we were in a dogfight with the defending champs.

"The middle eight, fellas!" I yelled as I walked up and down the sideline.

"We have lots of time. Let's do this," Chris said to the offensive huddle.

After a first down, Karri gashed them on second down for 18 yards, and we had the ball on the Monarch 30-yard line.

"Hippo! Hippo!" I yelled to the guys on the field and our sideline.

Chris received the snap from Bobby while Jared, in motion, went behind Chris for a backward handoff. After securing the ball, Jared took several steps forward, planted his feet, and threw a pass back to his left. Chris was wide open after drifting casually outside following the handoff. The only Monarch defender nearby was their pesky American corner. But Yasir knocked him off balance with just one hand, allowing Chris to sprint down the sideline for an easy score.

We had a much-needed touchdown to give us a nine-point margin at the half with a 23-14 score.

"Great job selling it, Jared! You're going to be the highest-rated QB in the league!" I said.

"Good call, coach! Honestly, I was not too fond of the gadget call then. I didn't think we needed to take a chance there, but it was beautiful," Saul told me as we walked into the dressing room.

"Thanks, brother. I can't help myself when we are just outside the red zone. We've done well with gadgets this year, so the guys believe and make it happen."

The only concern I had going in at halftime was two big injuries. Max and Ruben had to be taken off on stretchers, and either of them returning was doubtful.

Dresden did an outstanding job of not giving up big plays to our explosive offensive. Their strategy of rolling a safety over to the top to help with #20, who we attacked in game one, was holding our deep passing game in check. We were still moving the chains, but our drives were of the eight-play variety.

We faced a 4th and 3 from the 17-yard line on our next possession. We were in Heiko's field goal range, but I called a run play to Karri as fast as I could, hoping Saul or Berti wouldn't stop me and call in the field goal unit.

Bobby snapped the ball before all the officials' feet were set, and Karri busted through the middle of the defense for a 14-yard gain to the Monarch three.

"Great block, Brenden! Great job, my brother!" Jerome yelled from the sideline. He was right. Brenden and Bobby's double team had opened up a big hole. With Max out, Ludi was now playing right guard and performing well.

"Slot! Slot personnel," I yelled, getting Jerome back on the field for our goal-line running game.

"Black Porsche," I signaled and told Jonas in the headset.

Black Porsche runs behind our two best offensive linemen, Yasir and Brenden, but Karri was dropped for a one-yard loss.

"Dammit! What the hell happened?" I asked Jonas.

"It was #38 we talked about. He blitzed through the B gap, and we didn't pick him up."

'Black Porsche Q,' I signaled.

"Karri, look for #38!" I yelled, hoping he would hear me. "Remind me to kill Stefan when he gets to the sideline." On the snap of the ball, Karri faked across and blocked him. Chris went left and walked into the endzone.

We missed the two-point conversion but had a 29-14 lead early in the fourth quarter.

"Stefan! Why, why, why?!" I asked incredulously but wasn't really asking.

"My fault, coach; I should've seen #38 walk up. It won't happen again."

Karri tacked on another touchdown later in the quarter to put us up 36-14. Our defense played its best game of the year. With lots of subs in, the Monarchs scored a meaningless touchdown to make the final 36-21.

Outside the locker room, Saul and Buddy brought cases of beer and Radler's for us to celebrate our 5-0 record going into the 3-week break.

"Stefan, have a Radler on me, brother," I said.

"Thanks, coach. Sorry again about not taking care of the 'B' gap on the goal line."

"No need to apologize. Anytime a player who cares like you makes a mistake, it's usually on the coach. This one is on me. We discussed taking care of #38 but we needed more red zone work in practice. We will from now on. You've bought in from day one. I appreciate you."

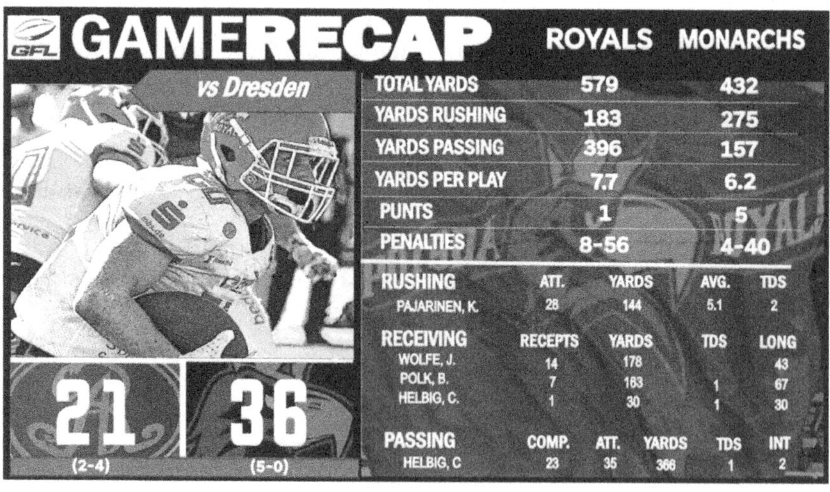

	ROYALS	MONARCHS
TOTAL YARDS	579	432
YARDS RUSHING	183	275
YARDS PASSING	396	157
YARDS PER PLAY	7.7	6.2
PUNTS	1	5
PENALTIES	8-56	4-40

RUSHING	ATT.	YARDS	AVG.	TDS
PAJARINEN, K.	28	144	5.1	2

RECEIVING	RECEPTS	YARDS	TDS	LONG
WOLFE, J.	14	178		43
POLK, B.	7	163	1	67
HELBIG, C.	1	30	1	30

PASSING	COMP.	ATT.	YARDS	TDS	INT
HELBIG, C	23	35	366	1	2

After the game, Jens and Buddy took me to a famous bier garten in Dresden, SchillerGarten.

“This is a very renowned place, coach! One of the most famous gartens in all of Germany. It originally opened in 1730,” said Jens.

"I'll help you with ordering," Buddy offered, "But trust me, if you don't get the Pork Knuckle, you'll regret it once you see how delicious mine looks."

We sat at a table with at least 200 others enjoying live music on the stage. As I looked out over the River Elbe, I couldn't help but appreciate the beautiful spot Jens and Buddy had chosen for us to celebrate being 5-0 at the summer break.

Pork Knuckle

Buddy’s recommendation was right on the money. The pork knuckle was fabulous and easily one of the best dishes I have tasted during my two-month stay in Germany.

"Coach Jackson?" I heard a voice call out as we were leaving. I turned around to see a man with his hand extended.

"I'm Austyn Carta-Samuels, the Dresden quarterback. I can’t believe we just bumped into each other, but I wanted to take the opportunity to meet you and tell you we knew what you guys were doing on offense."

Schillergarten

40

BACK TO TEXAS

July 3, 2022

"It's nice to meet you. It's fascinating to me that your older brother, KJ, led the team to its first-ever championship as the quarterback last year, and now you are the signal-caller."

"Well, KJ's actually my younger brother. And, yes, we've talked a lot about the pressure on me this season."

"We'd heard you tore your ACL in our game, so we didn't think you'd be able to play again this season."

"The doctors thought I tore it, but it was only a severe strain. I'll hobble through the season if I can."

“Now I have to know, how did y'all know about our offense? No one in America hardly has any idea about what we're doing."

"I was an offensive coach at the University of Missouri for five seasons, and we ran the choice route. One of our QBs, Drew Locke, set the SEC record for most yards in a season. We knew what to do today but still couldn't stop it. It was maddening. Tell Chris and your receivers great job. It looks like they have bought in 100%."

" Thanks, I will tell them. That's fascinating and another example that it's truly a small world. Y'all made us work for it today. We hit fewer big pass plays than we have all season. Please tell the defensive staff I tip my cap to them. Now, I have a favor to ask," I said.

“Sure, coach. What can I do for you?”

“If you’ve coached the Fast N’ Wide offense, would you be willing to do a Zoom call with my clients after the season? You’d bring a lot to the table for us.”

“No problem at all. I’d love to, just hit me up in October.”

DALLAS BOUND

One promise the Royals made to me was to help with flights for Tracy to visit in Potsdam, but I was homesick and asked them to fly me to Dallas and back during the break. Berti and the board said yes, so gratefully, I headed home two days after our big Dresden victory. Although I had a car now, Berti drove me to the airport so I wouldn't have to pay for parking for two weeks.

"Have a good trip, coach. Please do not decide to stay. We need you for the second half of the season," he said, joking.

"I'm coming back. I've got to bring Yasir some white cleats and, even more importantly, Buddy some BBQ sauce."

While in the Berlin terminal waiting to board the first leg of my flight to Zurich, I texted Jonas. *Any updates on Max and Ruben's injuries?*

Both are done for the season. Max is having surgery on his ankle, and Ruben tore his ACL.

Crap, I was afraid Ruben tore it but was hoping Max would be able to rehab and come back.

After surgery, if he works hard to return, he could play in the semi-finals. He's going to Denmark to have the procedure done and then stay there for rehab.

After the Rebels game, where our secondary gave up 400+ yards passing, Ruben moved to safety and played well against Dresden. Losing him was another major blow to our defense. Max had slowly come around to our new culture. Before the Rebels game, he was even admitted into 50 Strong. My head hurt thinking about once again reshuffling the offensive line.

TEXAS - FLORIDA - TEXAS

My flight arrived late at Dallas Ft. Worth airport. Although I could have taken an Uber home, Tracy insisted on driving the hour to pick me up at 1:00 a.m. On returning home to Heath, I had to stop at a 24-hour fast-food restaurant to take in some American calories.

There's nothing like fast food to make you feel like you're back home.

"Yes, I'll take a soft chicken taco, a grande burrito, nachos, an order of cinnamon delights, and a large *diet* Dr. Pepper," I said into the drive-thru speaker. "Honey, do you want anything?" I asked Tracy in the passenger seat of my Ford truck.

"It's good to have you home, baby," Tracy said, grabbing my hand.

"It feels amazing to be back. It feels like I've been gone for a year."

When I got home, I found two notes on my bathroom mirror. One said, "Two people are better than one, for they can help each other succeed." Ecclesiastes 4:9. I love you! T

The other was larger, written in crayon and on pink construction paper, "I'm glad you're home, Ranny! I missed you!" XOXO Coco

The following day Tracy, Coco and Tracy's mom, Gaye, and I would be making our yearly pilgrimage to the white sand beaches of the Florida panhandle. It's a 12-hour drive, but it's always worth it to hear the sound of the waves crashing on the shore and see the beautiful water.

We arrived and checked into our house in Rosemary Beach. Coco and I built sandcastles. We all soaked up the sun and ate terrific seafood each night. Unplugging and disconnecting on the beach with my family was indeed a blessing. For a few days, it was like football didn't exist. But as we pulled onto Interstate 10 and headed west to return home, the football coach in me returned. I started becoming preoccupied with our next opponent, the New Yorker Lions.

"Honey, I hear you always say "be where your feet are" to your clients. Can you give us 12 hours without watching the film or messaging Helbig while you're with us? It won't be long, and we won't see you again for several weeks." Tracy asked.

"Sorry, I'll do better. I'd stay here and 'satellite coach' the second half of the season if I could. We have a huge game when I get back and my mind is resetting to 'get ready' mode."

I spent my week in Texas doing Zooms with Fast N' Wide and Elite Coach Mastermind clients. It was incredible to be in the same time zone with them and to break down the lab results I'd learned in the first half of the season.

We also ate out almost every meal. Tex-Mex, BBQ, Steak, hamburgers, French fries...if it entered my mind, I asked if we could go there. The two weeks were wonderful mentally, but my physical health didn't fare well. I gained almost 10 pounds and enjoyed every bite. I knew I could work it off when I went back to Potsdam.

When I got on the plane, I dreaded knowing I wouldn't see Tracy again for over a month. After I made it through security and sat down, I found a red envelope with I MISS YOU ALREADY on the front. Inside was a handwritten note with the words, "I love you, and I can't wait to see you again." Tracy's support meant everything to me, and I was grateful.

I boarded the Lufthansa flight the Royals had set up for me. My ticket was 25C, so I knew I was either on the aisle or had a window seat. I never communicated with the Royals travel agent, but Berti had told him I am 6'5", so I was grateful he took care of me again on this long flight to Paris. As I approached the back of the plane, I realized the seat configuration was not the norm. The middle section had four seats instead of three, and 25C was an interior seat located slap dab in the middle. What?!? There's no way the Royals could have done this to me. It was going to be a miserable nine hours for me.

I sat down and tried to make the best of it. I wasn't going to say anything or complain to a flight attendant. I was going to suck it up and get through the ordeal. Within a few minutes, the lady in the row before me reclined her seat back and smashed my knees…

"Mmmphh," I murmured, trying not to be too loud. "I'm sorry, but I'm very tall, and your seat is hitting my legs," I said as politely as possible, considering the circumstances.

A gentleman seated next to her, her husband, I'm sure, said to me...

41

CAN CHRIS PLAY?

July 19, 2022

With a thick Scandinavian accent, "I'm sorry for your dilemma, but we paid quite a lot for these seats and will be using them to recline and sleep."

I decided to think about something else, the team, so I messaged our *Autobahn 80* group.

I'm on my way back, guys, and excited to find out what y'all think of the Lions. I'll give each of you your defender to evaluate within a few hours. Please have your report done by 1900 tomorrow evening. I can't wait to see you guys and hear what you did during the break.

Almost immediately after I hit send, my phone vibrated. It was a text from Seth Womack, former head coach of NYer for two seasons and who first got me interested in coaching in Germany.

(Seth) Hey, buddy. You're about to play my old team, the Lions, next, right?

(me) Yes, we're going to their place next week. They are second in the standings, so we must bring our A-game.

(Seth) You will need your A++ game. New Yorker is the standard of the GFL. They've won 12 championships and been the runner-up six more times. The head coach of the Lions, Troy Tomlin, is a friend of mine, and he runs the program as we do in the States. I know you guys are steam-rolling the league, but Troy's defensive coordinator is a retired Texas high school coach and knows his stuff. Be ready to see a defense that will go to the extreme to stop you.

(me) Thanks, brother. Jonas, my right-hand assistant, and Bobby, our starting center, were both at Braunschweig last season, so I've heard a few things here and there. I know they have the largest fan base in the league, so I'm excited to play in their stadium in front of a good crowd.

After a long flight, I was thrilled Conni, the Royals board member who provides team meals, was nice enough to bring me back to Potsdam from the airport.

"We have a big game this week, coach. Have you heard much about NYer?" Conni asked.

"Yes, ma'am. I've been working on them during the break. We're going to have a good plan for them. I'm hoping the time off will be what we need to take it to another level. I know the Lions will be the best team we've played this season, so we must play our best game of the year to beat them."

"Yes, they're a very good team. I suspect they will defeat Dresden when they meet. I hate TK decided to go there. I'm sure he'll play his best game of the year against us," Conni added.

Conni dropped me off at my flat. I collapsed for a two-hour nap and then started reading the scouting reports. Coaches should always make the players feel 10-foot tall and bulletproof. I promised we'd set offensive records, and we're on pace to do it, but this scouting report was the first time I felt like we were becoming arrogant. And it bothered me…

A lot.

At our offensive meeting, I let the guys know my thoughts the following day. "I'm concerned about this one. Maybe because of everything I've heard and read on the Lions, but winning at NYer will be a chore."

"We kicked their ass last season at NYer, coach. We got this," Yasir said.

"Here's what I know. They've had plenty of time to prepare for us. Their defensive coordinator is from Texas, so he has faced tempo for years. When I googled him, he said he was fired up to coach for the Alabama of the GFL. According to Bobby and Coach Jonas, he nailed it.

"They haven't blown people out like we have but are still undefeated at 4-0-2," Saul added.

"They'll have a good crowd Saturday. TK is also telling them what he learned about us at training camp. My friends over there aren't talking trash, but they are not scared of us, either," Bobby said.

"Wait till they see us up close and personal. We'll have something for TK and their big, slow defensive line," Jerome said.

"I'm all for us being confident, but my college coach always said this, and it rings true today- "Respect All, Fear None." Are we the better team? Yes, but the best team doesn't always win. The team that plays the best does," I said.

"Don't worry so much, coach. This game is on national television, and we'll give the Lions the disrespect they deserve," Yasir promised.

Jerome and Yasir are both studs. They can back up whatever they think and say, but I was worried this would permeate to the rest of our guys. I love instilling confidence more and more as the game approaches, but I'd have to be more demanding and 'attention to detail' this week to keep us grounded.

The following day, I read a message from Chris on WhatsApp as I left the office. *Fellas, I've ached all day and can't get off the toilet. If anyone has any medicine they think will help, please bring it to practice. I and my chapped butt will love you forever.*

What? Noooo! We can't have a functional practice without Chris. I texted Berti and Saul about my frustration with us not having a backup quarterback.

If Chris can't practice tonight, we should postpone it to Thursday. Maybe if we do, the board will get us a backup.

(Berti) Jonas is already on it. We're getting Chris some medicine to help his situation.

When I arrived at practice, I was nervous to see how Chris would be physically, but waited a little while to ask him. "How are you feeling?" I asked as he was loosening up his arm.

"I've been better. I'll try and make it through practice without crapping my pants. If you see me run off into the bushes, please ignore it."

"Thanks for fighting through this. As you're well aware, we'd struggle to have any practice without you. It means a lot that you're here. Thanks for being a real leader."

Helbig had a great practice, like always. He made all the throws like always and was sharp and focused mentally. He was his usual captain-like self, cementing his role as the true leader of our team.

The following day, Chris' condition did not improve; if anything, it slightly worsened. He showed up and pushed through the sickness, and we had a productive practice again. "At least it's Wednesday. These things take a few days max to run their course. You'll be good to go Saturday for sure," I said to Chris after the workout. I might've been trying to convince myself as much as Helbig.

"Yea, I'll stay at my flat on our off day tomorrow and get to feeling better. Jonas is headed to Berlin tomorrow to get me some stronger medicine."

FAAST FRIDAY

Friday's workouts are a mock game, where we work on situations and substitutions. We move quickly and are on and off the field in 70 minutes.

"You look better!" I said to Chris before we began our walk-through.

"I'm feeling a little bit better, but still having issues."

"Dang. Make sure you're staying hydrated. I'm shocked you aren't almost 100% by now, but tomorrow will be when you feel like Superman again."

"Yes, sir. I hope so. It's been a long week."

The following day, I was outside the cafeteria greeting players as they entered for our pregame brunch when Jonas walked up. "Since we don't have a restroom on the bus, Chris will ride with me to Braunschweig. He's still having to use the bathroom a lot. I'm glad he's tough. It'd be ugly without him."

I walked into the cafeteria with a million thoughts running through my head. How many points could we score with Jared as our *wildcat* quarterback? If Chris can play effectively, are we taking them too lightly? Do we respect them enough to win? To add to my stress, another shock greeted me when I sat down with my tray of food.

"Good morning, coach," Ludi said to me. "Have you seen Saul's shirt?" he said, laughing. I turned to see Saul walking near the front door. His shirt read…

42

TOUGHEST THING TO DO IN SPORTS

July 23, 2022

F____ YOU on the front and GO ROYALS on the back.

When it rains, it pours, as my momma always says. It wasn't my place to say anything to Saul, but we'd been fighting overconfidence since we returned from the summer break. At least he'd only wear it in Potsdam.

Wrong. After our three-hour bus ride, we pulled up, and Saul, who arrived early to help set everything up, was still wearing the shirt. He'd also taken our play board, where we track the number of times we snap the ball during the game, and arranged it to read "69" for all to see as we walked to our locker room.

What the hell? A massive shift occurred over our three-week break, and I didn't understand why. We were the talk of the GFL, this game was on national television, and we acted like we didn't remember what got us into this position.

NEKTON MENTALITY

Berti didn't ask me to speak to the team. I wasn't sure if he didn't want to impose or if pregame speeches didn't matter much to him, but today, I was only speaking to the offense. We met outside our locker room in a stairwell of the stadium.

"Get your phones out and queue up the video I just uploaded to Autobahn 80," I said.

"Hit play."

The video was a Shark Week trailer and a one-minute highlight of ferocious shark attacks. A massive shark jumps in the air and violently chomps down on a seal. It then thrashes back and forth, causing blood to go everywhere. The next shark was sinking his teeth into the protected arm of a diver in a cage while, at the same time, another shark was ramming the cage, attempting to destroy it.

"Pause it. Does anyone know what show this is advertising?"

"Shark Week. I watch it every year," Polk said.

"Exactly. The Discovery Channel has devoted a week of programming to sharks for years. Why? Because we are fascinated with this prehistoric killing machine. Hit play again."

A shark attacks a seal in open water, again leaping in the air, and ferociously bites it in half. "Pause it. Does anyone know what species of shark is the deadliest?"

"The great white shark," Stefan answers.

"That's correct. This next clip may be too old for you to know the movie, but it's iconic for people my age. I remember being in a theater when I was eight, scared to death watching it. Hit play." A rectangular float is being moved through the ocean by two paddling legs. The camera gets closer and closer to the legs when suddenly, a teenage body is flipped over, and he is fighting for his life. The boys nearby see the commotion and attempt to figure out what's happening, but they only see thrashing, red water.

"Get out of the water, get out of the water!" The crowded beach was now in full panic mode. Parents start running into the water to grab their children, but the boy on the raft never returns. "Does anyone know what this movie is?" I asked the team.

"Jaws, it's my dad's favorite movie from when he was a kid," Jared says.

"Jaws came out in 1975, and people were scared to get in the ocean for years afterward. In reality, sharks do not kill many people worldwide, but we have movies and television shows dedicated to them because they captivate us. Does anyone know about the DNA of a great white shark regarding how much it will eat? How about the phrase Nekton mentality? Does that ring a bell with anyone?" I asked.

"I can't remember exactly what it meant, but our special teams at Penn State used nekton mentality," Polk said.

"Nekton means cannot be satisfied. It makes sense to me he would nekton use it because elite special teams players must be relentless and on the hunt like a predator."

"A great white shark's DNA won't allow it to stop eating if food is present. They're literal eating machines. If there were a thousand seals that couldn't get away, a great white would eat himself to death. Today, we must play with a nekton mentality. We're going to attack, attack and attack some more. The GFL national broadcast is here today to see if we're for real. Can our offense dominate the Lions? New Yorker is a proud franchise, but they haven't seen anything like what they'll witness today."

An hour later, I stood on the sideline of Eintracht Stadium before the coin toss. It was by far the most impressive venue I had seen in Germany. Although modernized in 2011, Eintracht, the home of Braunschweig's largest division soccer club, is another facility built in the 1920s. The 360-degree stands with seating for 24,000 are all covered.

Speaking in German, of course, the #1 broadcaster team for SKY TV began the transmission for fans around the country.

"Welcome to Braunschweig, where SKY TV is excited to bring you the GFL *Game of the Week*. With the top offense in the league, the upstart Potsdam Royals take on the perennial power New Yorker Lions, who knows something about winning, especially at home," said Klaus Junger, lead announcer for the broadcast team today.

"I'm excited to see what Royal's American skill players, quarterback Chris Helbig, and receivers Brandon Polk and Jared Wolfe will do today versus the veteran Lions defense," said the color analyst Michael Baumgardner.

"Yes, Royals' new offensive coordinator, Randy Jackson's "*Fast and Loose*" offense, as he describes it, is leading the league at 50 points per game," said Klaus.

Thankfully, Saul changed his shirt to our normal coaching attire, but Chris didn't look as good. "I know you're tired of talking about your *situation,* but let me know if you need Jared to fill in if you feel terrible. I think we can run the ball and eat up the clock if necessary," I said.

"Yes, sir. I'll be fine. You may see my pants with a big stain on the back, but I'll play."

"Do you know what the toughest thing to do in sports is? I know you don't feel like guessing right now, so I will tell you. I always hear 'hitting a curveball in the major leagues' is the most difficult thing to do in sports, but it's not. The toughest thing to do is to ACT DIFFERENTLY THAN YOU FEEL. It takes incredible mental toughness to perform at your best when you're not feeling your best. Your performance will suffer if you let your emotions get the best of you. Elite performers know this and have the ability to act differently than they feel. I know you feel bad, but if you act the way you feel, it's over for us. Have you ever heard of Michael Jordan's *flu game*?

"Yea, it was before my time, but I've heard of him having a great playoff game when he was very sick."

"Correct. In the 1997 NBA Finals, the Bulls were in Utah, and Jordan had a 103-degree temperature. The team doctor tried to give him a shot a couple of hours before tip-off, but supposedly, Jordan was deathly afraid of needles and refused. I know it's easier said than done, but Jordan didn't let his feelings dictate his actions. He said he played because he felt obligated to his team and the city of Chicago."

"You don't owe us anything. You owe it to yourself to pass the mirror test today. I know you're tough enough to act differently than you feel, and because of that, you'll add to your legacy today."

KICKOFF

"The Royals have won the toss and will begin the game on offense," said commenter Klaus.

It finally happened. We went *3 and out* to start the game. Maybe Chris wasn't going to be Michael Jordan reincarnate after all. "What are you going to say to Helbig?" Jonas asked me on the headset.

"Nothing. I'm going to leave him alone. If I felt as bad as he does, I'd probably be in the locker room in the fetal position."

Heiko looked like he wasn't mentally ready to punt. The ball went off the side of his foot for an 11-yard kick. The Lions only had to drive 38 yards in six plays to take the early 7-0 lead.

On our next possession, Chris convinced me he felt okay by hitting Polk on a 49-yard "slant and go." Two plays later, Chris ran behind Brenden and Yasir for a 5-yard touchdown to tie the score 7-7.

Later in the quarter, Karri capped an eight-play drive with a one-yard touchdown. Unfortunately, our kicking game continued to haunt us, and the extra point was blocked.

"The kick is blocked! NYer Deshaun Ennels has it and is headed towards the Lion endzone!" Junger said into his mic. The Lions scooped up the ball and returned it 90 yards for a two-point play. As a result, our lead was now only 12-9.

"This is a huge momentum play for the home team! Just like that, the Lions are back to within three!" said analyst Michael Baumgardner.

Later in the quarter New Yorker kicked a 26-yard field goal, and the scoreboard read 12-12.

"The Lion faithful is starting to get into this one, Klaus," said Baumgardner.

"They are. This looks like it will be back and forth all day," said Junger.

My stomach hadn't felt like this since our red zone nightmare week one versus Dresden. I knew we were setting ourselves up for an upset with our attitude this week. We didn't look like the obvious best team on the field for the first time this season.

"How are we doing on TK (our former defensive end)?" I asked the offensive line on the bench.

"He's playing harder than he ever did in practice, but he's wearing down," Stefan said.

"Let's get in our heavy set and see how he likes Yasir being over there," I said. We began imposing our will with the run game. Channeling his inner Michael Jordan, Chris ran for touchdowns on our next two possessions to give us a lead of 26-12.

"The Royals offense is starting to get in gear now. The rumors of Helbig not feeling well today seem false," said commentator Baumgardner.

Our defense was playing terrific as well. New Yorker's starting quarterback was injured, so they were very one-dimensional. Berti smartly loaded the line of scrimmage and made it very difficult to run the ball.

"New Yorker must find a way to complete a deep pass to loosen up Potsdam defense. The Royals have nine players close to the line of scrimmage at times," said commentator Junger.

On our next possession, Heiko rumbled in from 3 yards out to increase our lead to 33-12.

Our defense forced another three and out. After the Lion punt, we had the ball on our 32-yard line with 92 seconds left in the half. "Move fast and be smart. We have plenty of time," I told our offense as we huddled on the sideline. After four completions, we had the ball on the Lion 18-yard line with ten seconds left in the half.

"Take one more shot here, coach, but then we will kick the field goal on the next play," Berti told me.

We didn't need to worry with the kicking tee other than for an extra point because Chris completed a pass to Jared, who caught it on the three, and then dove into the endzone. After another botched PAT, we took a 39-12 lead into intermission.

"We just scored four unanswered touchdowns, guys. I can't tell you how proud I'm of that second quarter. We looked like an eating machine, and their crowd's shocked at what they're seeing," I told the offense at halftime.

The third quarter was more of the same. We continued to run the ball at will and chew up yards. The score was 59-19 at the start of the fourth quarter. We continued to attack. Chris, who looked like he's never felt better, scored on a one-yard run with just two minutes off the clock in the fourth quarter. It was at this point that Berti approached me on the sideline. The entire country was seeing us dismantle the Lions.

"I know you want to score as many as possible, but Tomlin's a good guy, and I'll have to do a post-game interview with him. Please try not to score anymore," Berti said.

"I'm all for taking the air out of the ball, coach. We should put a dang backup quarterback in right now, but of course, we don't have one," I answered irritably.

"Ok, coach, you don't have to get testy. I know, I know," Berti said.

"Sorry, Berti. I was out of line there. It's just that we're all over here to win a championship and are one play away from disaster. It's ridiculous."

"It's ok, coach. I agree with you 100%. I need to pressure our board and get us a backup."

It was a total butt-kicking of a quality opponent on the road. Our offense amassed 504 yards with a terrific balance of 221 yards rushing and 283 yards passing.

"The Potsdam Royals made a statement here today. They look like the favorite to win the Northern conference after this dismantling of the New Yorker Lions," Junger said.

"I agree, Klaus. The Royal defense did its job but what a day by GFL rookie Chris Helbig. He ran for four scores and threw for three more. Finnish running back Karri Pajarinen, who didn't play in the fourth quarter, had 163 yards and one touchdown. American receiver Jared Wolfe caught eight passes for 122 yards and three touchdowns, while Brandon Polk had six receptions for 124 yards," Baumgardner added.

The offensive line had its best performance of the year. I gathered them and said, "Let's take a picture to commemorate this butt-kicking. You guys led the way today!"

I next found Chris and put my arm around him. "I'm so proud of you, big guy. Playing sick today is where legends are made. That'll go down as the 'Helbig Gut Game' for the Royals and me."

A few moments later, something happened I will never forget. The New Yorker fans began chanting, Booobbbbbyyyyyy! Booobbbbbyyyyyy! Booobbbbbyyyyyy!

Bobby went to the home side, where a couple of hundred fans were on the first row waiting to high-five him.

"Booobbbbbyyyyyy! Booobbbbbyyyyyy! Booobbbbbyyyyyy!" They continued to chant as he shook hands and was congratulated on his triumphant return after ten years and five championships of being a Lion. We had just set an opponent's scoring record in the most storied franchise in the GFL, and their fans were welcoming a returning legend. Where I'm from, boos and bottles would be the reception a returning player would receive, especially after the butt-kicking as we put on them. But Bobby is a class act, and the Lion fans are also. I stood there and soaked it all in. I took some pictures to give to Bobby, but I was also making sure I embedded this moment into my brain.

I made my way back to our side of the field when I saw TK still speaking with some of his old teammates. Around midfield, he approached me, smiling and very humble. He stuck his hand out to shake mine as he said, "Great game today, coach. You guys played amazing."

"Thank you, TK. Same to you. We knew we had to double-team you every play. I'm sure you expected that from seeing it all the time in training camp, though," I said respectfully.

"I want you to know something. I'm not too proud to admit this; I studied Fast N' Wide as much as possible during the break. I looked up everything online to try and get an edge, but nothing mattered today. You guys were awesome today."

"That's very nice of you to say. Trust me; I worked harder on the game plan for you guys than I have all season. I returned to the States for two weeks, but my mind wasn't ever very far from the Lion defense. Please tell Coach Ward (defensive coordinator) what a great job he does. I'm sure you guys will bounce back and go on a winning streak."

"I'll tell him. He's a phenomenal coach. I know I wasn't in Potsdam long this season, but you guys have something special going on. The Royals team we played today was more of a team than the one I played with last season. Good luck the rest of the way."

And just like that, the bliss was gone as quick as a snap of the fingers. A familiar voice brought me back to reality with…

"Hey coach, I've got bad news."

GFL **GAMERECAP**

vs New Yorker

	ROYALS	LIONS
TOTAL YARDS	504	273
YARDS RUSHING	221	119
YARDS PASSING	283	153
YARDS PER PLAY	6.5	4.2
PUNTS	5	6
PENALTIES	3-31	5-44

RUSHING	ATT.	YARDS	AVG.	TDS
PAJARINEN, K.	22	163	7.4	1

RECEIVING	RECEPTS	YARDS	TDS	LONG
WOLFE, J.	8	122	3	34
POLK, B.	6	124		49
HELBIG, C.	4	25		9

PASSING	COMP.	ATT.	YARDS	TDS	INT
HELBIG, C	20	37	283	3	

26 (4-1-2) 65 (6-0)

Back row: 77-Stefan Stefansson 66-Oskar Rüegg 81-Mat Dubicki 75-Brenden Oswin 54-Lukas Renner 67-Bobby Sövegjarto 53-Tim Waltner 62-Max Hocke

Front Row: 50-Mads Højen 89-Jerome Valbon 56-Ludi Röetzscher 78-Yasir Raji 20-Karri Pajarinen

BRAUNSCHWEIGER ZEITUNG

(Excerpts from the Braunschweig News)

POTSDAM ROYALS: NEW POWER OF THE NORTH?

The Lions had a pitch black day and rarely got the offense of the Potsdam Royals under control. New Yorker suffered a big setback in the tight play-off race.

The 65:26 over record champions New Yorker Lions of Braunschweig was more than just a gentle indication the Brandenburgers are the hottest iron in the North. It looked like a top game. Table leader Potsdam a guest of purser Braunschweig. Both teams were still undefeated at this point, but the Lions carried the burden of two draws around with them.

Although the first quarter ended 12:12, the Potsdamers erupted. The dual for first place in the north became a clear affair. Above all, Chris Helbig, put his stamp on the game for the Royals. The quarterback had four touchdowns of his own over the course of the game and threw for three more.

"Helbig was the best player on the field today. We didn't have an answer for him throwing or running. He is a problem for defenses. If I were able to cast an MVP vote, he would get mine. I love our team and we will regroup. We will get ready for Cologne next week and hope to see the Royals again in the playoffs," said, Lions head coach Troy Tomlin.

The guarantee of success for the best average scoring offense in the entire GFL is Helbig. The 24-year-old American has thrown the most yards and touchdowns this season. Jared Wolfe benefits the most from this. The wide receiver has already caught passes for 1,022 yards and is leading the league rankings by a whopping 200 yards ahead of his second-place pursuer Brandon Polk - by the way also a Potsdam Royal. The Royals have made themselves the top favorites for entry into the German Bowl with this resounding victory over the formidable Lions.

43

SAME SONG, SECOND VERSE

July 26, 2022

"It looks like Karri's foot is probably broken," Taka said.

"Dang it. I knew he was hobbling in the second half, but I didn't think it was broken. I know you can't tell me much this quickly, but any guess on how long it will take before he can return?

"It's hard to say. Probably around a month at least."

In the media room, the post-game press conference was underway. Yasir and Jonas, a defensive back, were also at the press table, along with Berti. "Jonas and Yasir, I have been to hundreds of press conferences, but this is the first time I've seen players show up without a shirt and wearing neckties. Can you explain what this is about?" a journalist asked.

Both started grinning and laughing a little. "We just thought we'd wear them in honor of the two ties New Yorker has had on the year," Jonas said.

"In a way, we are here to congratulate the Lions. At least they didn't tie today," Yasir said.

On the bus ride home, I started texting Berti and Saul. *I'm sure you guys know about Karri's foot. Heiko is a 225-pound bull, but he will need a backup. Any leads on a running back?*

(Saul) I'm already on it. If I don't kill myself driving and texting, I will have a few highlight videos for us tomorrow. A running back in London who played junior college ball for a year in Mississippi showed promise. I'm trying to find out where he plays now, but I will track him down. Also, the French league only has a few weeks left. Maybe, we can convince a back there to leave early off a team that sucks.

(Berti) Saul is the master at finding players in an emergency. He'll find us a backup.

I was a proud offensive line coach grading the film on Sunday. New Yorker had the biggest and most physical defensive line in the league, and we handled them. After rotating guys and losing Max for the season, our "best five" unit emerged. Our offensive line was among the strongest in the GFL, largely thanks to Yasir and Brenden on the left side. Yasir, an absolute beast at tackle, locked down Helbig's blind side like nobody's business. Brenden's physical run-blocking made him a force to be reckoned with at guard. Together, they were the best one-two punch in the league.

The only issue was, stop me if you've heard this song before, depth. We had one backup guard, Mads, and one backup tackle, Tim, who was injured more than he was healthy.

On Sunday evening, I posted in the Follow Us chat group. *I will sleep well tonight! You guys 'geh voras,' German for 'lead the way' against a good NYer defense!*

(me) Highlights from the grades:

> *No Loafs! - Zero OL penalties! - 10 of 17 3rd down conversions! - One sack (this is good for most teams, meh for us:) - Seven rushing touchdowns!*

(me) Has anyone seen Bobby today? Was he able to get in his flat, or was his head too large to fit in the door?

(Bobby) I'm good, coach. That was a fun win, but I'm ready to get back to work on the Crocodiles.

(me) Speaking of that, the "24-hour rule" of celebrating a win is just about up. We'll go over scouting reports tomorrow after our film session. I was impressed with their victory at Dresden. What are your first impressions of the 4-2 Crocs?"

(Yasir) They suck.

(Jerome) We will destroy them and be 8-0 on Saturday night.

(me) Coach Goodman says they have the best pass rusher in the league, a hybrid-type guy, #26.

(Yasir) He sucks. They're all trash. They all suck.

(me) Ok, I guess they all suck.

Before our meetings began, Saul walked into the coaches' office and said, "We may have the Czech league MVP coming to play running back for us."

"Really? Nice! How did you find him."

"One of my contacts in Poland told me about him. His name is Adam Žouželka. He's only 20 years and almost as big as Heiko but faster. I'm sending you his highlights to watch now. He had 264 yards in the Czech Bowl a couple of weeks ago."

"So, their season is over? Any issues with him being able to play with us as far as the GFL is concerned?"

"No issues. Adam's former team, the Prague Lions, needs to release him, but it would only delay it even if they don't."

"Why would he want to play again so soon?"

"To get paid. The Czech league doesn't pay players. He probably didn't even get a pregame meal from them. The GFL is like D1 versus NAIA for Adam."

"Sweet. When can he get here?"

"He's getting on a train tomorrow morning and should be at practice on Wednesday. He lives in a small town in the Czech Republic, so he'll have to take three different trains to get here."

After the film review, I opened the PowerPoint of the compiled scouting reports. According to most of our offensive players, we were playing a Prospects team.

Some of the comments were:

- Not great	*- Slow-not physical*	*- Not athletic / no moves*
- Lacks technique	*- Poor tackler*	*- Emotional*
- Gives away coverage	*-Not great ball skills*	
- No ball skills	*- Not much motor-slow off the ball plays high/gets fatigued*	

I posted my concerns on *Autobahn 80*:

I worried we didn't take the Lions seriously enough all week, and we played our best game of the year. I agree the Cologne defense is not as good as NYer, but I'm concerned again about the evaluations. Just call me an old worrier, but "they suck" will get you beat.

(Yasir) They suck, coach. I call it like I see it.

(Jerome) You always say It's About Us... If we practice how we are supposed to, then we'll beat the hell out of them.

(me) I love you guys, but these are famous last words of teams that get upset. I know y'all are tired of me saying this, but the best doesn't win. The team that plays the best does. The Crocodiles are a playoff team, and we have graded them 4s, 5s, and 6s.

PRAGUE PROBLEMS

That night, the head coach of the Prague Lions, Gabriel Herrad, contacted me on Facebook Messenger. I did a Zoom clinic on culture for coach Harrod a few years ago, so we knew each other.

(Gabriel) Are you guys trying to sign our running back, Adam?

(me) I was told this morning we were. Is he a good person and player?

(Gabriel) Coach, he just finished an entire season. He doesn't need to play with you guys now. This could be bad for his health. Would you want one of your players to do this?

(me) I'm new to all of this, but he won't be our starter. He'll give us some depth and get 7-8 carries a game. You should want him with us if he wants to play for another team. I'll take good care of him, I promise.

(Gabriel) I'm not going to release him. It is not ok that you guys are trying to sign him.

Just when I thought things would be stress-free for a little bit...I texted Berti, Saul, and Jonas. *Adam's coach is not happy we are signing him.*

(Saul) And...so????

(me) His name is Gabriel Herrad. I'm just relaying the conversation. He acts like he's heartbroken and is worried about Adam's safety.

(Berti) Will they release him? Nothing they can do about it, but they might block it for a while.

(Saul) It's nothing new. A GFL team which is a top league, wants to sign a small country player. The small team wants to keep star players whom they don't pay.

(me) This is bizarre to me. It's like a guy playing for a AA baseball team, and the major league manager wants to promote him, but his minor league team says no. This could be a big deal for Adam to get exposure in a larger league and get paid. I'm sure Herrad worries that Adam will enjoy the GFL and not want to return to Prague.

(Saul) One hundred percent. They don't care about anything but getting Adam back on their team.

I texted Jerome, our 280-pound tight end. *Can you play running back?*

44

ARE WE "IN FOOTBALL" OR "INTO FOOTBALL?"

July 25, 2022

On Tuesday morning, Berti was in the office, so I had a chance to run an idea by him and Saul in person instead of in a group chat. "The offensive players are starting to complain that some defensive players arrive later and practice doesn't begin at the set time. I want to propose a team meeting every day before we start. We could have them sit in the bleachers at 18:50 (6:50 P.M.), and we meet for 10 minutes before the walk-through begins. You're late if you're not sitting there with your shoulder pads on."

"This could be good. It would bring a formal beginning to practice instead of Coach Jackson yelling, "Walk-through!" Saul said.

I added, "It'd also help us with practice organization. Our practices move quickly until we work the kicking game. Most coaches are twiddling their thumbs while Saul works his tail off to get 11 players for a scout team. We could structure the meetings this way; Each coordinator, you, Saul, and myself could talk about our goals for the day. Saul's job would be securing scout team members for each phase of the kicking game, so we have 11 when the time comes. We close the meeting by allowing the players to have a three-minute players-only 50 Strong session. And, while they're talking, the coaches can go to the sideline and discuss whatever we need to for the day."

"I'm good with this. Let's try it and see if it helps," Berti said.

Before practice that night, I saw our newest Royal, our young, muscular Czech running back.

"Adam, I'm Coach Jackson. It's nice to meet you. I'm glad you're here to help us win a ring!"

"Thank you, coach. I'm happy to be here. The journey took a while, but I'm glad to be in Potsdam."

I'd texted our 50 Strong chat group earlier to let them know we'd start our team meeting system today, so when I yelled, "Team meeting!" all were ready.

Saul and I stood before the team, but Berti stayed with the other coaches off to the side.

I started the meeting by addressing why pre-practice team meetings were implemented.

"This is a new system for us, and I appreciate Coach Vogt allowing us to do it. We've had some complaints about practice starting on time, and we've had some issues with getting guys on scout teams. These pre-practice meetings will solve these problems and more. Offensively, I have two personnel issues to inform you about. Number one, Chris is healthy now. He told me his troubles are "all behind him"...get it? All behind him?"

"That's the worst joke you've told yet, and that's saying a lot," Yasir said, not even smiling, but I knew deep down he liked it a little.

"Secondly, I'd like to introduce you to our newest Royal, Adam Žouželka, a running back from the Czech Republic!" Everyone clapped for Adam. He gave a humble wave and was already sitting with Karri.

"We don't have anything new this week offensively. I'd say something about our trick play, but you guys on defense will find out about it soon enough," I said, smiling. "Oh yea, Adam isn't the only new running back I need to introduce today. Jerome Valbon is now our version of "Train 89" in the backfield!"

"Thank you, thank you, fellas. All heroes don't wear capes. I'm just one man. I put my pants on one leg at a time," Jerome said, waving and bowing from his seat.

Coach Saul

"Coach Saul, let's talk specials," I said.

"Thanks, Coach Jackson. Cologne is basic with its kick teams. They aren't trying to get an advantage; they want to be efficient. We should have a chance to block a punt. I posted this week's block scheme in Google Classroom. You should know your assignment when we get on the field. Speaking of punt block, if you are on scout punt, please stand up..." Saul went through each phase of the kicking game we would work on and had the scout team (service team) guys stand up. Not having to yell, "I need another guy for scout kickoff," should speed up practice tremendously.

After Saul finished, I looked at Berti, who was still standing off to the side of the team.

"Coach Vogt, would you like to say something to the guys?" I asked.

"No, I'm good. Let's have a good practice today."

"Ok, we'll finish each meeting with a member of 50 Strong speaking to the team. Today, Polk said he'd do it. Thank you, Polk," I said.

Jonas and I met Buddy for döners at PiPaSa that night after practice.

"What do you think, coach? Are we going to be ok with Heiko toting the mail this week?" Buddy asked.

"As long as he stays healthy, we'll be fine. We can rest him some in the passing game and even run Chris some, but don't get me started on why that's a bad idea."

"I'm working hard on that situation. If only we could find a European quarterback where we don't have to pay for a flight from the States. European quarterbacks are about as common as finding a good rugby player in Texas. On the other hand, running backs are easier, as you know. I'm not making excuses for us, just...."

"I know, I know, but 1,000 extra Euros to get an American over could keep us from a title," I said.

"I've called every board member and told them what's at stake. It's not every year you have an offense like this. We can win this whole thing. I don't care if we have to do a car wash and sell brats on the side of the road. We must get off our butts, raise some money, and turn Saul loose on locating a good backup."

"That'd be amazing. Thanks for helping with this," I said.

"Berti understands as well. He's gone from asking to practically begging. Jonas, let me change the subject, what do you think about our new back from Prague?" Buddy asked.

"He looks good. Once he learns what to do, he'll help us a lot. Right now, his head is spinning. Of course, he hasn't been released yet, so he may be unable to play Saturday anyway," Jonas said.

"You guys will find a way. We have all the faith in the world in y'all. On another note, how does the new kicker we signed from the European League of Football look?" Buddy asked.

"He seems like a good one. With Heiko about being our only running back for now, I'm sure grateful we have a kicker. If Heiko were to get injured, we'd lose three positions. I appreciate both of y'all. I'm off to grade some of tonight's practice before I get too sleepy," I said as I got up to leave.

As I began grading the offensive line, it looked like we were going through the motions. Everyone was blocking the correct defender, but not with the sense of urgency I was used to seeing from them.

On each play, I graded all five linemen on

- footwork
- assignment (did he block the right man)

- finish (effort)

Although it was almost midnight, I couldn't wait to give them my thoughts. I didn't care if I yelled into outer space where no one could hear me; I would keep warning them to stay humble and play like we were the underdogs.

(me) I know it's late, but I have a question: Are you "in football" or "into football"? If you're a student, are you "in school" or "into school"? Are you "in a marriage" or "into your marriage" if you're married? This is bigger than football. Going through the motions is for ordinary people, and we aren't average. The difference between being a dad and a daddy is effort. Winning the German Bowl doesn't happen on game day. The team who'll raise the trophy isn't going to practice from now till October; they'll be "into practice" till then.

Respect all, fear none. We didn't practice tonight like we respect the Crocs! They're not better than we are, but we must practice like they are. No one in the GFL can beat us if we are laser-focused. We didn't practice tonight with an obsession with being 8-0. We have one more chance to lock in Friday.

(Jerome) Sleep well, coach. Message received-we got you.

(Jared) Let's have our best practice of the year Friday!

(me) Thanks, guys. I love coaching this team; I just get worked up from time to time. :) This reminds me of a story about a [13]trap game I'll tell you before practice Friday...

Friday, at our pre-practice meeting, I spoke about the biggest trap game I could remember as a player when it was my turn to address the team. "In 1983, I was a junior at Tenaha High School in East Texas. My dad was our head coach, and we had a good ball club. In fact, we were the #2 ranked 1A team in the state at midseason, with a 5-0 record."

"In the States, especially in the South, teams have an annual Homecoming game where all the past alums are invited back to campus. The Homecoming queen is crowned, girls wear huge mums to the game, and there's even a dance for high school students afterwards. Nowadays, boys make extravagant proposals to ask their date to go to Homecoming with them. It's a very, very, very large deal. In Tenaha, the game is even moved to a Saturday so that other fans in the county can attend. In the morning, a parade takes place through downtown, adding to the festive atmosphere."

"Am I making this clear? Homecoming in Texas is a big deal!"

---

[13] Trap game - The Urban Dictionary defines a trap game as a game played against an opponent generally deemed to be easy to defeat. As a result, a person or team may not prepare as thoroughly as they would for a formidable opponent. Often this attitude and its attendant lack of preparation lead to a loss.

“Coaches normally schedule a weaker opponent so the alumni can see a victory. We never played well on Homecoming when I was in high school. I don’t know if it was because we had a different routine of playing on Saturday or were distracted by the dance afterward, but we didn’t play well. When I became a head coach, I constantly reminded our team that homecoming is for the graduates and not for them to attempt to keep their focus on the game and not all the pageantry. Remember, we're 5-0 and had scheduled a team not all that good - the Cushing Bearkats."

"What year is this again, coach?" Polk asked.

"1983...I know it was before your time, but it was still 11 versus 11 football."

"Did you guys wear facemasks?" Yasir asked, grinning.

"Yes, and we even had shoulder pads. Back to the story, We were a small school with around 30 guys on our team from grades 9-12 which isn't many, but it was enough that if someone got injured, we had a replacement. Cushing's record was two wins and three losses. They weren't very good. They came out for warmups, and we looked over there and saw 12 healthy players. I say healthy because they had one more player dressed out, but he had a broken leg and was on crutches. In small-town Texas, you dressed out if you could walk back in the 80s!” I said, smiling.

"We were the better team but lost homecoming 15-0. We got our butts’ kicked in front of a packed stadium, in front of fans from around East Texas, and didn’t even score a point. To this day, it's my most embarrassing defeat as a player or coach. During the game, they had more coaches than players on the sideline. They literally had one healthy player and one on crutches on the sideline! Texas is larger than Germany! How can the 2nd ranked team in a state lose this game?"

"You guys got the "big head" and looked past them," Leo said.

"No doubt, we didn't think they could beat us. I remember us, I included, talking about how they needed to be careful not to turn an ankle during warmups so they’d have 11. The one backup was 5'5", weighed 100 pounds, and didn’t play, so they kicked our butts with 11 players. If our minds were right and we respected them, we’d have won by 30 points, but the best team doesn't always win."

Jared jumped in and said, "Let's get our minds right. Lock in right now. When Coach Goodman calls a special teams unit, pay attention and get on the field. We don't need a player's only meeting today, coach. As Coach Luster would say, "Let's Go!"

45

DON'T EAT THE CHEESE...UNTIL OCTOBER

July 30, 2022

"Any word from Herrad?" Berti asked me as I entered the cafeteria Saturday at 11:00 a.m.

"He told me last night he was going to ask their team president to sign off on Adam, but he isn't sure it can happen before the game."

"What would the holdup be?" Berti asked.

"The president is on vacation in the Alps, according to Herrad. I guess he doesn't have internet service."

"I'm in contact with the GFL office. They're waiting for my email with the release from Prague."

"We have four hours before the game begins. It's obvious Herrad doesn't want him to play, so I'm not expecting the miracle," I said.

If the "Royal Lab" had wheels and were mobile, the tires would occasionally fly off in all directions. Dealing with Prague was one of those occasions. Playing in Germany would be a great life-experience for Adam. When I asked him what restaurant his favorite in Potsdam was, he told me he doesn't go out. "I cook chicken and rice every night," he said.

"Why don't you go out and eat a döner or pizza now and then? I'm sure Karri could take you somewhere?"

"I like chicken and rice. It's very good to me and easy to cook."

"Text him again now, please, and see if he can update the status," Berti said.

(Herrad) I'm going to play with my kids on this beautiful Saturday morning. I'll let you know if I hear anything; otherwise, I'll not answer any text.

I handed Berti my phone so he could read it for himself. He closed his eyes and said, "We won't have Adam play for us today. If we lose this one, we could go from the #1 seed to not getting a home playoff game."

"Let me have your attention, please," I said to the team in the cafeteria. "Does anyone know what this is?" I asked.

"It's a mouse trap," Mat answered.

"Exactly. Last night I told you about a trap game I'll never get over. A few weeks ago, Coach Luster and I gave you the "Vito versus Hart" story Bill Parcells loved to tell. Today, I will provide you with another Parcells analogy he used with his teams all the time.

"Coach Parcells occasionally reminded his team not to "Eat the cheese." Does anyone know what he meant by this?"

"Not get too cocky after a win?" Chris answered.

"That's correct. Parcells wanted to warn his players not to let success go to their heads.

"There were also other lessons. Elite cheese has to age. Years from now, no one will look back and say, "Man, that 7-0 Potsdam team was great in July." We're going to use a clip today from a movie most of you've probably seen. A swordsman is threatening to kill a guy with just a whip. Hit play."

"Oh yea, Indiana Jones about to mess this dude up," said Divine, a safety from New York.

The man swings his sword several times, making a production out of his skill for the large crowd surrounding the two men. After 20 seconds of watching the man work his sword, Indiana Jones gets an impatient look on his face, pulls out his pistol, and shoots the man dead.

"If we don't respect everyone, we could lose one we shouldn't. Get ready right now for a 4-quarter fistfight. They have weapons. Their QB and two receivers are leading the league in passing yards. We'll be in trouble if we assume we're going into a sword fight, but they pull out a pistol. It's tough to change your mindset at halftime."

"Ok, last movie scene. I'm not showing this one because it's too vulgar, even for grown men like us. Raise your hand if you have seen the movie, Gran Torino?"

Most hands go up in the air. "Someone tell me about Clint Eastwood's character."

"He was an old military veteran who helped an Asian family who lived next door to him," Tim, a backup tackle from Berlin, said.

"Yes, he was an 85-year-old racist who grew to love his non-white neighbors. In one scene, three street thugs are threatening his teenage neighbor. He sees what's happening and pulls his old pickup truck beside the curb.

One of the thugs says, 'What are you looking at, old man?'

"I'm paraphrasing because the language is terrible, but after he calls the thugs a very racist name, he gets out of his truck and stands there. He has a large pistol in his belt and says to them, 'Ever notice how every once in a while you come across someone you shouldn't have messed with?' Then he spits a large amount of tobacco juice near their feet and says, "That's me."

"You crazy man. What don't you get yourself outta here," says one of the thugs. Another says, "Why don't you get out of here before I kick your old wrinkly white ass!"

"Eastwood then sticks his hand in his jacket and slowly pretends to pull out a pistol (I imitate it with my right hand). He sticks his index finger out and points it at the thugs' heads."

"This guy's crazy!" one of them says.

"Get in the truck," Eastwood tells the girl. When they don't let her go, Eastwood pulls out the huge pistol in his belt."

"Hey pops, c'mon now," one of them says with the pistol pointing at him.

"Shut your face!" Eastwood tells him. "You guys don't listen, do you? Now get in the truck."

“They, of course, let her go, and she goes with Eastwood."

"Are we a great team?" I ask. All heads nod yes.

"Here is what a great team will do today. It will shut out the noise. It won't read the press clippings and play with a chip on its shoulder. A great team won't eat the cheese! Great teams win games they’re supposed to win. We’re the better team today, but we better have the mindset that Cologne is packing *heat*."

“We got here because we’re hungry to be great. Stay hungry today! One of our 50 Strong pillars is humility. Be a humble team that expects a worthy opponent to pull out a pistol."

"Do you guys know the world's best, most expensive cheese? It's called Royal cheese, and interestingly enough, it’s not yellow but red and black. It's produced right here in Potsdam. The reason it's so expensive is that it must be aged from exactly April 15th till October. If eaten even one day before, it tastes horrible. But in October, it tastes so good; it's priceless."

I take my right hand and point it at them slowly and deliberately. Finally, I say, "Bang, bang! Let's win #7 today!"

"I will always be grateful for the 2022 Potsdam Royals family. 50 Strong helped our brotherhood reach beyond the football field. We will forever be linked"

Jerome Valbon
#89 Tight End
Paris, France
2023 Team:
Potsdam Royals

46

SHOOTOUT AT THE ROYAL CORRAL

Game #7 vs. The COLOGNE CROCODILES

July 30, 2022

Two hours later, I was standing on the field and noticed the team music was even more vulgar and louder than normal.

"What's going on with our music near the 50-yard line pointing at their end of the field?" I asked Jonas.

"I've heard both teams have been talking trash on Instagram this week. This could be a crazier pregame than normal, and that's saying a lot."

Cologne now had their music also near mid-field, and it was becoming a test of audio superiority.

"Back home, when two people argue over a trivial matter, we call it a pissing contest. This music battle is the biggest urinating contest ever...so stupid."

"Coach, can you help us get the music situation under control?" Mats, our head official again today, asked me.

"Yes, sir, I'm on it."

"We might need a loss to get our focus back. It might happen today whether we want it or not." I said to Jonas.

'CIRCLE OF LIFE'
#11 Magnus Urth #14 Louis Christ

"Their two 'A' receivers are studs. I hope they don't pass it every play because we can't cover them," Jonas said.

Jonas was spot-on. Our defense had a much different assignment defending Cologne from the run-heavy Lions a week ago. Although they don't have much rushing attack, they average almost 350 yards passing a game. Our weakest unit is our secondary, so this was a tough matchup for Berti and Dave, our DB coach. After seeing what the

Rebels receivers did to us, I knew we needed to stay on the field, but with only one running back, it wouldn't be easy.

Cologne won the toss but elected to defer. Our first possession was just what the doctor ordered. We held the ball for 13 plays and kept their offense and studs on the sideline. Jared finished the drive when he caught a 10-yard pass from Chris to put us up 7-0.

"We're onside kicking this, coach. If Schumacher hits it as he did in practice, we have a shot at getting it," Saul told me.

#56 Ludi Rötzscher #50 Mads Højen

Despite our previous struggles with special teams this season, Saul's decision to onside was undoubtedly the year's highlight thus far. Schumacher hit it perfectly and was making new friends fast. Defensive back Jerry Bolton wrestled the ball away in the pile, and we had a chance to swing first again.

"Our ball! Our ball!" Jonas yelled into the headset as our sideline went wild.

"Great call, Saul! That's what I'm talking about! Let's leave those two studs on the sideline as long as possible!"

Six plays later, Chris scores from seven yards out to give us an early 14-0 lead, and Cologne hasn't touched the ball yet.

Once the Crocs finally got their hands on the ball, they worked it down the field with a long, 11-play drive. Quarterback Christian Strong, from Ontario, Canada, scored on a one-yard run to make the score 14-7.

It didn't take us long to get on the board again. After a Heiko eight-yard run, Chris found Polk on a go route for a beautiful 64-yard touchdown. Every defensive coordinator we faced was pulling their hair out, trying to figure out a way to stop our explosive passing game. We were still in the first quarter and had 21 points.

Maybe we weren't eating the cheese?

We had the Crocs right where we wanted them on the next possession. After an 18-yard sack on second down, it looked like we were about to force a punt when the Crocs completed a 72-yard bomb on 3rd and 27. "You've got to be kidding me. I may watch 10,000 more games before I die and never see 3rd and 27 go for 72 yards again. It just can't happen. For God's sake, can we let them make the catch for a 12-yard gain, make the tackle and get the ball back?" I asked Jonas.

On 1st and goal from the two-yard line, Cologne, without a strong rushing attack, decides to throw the ball on three straight plays. We sack them on second down, and their field goal attempt is wide right from the 14-yard line.

"Good job, D! Way to hold them!" I yell as I high-five defenders coming to the sideline.

We get in our no-back formation on our next possession to allow Heiko to rest. On the first play, Chris scrambles and finds Magnus Urth, our new import receiver from Denmark, alone down the seam. Magnus was wide open, with the Cologne secondary focused on Jared and Polk. He raced into the endzone alone to give us a 28-7 lead in the second quarter.

Cologne had too much firepower to keep them down all game. They started clicking offensively. They closed the gap to 28-14 with a 12-yard run, leaving us enough time to score again before halftime.

We did.

Our tempo was wearing them down already. Our two-minute offense worked to perfection for the third time in the last four games going into the intermission. Chris led us on a 70-yard drive in eight plays, finishing it himself with an eight-yard run.

At halftime, we were up 35-14 as we gathered in the shady area off to the side of our locker room. We controlled the game but committed three personal foul penalties in the first half. One on Yasir for talking trash to the defender he was blocking 10 yards down the field.

"I did it. I don't deny it. I was letting #59 know he sucks. I don't regret telling him. I regret the official hearing it. I mean, he does suck, just like I said in the scouting report," Yasir said.

I did something I don't often do; I bit my tongue and kept my thoughts to myself. Yasir is a stud and has controlled his emotions all season. I was not too fond of his attitude on the penalty, but it wasn't time for me to fuss…

Yet.

#8 Chris Helbig #89 Jerome Valbon

47

THEY'RE HUMAN, AFTER ALL

July 30, 2022

Cologne didn't just put away their sword and start firing bullets in the second half; the Crocs pulled out a .357 Magnum and started shooting directly at our defensive backs. Cologne's quarterback, Christian Strong, completed a 31-yard touchdown pass on their first possession to close the gap to 35-20.

To make matters worse, we began a friendly-fire barrage with penalties and turnovers.

After we drove the ball to the Cologne 17-yard line, we faced 3rd down and eight.

"Choice Dig," I said to myself and signaled in the call. "I think Polk will pop open here on the in-cut," I said to Jonas.

Chris dropped back and looked to his right for Polk. A defensive end beat Yasir to the edge on the pass rush for the first time all season. #59 violently inflicted the blindside hit on Chris, who had no idea it was coming. The ball popped loose, and the Crocodiles recovered.

"We're ok! We're alright!" I said, high-fiving guys coming off the field.

"My fault, guys. Damn, I let him get around me. It won't happen again," Yasir said on the bench.

Again, I didn't say a word to Yasir. He was cocky but never made excuses and wasn't now. He was mentally tough enough to brush it off and tell himself, "So what, next play."

"Offense! Offense!" Saul came over, yelling at us.

"Divine just recovered a fumble! Let's go grab the momentum back!" Jonas said to me in the headset. With three minutes left in the third quarter, we had excellent field position at the Cologne 43-yard line.

Second down and three is a passing down for me and most offensive coordinators in today's football. We have two more downs to run the ball and pick up the first down, so we have a free down to throw the ball down the field for a big play. On this 2nd and three, Chris did something he hasn't done all season, he forced a pass to our sideline, and the Cologne corner stepped in front for the interception.

Our two best offensive players made mammoth mistakes on two straight drives. We hadn't played like this all year. This is the recipe for losing a game you shouldn't.

"What the hell did Helbig just do?" Saul asked me.

"He forced one for the first time this season. I guess he and Yasir are both human, after all."

Cologne took advantage and drove down the field, throwing ten passes on the next 11 plays. At one point, we forced a 4th down and 10 and had them where we wanted them. The odds of an offense converting 4th and 10 are less than 10%.

"False start! The receiver jumped!" Berti said, pointing at Jackson, their receiver.

"Let's don't get cute here. Play safe and tackle them in front of the sticks," Chris said on the sideline.

Now it was 4th and 15, and we had them where we wanted them...again. That's until Strong fired his .357 to Jackson for precisely 15 yards and another ridiculous first down. Two plays later, Strong hit Jackson again for a 22-yard scoring strike. The Crocs went for two, and stop me if you've heard this before, Strong threw a quick out to Jackson to narrow our lead to 35-28 with nine minutes remaining in the game.

"Can you please get Clint Eastwood here to threaten Strong and Jackson?" I said to Jonas.

The Cologne kicker squibbed the kickoff on the ground, and Jerome, one of our up-backs, grabbed it and rambled to our 42-yard line, giving us terrific field position.

The offense huddled on the sideline.

"Alright, fellas, we're about to run the ball down their throats. We won't throw it unless we have to. We'll get in our unbalanced formation (both tackles on the same side) and run it behind you!" I said, pointing at Yasir. "Heiko, you've been a warrior, and we need you to be again for the next nine minutes. Put both hands on the ball and take care of it like it's made of gold. About every third play, you'll have your number called to run the ball!" I said, pointing at Chris.

We ran one play, *power left*, eight times in a row. We set the formation to our sideline and wore them out.

- Heiko for five yards
- Heiko for three yards
- Chris for five yards
- Heiko for 11 yards
- Heiko for one yard
- Heiko for nine yards
- Heiko for six yards

#78 Yasir Raji #75 Brenden Oswin #9 Heiko Bals

And finally, with 1st and goal from the three-yard line, Heiko punched it in to put us up 42-28. That drive is what makes Fast N' Wide special. When we needed to help our offense, who'd turned it over the last two possessions, we did with a violent run game. When we needed to help our defense, we bullied the Crocodiles. We didn't trick them. We didn't put the ball in the air. We ran it to our left eight times straight until we scored.

But Cologne wasn't done. They still had bullets in their clip.

Jackson, the receiver who was *taking our lunch money*, returned the kickoff to their 46-yard line. On the next play, Strong launched a deep one to Jackson, who I thought should need an oxygen bottle by now, for a 42-yard gain. "I think I'm having an out-of-body experience. I'm literally floating above the field on a unicorn. This has to be a dream," I said to Jonas.

I was so frustrated that I didn't care whether I was staying in my lane or not. "Can we please triple team #4?!? He's the only one they throw the ball to!" I said on the sideline to any defensive coach who'd listen. I know it didn't help, but having one receiver repeatedly make big plays is insane, and I was dying inside.

Five minutes were left in the game, and we held a shaky, at best, 42-34 lead.

"Hands, team! Hands team!" Saul was calling on the sideline, expecting an onside kick from Cologne, which is what they did. The Croc kicker hit the ball too strong, and it bounced out of bounds, giving us an amazing field position at the Cologne 41-yard line.

"You know what we're going to do. Cologne knows what we're going to do. Let's do it anyway!"

On 1st and 10, Heiko ripped the exhausted Croc defense for a 25-yard gain. After two more Heiko runs, Cologne called time out to stop the clock. Eventually, Chris scored from the one-yard line to seal the victory with a minute left in the game. We escaped with a 50-34 victory. We hadn't played our best game, but I was proud we did what we needed to do in the fourth quarter to finish it.

"Coach, would you like to say anything to the team?" Berti asked me at mid-field.

"I sure would, coach. Those guys didn't just have a saber. They had a dang canon! Heiko, great job today! You were a beast when we needed you the most! Offensive line, we ran the ball 15 straight times in the fourth quarter, and there wasn't a thing they could do about it! I'm a proud coach that we found a way to pull this one out after a rough third quarter!"

"The Crocs will be a playoff team. We may see them again, but we control our destiny now with three games left. We'll be the #1 seed if we take care of business," Berti said.

As I gathered my things on the bench afterward, I overheard a conversation between Leo, our best linebacker, and a friend in street clothes visiting with him postgame. His buddy said, "What was the deal with all the conversions the Crocs got on you guys? It seemed they got it every time they needed a first down."

I could feel the frustration in Leo's voice as he said, "I know! We couldn't stop them on fourth down! If we make them punt on fourth and long, we win this game 50-20 or even worse. We have to figure out a way to get off the field. Once, I was told I must stop and cover the running back if he releases to my side when I blitz on 4th and 15. We've never been told this. Coach said, 'When you're blitzing on a long yardage down, peel off when the running back is releasing. When you came off the edge, it created a huge window for Jackson to catch the dig. Know the situation next time.' Football is harder than it looks in the stands. It's my fault on that one. I watch a lot of film during the week. I'll make sure and remember this next time."

I didn't say anything to Leo then but would attempt to discuss this with his coach. "Football is easy, don't make it hard" needs to be discussed every chance possible. No player should ever stop his blitz (rush full speed through a gap) and do something different. That's how a blitzer's mindset must be. It'd be like asking a scorpion not to sting. It's in their DNA; they can't help it. A blitz is a feast or famine. It's the coaches job to know the risk when we send a defender on a blitz. The worst thing we can do is have Leo blitz half-speed, wondering if he should keep going. We didn't need a sack on 4th and 15. We needed narrow windows and knock down the pass for an incompletion.

Later, Buddy and I ate and drank in our VIP section when he asked, "Have you ever seen anyone dominate like #4 did today coach?"

"I can't say I have. I almost went in myself and tried to jam him at the line. I'm not an expert on our defensive scheme, but we can't allow one player to take over the game. The Rebels threw for 500 yards but had two receivers wearing us out."

“What happened today reminds me of a story my dad, Raymond, used to tell. He was a freshman basketball player at Tyler Junior College in 1958. They were ranked #1 in the country and routinely had a few locals watch practice. On this day, his assignment was to guard their best player, Jones, an All-American forward. Jones was killing him. He had made several buckets in a row. The old men sitting in the bleachers were 'oohing and aahing’.”

“The coach, Floyd Wagstaff, who the gym is named after, said to my dad, "Is there anything you can do, Raymond? Can you try something else? My god, he’s making you look bad, son!"

"The next time down the court, they ran the same play, and Jones again got the ball. This time, Raymond swung and hit him in the jaw, knocking him down. The two fought for a few seconds until the players separated them."

"Praise God, Raymond! You finally did something to stop Jones!"

"My point on this story is we didn't need to get any more personal foul penalties or play with less class, but we needed to go to the extreme schematically to stop #4.”

I got in the car to drive back to my flat. I was exhausted physically and mentally. The Royal Laboratory is becoming more and more complicated. The longer the season, the cloudier the picture is through the microscope. We were hitting our stride on the field offensively, but things were getting crazier by the day off the field.

My phone buzzed. It was a text from Mads Højen, our Danish backup guard, but more importantly, our only long snapper. Although we had only punted a few times, Mads was the only one we had who could snap the ball 14 yards to our punter.

Hey coach, I just want to thank you for all you’ve done for me. It was a pleasure playing for you. I’ve decided to accept a scholarship offer to Monroe Junior College in New York, so I’ll be leaving tomorrow. Good luck the rest of the way. I’ll be rooting for you guys to win it all.

What??? Mads is leaving??? Forget about a backup quarterback; we positively must find a long snapper.

GFL GAMERECAP

vs Cologne

50 (7-0) — 34 (4-3)

	ROYALS	CROCS
TOTAL YARDS	475	456
YARDS RUSHING	223	54
YARDS PASSING	252	402
YARDS PER PLAY	7.3	7
PUNTS	1	0
PENALTIES	10-87	10-90

RUSHING	ATT.	YARDS	AVG.	TDS
BALS, H.	15	113	7.5	
HELBIG, C	13	76	4.7	4

RECEIVING	RECEPTS	YARDS	TDS	LONG
URTH, M.	6	95	1	57
POLK, B.	4	99	1	64
BALS, H.	4	37		16

PASSING	COMP.	ATT.	YARDS	TDS	INT
HELBIG, C	16	30	252	3	

#94 Onni Soininen #81 Mat Dubicki

#15 Jared Wolfe

"Of all the great things we accomplished during the season, the thing I'll remember fondest was the white stripe and the meaning it had for us. When things were looking bleak, all you had to do was find and follow the white stripes!"

Brenden Oswin
#75 Guard
Brisbane, Queensland, Australia
2023 Team
Potsdam Royals

48

LET ME SHOW OUR TROPHIES

August 2, 2022

In mid-July, I received a message on Facebook Messenger.

(Pablo) Dear Coach, I am writing to you from Milano. I am the Director of Sports for the Seamen Milano football team. Next year will be in the [14]ELF. Is it possible to talk about you like our Offensive Coach in Milano (Italy)? As you know, it's a fantastic life experience. In a great country, great city, great team. Please let me know. My best. Pablo.

(me) Yes, sir. I would be interested in speaking with you.

(Pablo). SOUNDS GREAT! I'll write you back tomorrow (right now I'm really busy with my full-time job).

We did a preliminary Zoom interview in the next couple of days. After my experience in Potsdam, I had much more intelligent questions for Pablo, but I'd soon learn that asking questions wasn't in the equation.

Pablo spent 45 minutes telling me about his experience with American football and the Seamen.

"I spent time in California and Arizona learning about American football one summer. It was a very good time of discovery for me."

"We have been one of the premier teams in Italy for years now. We even had Joe Avezzano as our head coach for a season. Do you know who that is?"

"Yes, sir. He coached with the Dallas Cowboys."

"Yes! He came to Milano but tragically had a heart attack and died. We played in the Italian Bowl this season and lost to Coach Art Briles' team 21-17.

Our defense played very well, but we needed more offense. This is why we're looking

---

[14] ELF - European League of Football. The league consists of 17 teams located in Germany, Poland, Spain, Austria, Italy, Switzerland, Hungary, Czech Republic, and France, with plans to expand to 24 teams in 2025.

for an offensive coordinator. We've watched what you're doing with the Royals and think you would help us score more points."

"Thank you. I'm confident in the offensive system. Ironically, its foundation is from when Coach Briles was at Baylor years ago."

"We were very impressed with the 65 points the Royals scored at New Yorker. We know teams don't do that against the Lions."

"Thanks again. I do have a question. Who is the head coach for the Seamen?"

"His name is Paul Pokorny. He became our head coach in 2022."

"Did he fire the offensive coordinator?"

"No, the team's ownership and administration hire and fire all coaches."

"So, Coach Pokorny doesn't have a say in hiring the offensive coordinator for next season?" I asked but already knew the answer.

"Yes, he's involved, but he already knows about you and likes you."

"How can I speak with Coach Pokorny?" I asked.

"I will give him your contact information so you two can connect. Thank you for your time today, coach. Good luck this week versus Cologne."

I should have just let the situation end, but coaching in the ELF appealed to me. It's a multi-country league where a coach can see several amazing cities in a season. Milan might also be a city where Tracy and Coco would want to come to spend the summer.

Coach Pokorny and I corresponded a couple of times. I told him my family, and I would be in Venice in a couple of weeks, and if they were serious, I'd like to meet with them face to face. "I'm back home in Austria. The team is on holiday, but I'll see if I can get the Motti brothers to meet with you. They're the real decision makers for the team."

Tracy, Coco, and I traded a day in Venice for the two-and-a-half-hour journey across northern Italy to Milan. We arrived at the Milan Central train station. Instead of the team picking us up, we were given the address of owner Maximo Motti's real business, a real estate management firm. I asked Coach Pokorny if the Seamen would pay for our train fare from Venice to Milan, which he did.

Italy's very warm in early August, so we were hot and sweaty boarding the train after getting directions from Italian police officers outside the station. We were early, so we found a restaurant for a cold drink and for me to change clothes.

"This is brutal. I'm not sure how a team owner doesn't have the staff to pick us up at the train station," I told Tracy.

Milano Centrale Train Station

"Probably because this is a bigger deal to you than it is to them."

She has never been more correct. We walked into the main office of the real estate company, and there were at least 30 employees.

"Welcome, coach! Great to finally meet you face-to-face," Pablo exclaimed, eagerly shaking my hand.

"This is my beautiful fiancé, Tracy, and our even more gorgeous daughter, Coco," I said, introducing them to Pablo.

He led us to a spacious board room that had a large table at the center. Pablo was impressive with his medium height and muscular physique, making me wonder what his role was for the day. I didn't know Pablo's role today, but I'd be in trouble if it involved arm-wrestling him.

"Did you make it here ok?" Pablo asked.

"Yes, the train ride was fine. We walked around Milan and spent some time at a restaurant across the street to cool off."

You should have just come here if you were early. We have drinks here," Pablo said. He must have been reading my mind about why we spent money across the street when they had such a nice office.

"We have several interested people here who'd like to meet you. Please, make yourself comfortable, and we'll begin soon," Pablo said.

Six members of the Seamen organization eventually entered the room, and we all introduced ourselves. A man in his seventies, dressed and groomed very nicely, spoke first. "My name is Maximo Motti, and I'm the owner of the Seamen." Maybe I was wrong about my impression of the interview. This may be important to them after all.

"Thank you for coming to see us. We're proud of the Seamen organization and are glad you're interested in helping us transition to a much tougher European League of Football," Maximo said.

"Thanks for having us. We're glad we could see everything in person and sit face-to-face. I'm enjoying my time in Potsdam, but I learned things after I got there that I'd like to know before accepting my next position. Tracy and I are now engaged, so this is also a decision for both of us."

"We understand and agree that nothing should come before family. Not even football," Maximo said, smiling.

That was the last time I spoke for the next 30 minutes. The interview wasn't an actual meeting with a back-and-forth dialogue to see if we were a good fit for each other. Tracy and I got a crash course in the history and future of the Seamen by listening to Maximo praise the organization and explain how they would make the transition to the ELF. While I still didn't understand the hierarchy and power structure of the Royals, it was obvious who was running the show in Milan.

"We know you'll call the offensive plays and run your scheme, but the last coordinator only involved our assistant coaches a little. This is Giovanni Berti. He played for us for several years and now coaches the running backs. Will Coach Berti be involved in helping with the game plan?" Maximo asked, pointing at gentlemen across the table.

"Of course. I'll value any input from the coaches that are here. If I were to have access to coaches who spend the time I do on film prep, it would only help us. We have two excellent assistants in Potsdam, but neither can help with the game plan, so I use the players."

"We have excellent assistant coaches here. We were disappointed they weren't utilized more this season. So, we're glad to hear you would value them," Maximo said.

I was also curious to see if they had an interest in the mental game, so I added, "If you guys are interested in mental performance training, I can help in that area also. I helped guide some of the Royals players in April, and we established a players' creed called 50 Strong. If this works out, I can not only help us score more points, but I can also help create an intentional 'band of brothers' type culture."

"That sounds good. I'm sure we would want to help with this," Maximo answered but didn't want to know more about it.

I finally mentioned for this position to work, we would need a flat with two bedrooms and a car.

"Most of our American coaches only receive one-bedroom flats, but we can certainly look into what we can find," Maximo said. "We have a car the team owns that we allow coaches to use when they need one. You will not want to drive a car here most of the time. The trains will take you everywhere, and parking is difficult."

I had two interviews with a team that approached me about joining them, and both were infomercials for the organization. They either didn't know enough about the game or were too proud to ask questions. I also knew this wasn't going anywhere and that poor

Coach Pokorny paid for our train tickets and wouldn't be reimbursed for doing so.

"Ok, we appreciate everyone's time. Thanks for all the hospitality," I said, knowing they seemed to wish they hadn't moved their calendars for this meeting. It was time we got back to Venice, and they got on with their search for an offensive coordinator.

I got up from my chair to shake everyone's hands so we could head out when Maximo stopped me and said, "Just one more thing. Before you leave, please allow me to take you to my office and show you our Italian League Championship trophies."

49

ONE STEP FORWARD AND TWO STEPS BACK

August 12, 2022

With three games left in the regular season, we were the class of the Northern Conference. Our offense was as promised. We were averaging 52 points per game and 535 yards. Chris was leading the league in passing with 313 yards per game. Jared was the top receiver averaging almost ten catches per game and 190 yards. Polk, who teams started out double covering when the season began, was the fourth leading receiver averaging seven receptions and 135 yards per game.

Karri was second in rushing, averaging 7.5 yards per carry, after missing the last game and not playing almost three quarters against the Rebels. Although he would still be out for a few more weeks, Heiko ran well versus Cologne, and Adam was finally cleared to play.

I was Zooming weekly with my Fast N' Wide coaches in the States and was proud to show them our practices and games.

On Tuesday, my phone buzzed with a text from Saul.

Good news! We've been given the go-ahead to find a backup quarterback, and I've located one.

(me) That's great news, for sure! Can he long-snap :)

(Saul) His name is Robbie Patterson. He's from Oregon and was a part-time starter at the University of Montana. He looks like he can play. Look at his highlight video and let me know what you think.

(me) Good job. If he has two arms and two legs, I vote YES. Please get him on a plane as soon as possible.

Buddy and I met for lunch on Brandenburger Strasse, and I shared the good news about Robbie. "If you had something to do with the board allowing us to sign another quarterback finally... THANK YOU!"

"You're welcome, coach. I'm about the lowest man on the totem pole, but I talked about it every chance I could. On another topic, I've got something else I want to speak with you about," Buddy said. "Saul is yelling at our chain crew during the games. They are young players who are, of course, volunteers. They're threatening to quit if he keeps yelling at them."

"What? I agree Saul can be a lot, but I haven't noticed anything. We're trying to play fast, so I'm sure he's getting them to hurry so the officials won't hold us up."

"All I know is we don't have anyone else lined up to run the chains. Can you speak to Saul about how he is treating the boys?"

"I don't know, Buddy. If Saul is having the chain crew hurry, that's something I agree with. Let's do it this way; I'll listen during the game tomorrow and see if he's rude to them. If I hear something, I'll say something."

"A couple of them are friends of my son, and they're tired of how Saul treats them. We don't need any more drama than what we've had lately. I hope he'll lay off them."

"I understand. I'll be watching for it on the sideline tomorrow."

"Thanks, because if it were my son down there, I wouldn't put up with him yelling at him for a second."

GAME DAY

"Coach Vogt, thanks again for allowing me to speak to the team on game days. Guys, get your phones out and queue up a video I just uploaded. Hit play."

A mountain man is pointing his shotgun and about to kill a deer when suddenly, out of nowhere, a bear runs full speed at him from behind and begins mauling him. The grizzly bites the man on the leg and starts dragging him.

"Pause it. This is an iconic scene. I won't even ask this time because I'm sure all know this is *The Revenant*. Many film experts believe this scene won Leonardo DiCaprio the Oscar for best actor. Hit play."

In the intense scene, the grizzly bear fiercely attacks DiCaprio's character, biting his back and violently shaking him. The bear eventually stands on his back, seemingly assessing the aftermath. DiCaprio remains motionless throughout this ordeal.

"What's DiCaprio doing now?"

"He's playing dead, hoping the bear will walk away," Leo says.

"Let's find out. Hit play."

The grizzly begins to shake him to see if he's still alive. Satisfied DiCaprio is dead, the bear walks off far enough for DiCaprio to grab his rifle. When the bear returns to attack DiCaprio, he shoots it in the face. Now the grizzly charges him again and is on top of him, mauling DiCaprio for the second time. The bear isn't taking any chances now. It starts violently biting DiCaprio's back and slinging him around like a rag doll. After a few moments, it appears DiCaprio may indeed be dead. If not, he's headed that way.

"Pause it. Are we the grizzly or DiCaprio?" I asked.

"We're the grizzly, but we'll finish the job," Maciek, our Polish defensive end, said.

"How does this scene end? Anyone remember?" No one says a word. "Hit play."

DiCaprio grabs his knife and stabs the bear in the neck to death. They roll down a steep embankment, and the bear ends up on top of him and still almost kills him.

"Why is this message relevant for a professional football team? Because both teams have grizzlies, and both teams have mountain men hiding a knife. In high school, sometimes we knew we had the most talent, and as long as the bus showed up on time, we'd win. You college and pro guys know more about this than I do. We've dominated some teams for two quarters. We've been the grizzly, stood on their heads and roared and thought they were dead. The Rebels didn't lay there and die. The Crocs kept trying to stab us in the neck. Adler has a quarterback who's been an Eagle for a decade. He's going to fight back and not quit."

"Our 50 Strong pillars talk about preparation and humility. We've prepared, but we must also be humble enough to know they have some grizzly in them. Their coaching staff is thought to be the best in Germany. After the 51-17 butt-kick in week #2, they will have something different ready for us. They're in the playoff hunt at 4-3 and have the tiebreaker over Dresden. Back to our pillars, "Play Smart" means no dumb penalties. Let's keep our cool out there. Be your "Brother's Keeper" and take care of each other."

"How long will it take us to win this game?" I asked.

"All four quarters. We learned this playing against the Adler at Rostock. They'll play hard the entire game," Jerome said.

"We don't want it any other way, do we? Disciplined, relentless teams win championships. Let's go be the grizzly today, but don't take our foot off their necks!"

I felt good about the message. The guys were locked in and focused.

"How was the pregame speech?" Jonas asked me when I got to the field.

"You want to know how the pregame speech was? Ask me again in about four hours. But my fingers are crossed that they were listening. I think we'll be back to our old selves today."

I couldn't have been more wrong. The stuff was about to hit the fan. Sooner rather than later.

I went to the field after meeting with the offensive line before warm-ups. There weren't many people at the stadium yet, but a few female volunteers were preparing for the game and several kids were running around. Our speakers were on our 49-yard line, facing Adler. Our music, which is always vulgar, was so bad I didn't know people wrote songs with such disgusting lyrics.

"I'm that flight that you get on, international, First-class seat on my lap...!"

What the heck?! Are you going down this road again?! I thought about finding a wall to beat my head into until I passed out.

"Hey coach, please remember the chain crew, guys. If Saul is a jerk to them, please stop it," Buddy reminded me. I thought, geez, I've got a million things on my mind, but I said, "Sure, I'll pay attention."

Our warm-up was good, but more chatter than usual. Today could be a chippy game. After we kick our last extra point, we always get a repetition of our tight punt, where we snap the ball from our five-yard line and kick toward the middle of the field.

Today, the Adler was working their full offense and defense near mid-field when Heiko punted the ball right into the middle of them. They scattered and were not happy. Both teams began shouting at each other. Mats and the officials asked for both teams to go in and disperse. I was embarrassed for what seemed like the fourth pregame in a row.

"What the hell, Heiko?" I said to him angrily. "Why'd you do that?"

"Saul said I could."

For the first time in warm-ups, I didn't ignore the chaos. I looked at Saul and asked, "Did you tell Heiko it was ok for him to punt the ball into Adler?"

"I didn't understand he wanted to punt the ball directly into them," Saul said.

"That was no class all the way. I swear we act worse every pregame."

The locker rooms are across the street. Both teams enter the same doors and go down the same hall to their respective rooms. Teams are just across the hall from each other. I headed that way to make sure we didn't do anything stupid but also to speak with the Berlin head coach.

"I'm going to find their Coach Fatah and apologize to him for how classless we just were," I told Jonas. I waited at the door until a few Adler coaches, including Coach Fatah, walked up.

"Coach Fatah, excuse me, but I'm Randy Jackson, the offensive coordinator for the Royals. I want to apologize for all the crap you guys endured from us in pregame, especially when we punted your team. I've seen a lot since I've been here, but today was a new low."

"Thanks, coach. Yes, today's been crazy. Before warm-ups began, my 12-year-old daughter was with me on the field, and one of your defensive backs was cursing so loud on our end that I asked him to stop. He then cursed at me. I know these are grown men, but I should be able to have my daughter on the field and not get cussed or hear the music you guys play."

"I understand. I'm trying my best, but some of this is out of my control. What happened doesn't represent every Royal."

"Thanks, Coach Jackson. You're doing a hell of a job. Everyone in the northern conference knows you're making a difference in how the Royals are playing this season."

I walked into the locker room. Guys were going through their last-minute preparation for the game, going to the bathroom, applying eye black, wrapping more tape to their wrists, and anything else to kill the 15 minutes before we ran through the tunnel.

I didn't ask them to stop what they were doing, but I decided to give them some reminders. "I've got one question for you, fellas; Are you going to be the mauler or the maul-lee? Don't let all the crap and trash talk affect us. Play smart! Today will be a 15-round fight, and no one is worth a 15-yard penalty. Let's keep our mouths shut and maul them like a grizzly. He didn't say anything to him. He just abused him."

"Time to go, Royals!" Buddy said to the team. "Let's get to go to the tunnel."

"Everybody up! Everybody in really quick," Jerome said. "Let's keep our composure today and take care of business. We all know about the Adler and what they'll try to do today. They're a bunch of punks who'll try to get in our heads and get us to retaliate! Don't fall for it! Be a 50 Strong guy and play hard but play smart! Let's break it out, shut their mouths, and kick their asses!"

I waited until everyone left the locker room and then headed out. Walking down the hall, I saw the Adler starting quarterback, Zach Cavanaugh. I met him after the game in Berlin, and we had a nice talk. Cavanaugh's a 36-year-old Massachusetts native who's married to a local, and they have two kids. He seemed like a good guy, so I said, "Good luck today, Zach."

"You too, coach. Stay safe out there. Watch your back."

"Thanks," I said and kept walking to the field.

Wait a minute, did he tell *ME* to *stay SAFE*?

50

UNSPORTSMANLIKE AGAIN AND AGAIN AND AGAIN AND...

August 13, 2022

It was the defense's turn to be introduced to the crowd. As each starter's name was called, he ran through the tunnel to midfield to be greeted by the rest of the team.

"Starting at outside linebacker, number 27, Coooooodyyyy Crrrraaannnnsssttttonnnnnnn!!!!" our announcer said, doing his best “let's get ready to rumble” impersonation.

Our next defender appeared, running a few quick steps out of the tunnel. He turned towards the Adler bench and made a throat-slash gesture with his right arm.

"Did you just see that?" I incredulously asked Jonas, who was in our makeshift coaches' booth behind the Adler bench.

"No, I'm getting situated over here in the booth. A few Adler players told me to go to hell on the way up here. This is going to be an interesting day."

Me and Coach Saul

I looked around the sideline to see if there was any reaction from a member of the coaching staff to the throat slash. No one seemed to notice. "I know I'm an idiot, but I continue to be amazed by how classless we are sometimes.

Have you ever watched the old show '*Twilight Zone*?'"

"No, I've never heard of it."

"I figured you were too young. Well, we’re in the twilight zone right now."

Adler won the toss but deferred, so we, of course, elected to take the ball. This time, our offense didn’t get the chance to score on our first possession.

"He has a crease! He has a crease!" Saul shouted as Polk caught the kickoff at the one-yard line, then put on his afterburner and split the Adler kickoff team. He had one man to beat, the kicker, who had no shot to stop the fastest player in the league.

"Yes, sir! Yes, sir! We've been close all season. We finally "housed" one!" Jonas yelled into the headset.

The 99-yard return to open the game put us up 7-0 with 10 seconds off the clock.

"I wish there was an official record of the team that scores in less than a minute. We might have it," I said to Chris.

#3 Brandon Polk #24 Simon Alvarez
#52 Leo Bosch #14 Louis Christ

Berlin is a typical GFL team. Cavanaugh is an older version of Johnny Manziel with his playmaking ability and veteran savvy. The Eagles are averaging 35 points per game and are fourth in the league in total offense. They started the game with three straight pass completions to advance to our 31-yard line. Four plays later, Berlin ran around our right end from 10 yards out for the touchdown. The score was 7-7 with only four minutes gone in the first quarter.

After another excellent return by Polk, we set up shop at our 46-yard line. Heiko and Chris combined to run the ball down Adler's throat. Chris finished the drive with a nine-yard keeper over our left side. Saul dialed up a successful fake PAT where Jared completed a pass to Jerome to make it 15-7.

Our defense held Berlin and forced a Cavanaugh punt. For the first time, we were backed up, starting at our 13-yard line. The second quarter was starting, and it was time to see what our new back could do.

"Adam, it's your turn. Relax and have fun," I told the 20-year-old Žoužełka, who Prague finally released. He's a great kid. Adam's 100% a "Yes, sir," "No, sir," type and didn't mind sticking his face mask on a blitzing backer in practice. Karri had coached him every rep in practice, and they'd become good friends.

"Let's go, Adam! Trust the white stripes!" Karri yelled as the offense jogged onto the field.

On the drive, Chris hit Heiko, who was back at receiver, for 12 yards and Polk for a 26-yard chunk, but a holding penalty brought it back.

"They are giving us a five-man box when we're 4-wide. Let's give the ball to Adam and see what he can do," I said to Jonas.

Adam could run!

He showed his speed with a cutback on his third carry that went for 20 yards. "Adam's tapping the top of his helmet," Jonas said in the headset.

"Magnus, go for Adam and put Heiko at running back," I said. On the next play, Heiko burst through the line for a 34-yard touchdown. The score was 22-7 early in the second quarter.

Adam was bent over, catching his breath, when I said, "Dang it, buddy, if you'd stayed in, it'd have been you standing in the endzone."

"Yes sir, sorry, coach. I'm not used to our tempo yet. We didn't play this fast in Prague."

It looked like we were in complete control when our lack of discipline started raging like the grizzly on DiCaprio.

"Unsportsmanlike. Number 94 of the defense, late hit on the quarterback," Mats said into his microphone.

After our defense forced another punt, we returned to mauling ourselves with another big penalty.

"Unsportsmanlike. Number 25 of the defense, blindside block on a defenseless player," Mats said into his microphone.

"Unbelievable! Come on, guys!!" someone behind me yelled on the sideline. No kidding, I thought....un-freakin-believable.

We started on our 14-yard line, but after three plays, one of them a 47-yard bomb to Jared, we were on the Adler 28-yard line.

"Catalina wine-mixer! Catalina wine-mixer!" I yelled. Catalina wine-mixer is, you guessed it, a gadget play.

“Go, Hit!” Bobby yelled and snapped the ball to Chris, who was under center for the first time all year and not in the shotgun. Chris handed the ball to Polk, coming across the formation in jet motion. Polk then tossed it back to Jared on a reverse. Jared, who has six completions on the season, threw another strike to Heiko for a 15-yard gain.

But…there’s a flag.

"Unsportsmanlike. Number 15 of the offense," Mats said again into his microphone.

"What???" I yelled at Mats. "What the hell did #15 do? He's an accountant who helps old ladies cross the street?”

"He shoved an Adler player after the play. He's lucky we didn't toss him."

Et tu, Jared? I thought. If Jared is becoming bush-league, all hope is lost.

#50 Yasir Raji

"I'm not here right now. This is a bad dream. It's a Freddy Krueger-ish nightmare, and when I wake up, I'll be in a much better place...like hell or the dentist," I said to Jonas.

"Magnus, go get Jared," I said.

“What the hell? You’re one of the sane ones.” I asked Jared.

"That jerk was in Chris' face. I was protecting our QB1, coach. My fault all the way. It won't happen again, but they are talking more crap than any team I've ever heard, and I wasn't going to let him mess with Chris," Jared said.

I called five straight run plays to Adam. "Let's see if he taps out on this drive," I said to Jonas. On his fifth touch, Adam punched it across the goal line to complete the 86-yard drive and increase our lead to 28-7. Saul dialed another fake PAT, and Heiko kept it for the two-point conversion. We were up 30-7 with 7 minutes left in the half versus a playoff team.

"There's another flag on the field," Jonas said.

"Unsportsmanlike. Number 78 of the offense, taunting," Mats said for the fourth time in the quarter. Yasir's mouth had cost us 15 yards for the second game in a row.

"Dammit! I've never seen anything like this!" I yelled to no one in particular.

We were playing lights out offensively, but I couldn't enjoy it. A lack of discipline is a cruel mistress. It always costs you in big games. We wouldn't beat an elite team with our lack of self-control and arrogance.

"Guys, I know we're kicking their butts. We're ripping their flesh and swinging them around like we own them. But four personal foul penalties in a quarter isn't only embarrassing, but it might also be a world record for lack of discipline. We won't win it all if we don't learn to control ourselves. Mark my words and put them in 4" headlines. We'll win this game, but we need to think about the bigger picture. It's not about this game. It's about a ring!"

Adler scored to close the gap to 30-14.

Chris started dicing up the Adler again. He completed four passes and ran twice for a combined 36 yards. On second and goal from the five, Chris tossed a five-yard touchdown pass to Heiko right before the half ended. We'd again worked our two-minute offense to perfection and were up 37-14. We clinched the Northern Conference championship and home-field throughout the playoffs with a win, but I wasn't a happy camper.

We're in control, but I was more frustrated than at any point so far this season, and that was saying a lot. We played the most undisciplined half of football I could remember. It'd be unacceptable if my team got three personal foul penalties in a season, but no one was saying a word about it here.

I became madder and more frustrated with every step I took to our halftime area across the street. Pregame warmups were so bad now I had to apologize to our opponents, and we may have just set a new low for the game of football with four personal fouls in a quarter. We're going down a slippery slope that I couldn't stomach.

I sat down and grabbed a piece of yellow cake from our food brought from the sideline. I listened to our guys laughing and talking like they were oblivious to the embarrassment of the last two hours.

It took about a minute for me to go from mad to boiling to a nuclear fusion in my body. I stood up and faced the team and…

Went off.

"Does anyone have our 50 Strong posters that all the members sign after our pregame meal?!" I asked loudly. Anyone?! Can someone please go find it so we can burn it at the 50-yard line? We had four personal penalties last quarter! Are you kidding me? I'm sick and tired of this team playing like we don't honor the game! I talked about us not being arrogant for a few weeks now, but today you guys seem to want to show the world you don't give a crap!"

I was worked up now. The yellow piece of cake in my mouth was flying out into the air like confetti at a New Year's Day parade, but I continued my passionate rant. "Has any team, and I mean since the world began, won a championship committing four personal fouls in a quarter? No, damnit!" I answered myself quickly. No team has won a championship committing four personal fouls in a half or a game! In fact, I'd bet you as many euros as you want; Alabama doesn't get four in a freakin' year!"

"I wonder if the Patriots or Chiefs punt the ball into their opponent or throat slash when they run through the tunnel? I wonder if any Power 5 team puts their music box at the

50-yard line and points it at the opposition? Are you kidding me? There's nothing, and I mean nothing, professional about what we've done today other than from the snap of the ball to the whistle. All three phases are playing as well as we have all dang season, but we're so damn immature and undisciplined, it's no fun to watch!"

"Smart teams wear rings! Every penalty we get gives them a chance to pull out their knife and stab us in the face. I know I'm not the only one, but my family is a long way from here, and if I'm going to be separated from them for months, I want to coach guys who give a crap and play the game the right way! No one's worth a 15-yard penalty! Fifteen-yard penalties increase a team's scoring on a drive by 60%! We just keep doing dumb stuff! 'Play hard - Play smart! They seem like empty words right now! We worry about Instagram during the week. We talk trash before the game! Dammit, we act like we're 15 freakin' years old! We talked about 50 Strong, but I didn't see many of our pillars in the first half. Let's grow up and honor the game. Has anyone found our poster?"

I exhaled and walked away.

I found Berti, who was still walking up to the team area and hadn't heard a word of it.

"I thought they needed to be sent a message. We are in control and should win this one, so I took the opportunity to refocus us. I know you haven't given me the authority to chew out the entire team, so I apologize for overstepping my boundaries."

"You did what?"

51

YOU DIDN'T KNOW?

2nd HALF

"I came here to win a ring. We won't get one by being idiots before and during the game. I went off on them."

"That's fine with me. We needed to hear it. We act like we can't handle being good."

I walked away and composed myself. After a few moments, I returned to the offense to shift everyone's mind back to football and the second half. "Ok, guys, let's regroup, me mostly, and talk about what we'll do moving forward. I know in my heart most of you guys aren't eating the cheese or going to take your paw off their faces. I'm sorry some of you had to hear that."

"I'm extremely proud of our first half production. Kickoff return - amazing. Heiko and Adam - you guys are making them pay for not respecting our run game. Offensive line - we look as good as we have all season. Everyone comes over to the bench and knows exactly what we're doing and what adjustments we need. You guys have gone from asking me questions on the sideline to telling me the answers. Forget about finding me the poster to burn if someone could find me a brat or white asparagus to eat. I know I'm a hard ass and difficult most of the time, but I know football. I know what wins games and what loses games. We have all the tools to win games- playmakers, a violent run game, and great leadership; hell, we're even getting a backup quarterback next week. But please hear what I'm saying: smart teams wear rings. Disciplined teams wear rings, and undisciplined teams wear t-shirts that say 'Shoulda, Woulda, Coulda' on the front."

"If we return to 50 Strong, we'll wear rings!"

"We all know Cavanaugh is a ticking time bomb. He can make a big play at any time. We'll play it by ear and see what we need to do, but we're keeping everything the same for now. We'll continue to run and pass and light up the scoreboard. I love you guys. Let's keep our Royal paw on their faces."

I walked out to the field exhausted. I know they'll begin tuning me out if I keep hammering them about discipline, but I also can't sit by and accept the mockery of the game I see at times.

"Hey, coach! You got a second?" Buddy asked.

"I've got about two seconds, but that's it."

"Have you talked to Saul about how he's talking to the boys on the chains? They say it's bad again today."

"I know Saul's British and sometimes doesn't care if anyone likes him, but I've got to be honest. I'm glad the chain crew's moving fast. I haven't heard anything negative, but I'm pretty busy when we have the ball."

I decided to go to the source and speak to the boys briefly before we started the second half. "You guys doing ok, today?" I asked them. "We appreciate how fast you guys are moving. The quicker you guys go, the faster we can snap the ball. I know Coach Goodman fusses a little to get y'all to keep up with our offense, but he doesn't mean anything by it. Do y'all understand what I mean?"

"Yes, sir. We understand. The head official told us he would throw a flag on Coach Goodman if he yelled at us again."

"Ok, well, let's hope that doesn't happen. How about I buy you guys a brat or something after the game?"

"The first four minutes of the second half! Let's go, defense! Give us a three and out, and let's dominate this half of the middle eight!" I shouted and high-fived as I walked down the sideline while Schumacher was teeing up the kickoff. My dream of winning the first four minutes faded rapidly. On the first play, the Adler pulled out their knife. Cavanaugh hit ex-Royal receiver Max Zimmerman for a 42-yard *stab in the neck* to our four-yard line.

Two plays later, the score was 37-21.

The craziness continued. Before the kickoff, Mats walked over to the Adler bench and began speaking with Coach Fatah, who was as animated as I'd seen a coach. He pointed at Jonas in one of the three temporary press boxes the stadium provided for broadcasters, our coaches, visiting coaches, and our filmer to get 30 feet higher than ground level.

"They're telling me I have to come down!" Jonas said in the headset.

"What? Why?"

"The Adler coaches are telling the ref I can see their whiteboards, and we could be spying on them. This is ridiculous! We've been doing this all season."

Mats was now standing in front of the scaffolding and telling Jonas and our defensive coach they had to come down. Some of the Berlin players were pointing at our coaches as well. Mats came over to our sideline and explained the situation to Berti.

"C'mon, Mats! This is crap, and you know it," Berti said.

"Coach Vogt, I know this isn't your doing, but the city of Potsdam has to do better than this. Your coaches can probably hear the Adler staff with the tower so low and close to them."

"Why haven't you done this before now?"

"Because Coach Fatah was the first to complain about it."

The Adler smartly squibbed their kickoffs after Polk's opening house call. This kick bounced to Jerome at our 36. He made a guy miss, and we had excellent field position at the Berlin 43-yard line. We attacked quickly and efficiently. A Chris to Magnus touchdown pass of 21 yards capped a short four-play drive. Our point after snap [remember Mads left for New York] was wide, and we missed the kick to keep the score 43-21.

"That 'a boy, Magnus! Good job finding grass in the secondary and getting open!" I said to the offense at our meeting area on the sideline. "There's plenty of time left. Let's keep applying the pressure and score 60."

I saw Jonas standing behind the guys, so I checked on him when the offense broke it out to end the meeting. "Hey man, you made it over here. It'll be nice to have you on the sideline for a change," I said to Jonas.

"There's nothing nice about what happened! I was in the box doing what I always do when Adler players started looking at me and saying, “Nothing to see here, buddy!” They became more frustrated when we got a lead, which turned into screaming. Their coaches got involved, and one of their players even threw a full water bottle at me! They got the ref to come over, and he said I couldn’t be up there because it was right behind their bench. Unbelievable! The Adler players threw water at us and cussed us as we came down and left their area. The refs should be throwing them out of the game!"

"I swear they'll start making the Twilight Zone again, and the first episode will be about the GFL. They taunted and threatened you?"

"Yes! I may get the next unsportsmanlike penalty. I'm so mad right now! I can't believe the refs didn't do anything about it."

"I'm sure they didn't see any of it. Who would think a team would act like that? On second thought, I'm sure we would."

Back to the game, Berlin wasn't playing dead. They were fighting back. Cavanaugh completed a 15-yard bullet to close the gap to 43-27 with six minutes remaining in the third quarter.

The ensuing Adler kickoff again landed in Jerome's hands, and he returned it to our 47-yard line. Chris quickly completed passes to Polk and Jared to move the ball down to the Berlin nine-yard line.

"Is that a flag over there?" I ask Jonas.

"Yep, in our backfield."

"If it's a personal foul on one of us, I swear I'll go out there, and somebody will die. It'll probably be me, but I'll feel better either way."

Mats spoke to the umpire, then walked to the hash mark facing our stadium to announce the call. "We have two fouls on the play...Holding on the offense, number 75."

"Dammit! Can we get out of our own way for once?!" I asked no one in particular.

#25 Adam Žouželka

Mats continued, "Dead ball foul. After the play...Unsportsmanlike conduct…Number 90 of the defense, shoving the offense after the whistle."

"Yes! Thank you, Jesus! Great call, Mats!"

Heiko found the endzone running behind Ludi and Stefan two plays later, and we had a three-score lead again. It was 50-27 with two minutes left in the third quarter.

The drama continued in the fourth quarter. As usual, it wasn't over in the least. The Adler forced our only punt, then began a 10-play, 85-yard drive that was kept alive by a pass interference call on a 3rd and 13.

The connection of Cavanaugh to Zimmerman for a three-yard touchdown made the score 50-35.

The offense huddled on the sideline. We were backed up after Adler finally hit an outstanding squib kick that took two funny hops. Magnus was lucky to get his hands on it and return it to the 12-yard line.

"What do we do when we need to close out the game?" I asked.

"We run it down their throats," Brenden said.

"Yes sir! This is where you guys earn the big bucks," I said, pointing at the linemen.

"Adam, fist to chin ball security. Take care of the football."

We ran the ball five consecutive plays. On the fifth, Chris had broken free for an 11-yard gain, but an Adler defender punched the ball out from behind! A mass of bodies from both sides began fighting for the ball. Mats was uncovering players as best he could when suddenly, he pointed…to Adler's endzone.

"Dammit!" Chris screamed as he came over to the sideline. "Dammit!"

Cavanaugh was doing his best DiCaprio impersonation. He was trying to make the miracle happen. He'd done it many times before in his 10-year GFL career. The Adler started at their 44-yard line with five minutes remaining in the game, and the score was still 50-35. Cavanaugh ran it himself or threw eight straight plays to get Berlin deep into our territory.

Our defense put their paw back on the Adler's neck and forced a 4th down and five at our 19-yard line.

Cavanaugh threaded the needle again on an out route for a nine-yard gain and a first down. But...there was a penalty, and it was against the Adler!

"Holding on the offense, number 62," Mats announced to the crowd, who were making as much noise as 1,700 could make.

Now, Berlin had 4th and 15 at our 29-yard line. We had them right where we wanted them. Cavanaugh looked for his all-GFL receiver, Zimmerman, who'd gotten a little separation from our corner, Hjalmar. Our safety, Jerry Bolten, stepped in front and picked it off right before the ball hit its mark!

We knelt the ball three times and won another game that was more stressful than it should have been.

As soon as our team meeting broke up, I found the chain crew. "Hey boys, Great job today! Y'all follow me, and we'll get something to eat from the VIP area!"

After I got them a plate, I went to my car to grab my phone charger to call Tracy when I ran into Mats near the locker room.

"Great job today, Fast Football Randy," Mats said.

"Thank you. This team takes years off my life, but we find a way to pull it out."

"I heard what you said to Coach Fatah before the game. That was good of you to apologize to him. I'm sure he appreciated it."

"Thanks; I'm not used to how we act around here. One of us will have to change, or I will find a Zeppelin to jump out of."

"You mean.... you didn't know?" Mats asked.

"I didn't know anything. Know what?"

"The Royal's reputation. You didn't know this was their normal behavior when you took the job?"

"I had no idea. I'm not sure I'd ever heard of the GFL before last year. We don't hear about European football much back in the States. I got on the Europlayers website and uploaded my resume. Saul was the first person to contact me, so I accepted."

"Last season, in particular, it was tough to come here and officiate. We'd have to deal with so much extra stuff going on. It was like policing children as much as officiating football. I told you this early in the year, but the team has been much better this season until the last couple of games. You've made a difference in the program. I'm unsure why it has shifted back, but it's been a big change overall."

Oh, man. My mind was going full throttle down the rabbit hole of the last several months. I remember Saul asking me to help them with culture on our first Zoom, but I didn't realize the extent of what I'd walked into. Whenever I feel like we're becoming a team of professionals, someone throws a shovel of dirt on the 50 Strong casket.

I define culture as how a team "thinks, speaks, and acts." This is the magic of coaching, to get a bunch of individuals to point in the same direction, to truly want to be a part of something bigger than themselves. But there is only so much I could do as an assistant coach. I've written two books on turning programs around by installing an intentional culture. Why did Berti and Saul allow me to implement a players' creed but still be ok with or even promote the old ways? Maybe the Royals wanted to be different but didn't want a complete overhaul. We built a new program mindset from the ground up, and there wasn't anything left from the past regime. Now, I feel like 50 Strong is going head-to-head with FYGR.

And losing...

I was reminded of a story of a college basketball program that signed the #1 recruit in the nation. The head coach was ecstatic. He told the alumni they now had the "missing piece of the puzzle." Conference championships and possibly even national championships were on the horizon.

Except for one thing, the player was a cancer.

When the coach confronted him about his arrogance, selfishness, and work ethic, the player said, "I've always been this way and ain't changing now."

The coach admitted he'd never asked him about his character. He knew he was a once-in-a-lifetime player, so he hoped for the best. As soon as the recruit got on campus, things went south. It didn't take long to realize he wouldn't help the team win championships but would destroy them from the inside out.

The day after the season ended, the toughest and most frustrating in the coach's career, the player entered the transfer portal.

As I drove home, I knew this team had a decision to make. I wasn't sure what it would be, but I'd press the issue at our meeting on Monday. Our next film session would be the season's most "Tell the Truth" Monday.

My phone buzzed around midnight. It was a text from Buddy.

I'm hearing some things about your halftime rant you won't like.

GFL **GAMERECAP**

vs Berlin Adler

50 (8-0) — 35 (4-4)

	ROYALS	ADLER
TOTAL YARDS	456	425
YARDS RUSHING	269	144
YARDS PASSING	187	287
YARDS PER PLAY	8	6.7
PUNTS	1	2
PENALTIES	8-99	8-63

RUSHING	ATT.	YARDS	AVG.	TDS
ŽOUŽELKA, A.	16	101	6.3	1
HELBIG, C	7	86	12.5	1

RECEIVING	RECEPTS	YARDS	TDS	LONG
WOLFE, J.	4	80		47
BALS, H.	5	39	1	12

PASSING	COMP.	ATT.	TDS	YARDS	INT
HELBIG, C	14	23	2	177	

(North Champions)

"Being a part of the Fast and Wide offense last year changed how I view football. The simplicity of the offense and the amazing culture we had is what stood out to me the most. Coach Jackson's attention to detail and passion for the game helped me become a better coach. I'm grateful we will be friends for life."

Jonas Heck
Assistant Coach
Fulda, Germany
Head Coach Fulda Saints

52

FYGR OR 50-STRONG?

August 15, 2022

(Buddy) Some things were said at halftime after you yelled at the team that you wouldn't like hearing about.

(me) Really? Like what?

(Buddy) I'm not exactly sure, but I'm hearing about some bitching by the players after you walked away. They didn't understand why you yelled at the whole team.

I decided to do what I usually do in a situation like this, tackle it head-on. Delaying until Monday would only increase my frustration, so I took a deep breath and charged into the *Autobahn 80* chat like a bull in a China shop.

(me) I was told you guys didn't understand why I went nuclear at halftime. It didn't sit well with you, etc. My mindset was this...we're all sacrificing to be on this team. We can win it all, but we'll mess this up until we get more serious about being professional than a culture of disrespect. I'm only 1% of this team, but I seem to be the only voice who understands the importance of discipline and respecting our opponent. Only teams that are FFFFFFFFFING DOMINANT can disrespect everyone and win a championship like the Miami Hurricanes back in the day.

I'm frustrated my halftime talk didn't sit well with some of you. I have no interest in coaching a "Miami-type" team. I don't think we are, but some of us might enjoy it. We'll get our ass beat if this is what we want to be. Let me know if the BS we did today is what we want to be about.

Immediately after I hit send on the text, I knew I should've waited to address it in person, but, as a team, we'd gone down a long road to creating 50 Strong and a band of brothers' culture. Seeing it dissipating more and more each day was maddening for me. I was close to going to Bridge of Spies and jumping off. It wasn't tall enough to kill me, but I'm not a great swimmer so it might have done the trick.

Jerome, our elder statesman who'd become my part-time mental coach, also texted the group within a few minutes.

(Jerome) Appreciate you telling us all that but let's talk about it Monday face-to-face. But I can confirm we didn't bitch about you behind your back. When you returned, we

were all locked in and ready to go. We all got love and respect for you.

(me) Thank you, my friend. I will be able to sleep now. I want to win badly and am going to fight for it. I love that you guys are in my foxhole...I'm in yours. We have to, have to, have to get away from the culture of disrespect. Our message has been "It's about us" from day one, and as soon as we get on the field, we start mocking and ridiculing our opponent.

On Monday morning, Saul and I met with the entire offense. Instead of talking about our 50 points, 456 yards, and Adams' 101 yards versus the Adler, it was time to find out what we would be moving forward.

"Fellas, I'm going to speak to you from the heart right now. I'm sorry for my angry rant going too far at halftime. I knew we would win the game and thought it would be a good wake-up call. Coaches who are smart chew butt after victories, not defeats, so I figured I could refocus everyone. I have a lot of flaws; God knows I do. One of my biggest problems is anger and a lack of tolerance. At halftime, I did what I told you in our first face-to-face meeting I wouldn't do-be an angry coach. I know I've let some of you down in the past with my outbursts, and I want to apologize for that. I definitely crossed a line this time, and I'm truly sorry. Most of y'all know Jerome's my *get-back* coach when I fuss at players and officials. He and I have talked about everything, and once again, he's helped me see it from your perspective."

Jerome jumped into the conversation, "Coach, we're all grown men, and we understand we can't have seven unsportsmanlike penalties in two games. We know we shouldn't have seven in the season, but when you yelled at us like that the other day, it made me feel like a young child being scolded by his father."

"I get it 100%. This is why I wanted to address it with you guys and take full ownership."

Jared jumped in, "Let's all pledge to do better from now on. I got my first personal foul penalty ever in the last game, so I'm not judging anyone. If Coach Jackson is man enough to apologize, then I am too. I'm sorry, and it'll never happen again."

"Thanks, Jared. You and everyone in here have my word 'I'll do better. I'll still coach hard, don't get me wrong, but no more spitting yellow cake everywhere and threatening to burn 50 Strong," I said, getting the guys to laugh a little. Speaking of 50 Strong. I'd like to go to the next reason we're meeting today. The first time I was on a Royals' practice field was before we started training camp. Saul asked me to coach the offensive line for a 17U practice, so I jumped in to help. At some point that night, I went to get a ball out of our ball bag. I'm sure all of you know that on the top of the bag is a clear plastic opening where a team can place their logo or brand to identify the bag."

"That evening when I looked at the bag, it said, and still does, of course, F____ YOU, GO ROYALS."

A few guys smiled, but my tone was serious, and the mood was anything but jovial, especially for an 8-0 team that had just clinched home-field for the playoffs.

“Many of you met in this building in April and May and helped make a one-of-a-kind players' creed. At the time, I thought we were creating a culture, but we were instead replacing a culture of FYGR. 50 Strong has made an impact. I have no doubt it has. Our team cares about each other; our creed has helped foster this 100%.”

“But the team that took the field on May 21st against Dresden has changed, and I'm not sure why, but I’ll point out what I've witnessed the past month.

- The pregame music battles we've had with the other teams
- The throat slash by one of us coming out of the tunnel
- Punting into Adler
- The unsportsmanlike penalties
- The scouting reports. I see "Oh, the disrespect" typed in our chat. Champions respect their opponents.
- We didn't wear shirts, only ties to the NYer press conference.

We practice like we want to win a ring. Our offensive production is German Bowl quality, so why aren't we conducting ourselves like champions when it counts the most, at the games? It’s time for us to decide what we will be. It’s time to declare right now. I’m going to go “full Texan” on you right now and give you an example of this from the Alamo.”

"In 1836, the San Antonio mission, known as the Alamo, was surrounded by 1,800 Mexican soldiers led by General Santa Anna. There were only 200 Texans inside defending it. The Mexicans laid siege to the Alamo before attacking. A few days before the attack, Santa Anna sent a message informing William Travis, the commander of the Alamo, to surrender or his entire force would be killed. Knowing the odds were stacked against them, Travis gathered his men, removed his sword, and drew a line in the sand. To this day, when a big decision has to be made, the term "draw a line in the sand” is used.

“All but one brave soul decided to step up and defend the fort. They stood their ground for a grueling 13 days, fighting with everything they had and to the last man. But their sacrifice was not in vain. It became a rallying cry for the Texians, inspired by their bravery and determination. Six weeks later, under the leadership of Sam Houston, they avenged the Alamo and emerged victorious. The cry "Remember the Alamo" symbolized their unwavering resolve and played a vital role in their triumph.”

"I've been telling this story to my teams since my Middle School coach told it to us way back when. He pulled out a long saber from out of nowhere and drew a real line in the dirt. We literally crossed over the line as a team. I don't have to tell you what happened in the next game. I'll always remember the lesson in the commitment I learned that day. If we will be 50 Strong, let's commit to it right now."

"We have a decision to make. Are we going to be FYGR or 50 Strong? We can't be both."

I got up and made an imaginary line in the middle of the room. I looked each of them in the eye slowly and asked…

“What’s it going to be for you?”

53

THOSE WHO HUMBLE THEMSELVES WILL BE EXALTED

August 15, 2022

"50 Strong is why we're 8-0 and Northern Champions," Jerome said.

"As I said earlier, let's stop acting like children and get back to our pillars," Jared added.

"I want a ring. Disrespect is not how we'll get one," Chris said.

The meeting ended, and I felt a million pounds lighter. I felt a little bad about Saul on the spot indirectly, but I didn't come here not to hurt feelings. I came here to win and do it with a team of true professionals. I didn't hear from every alpha male in the room, but enough of them to create the momentum we needed.

"Coach Jackson, can I see you and Coach Saul in the office?" Berti said a few minutes later.

"Yes, sir. I want you to be in on this because it affects you through this season. Saul resigned from his position last night, and I don't know if he is leaving now or staying until the season ends."

He did what? Saul resigned? My mind was racing 100 mph.

After we were all seated, Berti asked, "Are you going to finish the season, or is your resignation effective immediately?"

"I'd like to finish the season."

"Ok, well, I'm grateful you'll finish the season, but I need you to start acting differently. We're 8-0 for the first time, North champions and I must apologize to people after every game because of what you're doing. You ignore the board and won't communicate with them. I consider you a very good friend, but I don't want to keep doing this."

Saul was calm and reserved. He showed no emotion as he did with me when I questioned him about Max missing practice a few months prior.

"Coach Jackson, I know you are frustrated as well. I'm sorry for the antics, but we'll do better moving forward," Berti said.

"Thanks. I'm glad we're getting this out in the open. One of the officials told me the other day the Royals are one of the most disliked teams in the GFL. I'm grateful to be here, but I would've joined another team if I'd known we would want to disrespect our opponents as much or more than we want to win games."

"The official told you we are among the most disliked teams?" Saul asked me, finally showing some emotion. "That's a bunch of BS. We don't have a bad reputation."

"I'm not arguing it, but we don't do much to create goodwill either. To give you an outside perspective, Tracy was shocked by the music we played during warmups at Kiel. There are women and kids everywhere, and our lyrics talk about every sex act known to mankind and some I didn't know about. It's the same at practice. I don't understand why we allow this."

"I have to admit. I don't hear the lyrics anymore. I tune it out, I guess, from all the years of hearing it," Berti said.

"Me too. I couldn't tell you what our lyrics are either," Saul admitted.

"If we're going to have a culture of winning the right way, shouldn't we hear the music?" I asked.

Later that day, I uploaded a movie clip into the 50 Strong and Autobahn 80 chat groups. The scene is Bob Ladoucer, head coach of legendary De La Salle football in California, walking into Dick's Sporting Goods while a parent and his son are exiting.

"Hey coach, great game Friday. Three more touchdowns for the beast!" the dad says as he lightly punches his son's chest.

"Yea, he played well. The whole team did," Coach Ladoucer said.

A convertible drives by the store entrance with four girls waving and saying, "Hey, Chris! Over here! Hi!"

"What's up?!" Chris says to the car as it drives past.

"Get ready to break that scoring record. I've got a place for the trophy all picked out," the dad says to Chris.

"Hey, Mickey?" Coach Ladoucer says to the dad.

"Yea?"

"Could I show you the thesis Chris wrote for my class on Matthew 23:12? It's amazingly insightful for someone his age. It's really terrific. You should read it," Coach Ladoucer says as he turns and enters the store.

Chris and Mickey walk to their car when Mickey says, "Matthew 23:12? What's he talking about? We're on our way to a championship! A state record!"

"Those who humble themselves will be exalted. Those who exalt themselves will be humbled," Chris says as he quotes the scripture.

"Exalted?" Mickey asks.

"Yea"

"You get 37 touchdowns in a season. Then you'll be exalted," Mickey says as he gets in the car.

(me) I know most of you are not Christians, but this movie clip shows where my heart is. The longer I've been in Potsdam, the more I have begun to rely on God to help me deal with the separation and missing Tracy and Coco, so I hope you guys don't mind if I share it with you. Can anyone comment on why this clip impacts me?

(Stephan) It's a reminder of our pillar, Humility.

*(Leo) We're crumb eaters continually chasing perfection. We don't *'BCD' because we are grateful to play the game we love.*

(Chris) Humble teams wear rings!

(me) Thanks, fellas. The only way the Rebels can beat us this week is for us to take them lightly and not respect them. We're the better team, but it's "the team that plays the best" and always will be.

54

ROBIN JOINS US IN THE BATCAVE

August 16, 2022

After wrapping up my Zoom session with the offense, I was preparing for practice this Wednesday for game #9 versus the Berlin Rebels.

Saul texted me with the news I'd been waiting to hear for a couple of months; *We had to fly Robbie into Frankfurt instead of Berlin. Jonas is driving to pick him up and bring him to the office. They should be here around 4:00 p.m. It'd be nice if you could come by and meet him if you have time.*

(me) Oh, heck yea. How far is it from Frankfurt?

(Saul) At least six hours round trip.

(me) Oh my. I'll have Jonas let me know when they're about to arrive so I can be waiting on him. I'll also get on the whiteboard and start teaching Robbie some of the offense.

When Robbie came around the corner to our outer office, I was taken aback by his size. Given his past as a starter at Montana, a well-known FCS school, I had expected him to be taller. Despite being listed as 6'0" on his profile, Robbie was at most 5'10". Shorter guys like Drew Brees or Bryce Young are the exception at quarterback. The only guys under 6' tall and playing 'big time' ball are either athletic freaks or extremely smart and accurate passers.

No offense to Robbie, but his highlight tape didn't show him to be a 4.3-speedster. Maybe his skill set would be similar to a Russell Wilson type; great decision-maker and leader.

"Hey, Robbie, nice to meet you," I said as we shook hands.

"Thanks, coach. It's great to be here."

"How was the flight? I'm sure you're exhausted."

"It was long but not too bad. I'm grateful to be here and get on the field again. I'll be fine after a couple of days."

"Don't worry about suiting up for practice tonight. I know you're just a couple of years younger than me, but I remember how exhausted I was for more than a few days when I arrived. If you can just follow Chris around and learn, that'd be great."

"I'll practice in full gear if that's ok. I'm ready to get with the guys and start repping the offense."

"Are you sure? You have to be wiped out."

"Yes, sir. I'm sure I'll crash afterward, but I'd rather be on the field than just watching."

"Tell me about your college experience."

"Well, I was a part-time starter at the University of Montana. As you probably know, Montana has an excellent program, so we were pretty good. It was a great experience for me to play in some big games."

I didn't take long to realize I didn't need to compete with him in *Words With Friends* or *Jeopardy*.

Fast N' Wide is basically *offense for dummies*, but within 15 minutes, Robbie told me he could run our day-one install of formations and play calls. I'd have to wait to see him throw the ball, but his intangibles jumped at me. He was confident but respectful and extremely smart.

One thing that's always bothered me about the current state of college recruiting is how much emphasis is placed on measurables. As a former head coach, height and arm length were often prioritized over factors like a player's passion for the game. It's frustrating to see this trend continue in the NFL draft year after year. I wonder if being a team captain moves guys up on NFL evaluations. It certainly would for me.

"Were you like me and had to convince someone to let you do this?"

"No, I'm single. No strings attached to get to be here. My dad and I live near each other, so not seeing him as much will be different."

"Our offense is simple. We should score a bunch of points Saturday, so I hope you can get your feet wet in the second half. I'll go ahead and draw up our base formations and our "Big 3" plays; our two runs and one drop-back pass. Don't worry about having everything mastered by Saturday. If we can get you in, I'll have you hand it off to Adam on power and zone. We mostly have "one receiver routes" where you know who you're throwing the ball to and don't have a passing progression. If I ever raise my voice for any reason, remind me how long I waited for you to get here!" I chuckled.

Berti sees us in the office, so he sticks his head in and asks, "How's it going, coach? Will you be able to sleep at night now that Robbie's here?"

"I'm heavy-eyed and on the brink of yawning right now! Yes, sir, I'll sleep well tonight. Robbie already knows 75% of the offense, and now he's about to teach me the theory of relativity and how fax machines work!"

I couldn't help but make this analogy, so I asked Berti, "Are you familiar with Batman and Robin?"

"Oh, but of course. Batman and Robin have fought crime in Germany and Metropolis since I was a kid. My son might be watching Batman as we speak on Netflix."

"Consider me Alfred, the butler who would like to introduce you to our newest Royal...Robin, I mean Robbie."

"At first, I thought that the idea of the players' creed and pillars was just childish and something that would not last a month, but each week, I started to understand the weight and importance of it. After playing over 14 years of European football, this was the first time I truly felt my team was my family. We were strong as a whole and

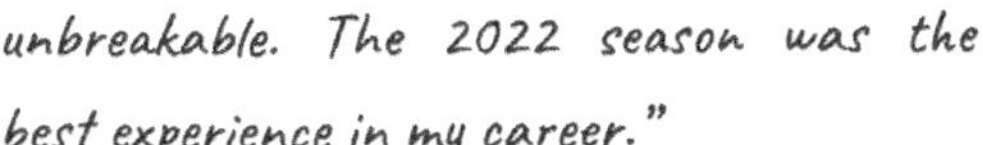

unbreakable. The 2022 season was the best experience in my career."

Mateusz Dubicki
#81 Tight End
Szczecin, Poland
2023 Team:
Potsdam Royals

55

STOP THE FIGHT, FRANK!

August 19, 2022

The next morning, we met at the Potsdam Main Station to board the bus for Berlin to play the Rebels. Berlin was statistically in playoff contention with a 3-4-1 record.

Pregame game pep talks to the team are dicey on the road. Most locker rooms are multiple small rooms, so there isn't a place to meet inside. Today, at Mommsenstadion, was no different. Mommsen Stadium was built in 1930 and reminded me of almost every other stadium we've visited, temporary scoreboard, covered bleachers, and a track.

"Team meeting outside in 10 minutes!" I said, walking around the locker rooms.

We utilized a park just across the street, featuring a railing surrounding the area where players could sit and gather.

"The last time we played the Rebels, Coach Luster and I gave you a boxing story for the message. Today, we'll get back in the ring, so to speak, for our rematch."

"The fight we'll break down is from 2002; Arturo Gatti versus Mickey Ward. Ring magazine tabbed it the fight of the year for 2002, and most believe the 9th round is the greatest in boxing history."

"Gatti was born in Italy and raised in Canada. He was a two-time world champion known as a *human highlight reel.* Ward was described as quite the opposite. He was a shy club fighter from Massachusetts who paved roads to pay the bills between matches. He quit boxing for three years because he was tired of losing before returning a couple of years before this fight."

"Ward, the one with red hair, was cut early in the fight. Both boxers were hurt in the third round, and as the slugfest intensified, both exasperated corners would threaten to stop the fight at various points. However, it was round nine when that became one of the greatest rounds ever."

"Hit play. This is round nine."

"I'm not sure about Gatti. He hasn't been in this type of war with as strong of a fighter as Ward before," said one of the announcers. After 26 seconds into the round, Ward knocks Gatti down. Gatti looks beaten and exhausted. He's on one knee, and his face is showing excruciating pain. He slowly rises, but the commentators believe he might be done.

"This one counts," one of the announcers says. "He may not be able to recover."

"I don't think so," says the other.

"Pause it. Did you guys catch that? The commentators think Gatti's done. Hit play."

Ward sees Gatti is wounded. He goes on the attack for the next 30 seconds, but Gatti hangs in and refuses to go down. "When the fight resumed, what did Ward do?" I asked.

"Ward's going up-tempo on Gatti. He's going as fast as he can, trying to overwhelm him," Mat says.

"I agree. Ward's exhausted, just like we may be at times today, but he smells blood in the water and is taking his best shot to finish him. I'm a firm believer in momentum. Ward has it and is using it to energize himself. Hit play."

"Arturo Gatti refuses to go down as Mickey Ward pounds away!" says the commentator.

With two minutes remaining in the round, Gatti stands his ground, and Ward stops punching. Ward is exhausted after the barrage.

"This is where Gatti has been dangerous," says one commentator.

"Mickey Ward should go to the body again," says the other.

"Pause it. What mistake did the announcer say Ward was making?"

"He should continue to hit Gatti with body blows," said Jared.

"Yes! Body blows today will be violence when violence is required. Body blows for us are taking the shot when it's legal and blocking through the whistle. We embarrassed them last time. They'll have enough pride to do whatever they can about it today. We need to be ready to give body blows and for them to as well."

"Hit play. Wait a minute, pause it again. Do you guys realize what you're seeing here? Everyone talks about toughness, we're going to be the toughest team on the field, but we are seeing tough personified right here. Both of these guys are 145 pounds or 66 kilos for my European friends and are battling their asses off. Now, hit play."

With a little over a minute remaining, Ward is in the corner, trying to hang on. He's having trouble standing up. When Gatti comes in close, Ward grabs him to rest. Gatti also uses the opportunity to stop momentarily, almost stumbling when the referee separates them.

"Pause it. Do you see? Both fighters are so dang tired they are practically holding each other up! Play it."

"Ward should go right back to the body!" says the commentator with 50 seconds remaining.

Ward connects three times and finds some juice. Gatti is taking the blows but not counter-punching.

"Pause it. Ask yourself in your mind right now… Who's going to win this fight? Hit play."

Ward continues landing punches on Gatti. "You dream of fights like this, but this is even more than you could ever dream of!" says the commentator, so excited he's struggling to find his words.

"Just imagine if you bought a ticket!" says the other commentator as Ward is now landing blow after blow, but Gatti won't go down.

"Stop it, Frank! [the official]. You can stop it anytime!" The commentator begs the official to end it.

"Pause it. Has anyone ever been this tired?" I asked the team.

"Where did I learn about Round 9 of Gatti vs Ward? Matt Rhule was previously the head coach of the Carolina Panthers but is the head man at the University of Nebraska. Coach Rhule believes in the importance of toughness. Next year when you watch the Cornhuskers play, find the guys with single-digit numbers. They're the ones voted 'toughest' by their teammates. Coach Rhule celebrates tough!

In 2018, he spoke about toughness to 400 coaches we hosted at North Forney high school. He shows round nine to his teams and asks them, "Do you want to see what real toughness looks like? This is it! If we can find 11 guys who are half this tough, who won't quit, we won't ever leave the field where the other team isn't beaten and exhausted. Coach Rhule's message is clear: his Cornhuskers will have some Gatti and Ward in them."

"Let's finish it...hit play."

With 25 seconds left, Gatti's walking zombie. "Frank's going to let the fight continue!" says the commentator.

"Gatti is too tired even to tie Ward up!" says the other. Then with 10 seconds remaining in the round, Ward is stumbling.

"Now Ward's tired!"

"Here comes Gatti!" as he connects on four straight punches. "Gatti's gonna survive the round!"

Ward lands one more blow himself. Both boxers have found yet another reserve to go back on the attack when we hear, "Ding, ding!"

"This should be the fight of the century!"

The clip ends, and I ask again, "Who won the fight? Wait a minute…who cares?! It doesn't matter because they both demonstrated what champions do. They were showing *extreme* toughness."

"Round nine was a laboratory of extreme desire, fatigue, and, most importantly, toughness. Were they being tough because they were taking and landing punches? Well…I guess that's some of it. The bottom line is they were fighting through their bodies' desire to quit. Both Gatti and Ward had to convince themselves not to give in to their exhaustion. Before the New Yorker game, I told Helbig that the toughest thing to do in sports is to act differently from how you feel. Gatti and Ward both conquered their minds' telling them to quit, and they kept going. What percent of the population would continue and make it through round nine? Before you answer, remember the average person dieting can't make it through the day without a cookie!"

"What is mental toughness? Being able to fight through the negative to get to the positive."

"Everyone close your eyes. I want you to feel the spirit of Gatti and Ward coming over you. I want you to feel their courage and tenacity, the determination that drove them to become two of boxing's greatest competitors. These men left it all in the ring; they put everything on the line for one moment of glory. They sacrificed their health, time with family and friends, and ultimately their lives in pursuit of greatness. There are lots of sports you could've chosen to play other than football that require a lower level of mental toughness."

"You chose a game that honors grit because you're to be an alpha male, a rare breed today. We're the better team, but they're capable. Get your mind focused right now that we're about to be battling in a heavy weight fight! Once the whistle blows, it'll be too late to realize we're in a bare-knuckle brawl. They still have a small chance at the playoffs. This is Rory's last home game, so he'll be amped up and talking more trash than 50 sanitation workers."

"Mental toughness is a decision and a choice. Choose to be both Gatti and Ward. Choose to be an extreme player. The type they've never competed against before. Choose to fight one more round…"

"Fight one more round.

When your feet are so tired that you have to shuffle back to the center of the ring, fight one more round.

When your arms are so tired that you can hardly lift your hands to come on guard, fight one more round.

When your nose is bleeding, and your eyes are black, and you are so tired that you wish your opponent would crack you on the jaw and put you to sleep, fight one more round—remembering that the man who always fights one more round is never whipped."

[Written by Jim Corbett, 1892 - the first heavyweight champion of the world where boxers wore gloves]

"Jerome, break us out!"

56

FEAR ONE KICK PRACTICED 10,000 TIMES

August 20, 2022

A few hours before kickoff, I was walking on the field when I heard a familiar voice. "Good day, Coach Jackson! I hope you had a great week. I might need your help with the music again today if you don't mind," Mats said.

"I will, but things have been quieter this week. We'll see in a few minutes when we start our pregame, but our focus has gone back to football and not shenanigans."

For the first time in what seemed forever, we were 50 guys locked in before the game. Before our last meeting with the Rebels, we stressed how mouthy and dirty they'd be all week. We didn't speak about any of it this time all week, and the warmups were fine. We got ready for the game like professionals. It was the first pregame without incident since Kiel over two months ago, and it was amazing.

"This is a good sign. I like where our heads are today," I said to Buddy and Jens as the team left the field.

"Good! We're the talk of the GFL for the first time in club history! Thanks again for coming here and helping make this happen, coach," Jens said.

"We should take care of business today. I'm hoping we get to see Robbie play in the second half," Buddy added.

"Me too. I'm sure the Rebels will do what everyone else has done lately: take away Jared and Polk and make us run the ball to beat them. Heiko and Adam have been excellent, but I'm glad Karri is back today," I said.

The GFL certainly knows how to put on a show regarding stadium entrances. The last time we were in Berlin to play the Adler, guys on Harley-Davidson motorcycles escorted the cheerleaders around the track before the teams ran through the tunnel. Today's entrance, however, became my favorite spectacle of the year so far. Two flame machines were positioned at midfield, shooting impressive fiery jets high into the air as both teams took the field.

One disappointing thing was that few people saw us take the field. Only around 350 spectators were there. The weather was gloomy with light rain, but the fact that our rivals were only 30 minutes away made it feel like a junior varsity game back in Texas.

The first half started ominously. On the second play, Chris tried to force one to Polk, who was bracketed by the Berlin secondary; their American corner made an excellent play for the interception. Everyone on the sideline was calm, like it was no big deal, which I loved.

The game plan was, to start with several passes in a row. We stayed on script for the next series. Chris completed two straight passes to Jared and a third to Polk on a screen. Now we were finding our rhythm moving down the field as we expected. I also wanted to get everyone involved early. Chris went to Magnus for 11 yards, then Heiko on consecutive plays for 13 and 11 yards to take us down inside the five.

“I’m not getting cute down here. Let’s get Karri back in his groove,” I told Jonas on the headset. Karri punched it over from the two-yard line, and we were up 6-0. The Rebels were penalized on the point after, so we sent the offense back out, and Karri once again found the endzone to make the score 8-0.

Our New Zealand defensive end, Zaire Ugapo, strip-sacked the Berlin quarterback, American Daryl Isom, and we recovered at the Rebel 42-yard line.

"Let's stay on script and keep tossing the [15]egg," I said to the offense.

And that's what we did. Chris completed passes to Jared, Polk, and Magnus to move us down the field. It was Adam's turn to score on 1st and goal from the seven-yard line.

The PAT attempt was blocked to keep the score at 14-0.

"Guys, this is the second PAT we've had blocked this year. I've gone a decade without having one blocked. How’s it happening?" I asked the offensive line afterward on the bench.

"It was blue protection, but I heard it wrong, so I thought it was red. I went right instead of left. Rory came through my gap," said Klaus, one of our backup linemen.

---

[15] Egg - a common term in Europe for an American football.

Instead of exploding like I'd done early in the season, I kept my cool for the most part.

"They have one player we must block, and that's Rory. We must know which direction we're protecting. Can we echo the call down the line, guys? I can hear crickets chirping because there's not a crowd here today, but we must help everyone go the right way." I said.

"Let's refocus and get back to talking offense. Great drive, fellas. We're dicing them up. Eventually, we'll go back to running the ball like normal. Karri, you and Adam don't get bored," I said, smiling.

The worst thing that could happen analytically happened next. The Rebels kept the ball for 14 plays.

It seemed like an eternity watching them run the ball and throw screen passes to make just enough to continue making first downs and keep our offense on the bench.

On 4th and goal, a Rebel receiver dropped the pass, and we finally went back on the field at our eight-yard line with eight minutes remaining in the first half. On second down and five, Adam burst through on our *power left* behind Yasir and Brenden for a 64-yard gain all the way to the Berlin 23-yard line.

We did what we almost always do after a big play...we ran a gadget. It was the running back version of *Hippo* we ran at Dresden. Chris threw a slightly backward pass to Jared, who pump-faked to his left, then threw back to Karri on his right. The Berlin corner played it well, but Karri made him miss and went up the sideline for an 11-yard gain and a first down at the Rebel 12-yard line. Three plays later, Chris completed a perfect seven-yard lob touchdown to Jerome on an RPO (run-pass option).

Once again, the extra point was blocked. I held my head in my hands in a state of bewilderment. I'm the offensive line coach and work with them on kick protection. It fell on my shoulders, but I felt helpless, not knowing if we would call red, blue, or white (the middle protection I'd used, used exclusively in my 31 years of coaching).

The score was 20-0 with six minutes remaining in the half.

"Jonas?" I said, getting his attention on the headset. I now wasn't as calm as before.

"Yes, sir?"

"Why do we have three different protections on the extra point and a field goal in the *Wide World of Sports*? Bless my heart; this is going to be the death of me! Everyone, and I mean everyone in the U.S., has the front-line step hard inside and block their inside gap. I give you advice when you don't ask, so I'm going to again right now. Bruce Lee said, "I don't fear the man with 10,000 different kicks, but the man with one kick who's practiced it 10,000 times."

This time the Rebels held the ball for nine plays. They finished this drive with the quarterback, Daryl Isom, running it in from the one-yard line. After the PAT, the score was 20-7.

"We've executed this all season long. Let's go full throttle tempo and put points on the board before halftime," I said to our team huddled on the sideline.

We started on our 35-yard line after the kickoff. On 2nd down and eight, Chris completed a post to Jared for 35 yards. After a short completion to Heiko, we called timeout to stop the clock.

The Rebels forced us to a 4th and eight from the 26-yard line.

I positioned Polk and Jared on opposite sides of the field to determine the best matchup. Our objective was always to create situations where an American receiver would face a non-American defensive back.

As stated in the book, American players normally possess a higher level of ability than most European players. Jared and Polk began playing football before age ten, meaning they've played more than a decade longer than most GFL players, faced stiffer competition, and received high-level, year-round training.

Jared was to the wide side, so I called a post to him.

"Go, Hit!" Bobby yelled as he snapped the ball back to Chris. Jared attacked the corner, stuck his outside foot in the ground, and broke his route inside. He'd beaten the corner and was open in the back of the endzone. Chris, as usual, was right on the money. The ball landed between Jared's "1" and his "5".

We're about to do what we always do. Score and grab the momentum right before the half. But...

57

THE TORTOISE AND THE HARE

August 20, 2022

The ball hit him in the chest and bounced away.

"Oh no! It went through his hands!" Jonas yelled into the headset.

The half ended with us up 20-7, but we'd left some meat on the bone. We played well offensively in the first half. We gained 255 yards with no sacks or punts. Our halftime adjustments (which are highly overrated) were nothing to speak of. Despite a few mistakes, such as an interception and a drop, everything was going according to plan. Overall, it was just business as usual for us.

The second half was the other end of the spectrum. It was half that I'd have to break down the next day to understand fully. I was about to enter a new type of Twilight Zone.

The Rebels decided at the intermission to not just slow the game down but to push the brakes through the floorboard with both feet. Berlin would do its best to turn this game into a remake of The Tortoise and the Hare poem.

The Rebels started their first drive of the second half at their 22-yard line and slowly, painfully, moved the ball down the field. They ran a play; Isom jogged over to the bench to get the call from the offensive coordinator, then jogged back. They broke the huddle and snapped the ball with three or four seconds left on the 40-second clock.

On the sideline, I turned to Jonas and Saul and said, "You know what's interesting? If Kevin Kelley were here [football analytics expert], he'd recommend we start blitzing more on defense. The numbers prove it's better statistically for your defense to give up a touchdown than to let the opponent keep the ball for eight or more plays. In the long run, giving up six points and getting the ball back throughout a game is better than allowing a team to eat up the clock."

Saul nodded in agreement and said, "Yeah, that makes sense. Helbig has been standing with us a lot this half. Maybe if we put more pressure on the opponent by blitzing on first downs, we can get them behind the chains. We might give up some big plays, but our offense can get back to scoring."

Their drive was eight plays (the threshold Coach Kelley said was too many), 78 yards, and ended with a touchdown. Berlin took an agonizing six minutes off the clock.

"They're certainly playing this correctly, according to Coach Kelley's analytics?" Jonas said.

"Yes, and it's killing me."

We were the hare once again. On the third play of our drive, Polk caught a 6-yard stop route, made the corner miss, and raced 54 yards for the touchdown, taking one minute off the game clock.

We wisely decided not to kick the PAT after having two blocked but failed to convert. The score was 26-14 Royals with five minutes left in the 3rd quarter.

Berlin continued taking their own sweet time snapping the ball on the next possession. They painfully delivered deliberate body blow after body blow with the speed of a tortoise. Isom was still jogging back and forth to the sideline between every play. They *matriculated* slowly down the field, finishing the 10-play, 78-yard drive with a 13-yard touchdown pass to cut our lead to 26-21.

I was feeling the pressure to score every time we had the ball. "We have to be perfect on every drive because we aren't going to get it back many more times," I said to Jonas.

"I know! They're playing keep away from us, big time."

#89 Jerome Valbon
#77 Stefan Stefansson

"Are you noticing if we're blitzing much? I don't think we are. Now's not the time to give Berti suggestions, but they're slowly bleeding us to death," I said.

We ran a total of four plays in the third quarter.

Three plays into the fourth quarter, Heiko broke around the left side for a 27-yard run to get us to the Berlin one-yard line. After a two-yard loss, I called Chris's number on a run play to the left side, and he punched it to give us a cushion again. The score was now 34-21.

Berlin's American receiver, Pollard, who caused us so many problems in our first game, was injured and not playing today (thank the Lord), but their other 'A,' Paul Morant, was inflicting damage. He fielded the kickoff at the seven-yard line and broke into the open field. Luckily Manase had the angle and pushed him out of bounds, but they had terrific field position at our 47-yard line.

The tortoise punched us again, slowly but surely. The Rebels, whose uniforms should've been "turtle green" instead of black, stayed true to their game plan and didn't panic. They ran for 12 yards, three yards, and 11 yards, and then Isom hit an open receiver for an 11-yard touchdown pass.

We were hanging on 34-28 with seven minutes remaining.

The same team we'd scored 81 points on and set the GFL records for yards in a game (783) was one possession from beating us. The Rebels were Gatti, who wouldn't quit. I was guilty of thinking we'd score 50 without any problem. We all thought today would be a leisurely *pleasure cruise*, but we were fighting for our lives and struggling to flip the switch in our minds to go to *battleship* mode.

"Like the boxing commentator said, "He should keep going to the body." It's time to run it at them and punch one in," I said to the offense.

We started on our 41-yard line. Karri and Chris combined to rush for 11 yards and a first down. Then, Karri broke a big run right up the middle for 41 yards to the Rebel 17-yard line. It was his most disciplined carry-on inside zone all year.

"Heiko, protect the ball and run over some guys," I said, giving Karri a quick break. The Rebels stacked the box, expecting us to run the ball. I called the same corner route we missed right before the half to Jared, hoping he would be open again. Rory, playing defensive end, had other ideas. Chris scrambled for a 1-yard gain and wisely stayed in bounds to keep the clock ticking.

Two more run plays left us with a 4th and one. We did what I've done for over a decade. We ran behind our best linemen as fast as we could snap it. "Psycho! Psycho!" I said as I signaled to the skill players to run the same running play as we did on third down. All 225 pounds of Heiko bent back to the left side hard, but an inside linebacker scraped between a gap and tackled us for no gain.

The tortoise was about to cross the finish line ahead of us. If we lost this game, I wouldn't get over it if I lived to be 100.

With three minutes and 30 seconds left to play, the Rebels could achieve the GFL upset of the decade if they found a way to score now.

Berlin was now playing at a normal tempo, but they still had time to run the ball, which we hadn't stopped much this half. After three run plays, the Rebels faced their own 4th and one, at their 17-yard line, and of course, went for it.

Isom play-action faked (bluffed a run play to throw a pass) and he was throwing the ball!

Incomplete! Game over!

"I see a dang flag!" I said to Jonas.

"Pass interference, number 52 on the defense, automatic first down," Mats said into his microphone.

The Rebels had new life and a new set of downs. Our defense stepped up again and forced a Berlin 4th and 3 on their 32-yard line with 90 seconds left in the game. Although, as Kevin Kelley would say, we played too much "bend but don't break," we could escape the nightmare if we stopped them here.They ran it to our left, and it looked like the back would get just enough when Michael Podroski, our corner, forced the fumble and recovered it himself!

#9 Heiko Bals
#14 Louis Christ

Now it really is game over!

In his exhilaration and relief, we'd finally ended the upset bid; Podroski did something I'd never seen before. He stood up and punted the ball into the woods behind the visitor's bleachers. Now, I absolutely, positively have seen it all.

"Did you see what the hell Podroski just did?" I said incredulously into the headset. "We almost went an entire game without doing something stupid. Will Berti ever realize if he starts fining guys for unsportsmanlike penalties, we might not be so undisciplined? Don't answer that; I already know that'll never happen."

As we were boarding the bus, I saw Robbie and Chris talking to each other. "I should have scrambled on the first play of the game. One great thing about our throwing choice is that it's the simplest pass play you'll ever run, but if the receiver's covered, don't force it. Scramble and make something happen with your legs or find a check down," Chris said.

"Yea, I noticed on film how many plays you've extended with your legs. Thanks for offering to go over the film with me tomorrow. I'm excited to break it down with you before we review it with Coach Jackson," Robbie responded.

"It's a great sight to see both quarterbacks getting along so well," I remarked, pleased with their camaraderie. "The only thing that could make this better is if one of you were European, allowing us to develop a creative two-quarterback package that would keep Polk on the field," I added with a smile.

On Sunday, I chose to break us down analytically before I graded the Follow Us guys. I shared the findings with my Fast N' Wide coaches on a Zoom call a few days later.

“Thanks for joining me today; it’s good to see everyone. Not to be 'Captain Obvious', but in today’s session, we will discuss how 74 is greater than 45.”

"Y'all all know about our 81 points in June versus Berlin. They held us to 34 on Saturday, and although that’s a 47-point decline from game one, we actually played very well again. We averaged 9.6 yards per play, didn't punt, didn’t give up a sack, and only had one turnover."

#11 Magnus Urth

"How’d this happen?"

"Our offense is a Lamborghini, but they drove a Pinto. Advantage us, right?"

"No. The Rebels' Pinto kept going, and going, and going while our Lambo was in the garage almost the entire second half."

"In game one versus the Rebels, we ran 74 plays for 783 = 10.6 yards per play. In game two, we snapped the ball 45 times (17 in the second half) for 432 = 9.6 yards per play."

"In the second quarter, we were up 20-0, had run 24 plays, and everything was going like the previous eight games."

"Although we nearly gained a first down on each snap in the rematch, we scored 47 fewer points. Why? Because we allowed Berlin to keep the most explosive offense in the history of Europe on the sideline."

"In the third quarter, we ran four plays for 64 yards (one a 54-yard catch and run). We averaged 16 yards per play, but it didn't do much for us because we needed to snap the ball more times."

“Last year, I had the privilege of interviewing Kevin Kelley on the Elite Coaches Mastermind about football analytics. One of the most important things I took away from our conversation was his statement, "The worst thing a defense can allow are drives of eight plays or more." He suggested that defenses should blitz and take chances to put the offense 'behind the sticks,' but they should also avoid letting the offense keep the ball for long drives. This advice can be a real game-changer for any football team looking to improve their defense.”

“What if we'd blitzed on defense as Coach Kelley's analytics would say to do? They would've hit us for some big plays, but we would have forced them to punt more. Either way, their drives would've taken less time. Instead, we sat back and played traditional defense. Berlin ran 32 plays in the second half, almost twice as many as us. What would've happened if we had brought pressure most every down? Would they've scored more? Yes! Of course, they would have. How many more points would they have? Let's say instead of 24; they score 38 or even 42, a full two more touchdowns. But we also would've stopped them a few times after only three or four plays."

"By doing the math, if we snap the ball 72 times (our average), we gain 700 yards and win the game 60-42. We're not in a nail-biter with three minutes left because the tortoise is about to creep across the goal line and beat us."

From Nixa, Missouri, Coach John Perry asked, "If this is true, shouldn't you go "Full Kelley" and onside kick it every time as well?"

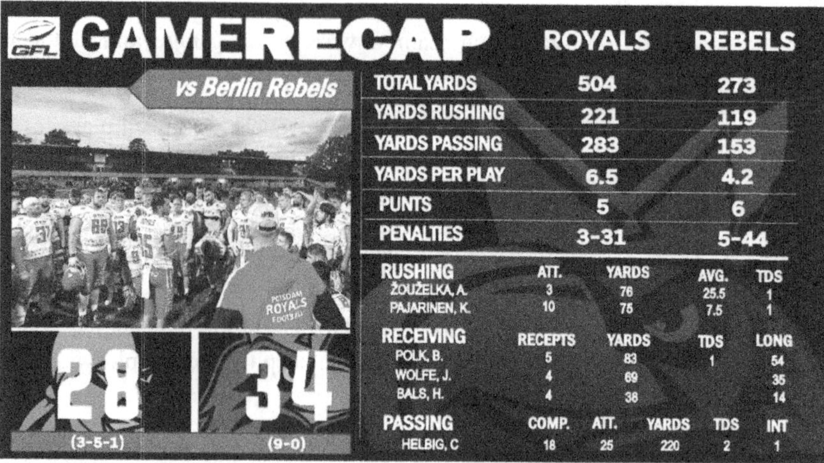

	ROYALS	REBELS
TOTAL YARDS	504	273
YARDS RUSHING	221	119
YARDS PASSING	283	153
YARDS PER PLAY	6.5	4.2
PUNTS	5	6
PENALTIES	3-31	5-44

RUSHING	ATT.	YARDS	AVG.	TDS
ŽOUŽELKA, A.	3	76	25.5	1
PAJARINEN, K.	10	75	7.5	1

RECEIVING	RECEPTS	YARDS	TDS	LONG
POLK, B.	5	83	1	54
WOLFE, J.	4	69		35
BALS, H.	4	38		14

PASSING	COMP.	ATT.	YARDS	TDS	INT
HELBIG, C	18	25	220	2	1

#4 Daniel Schuhmacher
#15 Jared Wolfe

HOBBY OR PRO?

August 27, 2022

We hosted the winless Dusseldorf Panthers in our season finale. Although the Panthers have been out of the playoff hunt for weeks, they did have a reason to play hard. They were playing to avoid being [16]relegated to the GFL 2 next year. In almost all European leagues, the team with the worst record moves down, and the GFL 2 winner takes their place. It would have kept them in the GFL 1 in 2023 if they could somehow pull off an upset.

It didn't matter if the Dusseldorf flew the ghost of Vince Lombardi in to be their head coach for this game, and they were allowed 80 seconds between plays. We should dispose of them without a problem.

While we maintained our usual routine of adhering to the scouting report and game plan, I decided to introduce another element to our preparation for this week's game.

(me) Guys, I have a challenge for you this week. Look back at the Rebels' game and make a "Nasty" cutup. Find two or three plays where you delivered a body blow, finished a block, took a big hit, whatever, and post in the chat. We will watch them together at the office tomorrow after the film review. If you don't have one this week, that's your challenge for Tuesday's practice!

A couple of hours later, a few clips started coming. Jared was the first to submit a play where he blocked for a run that broke down the sideline.

Adam and Karri, probably working together, posted cutups of each finishing runs by moving the pile forward and picking up blitzing linebackers. Polk followed them by posting a hit he took but held on to the ball.

---

[16] Relegated - promotion and relegation is a process where teams are transferred between multiple divisions based on their performance for the completed season. In a system of promotion and relegation, the best-ranked team(s) in the lower division are *promoted* to the higher division for the next season, and the worst-ranked team(s) in the higher division are *relegated* to the lower division for the next season.

(Chris) I'm still trying to figure out what I can post, coach. The OL does a great job of keeping me from having to be nasty!

(me) How about you post a gratitude clip of the big boys caring for you? Find a clip showing them working their butts off for you. Speaking of the big boys, Follow Us, guys, where are you on the "Nasty train"?!? We need to see plays where you're either Ward or Gatti!

A few more cutups were posted, but only some guys were able or willing to showcase examples of them being tough or exhibiting a nasty attitude on the field.

The following morning, I put the offensive line on the spot in our meeting at Simplioffice. "What's the deal, fellas? All of you chose football because you're alpha males. I don't have Instagram, but I hear some of you post individual highlights. I use social media to promote the team and Fast N' Wide, but I don't 'beat my chest' online and attempt to show people I'm tough. In other words, some people 'talk the talk' and don't 'walk the walk.' You can also say, 'Actions speak louder than words,' or 'What you do speaks so loudly I cannot hear what you say."

"Years ago, late one night on a lonesome West Texas prairie, three cowboys were sitting around a campfire when stories of which one was the toughest began to be told."

"I must be the meanest, baddest cowboy in Texas," said one of them. "Yesterday, a bull got loose in the pen and gored six of my buddies to death with his horns. I immediately jumped in and wrestled the bull to the ground with my bare hands. Beat that."

The second cowboy, not to be outdone, said, "That's nothing. I'm the toughest man in these parts. I was shot off my horse, scalped, and left for dead. On my belly, I crawled to the nearest fort 60 miles through the desert."

"The third cowboy listened intently and didn't say a word. He just stirred the orange hot coals of the fire with his bare hands."

"That's toughness. People don't believe what you say. They believe what you do. I need some 'Nasty cutups' that show what you do in the trenches."

Our quarterbacks were always in both film sessions, so Chris and Robbie were present. "Robbie, you played at a perennial power at Montana, so you know what toughness and nasty look like. Would the OL coach there be demanding nasty clips like I am? Am I being too hard on these guys?"

"The OL coach at Montana only speaks in curse words. So, no, sir, you aren't being too hard on anyone," Robbie replied.

Both our Tuesday and Wednesday practices were very good. Guys shared clips of impressive nasty in our chat, and I liked the new emphasis. We didn't seem like a team "eating the cheese" but one on a mission. It's a good time to refocus on the fundamentals when playing a vastly inferior opponent.

We were still adding players to 50 Strong periodically after practice, but I spoke to the entire team before we gave Jared the floor.

"We're not just practicing for Dusseldorf this week; we're preparing to deliver our best performance of the season," I emphasized to the team. "Great teams continually improve as the season progresses. I've never understood the notion of 'midseason form.' Our mindset must be one percent better each day until the German Bowl. It has always been and will always be about our commitment to excellence."

"This week's message before the game will focus on the difference between being a PRO and an amateur. Ask yourself, are you a pro, or is this a hobby? Are you a pro or a pretender? Professionals do their best when it means the most. Pros do their best when they feel like it the least. People told me football in Europe was a hobby before I came here. A bunch of pros will be on the field in Frankfurt in October, playing for the big trophy. Pros will take care of business Saturday. A pro will prepare to dominate his opponent regardless of whether he plays the New Yorker Lions or the Dusseldorf Panthers. This is a tough question, but who would you guess is the most professional player in the NFL?" I asked.

"Tom Brady?" Chris responded.

"That's a great answer. I completely agree with you. Tom Brady is undoubtedly a true professional. I'd be willing to bet he prepares the same for every opponent, whether the Bucs are playing the worst team in the league or the Super Bowl. Tomorrow I'll tell you about another quarterback who takes it to an unbelievable level. Today let's talk about another profession where elite performers are almost as rare as NFL quarterbacks and are just as relentless in their preparation."

"The profession I'm referring to is magicians. Once, I met the world's greatest coin magician and asked him how we got so good."

He said, "I've practiced every minute of every day since I was 14."

"How could you practice every minute when you were in high school?"

"I dropped out when I was a sophomore."

"It's almost impossible to make a good living or get paid by anyone doing magic tricks. The elite magicians travel the world, make a ton of money, and know 10 to 12 tricks. An amateur magician who does it for a hobby knows hundreds of tricks, stays home, and bores his wife and family with them."

You've heard me say this a few times, “You don't win games. You win plays”. Lock in mentally for the next couple of days. We don’t have to do anything fancy or complicated to win; we just need to focus on the task at hand and be professional about it. How we perform Saturday will tell the coaching staff if we're mature professionals ready to win the whole thing. I'm betting we are."

The next day, after our pregame meal, I continued emphasizing professionalism and not playing down to an inferior opponent. I got everyone's attention by asking everyone to close their eyes. "Now, think back to when you were ten years old. It’s Saturday at noon, just like it is now. You're about to go outside in the warm sunshine for three hours. Your mom hopes its four or five hours, but we'll say three. You get some of your friends and play all afternoon. Think in your mind right now what you'd be doing. Think about all the laughing, running around, and fun. You guys would be having. If you’re having trouble with this, think about being with Ludi when you both were ten years old. This should be easy. He’d be about the same height,” I said, grinning at one of my favorite Royals.

"Open your eyes. What were some of you doing in your mind?"

"Playing football, European football," Hjalmar says.

"How about you, Jerry?"

"I can remember just running with my friends. We ran and played tag. We didn't have any equipment or even a soccer ball.”

"That's what I’d been doing as well way back in the day. We’d have been having fun and not worrying about how we were doing it. But no one was paying us to play all afternoon. Here is how the U.S. government's tax office, the IRS, identifies a hobby: 'A hobby is any activity that a person pursues because they enjoy it and with no intention of making a profit. People operate a business to make a profit. Many people engage in hobby activities that become a source of income."

"A professional is obsessed. We talked about Tom Brady yesterday, but I have another one for you. Has anyone heard of Vikings' QB Kirk Cousins' maniacal weekly routine? Cousins breaks down his day into 15-minute segments. Everything he does is planned and executed to do one thing; be his absolute best when he takes the field."

Cousins is a creature of habit and finds comfort in a predictable routine. Here is his typical Monday schedule that never wavers; it doesn’t matter if they won by 30 or lost by 30.

- Wakes up at 6:00 a.m.
- Arrives at the facility at 7:00 a.m.
- Breakfast
- Lifts weights

- Rewatches the previous game, jotting down his thought in a notebook
- Watches the same game with Vikings offensive coaches
- Meets with coaches to get scouting reports on upcoming opponent
- Lunch
- Records his weekly podcast
- Heads home around mid-afternoon
- Then he does his "bodywork" - chiropractic and deep tissue treatment. He has people come to his house, and they spend about 2 ½ hours working on his aches and pains.
- Attends team bible study
- Comes home and tunes into Monday Night Football
- Goes to bed

"Cousins literally has a 15-minute color-coded spreadsheet from 6:00 A.M. - 9:00 p.m. seven days a week. For you guys who want to play for a long time, I strongly recommend taking a serious look at his approach and incorporating as many elements as you can. We rightly don't talk about this, but some of you are paid, and others aren't. None of us are paid much, but we would all be in the NFL and make millions if we could. Although we started playing football as a game, it either is, or we want it to be a business for us."

"Play today like football is the only way you're going to eat and feed your family. Does that mean you don't have fun? No! Does that mean we can't savor every second of playing with our buddies? Of course not! It means treating your job today like a profession, not a pastime or hobby. Every play you are on the field, take care of your responsibility with the same attention to detail you would if you were opening your own business. Alabama doesn't care if they are playing Georgia or Dusseldorf. Either way, they'll take the field like a bowling ball of butcher knives and play both teams with the same intensity and professionalism. The team that hoists the trophy in Frankfurt in October will be the one with the most professionals."

We played like a bunch of pros later that day from start to finish. We were focused and surgically took care of a bad team, ready for their season to end.

Polk, again proving he is the best returner in the league, took the opening kickoff back 91 yards for a touchdown. Next, he accounted for our first offensive score with a 24-yard tiptoe in the back of the endzone to put us up 14-0.

We executed a classic gadget play called 'döner' on the next possession, which I've utilized for over a decade. It involves a hitch route followed by a pitch-back lateral. In this play, Jared caught a short stop route and lateraled the ball back to Yasir, our left tackle. The entire team executed the play flawlessly, resulting in a 14-yard "Follow Us" touchdown.

The rest of the half was more of the same. The score at halftime was 37-7 Royals.

Robbie was able to play most of the second half. As I suspected, we didn't miss a beat. He rushed five times for 28 yards, but his speed and quickness jumped off the page. Robbie also threw our longest touchdown pass of the season, a 90-yard screen, to Jared on 3rd and 15. He drove the bus like a natural-born leader and performed like he'd been with us since April.

Another great sign for our depth was that Adam also looked great, scoring two touchdowns on the ground...

The final score was 66-7. We could now finally focus solely on the playoffs.

Jonas and I sat in the VIP area after the game, eating and drinking, when he said, "I have something I want to admit to you..."

GFL **GAMERECAP**

vs Dusseldorf

68 (10-0) 7 (0-10)

	ROYALS	PANTHERS
TOTAL YARDS	471	62
YARDS RUSHING	180	9
YARDS PASSING	291	53
YARDS PER PLAY	8	1.2
PUNTS	3	7
PENALTIES	6-68	6-25

RUSHING	ATT.	YARDS	AVG.	TDS
PAJARINEN, K.	13	136	10.4	1
PATTERSON, R.	5	28	5.4	

RECEIVING	RECEPTS	YARDS	TDS	LONG
WOLFE, J.	8	144	1	89
POLK, B.	5	76	2	24

PASSING	COMP.	ATT.	YARDS	TDS	INT
HELBIG, C	18	27	202	3	

Manase Time - Zaire Ugapo - Gianni Versace - Divine Buckrham - Stefan Kamanga
Yasir Raji (holding trophy) - Nick Klopsch - Heiko Bals

59

ALL GFL

Sept. 2, 2022

"When we had Zoom calls in January and February, I was a non-believer. Not in the sense that we wouldn't have success, but it can't be this simple, and we can't run so few plays and set records. I was wrong and can't believe how *wide of the mark* I was."

"Thanks, buddy. It means a lot that I've helped change how you think about football. You've got a few more decades in your career to attack defenses. Your teams could go down as the highest scoring in German history."

One of the most interesting laboratory results regarding European football is that nothing is certain. The NFL scheduled a European combine to scout for prospective talent the same week as the German Bowl, so the GFL had to adjust. Several league players would be invited, although the combine is 99.9% for publicity, so the championship was moved back a week. Coaches voted on a new playoff schedule with an open date between each game to avoid two weeks off between the semi-final and the German Bowl.

Our playoff schedule was now set...again.
September 10 - Round 1
September 24 - Round 2
October 8 - German Bowl

Another end-of-the-regular season announcement was made a couple of days later. The all-GFL team was announced.

(Saul) Congrats to our GFL All-stars for 2022! With our record-setting offense, we were well-represented on the offensive side of the ball this season, with four players named to the list.

Congrats to...
Yasir Raji - Offensive line!
Karri Pajarinen - Running Back!
Jared Wolfe - Receiver!
and last but not least...
Chris Helbig - Quarterback!

I'll post on social media for each of you this week, but I wanted to announce it to the team first. Each of you had remarkable seasons, and the Royals are proud of you! As always, some guys could've and should've been named an all-star but weren't.

The GFL doesn't name an MVP, but Chris would've won it hands down. He led the league in passing with 3,085 yards and 32 touchdowns. He also ran for 11 more scores. Jared also had the most receiving yards with 1,336 and 14 touchdowns. Karri was second in the GFL in rushing with 1,014 yards and 11 touchdowns while only missing two and a half games to injury. The one player that made it all go for us was Yasir, though. No opponent wanted to face him. He anchored the left side of our offensive line and had a dominant season.

The GFL only names five offensive linemen for 14 teams. If there would've been more (why weren't there?) Brenden would've made it and probably should've anyways. He graded extremely high all season and would've started at left tackle for most teams. Brenden's roommate, Jerome, who plays tight end, but is used like an offensive lineman, was the most punishing blocker in the entire league. I understand there isn't a category for *destroyers*, but when Jerome hit defenders, they went to the ground. Saul made a highlight video of his pancakes that should be a must-watch for every offensive lineman in the world.

Another travesty was Polk not being an all-star. Every team in the first half of the season focused their attention on him in an attempt to stop him, which allowed our other receivers to flourish. He was fourth in the league in receiving yards and had 11 touchdown receptions. And...he had run back two kickoffs.

I texted all four and congratulated them. We had the most offensive selections of any team in the league. Although we didn't have a defensive selection, Cody Cranston, with five interceptions, was a clear "should have been" omission.

The league coaches selected the all-star team, making me wonder if our reputation as the most disliked franchise contributed to the most glaring snub; Berti wasn't named Northern Conference coach-the-year. David Odenthal, the head coach of Cologne, was the choice. The Crocodiles qualified for the playoffs with a 7-3 record but didn't surpass preseason expectations or, unlike us, *weren't the talk of the GFL.*

I invited Chris, Jared, and Polk to lunch on Friday of our open week before the first round versus Straubing. I wanted to make a special effort to show my gratitude for all three of them being *Anti-arrogant Americans* and to give them my thoughts about how we would use them going forward. We went to an Italian restaurant near the Bridge of Spies with, of course, outdoor seating. It was also out of town a little, so it had easy parking, almost as important as the quality of food.

We sat down in the sun and ordered. Our waiter spoke English, but like 99% of all Potsdamers, he had no idea about the Royals or American football after asking why we were in Potsdam.

"Thanks for making time for me today, guys. I know there are other things you could be doing. First, thank you from the bottom of my heart for being all in on 50 Strong. All three of you started the process of us having a *foxhole culture* while we were still Zooming last winter. One of my biggest surprises early was finding out most Americans are arrogant look-at-me guys. Y'all are the opposite. The creed only works with you guys. Thank you so much."

"You're welcome, coach. I didn't know what to expect after being at 'Nova, but we made it special," Jared said.

"It was fun helping create something like we had at Penn State with guys who hadn't done it before," Polk said.

Chris added, "It was actually easier than I thought it would be. It's like they expected us to be jerks; when we weren't, we bonded deeply. We had good chemistry at Southern Utah, but I've made friends here for life. Karri and I hang out basically every day now."

After our pasta and pizza were brought to the table, I brought up another topic we needed to discuss. "The main reason I invited y'all here today is to express my gratitude, but we also need to discuss something important. Although both of you are in the top four in the league in receiving, we've made sure others got touches when we could," I said, looking at Jared and Polk.

"We may have to score 60 in the next two games to win, so we all need to be on the same page that our mindset will need to shift. We can't worry about injuries or stats or feelings anymore. This isn't something I'm going to make a big announcement about. In the year 2000, I was a young head coach at Paducah High School. We were 11-0, ranked #3 in the state playing another 11-0 team, Rankin, who was #2 in the polls. I thought I'd outsmart the defense in a second-round playoff game. I thought I would trick them by faking a handoff to our best player, a 215-pound bruiser, and handing the ball to our other back. It was 4th down and a goal from the one. What do you think happened?"

"I'm guessing you didn't score since the story fits this situation," Polk said, smiling.

"Yep, and we lost 13-12. I learned my lesson the hard way; never again will I sacrifice my best player as a decoy. From now on, it's all about having our dudes with the ball in crunch time. It's not about the opponent; it's about us. The playoffs are crunch time personified."

“You know we are all about doing what’s best for the team. The playoffs aren’t a time to worry about whether you get the ball. It’s time to do what it takes to win. There’s glory for everyone when you win,” Jared said.

“Chris, be ready to get the ball even more in short-yardage situations. Faking to a running back on the goal line is like a kryptonite for linebackers. They just can’t help but take a false step,” I said.

"I'm sure Cologne will play like everyone else and see if we can beat them running the ball. Don't worry about me getting injured. Give me the ball as much as we need,” Chris said.

"I agree that they might dare us to run the ball, but we need to find ways to involve both of you," I said, addressing Jared and Polk. Whether through screens, jet sweeps, reverse, or any other means, we must get the ball into our playmakers' hands. As the offensive coordinator, it's my responsibility to ensure that happens. On the other hand," I said, looking at Chris, "We have to be careful with how we utilize you. I'm an idiot if I don't take care of the league MVP on our playoff run. We need you on the field like I need some good fajitas right now."

"I'll be fine, coach. I'm made of steel." Chris said, smiling.

60

HOW A COACH LEARNED TO STOP YELLING...

Sept. 9, 2022

In July, I received incredible news from Charlie Scudder, a freelance reporter. He informed me that the New York Times had agreed to feature a story about my coaching journey in Potsdam. While I've had articles written about my teams in newspapers all across Texas in notable newspapers like the Dallas Morning News, the New York Times is the world's newspaper. Millions read its international edition across the globe.

"Coach, as much as I'd like them to fly me over, the Times is going to use a reporter from Berlin to come to watch a practice and take some pictures."

"I totally understand. I'm doing a Zoom with Fast N' Wide clients in a couple of days, where I will share what I'm calling my Royal Lab results from the first half. You are more than welcome to join us."

"That sounds great. Thanks for the invitation. I'll sit in and be a fly on the wall."

A few days later, I had a Zoom session with over 30 Fast N' Wide coaches from various parts of the United States.

"If you want to prove anything, you must test it. The Royal Laboratory has helped me prove and disprove many theories about offense and coaching in the first half of our season."

This meeting didn't focus on how we created 50 Strong. I reviewed our offensive stats, what worked well, and how I've needed to change my Texas High School coaching style because I'm in Germany coaching European adults. Many of the same coaches had sat in on the Zoom meetings with our players, so this Zoom was all about what I must do differently in the second half of the season and how it applies to coaching in the States.

"I've got to realize that I need to coach differently. Most 18-year-old Texas players have been playing since elementary school. It's not fair to expect players who have only played football for a few years to have the same level of understanding as someone who has been playing since childhood. I recognize that this was a mistake on my part, and I need to adjust my coaching style to meet my players where they're at and help them develop their skills and understanding of the game."

"I also have to know I can't punish a grown man for poor effort at practice like I could a teenager on a high school team."

"Coach, how do you get them to go hard if you can't punish them?" asked Chris Yeager, a high school coach in Alabama.

"That's a valuable lesson I've learned as a coach. In the past, I mentored my high school players and tried to be a father figure to them. We had team-building activities and ate together, establishing a certain level of trust that allowed me to discipline them when necessary. However, coaching adults in Europe is a different experience altogether. They haven't gone through the same rigorous offseason conditioning program as high school players in Texas, who spend over 1,000 hours getting bigger, faster, and stronger from December to August. In the GFL, players show up only when training camp starts, and they get to play football without paying the same price of admission. A 30-year-old player from Germany or Poland doesn't necessarily need or want me to mentor him. What he does want is the same thing as your assistant coaches, and even your players crave...more ownership in the process. We built our creed as I've done for years, but without many coaches, it forced me to lean on these guys more, and it has been great. *The more I've allowed the guys to help with game plans and scouting reports, the more it motivates them."*

Dr. Rob Gilbert, sports psychology professor and founder of The Success Hotline, was a guest speaker on our Zoom session, said, “Coach, can I add something?”

“Please!”

“People are motivated by two things: pleasure or pain. It would help if you motivated the employees in this laboratory with pleasure. Napoleon said, "A man will fight long and hard for a bit of colored ribbon." Ensure they are appreciated for their hard work, rewarded with monetary bonuses or extra time off. You’re becoming a much better coach because you can't use force to get what you done. You have to find ways for them to want to do it because you've convinced them they want to. This is the essence of coaching."

A few weeks later, a local freelance reporter from Berlin and a photographer came to practice.

"Hello, my name is Ella Schmidt. I'm excited to be here. Today will be the first time I’ve ever seen American football. I've heard about it and am excited to learn more today. We will stay out of the way, but thanks for allowing us to be here. Lena, our photographer, will also take some photos."

Ella appeared to be in her mid to late 20s. She was very professional but was probably assigned to fluff stories more than covering peace talks or economic summits. About halfway through practice, Ella asked me, “You seem very excited standing at the side of the court [her words, not mine] giving instructions. Is this normal for American coaches?"

"Absolutely. That's an excellent observation. There are many coaching styles, but players tend to take on the personality of their coach. If I want my players to have energy, I need to bring energy myself. Leading by example is an important aspect of coaching and sets the tone for the team."

A few days later, I was back on a call with Charlie. "Thanks, Coach Jackson, for being so open about your story. Ella and Lena said they got everything needed. I'm not sure when the Times will run the article, but I'll let you know when I find out," Charlie said.

I was thrilled to share the story of 50 Strong and how the players had accepted a Texan on our way to setting records with the Royals with Charlie. Our team's core values were groundbreaking for Europe and one of my proudest accomplishments as a coach. Thanks to the Times, the world would now hear about it.

Except for one thing... The article wasn't about 50 Strong. After the New York Times article was published, I was disappointed that it didn't focus on the team as much as I had hoped. Charlie and the Times editors focused on how I'd adjusted my coaching style from football-crazy, driven Texas players to European adults.

I texted Saul and let him know the article was published. *"The Times article came out. It didn't focus on the team as much as I was hoping. It was more about me not being a Neanderthal. Dang it."*

(Saul) "Yea, it made our players seem like a bunch of bums."

(me) "Sorry about that. I didn't know the slant the editors were taking with it. I told Scudder that the headline "A Coach Stops Yelling..." made my eyes big and actually made me want to yell. He agreed with me that the headline surprised him as well."

Even though the article didn't give as much coverage to 50 Strong and our players as I had hoped, Charlie still managed to provide readers with a glimpse of my 'Texan in Germany' coaching adventure.

Excerpts from the article…

'How a Veteran Coach Learned to Stop Yelling and Start Collaborating'

A longtime Texas high school football coach has spent this season coaching a German team. The experience helped him see that he needed to change his coaching style.

New York Times
September 9, 2022

Jackson's culture shock was magnified when he moved from Texas — where Friday night lights are a societal obsession — to a European league in which players are paid, but most consider football a part-time gig outside their main profession.

Back home, Jackson would often demand perfection from his high school players with punishment like extra plate pushes or running. He learned that he had to change his tactics and his mindset with his adult German players — and that he hadn't needed to be so firm during all those years in Texas, either.

Now, he asks more questions and tries to get more input from his players — and is encouraging his peers back in the United States to do the same with their younger teams.

"It's made me a better coach. I've always been a relational coach and believed a primary goal of a coach is to have players 'lay in traffic' for them, but I had to take it to the next level here. I wish I'd used some of these tactics coaching high school players, " Jackson said.

The new approach, he said, helped Potsdam shoot to the top spot in the league's northern division with an undefeated regular-season record. They play the Straubing Spiders in the first round of the GFL playoffs on Saturday.

"I have to have some gray area and understanding," Jackson said. "If I want to coach like I did in Texas, I need to go back to Texas."

"No one would describe me as laid back," he said.

Most of the GFL's European players learn football by watching YouTube clinics and Google. Players in their late 20s and 30s are recruited from all over the continent and with varying levels of skill and experience.

Americans are allowed to play, but only two may be on the field at a time. They wear big A's on their helmets so the referees can spot them easily.

Blending this hodgepodge of cultures and backgrounds can be a challenge in the ultimate team sport. Michael Vogt, the Royals' head coach, said he hired Jackson primarily because of his team-building experience in Texas.

"For him, it's not about him. It's about the team first," Vogt said.

"To get this group together and function together is probably the most important stuff. He found a way to get this going right from the get-go."

Chris Helbig, the team's American quarterback, said players had needed to adjust to

Jackson's intense style, and Jackson had needed to learn a new approach to coaching.

"He's changed some of his philosophy in the sense of, he can be a little more hands-off and give us a little more responsibility with things," Helbig said.

In Texas, Jackson said, his strategy was to "confront and demand." He would confront behavior 'below the standard' and demand it gets corrected. His German players have families and jobs that take up more time. He realized that he couldn't punish them for prioritizing those things.

"Coaching high school football players in Texas is like being a manager of a business 30 years ago," Jackson said. "Coaching in Europe — it's the modern employee now."

Jackson accepts that but doesn't always like it.

"It's hard for him to adjust, that people can't always come to practice," said Yasir Raji, a German offensive lineman on the Royals. He said he sensed that Jackson still got angry about it. "He wants people to sacrifice," Raji said.

"One of the best things I've done over here is rely on my players more; No one washes a rented car. The more ownership I've given them, the more they've bought in," Jackson said.

Jackson's Royals have smashed the GFL's record for the highest-scoring team, averaging 51.4 points a game. Only the fourth GFL team since 1999 to go undefeated, the Royals are hoping to go all the way to the German Bowl championship game in October.

"There's no doubt it has worked out so far," said Vogt, the head coach. "He does stuff to perfection."

"I wish I'd have used some of these tactics coaching high school players. We would have been better off, and my blood pressure would have been lower," Jackson said.

Jackson said he would not return to Potsdam next season but was excited to go back to Texas high school football. When he does, he said, he'll be a different kind of coach.

Despite the article not celebrating 50 Strong or our players as much as I'd liked, I was still thrilled we were featured in the New York Times. Millions worldwide would read about the 2022 Royals and our success. The article could lead to more Fast N' Wide clients and the Elite Coach Mastermind. It could open doors to other newspaper articles, podcast interviews, and publicity in the States. Maybe Netflix would call me, or ESPN would want to do a "30 for 30" on a Texas coach in Germany.

Well…none of that happened. Nada. Just crickets.

Maybe people aren't reading the newspaper anymore?

"It was much larger than football. Football was just the vehicle. For men from all walks of life to come together and share our bond, that was special."

Jared Wolfe
#15 Wide Receiver
Seaford, New York

GFL PLAYOFFS 2022
ROAD TO FRANKFURT
QUARTER FINALS
10./11. SEPTEMBER
SEMI FINALS
24./25. SEPTEMBER
FINAL
08. OCTOBER
SEMI FINALS
24./25. SEPTEMBER
QUARTER FINALS
10./11. SEPTEMBER
GERMAN BOWL XLIII
DEUTSCHE BANK PARK FRANKFURT
VS
VS
VS
VS
VS
VS
VS

61

200 FEET

Sept. 10, 2022

After a week of rest, we returned to the field on Tuesday evening to begin our preparations for our first-round opponent, the Straubing Spiders, who have a record of 6-4.

"Twwweeettt!" Saul blew his whistle and yelled, "Team meet!"

All the players were on time and in good spirits, ready to finally begin our playoff journey. "Good evening, gentlemen!" Saul said enthusiastically. "Welcome to the 2022 GFL playoffs! Some of you know how it works, but for those who don't, I will give you a short lesson. The bracket is set up like the NFL playoffs, minus the Wild Card round. The higher seed will always play at home. The top seed from the north division, "Your Potsdam Royals", plays the lowest seed from the south division, the hated Straubing Spiders. Not to get ahead of ourselves, but when we win, we'll host the winner of the second seed from the south, the Munich Cowboys, or the third seed from the north, the Cologne Crocodiles." Saul continued, "On the other side of the bracket, Schwäbisch Hall is the top seed, hosting the Berlin Adler. The second seed from the north, the New Yorker Lions, are at home versus the third seed from the south, the Allgäu Comets."

After he explained the playoff structure, Saul talked about Straubing's kicking game, then looked at me and said, "Coach Jackson, please take it away."

"Thanks, Coach Saul. Newsflash, guys, we will run the same plays we used in weeks 1-10, just faster and better. Let's talk about mindset for a few moments. Have you ever noticed that sometimes when you're driving to a new place, the trip there seems to take forever, but the drive back home always seems to go by faster? And, if I may say so, here on the Autobahn, it's even more exhilarating to drive both ways. By the way, in case you were on pins and needles wondering what this Texan thinks of the Autobahn, I'm a huge fan. The systematic driving where trucks must be in the far-right lane and how everyone moves over for the fast people in the far-left lane is pretty awesome. I commend each of you Germans for your orderly driving structure." I said, laughing but also sincere.

"Back to my analogy. Does anyone know why we always seem to get home from a new destination sooner than we did going?"

"Because we're familiar with the road?" Stefan asked.

"Yes, because we've been there and done that. But also because we have a goal. How long did it take us to get here? I can beat that coming home!"

I continued, "We're starting down a new road now. By the way, what's our record?"

"10-0!" a couple of guys said proudly.

"No! We're 0-0." Chris said, correcting them.

"That's right! Why are we 0-0?"

"We're in the tournament now. Everyone has the same record," Chris said.

"Back to my analogy. The playoffs are a winding road. Is it the same road we've been on all year, or did we exit off one Autobahn and get on another one?" I didn't wait long and answered my own question. "It's the same road. Look behind me. That's the same field we've played on all season. We'll be there again Saturday. If we were in Straubing, I bet their field would be 100 yards long and 53 yards wide."

"Next question. Are we going to win the game Saturday?"

"I've even heard this a few times; "You don't win games, you win plays," Robbie said.

"Exactly. There will be 175 total plays versus the Straubing, and each will have a history of its own. Our focus has to be on winning each and every play. Everything is important, but nothing's special. We've been down this road many times. We'll play a four-man defensive line this week for the sixth or seventh time. It's not about what round of the playoffs we're in or what the bracket looks like; it's about the road ahead. We had to go over the bracket and all that. I totally understand, but now we shouldn't talk about what round we're in again. We should focus on the road ahead. A pavement of plays. Win one play at a time until they tell us to stop Saturday."

Before Friday's practice, I asked everyone to bring their phone to our team meeting. "I want to circle back to Tuesday's point about us being on the same road as we've been all season. Get out your phone and find the video I just uploaded. This is a Toyota commercial from 2015 that teaches exactly the mindset we must have. Hit play."

A couple is driving a Corolla at night when a voice begins speaking. "Wherever you want to go, all you need to see is the next 200 feet."

"Pause it. What does this mean to us? The first few seconds already drives the lesson home, no pun intended."

"The 200 feet is all you need to see at a time," Leo answered.

"Yes! Each play for us is 200 feet on our journey," I said. "Play it."

The car now drives past a tractor pulling a large hay trailer. Next, it passes through a lightning storm and an ominous dark tunnel.

"Pause it." Now, I don't know why some idiot in Iowa or Texas is driving his tractor at night, but it's a hazard for the drivers," I said, smiling. "How is the couple going to get through to their destination? I think they're headed to Frankfurt."

"They're just going to keep pointing the car where the lights tell them to go. Two hundred feet, or as we would say, 60 meters at a time," Ruben said, who was on crutches and now the assistant secondary coach.

"Hit play."

"That's how life unfolds...a leap of faith. Even if you can't see it, your destination is out there." The couple is now driving past a huge grizzly bear and then through another tunnel where suddenly, things shift to pleasant lanterns floating in the sky.

#95 Norman Kullenisch #52 Leo Bosch
#66 Oskar Rüegg

"So just keep going. You'll get there 200 feet at a time."

"Are we going to win the game Saturday??" I ask as I hold my hand to my ear and lean toward the team.

"No!"

"Ja!" (yes in German) I said enthusiastically.

"Let's go win plays 200 feet at a time on this *Fast Friday* and again tomorrow against the Spiders!"

Game day was another beautiful September day. It was 72 at kickoff and partly cloudy.

Our first drive was a three-play *Stampede* (three memorized plays in a row as fast as we could go). On the second play, Chris faked a reverse and threw a deep crossing route to Sixten Dragen for 33 yards. Three plays later, Karri ran it over the goal line for a quick touchdown. The Schumacher PAT made it 7-0.

The Spiders, missing their first team all-GFL running back to injury, milked the clock with a 12-play 72-yard drive to tie the score at 7-7.

We attacked down the field on the first play of our next possession. Chris went over the top to Polk for a 54-yard touchdown. We executed a fake PAT with Sixten running it in on the left side, reclaiming the lead at 15-7 with six minutes left in the first quarter.

Straubing did their best to control the ball and keep us on the sideline. The Spiders mixed short passes and rushing plays for another 12-play drive to close the gap to 15-14.

After our own 12-play drive, early in the second quarter, we increased our lead to 22-14. Karri converted a 4th down and four at the Straubing 26, then four plays later capped the drive off with a five-yard score.

Straubing's lucky number must be 12. Painfully, their straight possession resulted in a 12-play drive for a touchdown. The key play was a 44-yard completion on 3rd and 23!

"I don't know who God's angry with on the defensive staff, but I wish they would go to confession or have an exorcism or something. Third and 23 should never happen! Damn!" I said to Jonas in the headset. Quarterback Zack Wright scored the touchdown from the one-yard line. They went for two, got it, and the score was now 22-22, much to our surprise.

A Chris-to-Polk touchdown completion of 16 yards finished the scoring in the first half. We kept the offense on the field, and Chris ran it in to increase our lead back to eight points, 30-22.

The Spiders had an excellent *first downs, then touchdowns plan*. The score was closer than we anticipated at halftime. I was grateful they weren't slowing it down like the Rebels did a few weeks prior.

Offensively we were rolling. For the first time in my memory, we didn't score in our two-minute drill at the end of the half, but I didn't have anything major we needed to address or change.

"We're playing lights out, guys, averaging around 10 yards per play. I love the discipline and execution. Keep winning plays. Keep applying the pressure, and eventually, their pipes will burst."

We owned the third quarter. Other than yet another Spider 12-play drive, we dominated the period and went on a 22-0 run. Our defense got in on the scoring on a Time 50-yard interception return. With 12 minutes remaining, the score was 55-22, and the game was over for all practical purposes.

Adam and Karri scored touchdowns in the fourth quarter, resulting in a final score of 66-25 in our favor. This victory allowed us to play a home *half-final* [semi-final] game for the first time in Royal's history.

We tallied 522 yards on the day [9.8 average per play], 281 passing, and 241 rushing. Chris threw for 273, Karri rushed for 100, and Polk had 100 receiving yards on five receptions.

"Good job today, coach!" Saul said as he sat down next to me in the VIP area for some post-game food.

"Thanks, brother. That was the most uneventful game we've had in a while. It was almost peaceful. I hope you don't take this wrong, but I want you to know I'm impressed with how you are handling everything."

“Thanks; I love the organization and always will. I'll do whatever I can to make Berti's life easier as well.”

Saul received a text and looked down at his phone.

"I hate to ruin our Zen-like state, but this is not good news....”

GFL **GAMERECAP**

VIERTELFINALE vs Straubing

66 (11-0) | 25 (8-3)

	ROYALS	SPIDERS
TOTAL YARDS	522	330
YARDS RUSHING	241	222
YARDS PASSING	281	108
YARDS PER PLAY	9.8	4.6
PUNTS	1	1
PENALTIES	9-96	2-10

RUSHING	ATT.	YARDS	AVG.	TDS
PAJARINEN, K.	13	100	7.7	3
ŽOUŽELKA, A.	5	40	8	1

RECEIVING	RECEPTS	YARDS	TDS	LONG
POLK, B.	5	100	2	54
WOLFE, J.	5	67	1	35

PASSING	COMP.	ATT.	YARDS	TDS	INT
HELBIG, C	19	23	272	3	

62

WHAT'S GOOD FOR THE GOOSE...

Sept. 13, 2022

"C'mon, Saul! Don't tell me something bad now. I'm at peace after a game for the first time in forever. If you have bad news to give me, can you wait until I've had a couple of Radlers?"

"Sorry, but misery loves company. I have two names for you...Strong and Jackson. Do they ring a bell?"

"Not a bell, but a gun blast in my brain. I still have nightmares and cold sweats about how they hammered us in game seven. You're about to tell me they beat Munich, so we must stop them again?"

"You might get your buddy Luster back here. He can give another pregame speech or, even better, bring his 21 guns!"

TUESDAY PRACTICE

The following Tuesday evening, we were about to disperse from our pre-practice team meeting when a player's voice from the front row grabbed everyone's attention. "Wait a minute. I've got something I'd like to discuss with the coaches present," Yasir said.

"Go ahead, sir," Berti said.

"We've heard several times this season that *no one's worth a 15-yard penalty*, and we agree. This season, we've had a couple of penalties on the coaches, which will cost us in the playoffs. Some of us feel like you, Coach Vogt and Coach Jackson must calm down on the sideline. We'd appreciate it if you two could be more under control."

Say what? Did I hear this correctly?

One of our players, who's received two unsportsmanlike penalties this season, is calling out Berti and me for our sideline conduct. I'm intense during games, but after 31 years, I know what I can say and the tone I can use. I know when I get *the look* from Mats to shut up and when to joke with them. Jerome grabbed my arm a few times and said, "Be careful, coach," or "That's enough," but I have NOT been flagged this season.

"Ok, I will do better in the future. I understand," Berti said.

All eyes now shifted to me, and it was my turn to respond to the statements from Yasir. "I won't apologize for how I act on the sideline. If you guys don't like how I conduct myself, I'll call plays from the press box," I said and then looked at Berti to let him know I was finished speaking and move forward.

"Ok…let's have a good practice," Berti said.

The next morning, I was still unhappy about Yasir being bold enough to call out Berti and me. All coaches want communication from players and to know the team's pulse, but if this was a major concern, our team meeting wasn't the place. It would be like me saying to a player, "you need to stop being a prima donna and selfish," in front of the entire team. At different times during the season, I had hard conversations with players, but they were always in private.

I put this message in our Autobahn 80 chat: *After contemplating the comments from Yasir yesterday, I've decided to actually go to the press box during games. It will be a blessing, as most things are. I'm not apologizing for how I conduct myself during games. Robbie and Chris are the most natural to signal plays in. We need to begin the practice tonight.*

About an hour later, Berti texted me. *Good day, coach. Can we please meet before practice today and go for a walk?*

Berti and I met about an hour before practice and walked around the beautiful Sportpark Luftschiffhafen athletic facility. We strolled across the street, past the Olympic bobsled training ramp and the track to a wide tree-lined biking and jogging path that borders the Havel River.

"I know you're upset, and I don't blame you, but I'm asking you to stay on the field Saturday and not go up in the press box. Our offense is the best I've ever seen, and we don't need to change anything now," Berti said as we walked.

"Coach, I've been frustrated with things I've never seen until I started coaching with the Royals. But last night was the final straw. It's one thing for players to make mistakes on the field, but when they start disrespecting coaches in team meetings, it's just unacceptable. I'll stay as far away as possible and call plays from a distance."

"I don't think Yasir came across the way he meant."

"I can't imagine how he could have meant it any other way."

"I know I'm a players' coach. I allow guys a lot of freedom to say and act the way they want as long as they perform. Every American coach we've ever had becomes frustrated by different things, but you're the first who has helped us shift our mindset.

Don't take Yasir's comments personally. It's simply a different environment here."

"I believe it speaks volumes about 50 Strong that Yasir felt comfortable enough to express his or the team's concerns. It's great that we've allowed them to speak their minds, but that wasn't the right time or place to do it. I'm incredibly grateful for how you've treated me over the past few months. Everything I've asked for, you've tried to do for me, but I can't change who I am. I can't be someone I'm not to please Yasir or anyone else who doesn't understand or like my coaching style. I never imagined being called out in a team meeting is standard operating procedure for German teams. I understand things are different here, but at the end of the day, football is football. Players play, and coaches coach. I can't do it any other way. I'll see how it goes tonight and the rest of the week before I decide how I will coach on Saturday. Let's leave it for now as a game-time decision."

63

CLEAR THE 'B'

Sept. 21, 2022

Have you ever felt like you've overstayed your welcome somewhere? Like at a dinner party at 11:00 p.m., and the one couple will stay even though the hosts are cleaning up?

Today was the Tuesday of the Cologne rematch, and the winner advanced to the German Bowl. We were 11-0 and on pace to be the first team in the history of Europe to average 50 points a game, but for me, the clock was ticking toward midnight. The Royal Laboratory was proving my theories would work, but I was increasingly becoming lonely and dejected. The problem was I shouldn't want to leave at all. But, more importantly, why was I feeling this way? I was missing my family and was ready to go home. I didn't want to get up and go to the airport, but I didn't just come to see the sights and coach some ball. I came to help win a championship and help people become more. The GFL moving the German Bowl back a week didn't help any. The past several weeks felt like all the 50 Strong momentum was fading faster than it was created. Most of the guys were all in, but some were extremely tired of being coached hard and were starting to let me know it.

My grandfather always said, "It's easier to pull a rope than push one." I was still excited to see it we could 'ring the bell' and win the German Bowl, but I felt like I was pushing a heavy rope.

After our summer break, it was as if the axis on *Planet Royal* shifted. We spent the next six or seven weeks seeing how much we could disrespect our opponents and still win. We were still scoring points, but that was secondary to me. My mission was to help create an intentional culture for the first time in Potsdam and probably in the history of the GFL. We were coming out of this funk, but I was still struggling with my own feelings. As someone who always wanted to be liked, I couldn't help but feel hurt that things were shifting in a way that was unfamiliar to me.

I believe that God uses difficult seasons to draw us closer to Him. If we didn't have several open dates throughout the year, the season would be complete by now, and I'd be back home. I decided to use this time "in the desert" to improve. During my free time, which I had plenty of, I listened to spiritual podcasts and books on improving my marriage. I prayed more often, and my perspective shifted, becoming more forgiving than I had been for years. Even when the season felt like it was dragging on, I chose to find gratitude and thank God for the blessings in my life.

Tracy and I spoke a few times daily, but his seven-hour difference made it difficult. I would set my alarm for 5 a.m., talk to Tracy before she went to bed, and then go back to sleep.

Another excellent habit I started was getting myself in shape and sweating. Instead of spending too much time indoors watching Netflix, I started engaging in daily workouts at Fitness First gym. It was also a good place to see some players outside practice or games.

WEDNESDAY PRACTICE

High-caliber players are harder to find in Europe than coaches, which says a lot. Coaches tended to be pretty hands-off with our starters, but our backups didn't always get off so easily. I don't recall ever seeing a starter getting reprimanded for lackluster effort or execution. The Royals' philosophy was to kill them with kindness so they would return.

"Hey, d-head! Can you read the card?!" One of our coaches asked a player attempting to replicate a Cologne play. Even after almost six months of the language, this comment startled me.

It must've been a full moon because we were just getting started on negativity at this workout. I'm intense during our 11 on 11 sessions versus the defense. Games aren't won by adding a new play that tricks the opponent. Fanatical execution of a few plays is how Fast N' Wide is designed. The simplicity blows away most coaches. If all 11 players execute their assignment, the play will be successful. You don't win games. You win plays.

Success lies in simplicity. Failure lives in complexity. My dad gave me one piece of advice when I became a coach in 1990: "Make sure if you're ever an offensive line coach, have simple rules that apply versus any front. If they have to block each type of defensive alignment, there'll be confusion, and a confused lineman causes punts or, even worse, turnovers. If your offensive line is confused, you'll be looking for a job soon."

Our backside tackle's rule is *Clear the B gap* on zone away (an inside running play). All defenses are designed for each gap to be defended, so there will be someone to block. For example, the left tackle is responsible for any defender in the opening or area between him and the left guard. He climbs and goes to a linebacker if no defensive lineman is in the hole.

This has probably been over-documented in this book, but Yasir is the best lineman I've ever coached or coached against. He is so athletic that he can help others and still get his defender blocked, but he didn't this time. He blocked out on the defensive end instead of going directly into the B gap, then went to his linebacker.

The key block on the play is the tight end's kick of the defensive end, so my eyes were there when I saw Yasir block out before clearing the B gap. He was then late to the linebacker inside. I didn't go crazy or get overly loud, but stopped the play and, from where I was standing 20 yards away, yelled, "Yasir, clear the B!"

"I did clear the B!" Yasir responded like I'd said something about his mom or his favorite soccer team.

Maybe the "good for the goose" comment from last week was in the back of my head, but I didn't respond well to being yelled at by a player. The fact Yasir didn't handle his assignment wasn't the issue. The issue was I'd had it with the culture of the player-coach. There has to be a hierarchy of how players speak to coaches. Although, after months and months of coaching where I confronted mistakes and demanded they be corrected, I couldn't tolerate the disrespect any longer.

"No, you did not! You chipped the end first!" I was now overly loud.

Yasir is also one of the smartest players I've ever coached. He would score higher than me on an IQ or aptitude test. But high intelligence can also be a liability at times if it keeps an individual from having a growth mindset. I fired back at him, "The four worst words someone can say are, "I already know that" and that's your mindset. Not once have you asked me to coach you this season, including now, because you already know!"

"You're right!" Yasir shouted back at me. "I know I cleared the B gap!"

"Get out of my drill! Get the hell off my field!"

A few minutes later, Berti was speaking to Yasir on the sideline. I walked over and said, "Is this what we're going to do here? Are we going to say the hell with any player discipline?"

"You shouldn't have yelled at me. If you shout at me, I shout at you back," Yasir said.

"We need to all calm ourselves and get back to football," Berti said.

No matter how hard an assistant pushes for change in a culture, it's almost impossible if the head coach is not the *tip of the spear*. We were preparing to advance to the German Bowl for the first time in the Royals' history, and a player felt like he was on the same level as his coach.

Later, I could hear Yasir explain his side of the story to teammates on the sideline. Everyone was hoping the situation would die down and go away. It was all I could do to let it go, but I did. This was the most alone I'd felt since I'd been in Germany. It seemed like no one had my back. "Tim, you're in at left tackle," I said right before we scrimmaged the defense again.

"Coach, is Yasir not going back in?" Jerome asked me.

"Hell, no, he's not going back. I may not be able to control if he wants to be coached, but I damn sure control if he plays." Jerome and I have had an amazing relationship all season, but he was frustrated with me and let me know it.

He looked straight at me and said, "If he isn't going to play, then I don't want to play either..."

64

THE 'HALF-FINAL'

Sept. 24, 2022

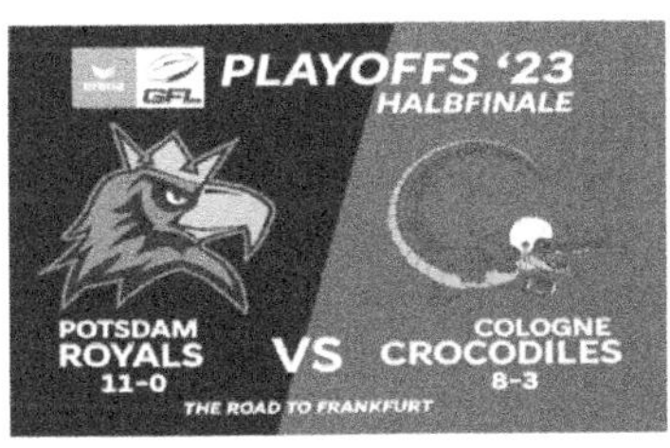

"Then I guess you won't play either. Right now, I don't care if anyone wants to play."

We made it through practice without anyone killing me or vice versa, but maybe I'd overstayed my welcome, and the dinner party needed to come to an end. We had our normal Zoom meeting the following day, reviewing the previous night's practice. I still needed extra high-blood pressure medication, but I wouldn't escalate the situation. I was, however, going to coach Yasir on the play in question.

"From my vantage point, you block out here and don't clear the 'B gap'. I'm not sure why you thought you did, but Leo is in the B gap, and he makes the tackle." Yasir didn't say a word. I advanced to the next play and started coaching again.

None of this book is my attempt to show anything other than laboratory results. I'm not attempting to paint a picture of the situation that I'm correct or that Yasir was wrong. We both had our share of fault for blowing up practice. But, explaining in the last chapter how these last few weeks were my time to become a better version of myself and get closer to God, it was clear that I needed to make it right between us.

I just couldn't get myself to do it.

The following day was Fast Friday, our mock game. Without any mention of the incident, I said, "Normal starters, you're in the first series."

It was the best I could do at the moment. And just like that, it was behind us.

Earlier in the week, I included information on the world's greatest international hockey team: the Soviet "Big Red Machine" of 1980.

I used pictures of the Soviets but cut and pasted our guys' faces to make it funny and hopefully fascinating.

Saul, who is excellent at marketing and creating graphics for the Royals' social media, posted on WhatsApp, *"Coach Jackson, that picture is so bad; it's sort of good :)."*

#15 Jared Wolfe #23 Nadim Merrikh
#78 Yasir Raji #24 Simon Alverez

At our Saturday pregame meeting, it was time to link the Soviet 1980 team with my theme for the week - RED ARMY.

"I will talk to you guys today about the 1980 “Miracle on Ice” game where the U.S. defeated the Soviets 4-3. I'm not going to tell you about how the U.S. did it. We're not the underdogs today. Our focus today is on the Soviets. A friend of mine, Mike Tully, is a retired sports reporter who covered an exhibition game between the U.S. team, a bunch of college guys, and the Soviet team two weeks before the Olympics. The Soviets won 10-3, but it could easily have been 20-0, according to Mike. He said they didn't belong on the same ice and described the game as a massacre."

"How good was the Soviet hockey team? Between 1954, when the Soviets began playing international hockey, and 1988 they won a medal at every competition. In 1979, before the 'Miracle', the Red Army played an NHL all-star team with 20 future Hall of Famers on the roster. The Soviets routed them 6-0."

"Hit play in our WhatsApp. It's a one-minute clip from the documentary *Red Army*." A highlight video began with the team while journalists commented on what made them great.

"They had a sixth sense about them. They had eyes in the back of their heads."

"Sometimes you feel without a look. Your partner must be there."

"The Soviets really perfected the weave."

"Festivov was number two in scoring, although he was a defender. He would go forward, and Markarov would draw back. Everything was like this (the journalist was moving his hands in circles), and no one knew who to cover."

"The goals they scored would highlight reel goals. They all touched the puck."

"The skill level of that team was astounding. They elevated hockey to an art form."

"No one could hold them down. What they did on the ice...they were the best."

The clip ended, and I said, "The Finns, no offense, Karri, played them 66 times in the 1970s. Their record was 2-63-1. What do you do when you can't beat 'em? “Success leaves clues”, so Finnish hockey coaches made a few trips to Moscow to see why the Soviets were kicking their butts. They discovered the Soviets practiced 1,200 hours a year—three times more than the Finns. The Soviets slept in military barracks 11 months out of the year and had the discipline to match."

"Did you guys catch that? Let me get out my phone and divide 1,200 by 365. That's three hours and 15 minutes a day! Just a second, they took a month off, so dividing by 335 comes to four hours a day! The Soviets had ‘three-a-days’ for 11 months a year."

"They earned the right to be the most dominant sports team in the world, but why does any of this matter today?" I asked.

"Because we should win this game," Maciek answered.

"Yes! We're the Red Army, and Cologne is capable, but they won't be the dominant team on the field today. An article about the Soviets says, 'They were the best team, even at the 1980 Olympics. They just happened to lose at the wrong time...It happens. 'How does it happen? From a football perspective, the Soviets were like an NFL all-star team defeated by a bunch of college guys. To make this very clear to us today, it was like the Soviets defeated the Americans 81-14 just two weeks earlier. Do you guys remember us scoring 81, and the next time we played the Rebels, they had to ball with three minutes left in the game to win? It seemed impossible, but it could've happened."

"We've earned the right to win, but the team that will be victorious today is the team that plays the best, not that is the best team. Could the 10-3 exhibition game blowout have been a factor in the 4-3 defeat in the Olympics?"

"Yes, sir. The Soviets became overconfident. They didn't take the Americans seriously," Mat said.

"Yes! It took a miracle to beat them. We didn't defeat the Crocs 81-14 last time. We have a great plan to stop #4 (the receiver), and they are a talented team. We’re the champions of the North, and if we go out and play like machines with execution and discipline, they don't stand a chance.”

“Play 50 Strong football today! Be your brother’s keeper, prepare even now, play hard and smart, be humble and always, always, always compete!”

65

THE WORST THING I'VE EVER SAID TO A PLAYER

Sept. 25, 2022

About 30 minutes before we began warmups, I was doing my walking-the-field routine and thinking about the game.

"Hey, coach!" Buddy said as he walked over to me.

"I heard you spoke about the Soviet hockey team earlier. I bet that made some coaches reminiscent of the good 'ol days."

"Really? Reminiscent like they miss being behind the wall?"

"Not behind the wall, but some aspects of communism. To some extent, my wife's parents and even she will nostalgically talk about how life was simpler."

"That blows my mind, to be perfectly honest with you. I guess we were taught the USSR was so evil, I can't comprehend longing for them to be my government."

"I agree, they don't necessarily miss the political system of the USSR, but they reminisce on the camaraderie and reliance on one another they had to have. My wife's parents will discuss how they didn't have many tools, so they'd borrow from neighbors. A few minutes later, they'll talk about how the other neighbor was a communist spy and would turn in non-conformers. We never think about aspects of life here in the States like this."

"I guess that explains why I totally understand no one speaks about Hitler, but anything Soviet in Potsdam is well-maintained. I've wondered why a statue of Lenin in a park is still around, or the Soviet military cemetery is the most manicured thing I see."

"Anyone behind the wall was taught Russian as a second language. Every *East German* older than 45 can speak Russian, and everyone younger learned English in school."

GAME TIME

It was a beautiful day for the game, with the temperature at a comfortable 63 degrees and the sun shining bright. Our players aligned inside our run-through tunnel to be announced like always, but one thing was different; they all had lit, burning flares in their hands. The bright flares looked dangerous to this old guy but were also amazingly cool.

#1 Manase Time

And the guys loved them.

"I don't know whose idea this was, but it's pretty dang awesome," I said to Saul on the sideline.

"Isn't it? The guys are loving it, and the pics will be amazing."

I was enjoying the new Saul. His demeanor on game day had changed 180 degrees. He was calm and collected; in fact, I was envious of how composed he was during games now.

We've scored a touchdown on our first drive in 11 of 12 games. It baffled me why teams allowed us to be ahead 7-0 when they touched the ball for the first time, but most teams did the normal *defer* if they won the toss.

Cologne won the toss and...Let us have the ball first.

Again, we scored a touchdown on our opening possession. A 16-yard touchdown pass from Chris to Polk completed an eight-play, 65-yard drive. Our two-point conversion failed, but the score was 6-0 with only three minutes gone in the contest.

The Crocodiles, who threw for over 400 yards in our first game, came out of the gate passing it again. A Strong to Jackson completion of 33 yards looked like it would set them up deep in our territory, but our free safety, Divine, knocked the ball out of Jackson's hands, and Manase recovered it.

Chris and our offense went back on the attack. After four plays, it was 2nd and three from our 41-yard line. Chris dropped back to pass and threw a wobbly completion to Jared for one yard, but 3rd and two weren't the issue. Chris was holding his throwing hand and jogging off the field. He wasn't hit on the play, so I didn't think it could be very serious.

I grabbed Robbie and said as quickly as I could, "Go make it happen. Let's see you do your thing." I called a quarterback run play behind Brenden and Yasir. Robbie picked up five yards and moved the chains for a first down.

I didn't have time to wonder about Chris. We play too fast to think about anything other than the next call. Ten plays later, Heiko barreled his way into the endzone for a 2-yard touchdown. With one minute gone in the second quarter, it was 13-0 Royals after the point after.

"Great job, Robbie. You looked like you'd been with us for months. Did anything happen out there you weren't expecting?" I asked.

"No sir, I feel great. They look like they are double-covering Jared and Polk, so running the ball wasn't a problem."

Taka and our assistant trainers were looking at Chris. "What's the status? Does it look like he'll be back in the next series?" I asked Taka and Chris.

"Not yet. We are seeing if we can tape up his thumb and if he can throw," Taka said.

Our defense was playing like I hadn't seen in a long time. It was a real treat to watch. Our defensive staff schemed to neutralize Jackson, their stud receiver. And it worked like a charm. We decided that if their tight end caught an eight-yard pass, it wouldn't be enough for them to beat us. We had a plan, and we executed it flawlessly. We double-teamed Jackson and made the European guys beat us.

On 4th and one from our 15-yard line, Strong misfired, and we took over again. Chris was still at the trainer's table with Taka.

"Let's give 'em more of the same guys. If they continue to play on Yasir's inside without a linebacker on the outside, we'll keep blocking down and going around," I said to the offense.

Robbie led us down the field again. He went around our left side for 25 yards on the drive's fourth play. On the next snap, he connected with Polk for a 40-yard touchdown. After our successful two-point conversion, we'd increased our lead to 21-0 in the middle of the second quarter.

"We're playing like the Red Army! I shouted to Chris as I walked up behind him and put my arm around his neck to hug him. "Robbie's getting it done for us!" I said but was now looking at his face.

I knew in a split second I'd just made one of the biggest mistakes of my career. Chris wasn't smiling or joyous. His eyes were red, and he was tearing up...

66

"GERMAN BOWL! GERMAN BOWL!"

Sept. 24, 2022

"The doctor thinks my thumb is fractured. I'm about to leave and get an X-Ray to make sure, but he thinks it's broken for sure."

Holy crap. The past few weeks have been bad, and I've made things worse. I'd convinced myself Chris was indeed Superman. We'd gone so long without a backup, and he'd played through sickness, blindside hits, and everything else a starting quarterback deals with.

"Oh man, Chris...I'm so sorry. I've said some stupid things, but this takes the cake. I'm so sorry I didn't find out more about your injury coming over to you. Since you weren't tackled, I assumed the best and figured you'd be ok, especially for the German Bowl in two weeks."

"It's OK, coach. I know you didn't mean anything by it. It's just this always seems to happen to me. In high school and at Southern Utah, I was injured both times before the championship game and didn't get to play in either. I can't believe it just happened again."

"I can't believe it either. You're the reason we're here today. How did you injure your thumb?"

"I hit it on Karri's helmet after I released the pass to Jared. I knew immediately that it wasn't good."

Chris is a fellow believer, so I knew this would mean something to him. "You know, God is in control. Let's pray for a miracle."

My stomach was churning with a feeling much worse than the aftermath of the big nuclear meltdown Yasir. I've made a lot of mistakes on this field. I'll never forget the horrendous blunder I made in our first game, thinking it was 3rd down when it was actually 4th. I've been harsh on my players at times, and I even lost my cool with a referee once or twice. Now, the last time I'd stand on this sideline, I'd made the biggest error, and no one could fix it for me. No one could save me from this debacle. I'd hurt the guy who had my back all season and the months before on our Zoom calls.

Damn…how could I be so stupid?

"Punt return alert!" Saul shouted on the sideline. "Jared, get ready!"

I had to shake out of it and finish the half. "I'm sorry again, buddy. I love you and wouldn't have ever said anything to hurt you on purpose."

"Don't think about it anymore, coach. Now's not the time for pity. Go coach up, Robbie, and let's win this game."

#19 Jonas Gacek #2 Divine Buckrham

I gathered the offense up on the sideline and made sure I looked different from how I felt. Six minutes were left in the first half when Jared fair-caught the Croc punt to set us up at our 35-yard line. "Let's get in trips to the field again and see if Cologne will keep letting us block down and pull Brenden around. Karri, you're doing a great job of finding work [someone to block]."

Playing fast wears down opponents physically, but tempo forces defensive coordinators to stay basic with their game plan. Cologne aligned badly to our single receiver side, and we kept sticking the knife in the wound.

"Jonas, until you tell me they've made a change, I'm calling the same play over and over."

"Understood. I'll let you know."

'Three right, South Lambo Q,' I signaled repeatedly and as quickly as possible.

Cologne was beaten by alignment. They simply didn't have enough defenders to our single receiver side. Yasir was at the point of attack and crushed his man inside. Brenden pulled around and sealed the inside linebacker. Karri was an extra blocker who went to block their all-league safety.

'South Lambo Q' worked time after time:

- Patterson for 11 yards
- Patterson for 9 yards
- Patterson for 12 yards
- Patterson incomplete
- Patterson for 10 yards
- Patterson pass complete to Heiko for 18 yards
- Patterson touchdown run for 5 yards

As we went in at half-time, up 28-0, I could feel the mixed emotions in the air. On the one hand, we were in the driver's seat to play for the championship, but on the other hand, a cloud of darkness loomed over us. Despite our lead, it was hard to feel good at the moment. We all knew how tough it'd be to play without Chris in Frankfurt.

THE SECOND HALF

Cologne was a good football team, especially offensively. They came out of the intermission determined to make it a game by driving 70 yards in five plays. The big plays on the possession were two completions to their tight end for 43 and 26 yards, but #4 wasn't the guy, and we were fine with this. I'm a former tight end, but receivers make big money because they are explosive. We were keeping Jackson in check for now.

Both teams scored two touchdowns in the third quarter. The Crocs continued to throw the ball, but we were content to take the low-hanging fruit and run the ball against a defense that was still aligned to stop Chris from throwing to Jared and Polk. Karri scored from nine yards out, and Robbie scored on a five-yard run near the end of the third quarter. We held a commanding 42-13 lead.

Cologne continued to throw the ball, but our defensive secondary played one of the best games in The Royals' history. Divine ended the first drive of the fourth quarter with an interception at our one-yard line. The party was starting to happen in the stands. Board members were coming down to the sidelines to participate in this special moment unfolding.

As a championship offense does, we went 99 yards in 12 plays to score one more time. Heiko scored the last Royals touchdown of the season in our home stadium from five yards out to increase our lead to 49-13.

Cologne added a score late to make the final 49-21, but it wasn't that close. The game was an exclamation point on our dominance of the Northern Conference this season.

Players doused Berti with Gatorade as the seconds ticked off the clock.

Schumacher, our kicker who joined us in July, was waving our huge Royals flag to the crowd.

Dave, our secondary coach, and the defensive backs were taking pics together, celebrating their momentous effort of shutting down the Croc passing game.

As happy as everyone was in May when we defeated Dresden for the first time, this moment took it to another level. As always, the players walked through the crowd to thank them for their support, but this time, Yasir grabbed the microphone in the announcers' booth in the middle of the bleachers and started chanting,

"German Bowl!"

"German Bowl!"

"German Bowl!"

I made my way to the VIP tent but decided quickly I wasn't in the mood to celebrate. As I was making my way out of the crowd, Hjalmar Nielsen, defensive back, introduced me to his father from Denmark.

"You have a fine son, sir. He is enjoyable to coach and always gives 100% effort," I said, shaking his hand.

"Thank you, sir. We're proud of him."

"Coach, I've told my father about how you have helped the team this season in so many ways," Hjalmar said.

"Thanks, buddy, that means a lot."

"I don't know if you understand this, but there aren't coaches like you in Europe. We do things differently here with 50 Strong, our WhatsApp and how we practice. I want to thank you for what you've done for me and the Royals."

"Wow, that means more than you know. It's been a bitter-sweet day for me," I said as I excused myself and began walking to my car. Hjalmar had no idea what those words meant to me. He just had my back and didn't know it.

Beer and food flowed for a few hours after the game ended, but it wasn't my time to enjoy it. This moment was for the Royals' current and former players.

"Congratulations, coach! This is an epic thing for the Royals," TK, our former defensive end, said, sticking out his hand to me.

"Thanks very much. I'm happy for everyone who's put in so much work over the years. I'm impressed you're here."

"These guys are still my brothers. I'm happy for them and wanted to be here to see this in person."

"Coach, come grab a Radler and celebrate with us!" Buddy yelled from near the VIP tent.

"I appreciate it, my friend, but this moment is for the players and all the volunteers who've made it happen. I'm going to go home and watch the film."

I called Tracy in the car as I drove away.

"Congratulations, babe!" Tracy said immediately.

"Thanks, if only I felt like celebrating. Unless Chris really is Superman, and his thumb is made of steel, we'll be between a rock and a hard place in Frankfurt. Speaking of Frankfurt, can you get your boss to let you come back one more time?"

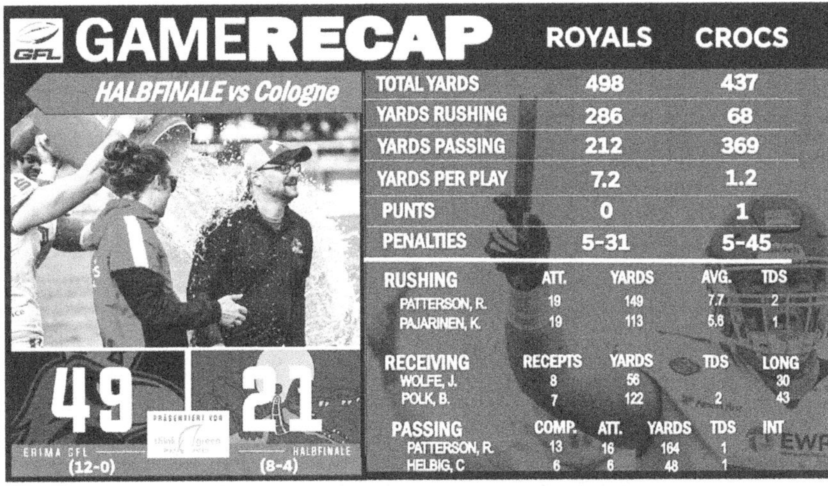

	ROYALS	CROCS
TOTAL YARDS	498	437
YARDS RUSHING	286	68
YARDS PASSING	212	369
YARDS PER PLAY	7.2	1.2
PUNTS	0	1
PENALTIES	5-31	5-45

RUSHING	ATT.	YARDS	AVG.	TDS
PATTERSON, R.	19	149	7.7	2
PAJARINEN, K.	19	113	5.8	1

RECEIVING	RECEPTS	YARDS	TDS	LONG
WOLFE, J.	8	56		30
POLK, B.	7	122	2	43

PASSING	COMP.	ATT.	YARDS	TDS	INT
PATTERSON, R.	13	16	164	1	
HELBIG, C	6	6	48	1	

POTSDAMER TAGESSPIEGEL

(Excerpts from the Potsdam Daily Mirror)

As so often this season, the Potsdam Royals footballers let it rip again. Before the game with pyrotechnics and fireworks, on the pitch with quick moves and touchdowns. In the GFL semi-final, the Potsdam Royals beat 2,431 spectators in the Luftschiffhafen stadium to the Cologne Crocodiles with a deserved 49:21, making them in the final in Frankfurt am Main for the German Bowl and making history.

"We had a good plan, but one could only hope before the game that it worked out so well and that makes it even nicer," says Royals coach Michael Vogt after the game. "Now we're in the final and of course we want to win the game." In the final on October 8th, his team will face the Schwäbisch Hall Unicorns, who beat the Allgäu Comets 33:8. But there's already a bit of celebration today: "We'll definitely have a beer or two," says Vogt.

67

YOU SHOWED US HOW TO BE A TEAM

Sept. 25, 2022

I knew I couldn't fall asleep, so I did the next best thing, I graded the film. Why couldn't I sleep? Because now I have much bigger problems than I did a few hours ago. If you'd asked me a day ago what I'd change, it would be to be back in Texas with Tracy and Coco.

I've heard before that if you want to solve your problems, get a bigger problem. My perspective has officially changed...now we're going into the German Bowl without the heart and soul of our team, our QB. We can dress out 50 players each week, and the one we absolutely need the most is our quarterback, Chris Helbig.

The next morning, I watched my friend, David Griffin, from Community Life Church in Forney, Texas, deliver a sermon on YouTube. It was like David was preaching directly to me because his message was titled "The Power of the Overcomer". I've known David for several years and love listening to him because he is not only an amazing man of God but a sports guy. Today he would speak to me as much as any pastor has in years.

"It's awesome when Tom Brady or Michael Jordan wins the championship, but it's magical when someone who has been benched perseveres and finds a way to lead their team to victory. All of you know I'm a huge 'Bama fan, so I'm going to tell the story of a Tide overcomer, Jalen Hurts. In 2018 Hurts was benched in the national championship game and replaced by freshman quarterback Tua Tagovailoa. Hurts didn't sulk or give up — he stayed focused and encouraged his teammates as Tagovailoa led the team to victory."

"The following season, 2019, Hurts was Tagovailoa's backup until the SEC championship game. Tagovailoa was injured in the fourth quarter of the SEC Championship. Jalen endured and eventually found success. Hurts came off the bench to lead scoring drives in a 10-minute span to lead a 38-35 comeback victory and seal a fourth straight national title-game appearance for Alabama. Jalen was ready when his time came. I think of Hurts anytime I use one of my favorite quotes, "Failure is never fatal" by Winston Churchill."

"Today, Jalen Hurts is one starting for the Philadelphia Eagles and will sign a massive contract in the offseason. He's going to continue to get better and better because he is an overcomer. Even Auburn, Georgia, and Texas fans should be rooting for him. You

Aggies out there probably don't know who he is but see if there's a Baylor grad near you; they'll explain everything," David said, chuckling.

"We'll all face trials and tribulations in this life. We'll go through hardships but can all focus on overcoming them. Jesus Christ was the ultimate overcomer. He had to overcome the cross and now sits on the throne. Jalen Hurts was ready when his time came again. What choice will you make when facing a hardship completely out of your control?"

I then drove to Potsdam main station to work out at a local sports club, Fitness First. All Royals players and staff members have free access to lift, do cardio, and unwind in saunas. My routine was to work cardio on the stair climber, then weights, and cardio again before hitting the sauna. I wasn't the hardest worker in the facility, but it helped me mentally as much as anyone. I usually spent two hours listening to podcasts and audiobooks while I sweated a little. Today, the gym was fairly quiet. There are always a few Royals coming in and out, but the afternoon after a big win, I didn't expect to see many and didn't. I got off the elliptical machine, went to the free weight area, and was about to start working my shoulders with dumbbells when a voice stopped me.

"Coach, have you spoken to Yasir yet?" It was 18-year-old Tristen Güther, an up-coming stud receiver on our Prospects team and our color commentator for the Royals live streams.

"No, Tristen. I haven't. I know I need to, but it seems like my message is getting old to some guys, Yasir being one of them."

"What do you mean, coach? You must make this right. We have something special happening here, and it's because we're a team for the first time."

"Thanks, Tristen. I'm proud that we created our creed and have a team that cares about each other, but I've become more and more frustrated from being the only one fighting for us to be disciplined. Yasir isn't the only one, but he's tired of me coaching the way I do. But you know what? Coaching the way I do has made Yasir a better football player than he was a year ago."

"You must talk to Yasir and make this right between you. You should be proud. You showed us how to be a team."

"Ok, I get it. You're exactly correct. I'll make amends with him."

I walked away, amazed by the insight of Tristen. He hadn't participated in our 50 Strong meetings in training camp and wasn't a regular at our practices. Tristen spoke from the heart about the rift between Yasir and me. He was spot on. How could a teenager be so wise? I stopped and turned to him and said, "Thanks Tristen. You're an amazing kid."

Before I left the gym, Yasir, who worked out daily, came in. I went over and looked him in the eye and said, "I want to apologize for going off on you the other day. I'm sorry I lost my temper."

"I'm sorry too, coach. I should've shown more restraint as well."

We shook hands and continued to talk. I said, "We're both alpha males and sometimes alpha's butt heads. I'm an old goat who should control my emotions more. Like in a marriage, coaches shouldn't let the sun go down without making things right after a confrontation. I was also wrong for not coming to you sooner."

"It's ok, coach. I'm just as guilty. I let my pride keep me from repairing things, and I shouldn't have."

"Tristen (I pointed across the gym where he was still working out) talked to me a little while ago and reminded me we have something special happening, and you and I must be good for it to continue. We shouldn't let anything fracture what we've worked hard to build."

"I agree. I would've continued doing my job and not be hard to coach, but burying the hatchet is always best."

"I want you to know I'd still be having this conversation if we'd lost yesterday. This has been a lifetime experience for me, and you've been a big part of it. I've loved working with you. You've made me a better coach."

"Thanks, coach. I loved this year and being coached by you. We're going to win by dominating 'Hall up front. They're very talented, but the Southern Conference is weaker than the North. They will not have played a team as good as our offensive line."

Later that evening, I started my research on the Schwabisch Hall Unicorns. Before I break down the game film of an opponent, I do my best, *Sherlock Holmes*, to find out everything I can about them. Twenty years ago, I listened to Pete Carroll, then head coach at USC, say before we ever watch our opponent on film, we should research their stats. We should know their play caller's personality and their top performers as much as possible. If we realize their run/pass ratio or who is their leading tackler, we'll be a smarter dissector of the video. It'll make the picture much clearer.

I don't overthink our opponent's defensive scheme. My goal is to determine the foundation of their defensive structure. How do they align on day one of training camp? I want to know their base fronts and coverages 100%, but our wide splits and tempo will force simplicity on our opponent's game plan. The GFL stats page (stats.gfl.info) is simple but does a great job showing game histories, team and individual stats from 2007 to the present.

After this, I want to know who their "#11" is, their worst defender. There are 11 players on the field at a time, and one of them is the worst. He isn't getting any better during the game, so I must identify and attack him.

One of the core principles of Fast N' Wide is "the game isn't hard, don't make it hard". Many coaches want to overcomplicate football, but it'll always be about matchups. How can we get our best player on their worst player? Is "#11" a corner? We must be so simple with our formations and plays that Jared and Polk can attack this corner. Is their worst player a defensive lineman? Then that's where we want to run the ball. Even if he is on the other side of the field from Yasir, we can get in our unbalanced set and crush him with our best.

Schwäbisch Hall is not a typical GFL team. They have their two 'A' defensive backs, but they also have several 'unicorns' (no pun intended), dual-passport guys like Jared.

What most interested me was discovering 'Hall's head coach is a Texan. John Neuman, 39, grew up in Fort Worth, then graduated from McMurry University. In 2005, he played quarterback for 'Hall, stayed on as a staff member after his career, and worked his way up to head coach in 2016.

What are the odds that in the championship in Germany, the head coach of one team and the offensive coordinator of the other are from the Dallas-Fort Worth area? It's just another reminder of how small the world has become and Texas's global impact on the game of football. The fact Neuman is from Texas means he understands the DNA of team football. 'Hall plays like a team that I've fought for us to be all season—disciplined. *Most games are not won...they are lost.* 'Hall doesn't beat themselves with poor execution or undisciplined play. They are a well-coached unit that is a product of a top-to-bottom system being in place.

The Unicorns have won two German Bowls under Neuman (2017 and 2018) and finished second twice (2019 and 2021). Offensively they were averaging 43 points a game and leading the GFL defensively by only giving up 15 points and 242 yards per game. They don't have the legacy of the New Yorker Lions, but under Neuman, no team's been better. The bottom line is they're the big bad wolf from the South.

I looked up the stats from the 2021 semi-final game that we lost in Schwabisch Hall 28-19. The Unicorns committed two penalties on the day. The Royals were flagged 19 times for 170 yards.

Nineteen penalties! That can't happen again.

I immediately called Buddy and said, "I'm sorry to phone you this late, but I'm looking at the stats from the 'Hall playoff game last season. Nothing jumps out at me except the penalties. We had 19, but they only had two. I'm not sure I've ever seen one team have 17 more penalties than the other team! Did they get some home cooking from the officials, or did we act as we did versus Adler a few weeks back?"

"No, we looked like we did after this season's summer break. We false-started, jumped off-sides, and had a few personal fouls. It all started before the game, though."

"You mean on the field in warmups?"

"No, our locker room was very near theirs, like normal. We decided it would be good to taunt some Unicorns while they were still in their locker room."

"You've got to be kidding me. Really?"

"Yes, you know I'm the one who always gets the team for the officials, so I was back there. A few of our guys opened the 'Hall locker room door and started cussing them and telling them how we would kick their asses. It was classless mayhem for a few moments. I've seen a lot of trash-talking in my time with the Royals, but nothing like this. I think you can search it on Instagram and see how bad it was."

"Ok, thanks. This story explains the 19 penalties a little more. It also helps me understand the monumental struggle we've had keeping 50 Strong on track."

"You have no idea, coach. You and the new players have changed and helped this team more than you'll probably ever know. I wasn't sure if the Royals' vets would buy in, but they also have, for the most part."

"Neuman and his staff have the Unicorns so disciplined that we're going to have to play our best game of the year to have a chance."

"We have a tougher task without Chris, but we won't be embarrassed by how we act before or during the game. Make sure you look at 'Hall's competition from the South. They've won 62 straight regular season games, but the teams down there aren't nearly as good as who we've beaten to win the North."

"Sixty-two straight is amazing, even in the weaker Southern Division. It means the Unicorns haven't lost a game in six years," I said. To give some perspective, the longest regular season winning streak in the NFL is 28, by the Indianapolis Colts from 2008-09.

Around 1:00 a.m., I finally went to sleep after watching three games. Yasir and Buddy, both smart football guys, were correct in their Southern Conference evaluations. They don't play as physical a brand of ball. Maybe we can run it at them and turn the tables on what opponents attempt to do to us...keep their offense off the field.

Just as I was dozing off, my phone buzzed. It was a text from Saul.

Do you remember the American running back we had last year...?

68

OFFENSIVE CAPTAINS

October 5, 2022

(me) Yea, you mean Johnson, who was with you guys last year?

(Saul) Yes, I'm contacting him about coming back for the German Bowl. He is an absolute stud.

(me) I agree he is but what about Karri? Polk would also have to come off the field because Robbie and Johnson would be our two A's.

(Saul) It's not 100% something we should do, but I wanted you to think about it. It's common for teams here to add a player for the championship game. Trust me, 'Hall will have one or two new players.

(me) Chalk this up to another mindblower for me. I would struggle to tell Karri and Polk they're not starting after being absolute studs for us on and off the field.

The following morning, I sat outside the bäckerei (bakery) near my flat, eating a swine ear and drinking coffee. I knew Chris's surgery was coming up and wanted to check on him, so I texted him.

Good morning, buddy. How are you feeling?

(Chris) I'm doing ok. My surgery is tomorrow, so I'll be glad to get that past me.

(me) Any more news on the prognosis?

(Chris) No. The doctor told me it would be a miracle for me to be able to play.

(me) Let's pray for the miracle, then. Our God is a big God. He's still in the miracle business.

A few days later, I asked our Americans to meet me at the office and help finalize the game plan. Berti stepped in and said, "It's official. Chris is out. The doctor wanted to give him hope, but it was impossible. After a complete fracture, no one could grip a ball, much less throw in two weeks. He went in for his follow-up this morning and was told he'll need another surgery in two months."

"Dang, I knew it was the longest-long shot ever, but I hate it, especially for him. He's coming up here later this morning to help our game plan. I've asked him to be our quarterback coach for the next ten days. Hopefully, that will take his mind off not getting to play."

Jared, Polk, Robbie, and I all did our best to let Chris know we were sorry, but he wasn't having it. "Guys, it's football. It sucks, but it happens. Coach Jackson asked me to help coach you, Robbie, and if that's good with you, I'm all in," Chris said.

"Heck, yea. I'll take any coaching or advice you'll give me. Thanks," Robbie responded.

As we watched the film, Robbie said cautiously, "I know you've already told us we aren't changing much because of this situation, but what do you think about allowing me to sprint out?"

"Hmmm," I said, mulling it over.

"I like it. Getting Robbie on the move outside the pocket will be good," said Chris.

Just then, Brenden, Jerome, and Yasir walked into the room. "Hey, guys. What are y'all up to?" I asked.

"We heard some planning was going on here and want to help. Is that ok?" Jerome asked.

"You bet. Y'all pull up a chair."

Everyone threw out ideas and opinions on how they aligned to different offensive formations and who was "#11" and "#1," Hall's worst and best players.

"I've got an idea already, but anytime you formulate a game plan, you must answer this question first; "How will they line up to our top three formations?" If Chris' right hand were ok, I'd ask him to draw their defense up for us, but we better ask someone else. Does anyone mind drawing?" I said with a laugh.

"Too soon, coach. Too soon," Chris said, smiling for the first time since the Cologne game.

Later that night, I texted Berti and asked him for one last favor. *I know y'all have been very good to fly Tracy over twice, but could you ask the board if they'd get her to Frankfurt to see the German Bowl? I'll understand if the answer is no, but it would mean a lot to us.*

(Berti) I'll ask them tomorrow and let you know. I hope the answer will be yes. She needs to be here if possible. Of all your pictures together, if we win, a pic of you two holding the GFL trophy would be the best one yet!

GAME WEEK

Although time marched slowly with no game, championship week had finally arrived. We had a walk-through session on Monday to help Robbie feel more comfortable. But we didn't have a great practice on Tuesday. Toward the end, Berti told me, "We could practice tomorrow or every day this week, and if it's like this, we won't get better." Berti was correct. One of his strengths is his ability to read people and situations, and I agree with this assessment. Tonight's practice was a bunch of guys going through the motions.

One laboratory result that has proven correct time after time has been player input. The more I've allowed the guys to help, the more quality information I've received. I decided to ask one of our veterans what he thought.

"Robbie did a good job tonight, but overall, it was lackluster at best. What do you think was the deal?" I asked Bobby.

"It was a little too long. It feels like we've been out here longer than we'd been going since we started the playoffs."

Bobby hit the nail on the head. Our practices had been closer to 90 minutes the last six weeks, but we were over two hours tonight. I was at fault as much or more than anyone for this. Berti and Saul were both great about letting me have input in our practice plans. It was a reminder if we needed two hours in our 13th game, we were trying to do too much.

(me) Fellas, I'll get with Coach Vogt, but we'll shorten up practice for tomorrow. One thing we need to discuss is our upcoming vote for offensive captains. During tomorrow's Zoom, we will discuss what real captains do for their teams.

The following morning, after we went through practice and grades, I began to break down a picture of an elite captain.

"The last few years as a head coach, I'd invite eight to ten players for lunch each week. We'd discuss their goals and how they could be better leaders. I also shared some of my experiences growing up and asked them about their interest outside of football. After 30 minutes or so, I'd pull out this book...The Captain Class."

"Sam Walker researched what separated very good teams from true dynasties. He determined the one aspect truly elite teams have in common is non-traditional captains. The teams had captains that weren't necessarily the best players but were the most valuable team members."

Last year I interviewed Walker in an Elite Coaches' Mastermind class. He and I went deep into his research. I will use some of our discussion to show you what he discovered about the most crucial ingredient to having an elite team.

Sam said, "All coaches want captains like Carla Overbeck on their team. Carla was the U.S. women's soccer team captain when they won the World Cup in 1999. Everyone remembers Brandi Chastain for winning the championship with a penalty kick and then taking off her shirt in celebration. Still, Carla was the key to why gold medals were placed around their necks."

"Carla was the oldest at age 34 and the team mom. She carried her teammates' luggage and dropped it off in front of their doors at hotels. She filled water bottles and brought them to the field. And in terms of leadership, Carla was a listener, a servant, an encourager, and anything else her teammates needed. She didn't care about the limelight or praise; she cared for her comrades. Carla stayed home when the team was invited to visit President Clinton at the White House. She said her daughter's laundry was piling up and couldn't wait. She was too busy serving her family to attend the White House celebration."

"Most people associate great captains with being an all-star. Although an unbelievable competitor, he didn't bring others along." Walker talks about Michael Jordan and why he wasn't a good captain.

I continued the video of our interview together. Walker said, "Jordan was big on personal attacks. I mean, he would just cut people down in a way that hurt their feelings, which is not what great leaders do. Great leaders will dress people down but always make sure they're talking about the team and their goals and not making it personal."

"So, you're telling me a great team needs a water-carrier servant more than the best player in league history?" I asked Walker.

"We'll all take the best player in the world on our squad, but if he or she doesn't put their arm around teammates and serve, they shouldn't ever be a captain."

I stopped the interview recording and said, "The guys you vote for as an offensive captain shouldn't be the best players on the team but the best connectors—the guys who were the glue that held us together during the season's storms. The dynasty teams Walker researched all had captains that kept the team together as a family behind the scenes."

The next slide is a picture of Dallas Stars hockey player Jamie Benn with the quote, "*Captain Benn Wastes No Time Welcoming First-Round pick Riley Tufte to the Stars.*"

"Think back to the guys who welcomed you to the Royals when you decided to join us. Vote for a captain who made you feel like part of the family as soon as he could."

"The last clip is Bruce Bowen of the San Antonio Spurs describing his teammate Tim Duncan."

Bowen says about Duncan, "The Hall of Famer that Pop started to recognize as one of the best ever wasn't because of the MVPs or championships. The teacher in him began to take shape in helping others become future Hall of Famers through the example of selflessness. Tim started to see the big picture of what it meant to make it about the team, not him. He didn't make it about him. He made it about the team".

The last slide was motivational speaker Inky Johnson speaking about leadership being action and not words. "I often say if you watch a person's actions, you don't have to listen to their words. They're going to tell you everything you need to know. You watch a person's example in spite of what they say."

I concluded the lesson with reminders of the characteristics of true leadership. "When you vote for a captain tomorrow, vote for one that made it about the team this season. Even though he might be an elite player, it was always about the team. We have some of those guys. We have several quality guys that fit the criteria above. There is no greater honor than being selected as a captain by teammates and coaches.

The following morning, I posted a link to a google drive quiz that had spaces for four names to be chosen.

*(me) *Remember- Captains are not the best players ON the team. Captains are the best players FOR the team. When you vote, think about the guys who were:*

-pivotal in helping us win the Northern Conference by elevating other players' performance.
-the hardest workers on the team. The ones I don't want to let down.
-the ones who have my back when the 'stuff hits the fan'.
-the ones who took massive action. They didn't just talk about it; they were about it with every practice and game.
-the ones who are teachers and show examples of selflessness.
#captainsarewatercarrierservants

Later that night, I posted on Autobahn 80...

The captain voting results are in. Congrats to all four of you! The 2022 Royals' Offensive Captains are....

THIS SENT A CHILL DOWN MY SPINE

October 6, 2022

In alphabetical order:
Chris Helbig
Yasir Raji
Jerome Valbon
Jared Wolfe

All of you guys made us better this season! All of you were unselfish, hard workers and led from the front. Thank you! We'll select two of these guys, again by vote, to represent us on the field for the coin toss in Frankfurt.

Berti and the board came through and purchased Tracy a plane ticket. There aren't many ways coaching in Europe makes you feel special, especially compared to Texas, but getting Tracy a plane ticket was more than special. There is a direct flight from Dallas to Frankfurt, so it made the travel much easier. I cleaned my flat and packed to go back with Tracy the day after the game.

Brenden was our only player invited to the NFL International Combine in London on October 3rd and 4th. (the Combine the German Bowl was moved to accommodate). He missed the last two practices before we left for Frankfurt to attend the combine, but it wasn't a big deal. We were happy he was one of 20 players getting a chance to show his talents.

What was a big deal was he got very sick during the combine and hadn't recovered yet.

(me) How are you feeling today?

(Brenden) I'm doing my best, coach, but I am still sick as a dog. I think I caught the 'C' flu at the NFL combine. I take every drug they give me, but I feel terrible.

(me) The game is two days away, so I bet you'll be good by then. If I need to, on Saturday, I can tell you the same Michael Jordan story I told Chris....:)

(Brenden) Ha...that's ok, coach, not that I don't love your stories, but...I'll be fine.

TO FRANKFURT

Jonas drove me to Fulda, his hometown, where I took a train to Frankfurt for the last hour of the journey. About 1/2 way to Frankfurt, an older man, traveling alone, entered our car with a bicycle and was wearing riding gear. A teenage boy got up to use the restroom, then returned to his seat. The man with the bike was next to enter the toilet, but a few seconds later came out and pointed at the teenager.

He said in German, "Come back in here and clean this up. You know you should lift the lid." (making a motion with his hands). He didn't raise his voice at the boy, but the tone was stern, especially considering he didn't know him.

The teenager got up and went back to the restroom. He looked ashamed to be called out but cleaned the seat and returned to his seat next to another teenager he was riding with.

"Bitte[thanks]," the man said as he entered the restroom.

Every American reading this knows how this incident would've escalated if the same scenario had occurred in any of our larger cities. The older man taught this boy a lesson he wouldn't soon forget, the lesson of German awareness for others. This incident was Germany for me in a nutshell. As ready as I was to get back home, I respected and would miss German cleanliness, manners and politeness.

After arriving in Frankfurt, I took a taxi to our hotel. Buddy and Jens were in the lobby setting up banners and shirts for the players' arrival later that evening. "Hey, guys. Good to see y'all. How is everything?" I said.

"It's good, coach. We're putting sponsor banners in the lobby so we can use them for publicity advertisements. Being in the championship is a good way for us to increase sponsors for next season, and we have to find a way to pay for the cost of playing in the German Bowl," Jens said.

"What do you mean to pay for us to play in the German Bowl? Doesn't the league cover our expenses?"

"Ha! It's costing us 21,000 Euros to house the players here for two nights. No, they don't pay for anything. After the German Bowl last year, the Monarchs complained very loudly that it took them months to fundraise to pay for their cost. It's very expensive to bring this many players and coaches for two nights."

"This makes it even more special to me that you guys paid for Tracy to fly over. I'm very thankful, my friend."

"You're most welcome. We're grateful to you for coming here this season. I've never seen a team like this before. You made us a team. It's one thing to take guys from Texas who grew up similarly, but creating a team from men who grew up differently is special. Thank you again for coming!" Jens said with his hand on my shoulder.

"Jens, I bet this is the tenth time you've told me this since the playoffs started. It was my honor, brother. Do you guys have any news on Brenden?"

"He's riding over with a few of our board members today. We didn't want him to get anyone else sick if he's contagious," Buddy said.

The next morning, I went to the airport and picked up Tracy. It was an amazing feeling to know we wouldn't be separated again. We grabbed a bite to eat then I let her crash while I went for a walk. As I was returning through the lobby, I overheard Berti speaking with a gentleman I soon learned was Robbie's father.

"Hello, sir. I'm Royal's offensive coordinator, Randy Jackson," I said, sticking out my hand.

"Hi, coach. I'm Richard Patterson. Nice to meet you as well."

"That's awesome you were able to come for the game. I know Robbie appreciates it."

"Yes, I'm excited to see Robbie play. I still can't believe he got on the plane in July to go to Potsdam."

"Really? Did you not want him playing in Europe?"

"Oh no, it's not that. I'm sure he didn't tell you, but his mom passed away almost the same time he was leaving for Germany. We buried her two days before Robbie departed. He was devastated but said he'd committed and would keep his word."

"That's incredible. I knew Robbie was special but didn't realize how he'd just dealt with his mom's passing and then adjusted to life in Germany. It makes me believe even more in his mental toughness."

"He's not the biggest quarterback in the world, but there aren't any tougher or who will compete any harder," Richard said.

Later that afternoon, we had our last practice of the year. I was excited to see Deutsche Bank Park, which I'd heard so much about from the team.

Jonas and I took his car and rode to the stadium before the team so we could check it out before practice began. Deutsche Bank Park was as advertised! It is a modern facility that would hold its own in the States. The arena was built in 2005 and has a capacity of 51,500. It's the home of a first-league soccer team, the Eintracht Frankfurt. Its most notable feature is its convertible-style retractable roof, which we were told would be open for our game.

I entered the stadium and saw Schwabisch Hall in the stands taking their team photo. Every player wore dark green clothing with a Unicorn logo on the front. The coaches' attire was synchronized as well. The Unicorns looked like a unified, organized, real football team. Standing there looking at them from a distance sent a chill down my spine. We weren't playing an organization worried about having boombox wars with us in pregame.

STAY OFF THE FIELD

Our bus arrived a few minutes later. We were taken to our locker room and introduced to the field turf supervisor, Henri Müller.

"Gentlemen, welcome to Deutsche Bank Park! We're honored to host you for this momentous occasion. I'm in charge of the turf here; it's not just my job but my life. Because we don't want to incur any damage to the grass before our game tomorrow, you'll be practicing today across the street. In fact, you'll also warm up there again tomorrow before the game. After your workout today, you'll gather back in the stadium for your team picture. Please proceed to the other side of the stadium for your photo by walking only on the sideline."

Then Henri held up his cell phone and said, "We don't advertise this, but we have heat sensors all over the field. We're notified if a small animal wanders onto the playing surface. Please don't step on the game field for any reason."

"Wait, we must practice and warm up outside the stadium?" I quietly asked Jared and Chris, who were standing near me with amazement in my voice.

"Maybe first-league soccer in Germany is more important than Texas football?" Bobby said, smiling.

"I realized that a long time ago, brother! I only thought football was a religion in Texas. Soccer is like BBQ, guns, pickup trucks, and football combined here!"

We walked outside, and the first thing I realized was our field was a soccer-only surface. There were no markings for American football. The German championship didn't allow teams to practice with lines the day before. I'm sure Bobby knew what I was thinking…

"Hey, Coach Jackson!" It was Kevin, an old colleague from Texas who's been teaching and coaching at Ramstein Air Base near here.

"Hey, buddy! You told me you were going to come today, and you did! It's good to see you!"

LAST 50 STRONG MEETING

The last 50 Strong meeting was at 9:00 p.m. in our hotel conference room. Saul stood outside the door, passing out the special t-shirts he'd created for everyone. We'd gone from an "F YOU" shirt before New Yorker to 50 Strong t-shirts in two and a half months. I'm sure I was the only one who thought about this, but it was cool to see.

We'd have a team meeting here tomorrow morning, but tonight was time for the players to lead. There were approximately 60 players in the room seated in plastic chairs. None of the coaches said a word. Jared stood at the front of the room and said, "We've come a long way since we met at the office in April and May, creating our creed. In our first offensive meeting, Coach Jackson showed us an ad from the ship Endurance that read, 'Men wanted for hazardous journey.' It's been a journey and then some. In every season, a team will go through trials by fire. There'll be injuries, bad calls by officials, bad bounces, arguments, jealousy, close calls on games we could have lost, and a million other things. 50 Strong didn't keep all of it from happening, but it helped buffer the storms. I have been a part of many teams, but this one stands out as the most unified and together of them all. Joining 50 Strong back in May was something I won't ever forget, and seeing others invited as the season progressed was amazing. We're extending a warm welcome to those who still need to be invited to our brotherhood tonight. It's going to take all of us tomorrow. Together, we will be champions."

"If you've agreed to introduce a new member, please come forward at this time," Leo said.

The last few guys were introduced into 50 Strong. Johnni (pronounced Yan-ee) spoke such poor English that he asked Stanley, another defensive lineman, to translate for him. Guys who never talked much opened up about being a part of a brotherhood.

"I've always heard about what a true team is but haven't ever been a part of one til now. I'll never forget this group of men," said Lukus Fischer, a backup linebacker. Like many players, Lukus had played with the Berlin Rebels and other area teams for several years before joining the Royals this season.

"I've only been here for a few weeks but loved my time as a Royal. We don't just show up for practice and games. We have a bond that's real. Thank you for allowing me to be 50 Strong. I'll always be grateful," said Pierre Kamanga, a backup guard from France who signed with us in early August.

Chris stood up and said, "Even though I can't play tomorrow, I'm still thankful to be in this room with every one of you. I lived in Europe for six months with guys I'd never fathomed meeting. All because of the game of football and because we all decided to be Royals. I hate to think about it ending tomorrow, but it is, so let's end it with a ring."

"Everyone knows this weekend will be the last time this team will be together. Look each other in the eye and go get your mind right to play for everything we've worked for tomorrow," Jared said to close the meeting.

GAME #13
TWO-DEEP DEPTH CHART
GERMAN BOWL, FRANKFURT

QB	**#13 ROBBIE PATTERSON** **U.S.-OREGON** (Montana)
RB	**#20 KARRI PAJARINEN - FINLAND** #9 HEIKO BALS - GERMANY #25 ADAM ŽOUŽELKA - CZECH REPUBLIC
WR	**#3 BRANDON POLK - U.S.-VIRGINIA** (Penn State) #11 MAGNUS URTH - DENMARK
WR	**#15 JARED WOLFE - U.S.-NEW YORK** (Villanova) #14 LOUIS CHRIST - GERMANY
WR	**#12 SIXTEN DRAGEN - GERMANY** #9 HEIKO BALS - GERMANY
TE	**#89 JEROME VALBON - FRENCH CANADIAN** #81 MAT DUBICKI - POLAND
LT	**#78 YASIR RAJI - GERMANY** #53 TIM WALTNER - GERMANY
LG	**#75 BRENDEN OSWIN - AUSTRALIA** #66 OSKAR RÜEGG - GERMANY
C	**#67 BOBBY SÖVEGJARTO - GERMANY** #56 LUDI RÖTZSCHER - GERMANY
RG	**#56 LUDI RÖTZSCHER - GERMANY** #74 STEFAN KAMANGA - FRANCE
RT	**#77 STEFAN STEFANNSON - ICELAND** #53 TIM WALTNER - GERMANY

70

IT'S DO OR DIE...NOW OR NEVER

Oct. 8, 2022

We met at 10:00 a.m. in the hotel meeting room for final prep and our first game day team meeting of the year with video.

Video is an excellent way to give players one last look at how we will win. I use it as another Pygmalion tactic, a psychological phenomenon where higher expectations lead to improved performance. NFL Hall of Fame coach Jimmy Johnson talks about how he used the Pygmalion theory several times in his book *Swagger*. My mindset has always been that coaches should make players feel "10 feet tall and bulletproof," but Johnson took it to another level. "Our approach was completely different than other coaches. Our approach was, 'Hey guys, we're gonna kick their ass because we're better than they are," Johnson said in *Swagger*.

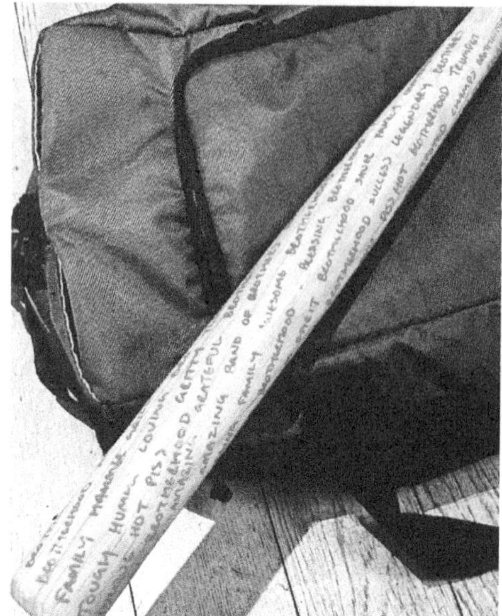

Another way we attempted to brainwash our guys with the Pygmalion effect was the theme for the game; BYOB - Bring Your Own Bat.

I led us through a cutup of the 'Hall defense versus various offenses in the Southern Conference. Teams that did not have Jerome, Yasir, Brenden, or our battering run game.

“We will be the most physical team 'Hall has ever played. No offense to the GFL, but all I see from most teams are four-wide, "dink and dunk" offenses. We're not just going to score more points than they've given up this season. We're going to leave them bruised and battered," I said.

Saul ordered a bat on Amazon and had the players sign it. "If you still need to sign the bat, please do it before you leave. Remember, write the one word on the bat that this team means to you," Saul said.

Berti chimed in, "I have one more thing to say before we conclude. Today is the most important game you'll ever play. We've worked hard to qualify for this chance. Now is the time to show what you've got. Don't hold back and give everything you have in this game. It's *do or die*. There are no second chances. The winner will be remembered forever, and the loser not so much. Today is *now or never*!"

Berti had mentioned "It's do or die" to the team several times throughout the week. It's a mistake coaches all over the world make all the time. Not that Berti would or should know this, but making a single game or event special goes against mental performance training fundamentals.

Everything is important, but never make anything special. I regularly remind my Fast N' Wide and Elite Coach Mastermind clients: "Never use the 14 killer words."

The 14 killer words are:
"This is it."
"It's now or never."
"It's do or die."
"There's no tomorrow."

Human beings don't perform well in special circumstances. They execute their best when it's important. John Wooden, when asked who would win at the Final Four, replied, "I can tell you who will win—the one who plays the most like they practice."

It reminded me of many years ago when I was watching the nightly news. They reported how former President Clinton had a serious heart operation that day, and they interviewed the head of the surgery team. When asked how it felt to operate on a former president, the surgeon said, "We knew it was President Clinton, but we treated him like any other patient." The surgical team didn't make the operation special, just important.

I didn't know when I would get the opportunity to speak to the team or the offense before the game, but I was going to remind them that we would win today by playing how we've played all year; fast, physical and one-play at a time. We wouldn't win the German Bowl, but we'd win the most plays. It was quiet on the offensive team bus as we headed from our pregame meal to the stadium. The German Bowl isn't the spectacle of the Super Bowl, but things would move fast once we started our pregame warm-ups. Once we got to the stadium, it would be chaotic, and I probably wouldn't have time to give a pregame speech, so I'd take this opportunity now to say what was on my heart.

"I want to thank each and every one of you for what you've done this season. I'm honored to be on this bus with you today. I'll never forget being here, right now with guys from all over the world, about to battle our butts off."

"We've come a long way to get on this bus. Nothing's gotten in our way this season. Our first practice in April was on a field with no lines. Our last practice yesterday was on another field with no lines, but just like all of our other obstacles, it didn't matter. We just stayed in the foxhole together and found a way. We're going to find a way again today."

"I'll always remember getting to be with this group on this bus. It doesn't matter where you've played before or where you'll play in the future. This bus is special. I'll always treasure this ride to the stadium and getting to look at each of you who are about to lay it on the line. I won't let you down today."

"We won't let you down today, coach," Jerome said.

The attendance for the last several German Bowls has averaged around 15,000, but today's crowd was slightly less than 10,000. The tickets were $58 each, which, stop me if you've heard this, blew my mind. From a marketing standpoint, you'd think the league would do whatever it took to get 20,000 fans in the stadium. The Royals received one complimentary ticket, so even Berti had to purchase tickets for his family.

Schwäbisch Hall's crowd was significant in comparison to ours. They had at least three times as many fans as we did. Not only was 'Hall just two hours from Frankfurt, but their fans also expected to be there. Today was the Unicorns' fifth straight German Bowl appearance.

Before the coin flip, I walked over to Robbie, who was warming up on the sideline, and said, "Your dad told me your mom's funeral was only two days before you left to come to Potsdam?"

"Yes, sir."

"I know it took a ton of strength to get on the plane, but God had a plan for you. He knew you would be in this situation today. He made you for this. I don't know what will happen today, but I know God built you to be our quarterback for this moment. Go

be great," I said, walking away to give him some space to prepare for the game mentally.

The players voted for Jared and Jerome, from our four offensive captains, to join Leo and Cody for the pregame flip at midfield. Schwabisch Hall won the toss but deferred. For the first time all season, I agreed with their decision. They wanted to see what Fast N' Wide would look like without Chris Helbig at the helm.

'Hall kicked it deep, and Polk did what he's been doing this season. He took it all the way back for six! Our small crowd went nuts, as did our sideline. We couldn't have scripted a better beginning to the game.

"Oh, F me!" I heard Saul yell with his hands on his knees.

"What happened?" I asked Jonas into the headset.

"There is a flag down. I bet it's a block in the back."

It was. Instead of starting the game with the ultimate momentum, we had 1st and ten on our 15-yard line.

Our opening drive was masterful. For the 12th time in 13 games, we started with a touchdown out of the gate. We controlled the ball for 15 plays, ten rushing and five passing. Robbie looked every bit the part. This moment wasn't too big for him.

If I had to guess, we were around a 14-point underdog, so we knew we had to take some chances. The Unicorn's kickoff return team aligns very tight with their front line, meaning there is a ton of space to onside kick near our sideline and have a high probability of recovering the ball. During our preparation, I showed Saul our "two kicker system" we'd used at North Forney. Schumacher and Heiko both did a fine job executing the onside kicks, so Saul agreed to put it in the game plan.

Other than the kick, the key to the onside is blocking the farthest aligned outside on the front line. We must *take him out* so our outside guys can recover the ball.

"Tweet!" the head official blew the game in for play. Heiko approached the tee, faked the kick, and veered to the right. As he passed by, Schumacher came from the other side and hit it perfectly to our sideline to the left. 'Hall adjusted well, but we also didn't do our job. A Unicorn from 15 yards deep sprinted up to the front line after Heiko veered off and got in the perfect spot near our sideline. He caught the ball cleanly after the first bounce. Our player assigned to block the closest Unicorn to the sideline didn't see him rotate, so he fielded it unmolested and went 35 yards for an easy 'Hall touchdown.

The kicking game was not our friend early. We blocked in the back to bring back a return for a touchdown, failed on a fake PAT, and then gave up an easy score on the following kickoff.

We battled back on our next possession. Our second drive was almost a carbon copy of the first. Karri converted a fourth and one at the 'Hall 42-yard-line, our first of five 4th down attempts on the day, to keep this one going. He finished the possession with a four-yard touchdown run with 1:19 left in the first quarter. Robbie completed an 18-yard pass to Jared and also ran three times on the drive.

"You're playing awesome, brother! I'm proud of you!" I said as I high-fived Robbie as he came off the field.

"Thanks, coach. I'm almost positive they know our signals. Before we snap the ball, they're saying what's coming," Robbie said.

"Yes! They know our signals 100%!" Karri said.

"Ok, no big deal. I need everyone to lock in on this…I'm now the *dummy* signaler, and Chris is going to be the "live" one. Everyone give me a thumbs up that you got this."

Brenden looked like death warmed over on the sideline. "Are you ok?" I asked, already knowing the answer.

"I'll be alright."

Jerome came up behind me and quietly said, "Brenden will never take himself out, and he's dying. I know he's my roommate, but I'm worried about him."

"Kamanga, you're in the next series at left guard," I said.

We signed Stefan Kamanga in late July when Mads left for junior college in the Bronx. He spoke very little English but was strong as an ox. Jerome helped us both translate "Texan to French" and back. Brenden laid down on the bench and tried to survive the afternoon. If he looked any better in the second half, we'd try again, but I already knew he wasn't going to.

"Jonas?"

"Yes, sir?"

"Kamanga's in for Brenden. Watch him for me if you can. If he goes to the right place, we'll be fine. If he doesn't, I'll try Oskar next."

We were in a good place offensively. In two drives, we'd run 28 plays for 146 yards and did something we'd desperately needed; control the clock and keep 'Hall's offense off the field. The first quarter time of possession was 10:29 to 1:16. Although the Unicorn ran back a kick, they only ran three plays in the first period.

Things soon changed.

The Unicorn offense got cranked up and began to run down our throats. 'Hall went 64 yards in just six plays with three explosive runs of 28, 12, and 15 yards. Their quarterback, Ryan Hennessey, muscled his way in from the one-yard-line to finish the drive. The successful PAT put the Unicorns up 14-13 early in the second quarter.

On our next possession, we luckily started at our 43-yard-line after the 'Hall kicker booted the ball out of bounds. The Unicorn run defense stiffened and made it more difficult on us. Robbie hit Sixten for 14 yards on a 2nd down and 12 to take the ball to the 'Hall 34-yard-line, but the drive stalled. We went for it on 4th and 4, but the pass to Jared fell incomplete to turn the ball back over to the Unicorns.

'Hall gashed us on the first two plays of the drive with runs of 17 and 14 yards. Three plays later, Hennessey connected with an open receiver for the 31-yard touchdown pass. The PAT was wide left, but in a little over two minutes, Schwabisch Hall increased their lead to 20-13.

"We're good, fellas. I said to the offense as we started on our 36-yard line. Let's go over the top with a play action to Polk on first down."

"Good call, coach. We've run it enough. The safeties should bite on the run action to Karri," Jonas said.

"I agree. We need to take a shot here. Even if it's incomplete, it sends a message and will loosen them up."

I was about to learn a hard lesson on why the Unicorns had won 62 straight regular season games. They were the best-coached team in the GFL. The 'Hall defensive plan was to make us earn everything and not give up deep completions to Polk or Jared.

Robbie faked the ball to Karri, then faked a reverse to Jared, stepped back, and let it fly to Polk on a deep post pattern. The ·American safety, Aaron Spectrum, was disciplined. He didn't step up on the run fakes. His job was to stay deep, and he did. Robbie's pass was a good one, as was Polk's route, but Spectrum barely undercut it for the diving interception on the 'Hall 20-yard line.

"Dammit!" someone on the sideline yelled as our guys came off the field.

"We have to stay positive here. We've got to keep Robbie's confidence up," Chris said, standing beside me.

"Agree, it was a good ball, just a better play by them," I said.

The offense met in the bench area like always. We were in a position we hadn't been in all year. We were behind and facing a defense that we couldn't run the ball for five yards a pop to make first downs.

"I thought I had him, coach. My fault," Robbie said with a frustrated look of determination.

"You're good, buddy. Keep playing your butt off and playing to win. Don't worry about anything else."

"Great job, OL! I'll make up for it in the next series," Robbie said to the big boys.

"We're good, fellas. We're moving the ball. We took a shot, and it didn't work, but we'll be fine. Something good's about to happen. We're due to catch a break, and when we do, we'll pounce."

“Just keep fighting. We’ll find a way,” Jared said.

The Unicorns went on an 11-play, 80-yard drive to eat up the rest of the first half and increase their lead to 27-13. We were in trouble going into the intermission, and everyone knew it. Our heads were down, and our body language wasn't good.

"Keep your head up! We've just begun to fight! We're just getting started!" Jerome yelled as we entered our locker room.

71

MAYBE MY LAST STADIUM

October 8, 2022

"We'll start our first series with our [17]wildcat package. Jared, Polk, and Heiko, in that order. Our defense will stop 'em and get us the ball back. We've found a way to impose our will all season. We'll do it again in the third quarter," I said to the offense in the locker room.

We installed a wildcat quarterback package so we would have a way to finish the game if Robbie got hurt, but also to give us a three-play series of "ground and pound" with three different guys rotating at QB. Though we were down by 17, it was still early in the third quarter. We needed a touchdown but also were desperate to keep the Unicorn offense, which has yet to punt, off the field.

#20 Karri Pajarinen #15 Jared Wolfe

Jonas and I walked over by ourselves, and I asked him, "Who #92, the nose guard? Is it just me, or is he new?"

"Yes, he wasn't on our scouting report. As Saul said, it's not uncommon for teams to sign guys for the German Bowl."

I always attempt to speak life into my teams. A coach should *paint the picture* of achievement, and the team is likely to create it. Success becomes a self-fulfilling prophecy. "Something good's about to happen because we're going to make it happen! We played a brilliant first quarter. Then they did in the second. It's our turn again! Let's goooooo!" I said to the offense as we left for the second-half kickoff.

The third quarter began like the second ended, with a 'Hall score. Tom Schweiger booted a 26-yard field goal to give the Unicorns a commanding 30-13 lead. They'd scored 23 unanswered points, and we had to figure out how to stop the bleeding.

---

[17] Wildcat - is a typical name for a formation in which the ball is snapped not to the quarterback but directly to a player of another position lined up at the quarterback position.

"Win plays! We won't score 17 points on this drive to tie it up, but we can win first down, second down, and so on. Win plays! Let's bloody their nose here and go wildcat as fast as possible." I said to the offense.

On our next possession, we again started with an excellent field position at our 44-yard line. We managed to run nine plays but only gained 32 yards. The 'Hall defense was in full *run-stop* mode and had defensive backs good enough to cover us without double-teaming Jared or Polk every play, especially on 1st and 2nd downs.

On 4th down and five from the Unicorn 24-yard line, Robbie couldn't squeeze one into Polk for the first down, so the ball went back to 'Hall.

Our defense stepped up and forced the Unicorns to punt.

"Let's get in our ultra-heavy set, Bucees, and see what we can do with Robbie carrying it," I said to Jonas and Chris on the headset.

We had some success with Robbie running behind Yasir and Jerome to our sideline. He went for 11 yards on first down, then nine, and then 16 on three consecutive plays. On 1st and ten from the 'Hall 39-yard line, I said, "40, 40," which is our choice play to Jared. Chris signaled it in, and I "dummy signaled" a false play. The ball was on target, but Spectrum, the American safety, made contact with Jared early and was flagged for pass interference.

Karri ran the ball twice to give us a 4th and one at the 'Hall 17-yard line. "East Porsche, East Porsche," I said into the headset. "Hurry, hurry!" I said knowing the offense couldn't hear me.

"He got it!" Jonas said as Karri barreled his way for three yards for the first down.

On the next play, Robbie hit our slot receiver, Sixten Dragen, who was getting single coverage for the 14-yard touchdown. "Great job! We're still in this!" I said, high-fiving the guys coming off after the PAT to close the score to 30-20.

We tried another onside kick that 'Hall recovered. They scored three plays later to make the score 37-20 with four minutes remaining in the third quarter.

We were still fighting. We didn't panic and continued running the ball with Robbie and Karri. Robbie scored on 3rd and goal from the two-yard line to get us back in striking distance. The drive covered 65 yards in 11 plays to cut the 'Hall lead to 37-27 with 7:30 left in the game.

Schwabisch Hall took the kickoff and went on a drive that sealed our fate. They took seven minutes off the clock with a 12-play drive. On 4th down and eight, with 59 seconds left, Hennessey completed a 16-yard touchdown pass to Aurieus Minton to end all hopes of the upset.

GFL GAMERECAP

GERMAN BOWL XLIII

27 (12-1) — 44 (13-0)

	ROYALS	UNICORNS
TOTAL YARDS	344	410
YARDS RUSHING	188	257
YARDS PASSING	156	153
YARDS PER PLAY	4.7	8.2
PUNTS	0	1
PENALTIES	7-66	10-84

RUSHING	ATT.	YARDS	AVG.	TDS
PATTERSON, R.	17	92	5.1	1
PAJARINEN, K.	24	85	3.3	2

RECEIVING	RECEPTS	YARDS	TDS	LONG
WOLFE, J.	6	45		18
DRAGEN, S.	5	62	1	23
POLK, B.	5	38		15

PASSING	COMP.	ATT.	YARDS	TDS	INT
PATTERSON, R.	17	26	156	1	1

"Thank you for fighting your butt off today," I said to Jared as he came off the field when the final gun sounded.

At midfield, I shook coach Neuman's hand and said, "Excellent plan today. You guys defended us better than anyone has all year. I tip my cap to you and your staff."

"Thank you, Coach Jackson. You did a great job this season."

We had a post-game ceremony at midfield. Jens placed our runner-up medals on every player and coach's neck.

"Thank you! You've made us very proud! Thank you!" he said to every one of us. Berti was consoling his two young kids, who were crying and couldn't hide their disappointment. I walked up to Berti and shook his hand. "Thanks for everything this season. I appreciate all you did for me and for allowing me to be on your sideline," I said.

"Thank you, Coach Jackson. Thanks for everything."

I next found Saul and said. "Thanks, brother. Thanks for hiring me and helping take care of me."

He hugged me and said, "You've taught me more than you know. Thanks for helping us this season."

It felt good to hear that. I didn't know what Saul would do next, but he's extremely intelligent and could be an amazing coach if he shifted more to 50 Strong and less to FYGR.

I found Tracy, who'd walked down to the first row of the bleachers.

"Good job, babe. I'm proud of you," she said.

"Thanks, honey. We did our best. I'm proud of Robbie and all of them."

My friend Kevin, who'd sat next to Tracy during the game, was also standing there, so I asked him if he could take Tracy and I to the hotel. "Let me find a few guys and say bye."

"Ok, we'll be waiting for you on the concourse right outside the stadium," Kevin said.

I shook hands with several players but honestly didn't know if they were glad to be rid of the guy who demanded so much.

"Coach Jackson."

"Yes," I said, turning around.

It was Max, who'd come up with our white stripe, but broke his ankle in July. He was coming up to me with his hand out.

"I know we had our differences, especially early on, but I'd get in your foxhole any time. Thanks for what you brought to the Royals this season."

"Thank you, Max. That means a lot. I'd be on your team any day of the week as well. Do you think you'll return next season?"

"I don't think I'll play again. My internet business has really started taking off."

“If you’re ever in Texas, hit me up, and we’ll go see a high school game that’ll blow your mind.”

“I may take you up on that, coach!”

Another voice I didn't recognize said, "Coach, can we take a picture together?"

It was Lukas, the backup linebacker from Berlin. Lukas was someone I'd only spoken to a few times. After games a few times, I'd see him, his wife, and their pit bull, named Margarita, and say hello, but I was very surprised he wanted a picture with me.

"Sure, buddy. I'd be honored."

"Thanks for coming to Germany this season. It was very good to learn football and teamwork from you."

"Thanks, Lukas that means a lot. Tell your wife and Margarita I said hello."

Just like Chris said at the last 50 Strong meeting, I'd met so many amazing men from all over the world because of football. Whether they knew it or not, they'd all changed my life.

Another relationship I was grateful for was the one developed with our head referee for most of our games, Mats Schweiger.

Mats wasn't on the field officiating today but was the logistics coordinator for the crew who was calling it. "Good job today Coach Jackson," Mats said, sticking out his hand.

"Thanks, my friend. We had to be perfect in all three phases today, but as you saw, we weren't. But I was proud we kept fighting."

"Schwäbisch Hall is a very good team. Unlike most teams in the GFL, they don't beat themselves. I hope we can remain friends. I'll be in Dallas next spring for a football officials conference. Maybe we can meet and break bread together if that's not too far from where you live."

"It's not far at all, brother. The Tex-Mex will be on me. Please thank all the officials here for putting up with me and my high-maintenance personality on the sideline."

Kevin, Tracy, and I walked about a mile to his car. I looked back at Deutsche Bank Park one last time. It was the last stadium I'd ever coach in. As we got in the car, Kevin asked me, "I know you're disappointed you didn't win, but as someone who's coached American football in Germany for eight years, you should be very proud of how you guys played. This was Schwabisch Hall's fifth straight time in the German Bowl. Teams don't knock off a dynasty on their first attempt."

"Thanks, brother. I know you're right, but feeling good right now is hard. Their defense was as good as advertised, but Robbie exceeded my expectations. Our offensive line played pretty well, considering we didn't have Brenden most of the game. We ran for 200 yards against the best defense we've seen this season that knew we didn't have the league MVP."

"Yeah, I definitely agree. I'm a bit of a football nerd, as you know, so I always keep up with the stats. Robbie went 17 for 26 passing and had 156 yards. Plus, leading the team with 92 yards rushing was huge."

As we drove, my mind started to wander. I knew I'd never see most of those guys again and wondered if my six months really mattered in the long run. Were the guys I coached grateful or glad they wouldn't have to put up with my intensity anymore?

The 2022 Royals broke through to new heights. We made history by advancing to the German Bowl for the first time. We were the only team to score 50 points a game in Europe, but as Achilles said,

"Would anyone remember my name?"

Did I make a difference?

I wondered.

72

50 STRONG > 50 POINTS

October 9, 2022

I met Buddy and Jonas in the hotel restaurant the following morning for an early breakfast.

"What time's yall's flight back?" Buddy asked.

"10:55 a.m. Tracy's meeting me down here in a little bit. We'll take a cab around 8:15. Thanks again for everything. I was lucky to have you both. I don't know what I'd done without either one of you guys."

"The pleasure was all mine. I learned a ton that we'll continue to use in Fulda," Jonas said.

"How're you feeling this morning after you had some time to sleep on it?" Buddy asked.

"I will know for sure once I make myself watch the film, but we played ok on offense. My first thought is I needed to do a better job creating big plays for Polk and Jared. Robbie certainly gave us a chance. Please tell the board 'thank you' again for spending the money on him. Regarding the entire season, I'm proud of how we attacked the GFL. We didn't have a long snapper in the last six games, and we still survived by scoring on most drives. With our talent, it was like taking an AK-47 to a knife fight most of the time."

"Watching all the big plays and how fast we snapped the ball was fun. I sure hope we do the same stuff next season," Buddy said.

"Seriously, what are your thoughts on how everything played out? I know you were frustrated the last couple of months. Now that the dust is settling, as you say, are you happy with 50 Strong? Did the team point to True North?" Jonas asked.

"I don't know for sure. I think ears become deaf to a lone voice, whether positive or negative. There weren't a ton of guys coming up to me and thanking me after the game last night. Most are glad this cranky codger will leave them alone now."

"That's just not the German way. You should know that by now. We don't show emotion if we don't have to," Jonas said.

At that moment, six players walked into the restaurant and sat down. Most were defensive players, except for two offensive linemen, Brenden and Tim. After they got settled, I walked over to say my goodbyes.

"You look better, Brenden. Yesterday, I was preparing a cremation box for your ashes," I said.

"I feel better, coach. I'm sorry I let the team down. I would have played every snap if you'd asked, but I felt absolutely horrible."

"I know you did, brother. I appreciate you trying. I'll always remember you playing as long as you did. Legends play when they want to the least."

Jonas, a defensive back, asked me, "What did you think about 50 Strong this year, coach?"

"We were just talking about that over there," I said, pointing to Buddy and Jonas. "The more important question is, 'What did y'all think?"

"We loved it. We're just sitting here talking about how we'll use it for next year," Jonas Gacek replied.

"The creed was amazing, coach. This is the most together team I've ever played on," said Jerry, the defensive back who thought I was having a heart attack in warmups a few months back.

I gratefully said, "You guys bought into the creed as much or more than the imports. I'm grateful it made an impact. Thanks, from the bottom of my heart, for trusting me and 50 Strong. It is another reason I've fallen in love with German people. Other than the ones on bicycles who give me the look when I almost kill them."

I looked over and saw Tracy grabbing her coffee and some fruit to eat on the ride to the airport. "I can't wait to see how you guys do next season. Thanks again for pointing True North with me. I will be watching with my Royals gear on and rooting for you guys every game next season."

As I said my final goodbyes to Buddy and Jonas, Tim Waltner, a backup offensive tackle, approached me.

"Excuse me for interrupting. I know you two are trying to catch your cab, but I wanted to say this while I can...I loved you being my coach. Thank you for everything," Tim said, half hugging me, which was like a bear hug for Germans.

"Thank you, Tim. I loved coaching you, brother. Remember, you promised to let me sleep on your couch in Berlin if I ever needed to. Tracy and I may take you up on that one day!"

"I hope so, coach. Be safe on your journey home."

Buddy and Jonas walked us out of the hotel onto the sidewalk. Buddy said one more thing to me, "The Royals changed this year and for the better. We were more disciplined and looked like a team. I can't tell you how much fun it was this year playing fast and scoring so many points. I know you were happy with us being the first team in Europe to average 50 points, but your legacy is 50 Strong. 50 Strong changed us forever."

"Thanks so much, my friend. This place changed me forever as well. Let's all three continue to be good friends."

Tracy and I got in the cab. I didn't get to say goodbye to lots of men I'd become close to over the last six months, and it bothered me. The team was put together for a mission, and now the mission is over. As quickly as we became a team, the team was no more.

The ride to the airport was quiet. Tracy and I were lost in our thoughts. I couldn't shake the feeling of remorse that we came up short in the finals. She held my hand and looked into my eyes. Tracy gave me a smile of encouragement and said, "I couldn't be prouder of you. I know you made a difference over here. The Royals couldn't have done this without you."

"Thanks, honey. I hope the Royals will use a few things we started this year, and the players who move on to other teams will take it with them as well."

We finally arrived back in Texas, but I wasn't craving fast food this time. A 5-year-old beauty queen was waiting for me at the airport.

"Ranny, Ranny!" Coco yelled and hugged me. "You can never leave me again…"

"Don't worry, baby. I'm staying with you and your mom FOREVER."

EPILOGUE

We made it home, and Coco and grandma 'Gigi' (Gaye) had a "Welcome Home" cake waiting for me. As we ate a piece, I couldn't help but feel as grateful as ever to be where I belong...at home with the ones I love.

After about a week at home, Tracy said, "Hey honey, how about picking up some doughnuts for breakfast?"

"Sure, no problem."

I entered the doughnut shop, and a weird feeling came over me. I knew it was in vain, but I looked in the glass case and then asked, "Do you have any swine ears?

"I'm sorry, we don't. I don't know what that is, sir."

"Well, if you ever taste one, you won't forget it."

I went over to Germany as one person and came back as another one. Of all the results that came back from my laboratory, the most significant were the changes I underwent on a personal level.

I gained new perspectives on life and became more open-minded. I wouldn't trade living in Texas for anything. Still, the experience of living in a new place and being exposed to different cultures gave me an appreciation for other people's beliefs. We should do a better job with gun control, recycling, and the environment in the States. Of all the discussions I had with players and coaches, not one European could understand why we don't do something about all the mass shootings we have. As I mentioned in Chapter 37, most Europeans have never seen a gun.

The experience also taught me the importance of self-reliance and independence. I had to navigate unfamiliar situations and overcome language barriers. "Just use Google Maps" didn't always work for me. Because of it, I had to figure it out and became a more confident problem-solver.

The German people I met were very polite and unassuming. If you rode a train in Germany, you would be impressed with how sensitive the Germans of others. No one is talking loud on their cell phones or cutting off other passengers. Everyone is courteous and respectful. Once I got off a train and left my backpack behind. After I'd walked 50 yards or so from the stop, a lady yelled, "Excuse me, sir, is this yours?" I had 300 Euros [$300 dollars] in it, my laptop and, most importantly, my passport! "Only in Germany" was the thought that went through my head after I thanked her for being so kind. Do you think that would have happened in the good 'ol U.S.A.?

After I returned in July, things went "sideways" for over a month. We became full of ourselves and wanted to be 50 Strong and FYGR. I'm grateful 50 Strong won over.

These weeks of fighting for our culture, and being lonely and homesick, made me realize that I needed to get grounded to keep my sanity. By grounded, I mean becoming more intentional and deeper with my relationship with God. I knew that if I had a foundation with Him, He could help me through the turbulent times of being away from my home and family. I started praying more, reading my Bible, and becoming more aware of His presence in my life.

Early in Potsdam, I inquired about returning for the next few seasons. I asked them if the salary could become high enough that Tracy could quit her job and find us a flat large enough for the three of us. Although they wanted to make this work, the reality is that European football is much less lucrative than it is in the States, so they couldn't afford to give me what I was asking for.

By the second half of the season, I realized my family needed me at home 12 months a year. I was making a name for myself over there, but I wouldn't miss out on any more special moments with Tracy and Coco.

Tracy and I are engaged and will be married in the fall of 2023 in the Bahamas. My next on-the-field coaching will be a seven-year-old soccer or softball team with Coco.

A few weeks after being back, I opened my email.

You Have a New Message From Europlayers

Coach Jackson, The Hamburg Sea Devils are looking for an offensive coordinator. Would you be interested? It will pay 2,000 Euros a month and one meal a day in addition to the usual travel, accommodations, cell phone, and health insurance as well....

My old me would have been tempted to ponder "what if". What if Chris had been healthy for the German Bowl? What if I could take Fast N' Wide and set records with a European League of Football organization? What if some of our players would come with me and we establish another players' creed?

The new me knows what's most important; my team in Texas...my family.

One lab result that did prove 100% positive was that my DNA is that of a coach. Every fiber in my being wants to help others do their best and to become more. I'm still going to coach others as long as I can. I will coach Fast N' Wide to coaches nationwide and keep growing the Elite Coaches' Mastermind.

My passion for coaching and helping others succeed has never been stronger. It took me six months of writing full-time with the help of my editor, Dr. Rob Gilbert, to write A Royal Season. I've loved every minute of it.

A Royal Season is an amazing story of how a few players and coaches helped transform us into a team that broke records. This book is 125,000 words longer than my previous two books put together. But I had to include every detail of the journey from start to finish. I look forward to seeing the positive results that my readers will have after getting to be a member of the 2022 Royals.

I didn't hear from Berti or Saul in the offseason. They had a new team to get ready and start the process all over again. I wear my Royals gear around the house and will always be proud and grateful to have been on the sideline in 2022.

But did I make a difference with the Royals?

In April, I got my answer. Saul sent me the greatest text message I could've ever received from him. There were no words, just a photo. My eyes watered a bit, and my heart was full looking at what he was leading the 2023 Royals through again this season…

A days later, Jerome sent me this text:

I wanted you to know we did the Creed again this year. The guys decided to call it "As One" because they wanted it not to be just about the players dressed or on the team but also the people helping out at the games, the fans, and the kids from the youth teams. Your teaching will forever be part of the team.

My experience with the Royals changed me forever, but more importantly, my impact is still resonating with the Royals. Life is good.

*Warning for Fast N Wide Coaches Only

After I'd been home for a few weeks, I decided to report my findings from the Royal Laboratory. Fast N' Wide had grown to over 100 programs, so we had a turnout for the session I was offering on the "7 Laboratory Results from Germany".

I shared my screen and asked the same question every Zoom presenter asks worldwide:

"Can everyone see my presentation?"

"I have treated these six months in Germany as a scientist would in a laboratory. I'm not sure how many experiments I did, but it seemed like it was daily.

EXPERIMENT #1 - DID FAST N' WIDE 'BLITZKRIEG' THE GFL?

CONCLUSION: *YES!*

Last season, our team set some impressive GFL and Royals records. We averaged 50.5 points per game, gained 509 yards, and only allowed seven sacks throughout our 13 games. Although we went for it on 4th down 22 times (converting 62%), I will always be proud of us for only punting 12 times all season.

The Observed Results:

1. Tempo worked: We snapped the ball faster than anyone in the history of the German Football League, and I'd be willing to be ever in Europe. Because of this, defenses stayed in base looks and focused more on being set when the ball was snapped than dialing up exotic blitzes or giving us different looks. We scored on the first drive in 11 of 13 games and in the first minute five times.

2. Simple wins: 73% of all our plays were from our "Big 3" (zone/ power/ choice). We always had different formations, and gadget plays each week, but we executed at a high level because we became very good at our 'day one' plays.

3. We were explosive: The team with the most plays of 20+ wins 81% of all games (the highest analytical factor). We averaged 7.5 explosive plays per game. Early in the season, when defenses didn't understand how many deep shots we'd take per game, Helbig torched secondaries with touchdowns of 50+ yards regularly. In the second half of the season, defenses shifted their focus to stopping Polk and Wolfe. We had fewer and fewer 'Michael Irvin' situations as defensive coordinators started saying "uncle" and resorted to just trying to

contain us and not give up the 50-yard touchdown. Once this happened, Karri and the company hit more runs of 20+ yards.

4. Get the ball to your best players: We had very good players and got the ball in their hands. Fast N' Wide is based on 'taking what the defense gives you' (see result #3 above). We set records in the passing game but also had a physical run game. We ran the ball to close out games on several occasions.

2022 GFL OFFENSIVE STAT LEADERS:

SCORING
#3 - Heiko Bals - 125
#5 - Karri Pajarinen - 106
#6 - Brandon Polk - 102

RUSHING YARDS
#2 - Karri Pajarinen - 1,301

PASSING YARDS
#1 - Chris Helbig - 3,406 yards

RECEPTIONS
#1 - Jared Wolfe - 102
#4 - Brandon Polk - 77

STATS LEADERS GERMANY

RECEIVING YARDS
#1 - Jared Wolfe - 1,504 yards (2nd All-Time in GFL history)
#3 - Brandon Polk - 1,382 yards

RECEIVING TOUCHDOWNS
#3 - Brandon Polk - 15
#3 - Jared Wolfe - 15

AVERAGE YARDS PER RECEPTION
#3 - Brandon Polk - 17.9
#6 - Jared Wolfe - 14.7

LONGEST RECEIVING TOUCHDOWN
#1 - Jared Wolfe - 89

ALL-PURPOSE YARDS
#3 - Jared Wolfe - 1,999 (158 per game)

EXPERIMENT #2: Can FNW work with only 1.5 assistant coaches?

CONCLUSION: *YES!*

"Why do I say 1.5? Saul wore about 100 hats for the Royals. He did a great job coaching the receivers at practice but didn't have time to grade their performance at practice or games. He was also the special team's coordinator, which he does with basically no assistance, so he didn't help during games or with the game plan.

Although I had an offer from a well-intended board member originally from Texas, Jonas was the only coach who helped me during games. He was also the head coach for his hometown team, the Fulda Saints, so he returned there every week after our game and didn't return until Tuesday."

I had two choices:

a. Make the plan for the week alone and tell everyone on Monday.

b. Involve the players. Like the creed, the more someone is allowed to create something, the more ownership and buy-in they'll have.

Necessity is the mother of invention, so I got creative. Our players were the same age as some of my past assistant coaches, so why not use them more? Our three American receivers help me game plan each Monday after our meetings.

"The best discovery, though, was player scouting reports. Each starter and primary backup evaluated the opponent he was likely to face. Chris broke down coverages, Karri, opponent blitzes, and our tight ends opponent's red zone defense."

"I have a question, coach. Did you start doing scouting reports this way before or come up with it during the season?" asked Neil Weiner from Baton Rouge, Louisiana.

"Good question. I had a lot of alone time at my flat, and my mind was racing about how bad we were after the first game. One person doing all the planning and then telling everyone what the plan is doesn't work in any organization. I had to come up with something, or I would drive myself insane. Getting the guys to help me more directly resulted in us being inside the red zone four times against Dresden and not scoring.

The Observed Results:

1. Before game #1, I was a dictator with the offense. Leadership involves others.

2. The players owned stock in the company. See take-home #2 above - the more I have allowed the players to be involved with game planning, the more they are invested.

EXPERIMENT #3: Can a high-tempo, high-repetition offense work with very little depth?

CONCLUSION: *"Yes!"*

"Fast N' Wide is the perfect offense for Germany because we use one-receiver routes. We have two studs outside, Jared and Polk, who cannot come off the field. Once we identify 'Michael Irvin', we throw to that receiver. The other one can rest. Our scheme is also so simple we can move every receiver around to get the matchup we want."

"Going back to wishing I understood more about how the GFL works, the fact we didn't have a backup quarterback was crazy. That being said, Chris was not taking a beating because we seven-man pass-protected most of the time. We have only given up an amazing seven sacks in 13 games, but we led the league in passing yards."

The Observed Results:

1. Football is and always will be more about the players than the plays. Go to the extreme to find ways for them to have the ball in their hands.

2. Be so simple, your best players can move around, and you can attack their worst defensive back.

3. Your quarterback is your 'queen in chess'. Protect him at all costs. We also use eight-man pass protection at times.

4. It's not the lettuce's fault. - "When you plant lettuce, if it does not grow well, you don't blame the lettuce. You look for reasons it is not doing well. It may need fertilizer, more water, or less sun. You never blame the lettuce."
   Thich Nhat Hanh, Buddhist Monk, father of "mindfulness".

   It's not the player's fault if they were not born with freakish athleticism. Bad coaches blame players. Good coaches help them succeed. We helped our offensive linemen in run and pass protection who needed help. Who is the opponent's best defensive lineman? Double-team him!

EXPERIMENT #4: Did we build an intentional team-first culture with mercenaries?

CONCLUSION: *YES!"*

"We had voluntary team meetings in training camp and implemented a players' creed we call 50 Strong. The players came up with the standards of conduct and defined them. After each practice, the guys in 50 Strong can invite new members. We have a poster for new inductees to sign before each game."

The following slides were the 50 Strong pillars and more detail about how the creation of the creed unfolded.

"I'm quite sure 50 Strong is the first players' creed in the GFL and probably in European football. Our 12-1 record was a product of our team culture as much as Fast N' Wide."

The Observed Results:

1. "People are people. Our 20 and 30-year-olds will point in the same direction if you give them a target."
2. "You are 'in on' what you are 'in with'. The players created 50 Strong. They admitted new members periodically, and it worked. Receiver Jared Wolfe said in an interview for a German newspaper, "We have a created 'family culture' that cannot be broken." Good stuff!"

"Coach, do you mind if I interject something here?" asked Dennis Dunn, a legendary coach from Louisiana who's won nine state championships.

"Heck, no! Please teach us something, brother."

"As some of you know, in addition to being a head coach, I'm also a full-time pastor. I used this story recently with my congregation. It's called 'The blind men and the elephant'."

"A king brought out an elephant and challenged six blind men [who'd never touched an elephant before] to see if they could determine what the animal was.

The first one happened to put his hand on the elephant's side. "Well, well!" he said, "This is a large, thick wall."

The second felt only of the elephant's tusk. "My brother," he said, "you are mistaken. He is not at all like a wall. What I'm touching is round and smooth and sharp. This is a spear."

The third happened to take hold of the elephant's trunk. "Both of you are wrong," he said. "This is a snake."

The fourth reached out his arms and grasped one of the elephant's legs. "Oh, how blind you are!" he said. "It is very plain to me that this is a tall tree."

The fifth was a very tall man who happened to take hold of the elephant's ear. "This is simple; it's a huge fan."

The sixth was very blind indeed, and it was some time before he could find the elephant at all. At last, he seized the animal's tail. "O foolish fellows!" he cried. "You surely have lost your senses. This elephant is not like a wall, spear, snake, or tree; neither is he like a fan. But any man with a par-ti-cle of sense can see that he is exactly like a rope."

Each believed he knew just what the king brought out before them, but all six had a different perspective and mindset. You found yourself in a place where the guys love football, but it's not year-round, and coaches can't make a living coaching it. You did a great job of getting them to all "touch the same part of the elephant" from where I'm sitting."

EXPERIMENT #5: Did an assistant coach impact team culture, or does it have to come from the top?

CONCLUSION: *Mixed results, but best when it comes from the top.*

"50 Strong was revolutionary. I will always be proud of it and believe we had the greatest change from one season to the next from any group I've been a part of, but…"

"An assistant coach can only do so much. Head coaching jobs are normally vacant for a reason; the team wasn't any good previously. When I took over as a head coach to Mesquite Poteet [1-19], Grapevine [1-9], or North Forney [4-6], they all had losing records and loser mindsets. All three became winners when they began to believe they could win. In Texas, you can replace assistant coaches at some places, and I always hired new guys when I could. Players can smell a rat from a mile away; they have to believe you believe. I wanted to surround myself with coaches who believed as much as I did.

On my first day on the practice field, I saw "F___ You Go Royals" on our ball bag, and I knew it wasn't going to be instilling a new culture, but my job was going to be much more difficult. Not only did I have to change a toxic environment, but I also had to do so without being the one in charge.

Experiment #6: Did a Texan go to Germany and fit right in?

CONCLUSION: *"No!"*

The "Main Thing" wasn't the "Main Thing" for me as I learned to live in Europe.

Organizations should consider the old environment a new employee has left. The attitude of "It's different here, and they'll get used to it" is tough. Instead of me being able to focus on football and learning 30 new players, I was also attempting to navigate Germany. For a 54-year-old Texan, this was no easy task.

"I was friends with the Royals' president and attempted to convince him there should be an onboarding process in the months leading up to arrival. My plane landed three days before our first team meeting. There will always be a transition period when anyone takes a new job because every place is different. Still, Europe, for me, was like going to another planet. Instead of being able to focus on training camp, I was learning how to live there."

"Everyone speaks English, so there won't be a language barrier" didn't hold up. While it wasn't absolutely necessary to speak German, it would have made life easier. Teams should offer basic language classes before Americans arrive."

"When interviewing for a job, you should 'Sherlock Holmes' it, meaning leave no stone unturned to find out everything you can to ensure you are a good fit. Nothing happened that ever made me regret coming over. But between October, when I signed my contract, and April, I could have learned things like conversational German, how the GFL operates, and the Royals' structure. Even things as basic as "Here is where you will be living and here is how you will get to the office, to practice, how you will get to downtown," etc., would have made the transition much easier. The Royals should provide Zoom sessions for Americans coming over for the first time, especially middle-aged coaches."

"When the Royals provided me with a car after two months, it was monumental. Again, 99% of Americans drive. Could I get around on a bike and the train system? Yes, but it was not easy or comfortable.

The Observed Results:

1. Help your new people with the culture. Have an onboarding process for new hires.

2. Make them feel special on the first day. Saul and Ruben greeted me at the airport with a Royal T-shirt. It was a special moment I won't ever forget.

3. Give them 'orientation information' before they begin on day one. Provide them with as much information as you can before they arrive.

4. Take into account who is joining the team and make the transition as easy as possible. Anytime someone has to deal with things other than their primary job, it takes away efficiency.

EXPERIMENT #7: Has Zoom replaced in-person when it comes to performance?"

CONCLUSION: *"No!"*

In other words, is it enough to tell them? No! The highest form of teaching is modeling. We met three mornings a week in Potsdam, and each one was necessary. But the things I mark as 'critical' for correction must be worked on again on the field. It seems like everything goes back to the red zone. If we don't fix it completely soon, I will have to figure out how to get counseling over there. We discussed #38 all week when we played Dresden for the second time. I was livid when he came through the 'B' gap, but an elite coach would have worked it on the grass more.

You can't just tell them. Most of our guys have only played football for three or four years. Although they are grown men, they are like a freshman in high school when it comes to football savvy.

The Observed Results:

1. Practice makes perfect. The teaching cycle must be followed.
   a. plan twice as long as the activity.
   b. Describe it.
   c. Model it.
   d. Allow them to do it physically.
   e. Test them

EXPERIMENT #8: Is it possible to get players to play hard without yelling at them?

CONCLUSION: "Yes!"

"This is the biggest learning curve for me of the season, even more than using the players more game-planning. Although the skill level is higher than I'm used to, the mindset differs greatly. There is no structured, mandatory offseason in Europe, so some or most use training camps to get in condition. In Texas, a 17-year-old will walk over hot coals and broken glass for twelve months a year to play ten games. Schools do not have interscholastic sports here, so everything is 'club'. If you want to play on a team, you pay and are included. Don't get me wrong, the Royals are not a club team, but the no-offseason where you earn your right to wear the jersey hit me in the face."

"Another big difference is the lack of professional coaches. Like club teams, the coaches here have a 'day job' and coach in the evening. Two of our offensive linemen coached the OL last year for their team, and one of them, Yasir, did it for the Royals."

"Does this mean the players and coaches don't love football here? Not at all. It means football is not life and death here. I've always been a confront and demand coach. I still believe in this style, but I had to change, and I think for the better. I had to figure out how to get guys to play hard without punishing them. Once, I made the offense go to the sideline and return more enthusiastically, but I couldn't 'up-down' a 30-year-old.

"Even with adults, the coach-to-player relationship should be a father-son dynamic. Praise, praise, praise, demand the standard be kept, correct with love, and praise again."

"There must be a standard, and every coach on staff should enforce it. I led warmups most of the season, and some of the defensive players wouldn't finish through the line. No one said anything to them. In August, I finally "blew a gasket" on a couple of them, but it was awkward with me not being their coach or the head coach. When I was in charge, every coach would hammer anyone not finishing a drill. In Potsdam, no one else seemed to care. If only one coach demands total effort, they will get tired of the message."

The Observed Results:

1. What you celebrate, you cultivate. Effort can be the result of positive affirmation. The optimal ratio is 5:1, with five positives for every negative comment.

2. Joke, have fun, use nicknames, and anything else you can think of to create an 'I want to be here' environment so that when it is time to correct a mistake, the player is not resentful.

3. Never make it personal. Correct the body part and the technique. Praise the person.

4. All coaches must demand that the 'standard is the standard' I'm proud of how much influence I had in helping the Royals be more disciplined than in the past, but if only one coach is the "bad guy", some will resent him.

EXPERIMENT #9: After my experience in Germany, do I have two words that I gratefully want to share with the German people?

CONCLUSION: "Absolutely! - Danke schön!"

Other books by Randy Jackson

ABOUT THE AUTHOR

Coach Jackson is truly an impressive figure in the world of coaching. With 21 years of experience as a head coach, he has become known for his ability to turn programs around. He is an expert in creating a championship culture and has even been the architect of the highest-scoring offense in the history of Europe. He is a successful coach and a best-selling author, leader of Fast N' Wide and the Elite Coaches Mastermind, keynote speaker, and certified mental performance coach. He has clearly dedicated his life to helping others achieve their goals and "clearing the path" for them.

Randy 'coaches coaches' with members worldwide learning to play faster and score more with his Fast N' Wide offense. Through his first two best-selling books," "Culture Defeats Strategy" and "Culture Defeats Strategy 2," - Coach Jackson has shared his innovative and revolutionary ideas with countless people, inspiring them to reach their full potential. His online resources and programs are highly regarded, offering powerful tools and strategies for coaches and their teams. Above all, Coach Jackson is committed to making a difference in the lives of everyone he works with, ensuring that his clients are successful and fulfilled. His belief that helping others achieve success can create a better world for all is a testament to his selflessness and dedication. With over 32 years of coaching experience, Coach Jackson is a true leader in his field, and he is grateful for any impact he has made to help coaches or leaders.

Randy and Tracy are happily engaged, and they have a beautiful daughter named Coco who is six years old. They live in Rockwall, Texas, and enjoy spending time together as a family. Randy is a devoted partner and father, and he works hard to provide for his loved ones. Tracy is a loving mother and fiancée, and she cherishes every moment with her family. Together, they make a strong and supportive team, and they are excited for what the future holds.

Made in the USA
Middletown, DE
03 July 2023